The Engineering of Software

Technical Foundations for the Individual

The Engineering of Software

Technical Foundations for the Individual

Dick Hamlet   Portland State University

Joe Maybee   Software Engineer, Xerox

Addison
Wesley

Boston San Francisco New York
London Toronto Sydney Tokyo Singapore Madrid
Mexico City Munich Paris Cape Town Hong Kong Montreal

Senior Acquisitions Editor: *Maite Suarez-Rivas*
Project Editor: *Katherine Harutunian*
Executive Marketing Manager: *Michael Hirsch*
Production Services: *Ecomlinks, Inc.*
Composition: *Windfall Software, using ZzTEX*
Text Design: *Ecomlinks Inc.; Paul C. Anagnostopoulos*
Technical Art: *Horizon Design*
Design Manager: *Gina Hagen*
Prepress and Manufacturing: *Caroline Fell*

Access the latest information about Addison-Wesley titles from our World Wide Web site: *http://www.awl.com/cs*

The programs and applications presented in this book have been included for their instructional value. They have been tested with care, but are not guaranteed for any particular purpose. The publisher does not offer any warranties or representations, not does it accept any liabilities with respect to the programs or applications.

Joe Maybee wishes to point out that the views represented here are not necessarily the views of Xerox.

Library of Congress Cataloging-in-Publication Data

Hamlet, Dick.
   The engineering of software : technical foundations for the individual /
Dick Hamlet, Joe Maybee.
      p.   cm.
   ISBN 0-201-70103-0
      1. Software engineering. I. Maybee, Joe. II. Title.
QA76.758. H35 2001
005.1—dc21   00-39000

2 3 4 5 6 7 8 9 10—DOH—04 03 02 01

For Corinne, with love

For Jan, Annie, and Julie, with love

Contents

5   The "Life Cycle" of Software   83

PART III   Design and Coding   209

11 Software Design   211

18   Wrapping up Design and Coding   381

PART IV   Testing   395

19   Software Testing   397

Foreword

I love the field of software. In my nearly 50 years of being a software professional, I have worked in industry (aerospace), taught at a university (Seattle University software engineering program), and helped steer the field (at the Software Engineering Institute, Carnegie-Mellon University). It has been a heady ride, from the very beginnings of the field to the relative sophistication of today.

Because of all that, I am fairly intolerant of software hogwash. And there is all too much hogwash in the field: over-promised, hyped technologies; advocacy research that lauds rather than explores; gurus selling software snake oil and promising miracle cures. There is so much hogwash in the field that I often think of myself as a "contrarian"—I have even been accused of being a "curmudgeon"—as I tilt at the windmills of the hogwash-purveyors.

All of that is prelude. When I examine a book on the software engineering field, I first look at it to see what it does with hogwash. I like what Hamlet and Maybee have done here. They have presented the facts of software engineering, untempered by hogwash. Their collection of software principles is straightforward and supportable. Their belief in focusing on product more than process may not synch with today's old husband's tales of the field, but it is a practical, workable view. When they deal with controversial topics, often as not they present their positives—and their negatives—allowing the reader to decide about their value.

Do I like this book because my software-field relationship with Dick Hamlet goes back over 30 years? I hope not. One of the benefits of being seen as a curmudgeon is that you can call a spade a spade, and people expect it of you. If I didn't like what Dick (and Joe) wrote here, I would have said so. But this book is well-written, sensible, and very readable, nicely meshing the theory-based state of the software art with the pragmatism-based state of the practice.

That's important. Many fault practice for being ill-informed about theory, and others fault theory for being irrelevant to practice. But both theory and practice are vital to the future of the field. The software engineering student had better be familiar with both of them.

I like to tell people that "my head is in the theory of computing, but my heart is in its practice." At this point in the history of the field, the number of people who choose to be a part of that "club" is fairly small. But I have a feeling, after you've finished with this book, that you may join me in my club. If you do, welcome!

Bob Glass

Software is arguably the most interesting engineering product ever invented. It is freed from almost all the limitations of the physical world, and therefore able to accomplish apparent marvels. It does not cost anything to reproduce once it has been designed and implemented, it does not wear out, and it can in principle solve difficult problems perfectly.

But often software does not fulfill its promise, and the culprit when it fails is complexity and loss of intellectual control by software developers. This book is about the engineering techniques and ideas that can be used to realize better software. These are collectively called "software engineering." The software-engineering discipline is very new as branches of engineering go—it was conceived only about 30 years ago—and even its best practices are not yet widely used. There are serious questions about whether it will ever attain the status of (say) civil engineering, with professionals who routinely succeed in large projects using a firm body of knowledge.

We believe that software engineering will become a well defined and respected profession, and we hope that this textbook brings together some of the knowledge that will be its basis.

The Software Engineer

The growth of software in the lives of people throughout the developed world is unprecedented. And although some software is no more than entertainment (for example, video games, and far too much of the traffic on the Internet), most of it has real potential for improving the way things are done in the workaday world, and helping people to live better. The corresponding danger inherent in software is that if badly done, or used wrongly, like any potent force it can cause misery. It is the business of technical experts to see to it that the potential is realized and the dangers are avoided. The struggle goes on every day, in every software project, and it will always be with us. Everyone has encountered the explanation for poor service that "the computer won't allow that." Software developers, when they hear those words, know that there has been a failure of the development process. The requirements were not thought through carefully enough, and were incomplete. Mistakes were made in the design or implementation. Testing was inadequate. And ultimately, the developers did not take responsibility for their mistakes and fix them.

Throughout this textbook we emphasize the technical knowledge and skills that a software engineer must have. It is our position that the whole of software development is based on individuals who know what they are doing in making software. Given the technical expertise—the engineering—software development can be organized in many different ways, and if a software project is at all complicated, it must be organized and controlled to succeed. But the team skills that are essential to cooperative work, and the management skills to direct individuals and teams to solve problems in concert, come on top of the base of engineering skills.

We have tried to explain what a software engineer should do, and what is needed to do an engineer's job. If other engineering disciplines are any guide, a software engineer reading this book (say) 20 years in the future will find it hopelessly primitive. The future engineer will know things by heart that today are thorny open problems, and from the welter of half-understood principles and techniques we present, will be sure of what is important and fundamental, and what was a fad of the moment. Meanwhile, there is a lot of software development to be done, and engineers have never been content to wait until they understood everything to tackle difficult problems.

The Audience for this Textbook

Portland State University, like many schools, teaches computer science starting with programming classes and discrete mathematics, and at the end of the program there are project courses in compilers and operating systems, and a "capstone" course in designing a software product for a real customer. We observed that students had a hard time making the transition from small, well-defined assignments required in a data-structures course, to the term-long, medium-sized projects of the upper-division classes. Software engineering seemed to be the discipline that was lacking, and this is the textbook for a course in the middle, teaching technical skills. In this course, students learn how to build software, including specification, design, and testing, to complement their algorithmic and implementation skills. The course is a practical one, but it includes challenging technical material. Existing software engineering texts were inadequate for such a course, because they survey the field rather than present details of doing the engineering, and they include too much material on teamwork and management skills. Our students need to know how to do the basics themselves.

This textbook is addressed to the individual developing significant software, and neglects the cooperative and management aspects of development. It attempts to convey practical information on building software, in sufficient depth that the techniques can be used immediately. Projects are the best way to learn these techniques, and as the Portland State course is taught, it is a project course. We prefer to include details on one particular method than to give a superficial treatment of many methods. As a text, this book is suited for a course at the junior undergraduate level, *before* students have to attempt significant software projects.

As the book has grown over more than five years of use, we have tried to keep in mind the beginning software engineer. We added material that may be needed to replace computer science courses taken long ago (or never taken), such as logic. We included details that are essential to the more intense environment of projects in the commercial world. Some management aspects of software engineering are included, in the form of notes on "how the other half lives." We hope that the result is a text that can be used for self-study, to learn the technical skills that are the basis of software development. Working engineers who came to software development without formal software-engineering course work should be able to catch up by reading this book.

We two authors each have experience in both the industrial and academic setting, but Maybee is primarily a working engineer and Hamlet is primarily a researcher and teacher. There were not many times when we were in conflict about what to include and how to present it, but when conflicts arose, we tried to include both points of view.

Features

The conventional "waterfall" development cycle is used in organizing the material, but only as a presentation device; no particular development process is assumed.

Testing is given a central role in the book. Test plans are introduced at the beginning, and testing issues are treated throughout. Thinking about testing during requirements analysis, design, and implementation is a way to reveal problems in those other activities. Testing and quality assurance are not add-on activities begun after the software is complete.

In the description of the specification phase, first-order logic and its implementation in Prolog is used to give the ideas that underly formal methods of software specification.

The design and implementation phases, usually neglected in software engineering texts, are treated in detail. The design part begins with a chapter on practical lore, and then covers six important design methods in detail.

Each method is illustrated with an example that is carried through to executable code in C, Java, or a UNIX shell script. In a one-term course, there is time to present only the instructor's choice of about half these methods, but the others are available as self-contained examples the reader can emulate should the need arise.

Finally, material is included on the social and ethical responsibilities of software engineers.

Each chapter ends with a collection of review questions and references to the current and classic computer science literature. A section called "How Does it Fit?" at the end of each chapter contains exercises that explore the student's understanding of the material in depth. Many of the questions have been drawn from examinations.

Supplements

Addison Wesley maintains on-line information for this book at `www.aw.com` `/cssupport.` Course instructors can obtain solutions there to "How Does it Fit?" exercises, and overhead projection slides for class lectures. Solutions are available exclusively to instructors using this text for a course. For more information, contact your local Addison-Wesley representative. An Instructor's Guide is also available, which includes sample term-long projects, and suggestions for presenting and evaluating the material in a one-term course, based on experience at Portland State.

Acknowledgments

It is usual to thank the generations of students who were (without being asked) the "beta testers" of this textbook. As one student put it on a course evaluation form, "Hamlet should pay attention to teaching instead of book writing." At the outset of the project, we were fortunate to get a sound review of the technical writing (alas, for only part of the book) from Linda Keast. Maybee had special difficulties in combining teaching and writing with his full-time job; the Xerox management and staff were flexible and understanding.

Our sincere appreciation to the following reviewers who gave valuable feedback and numerous accurate and insightful comments. Their contribution has certainly enhanced the quality of the final product.

Henry A. Etlinger, Rochester Institute of Technology

Jack R. Hagemeister, Washington State University

William Lively, Texas A&M University

Robert J. McGlinn, Southern Illinois University, Carbondale
John Noll, Santa Clara University
C. V. Ramamoorthy, University of California at Berkeley
Shmuel Rotenstreich, The George Washington University

We would also like to thank and remember the late John Gannon of the University of Maryland for providing input at the initial developmental stage of the book.
Thank you all.

PART I

Engineering and Software

▼

So-called software engineering is the commonly accepted name for the process of developing software. The name reflects something of the human tendency to make what we are doing sound more impressive, as "garbage collection" could be called (and is called) "waste-management engineering." But for better or for worse, software developers have decided to call themselves engineers. This introductory part of the text examines the field of engineering, and what software developers do (and what they *should* do), to see how well the name fits.

The concept of a "life cycle" of software, a separation into somewhat arbitrary phases of development, is introduced.

The viewpoint of this text, that technical skills lie at the heart of building (that is, engineering) software, is presented with an introduction to an alternative view—that software engineering is really just a form of engineering management.

Finally, Part I closes with a chapter on software testing, the final part of development, but one that can and should be distributed throughout the whole process, starting immediately with a test plan.

Concepts
of Software
Development

Almost every printed article on computing, in newspapers, popular magazines, even in professional and technical literature, begins with a statement of how important and ubiquitous software has become. Some of these articles go on to stress the potential dangers of putting so many eggs in the software basket. And indeed software is increasingly entering our lives, with great potential benefits, and corresponding great risks. But software is not a phenomenon that occurs naturally in the world. People make software, as they make other artifacts like houses (although to be sure not in quite the same way). In making software, the people can do a good job or a poor one, and the resulting software will directly reflect their care and skill. "Software engineering" is a name for the collection of skills, ideas, and procedures intended to help people do a good job. To emphasize that our subject in this book is the technical skills for an individual, we have turned the name around into "the engineering of software."

1.1 Separation of Concerns

Software engineering is built upon one of the basic ideas of rational thought, an idea that is almost too obvious to write down, yet profoundly useful and important. Here it is:

> In thinking about something too complicated to master, don't try to do it all at once. Break it down into less complicated parts, and concentrate on each one in turn.

Any kind of a decomposition of a difficult problem will be helpful in solving it, but some ways of pulling it into separate parts are much better than others. First and foremost, the parts have to *be* separate. If the division is not clean, one part will intrude on another, allowing the whole problem to sneak back into consideration. A second desirable quality of decompositions is called "separation of concerns." It is very helpful if each part comes with a restricted set of important issues and characteristics. Then when thinking about (say) part A, it will be necessary to deal only with (say) issue X that is relevant to A, not issues Y and Z that apply only to other parts.

For example, imagine capturing a complicated story, perhaps a description of some real event that took place. The most obvious decomposition is temporal; as Lewis Carroll advised, one should tell the story as follows: "Start at the beginning, go to the end, and then stop." Perhaps the event to be described has some natural demarcations in time, such as a number of days over which it took place. But in a temporal description there is no separation of concerns: each part of the story is handled in the same way as any other part. Another decomposition of a story might divide it geographically, into parts that happened in different locales. Now there is separation of concerns, since some locations will be more important than others, and each location will have a set of unique features upon which to concentrate.

Software engineering uses several dichotomies in decomposing the problem of developing software.

> "While he was at his uncle's villa in Spain, Robert was never sure if his rusty Spanish let him grasp the situation."

1.1.1 Management vs. Technical

Management and technical issues are completely different—the problems of running a large multiperson project are different from those of doing the work itself. Both are vitally important to software engineering. For an individual doing all software development, however, the managerial/technical distinction doesn't make much sense. One person could put on a "manager's hat" and tell herself what to do, then replace it with an "engineer's hat" to do what she was told and write a report about it, then switch hats again to read the report, and so on. But that's silly. "Management" for an individual simply becomes the activity of making a plan that can be consulted as the work proceeds.

Know How the Other Half Lives

This book is addressed to a technical audience, to engineers. One of the most important conditions of engineering employment is the freedom to *be* an engineer—to work with technical problems, and attack them in a skilled, technical way. The paradox is that this desirable situation must be established and maintained not by engineers themselves, but by their management. A good engineering manager in a company that values engineering spends a lot of time creating the right environment in which subordinates can work productively. The manager deals with the politics, the larger business and personnel issues, and the day-to-day nontechnical disasters that engineers don't want to face. The manager acquires resources like state-of-the-art workstations for engineers to use. The manager insulates engineers from the demands of other people in the company, who have their own important problems (like how to pay the bills next month, how to please a demanding customer, etc.). The manager is a champion for ideas coming from engineers, and sees that they get a hearing up the administrative chain.

Enlightened engineering management is not an altruistic or one-sided enterprise. Engineers need managers, and companies need engineers who are not managers. The reason is once again rooted in separation of concerns. A good engineer is not a good manager, and vice versa. Hard technical problems require concentration and all the attention and skill that a human being can bring to bear. Everything else must be pushed aside to solve them. So the best engineers have no time for anything but the problem on which they are working. However, everything else *cannot* be pushed aside—and if someone doesn't deal with the real world as it impinges on an enterprise, that enterprise will fail. The contract will be lost, the customers will be unhappy, the company will go bankrupt. However much engineers would like to deny it, even their own work needs directing and controlling. It is all too common for even the best technical people to get lost in some trivial or misdirected aspect of a problem, and waste their time while important other aspects are neglected. It is a manager's job to see that this does not happen.

One of the most important decisions an engineering student can make during schooling is a choice of "which side are you on?"—to be a part of the technical work, or a part of managing that work. A few people can do both; most of us can't. If your bent is to be an engineer, you'll be unhappy as a manager, and always trying to get your fingers into the "real work." If you lean to management, you'll be impatient with the narrow technical view, which seems to ignore all the political and human issues that "really matter."

This book is almost entirely concerned with the technical details of the engineer's craft. Some readers will have made up their minds which side they want to be on, whereas others will keep their options open. The authors are themselves solidly in the "engineering" camp. Learning about what software engineers do is one way to help make the choice. However, it is often important to "know how the other half lives." Managers are human, and not very many of them hold the ideal view that they exist to help their engineering subordinates. The majority of well-meaning managers probably believe that it is the other way around. A minority of managers are not well meaning, but more interested in their own power and their own careers than in any technical issues. In dealing with management, engineers can benefit from understanding the larger context in which they work. In that spirit we have included some information about the way in which software development fits into the world.

You Don't Have to Love 'Em

For all that it helps an engineer to understand the larger context in which engineers must work, and it is also crucial that managers understand the nature of the engineering that they supervise, there is a real and natural antagonism between the two camps. It is very human to blame anyone but yourself when something goes wrong, particularly if the other person is not one of your "own kind." So engineers grouse about their incompetent managers who couldn't even write a "Hello World" program, and managers sometimes think of their employees as children who must be told to use the toilet.

Both sides could be better critics. An engineer might ignore all the company politics, yet can be relied upon to tackle and quickly solve hard technical problems that baffle everyone else. Such an employee may be personally repugnant or incomprehensible to a manager who is the exact opposite, but the manager would be a fool not to value the engineer and help with the necessary politics. What a manager would better criticize is an engineer who doesn't solve assigned problems, and the better politician that engineer is, the worse for everyone. Similar remarks apply to an engineer's criticism of a manager. Since the manager isn't doing the programming, such skills may not be relevant. But a manager who doesn't provide needed resources, or who abuses supervised employees by blaming them to save his own neck, or who does not competently convey employees' concerns to managers higher up in the company, is not doing his job.

A little understanding goes a long way in the difficult relationship between manager and engineer. It is difficult to be generous and forgiving if one does not understand what is driving the other side.

1.1.2 Teamwork vs. Individual Effort

It is entirely legitimate to see engineering as a separate discipline whose concerns are often diametrically opposed to those of management. An engineer who believes that a similar dichotomy exists between working in a team and working alone is on much shakier ground. The psychological component of the issue may be the same: engineering does attract the "loner" who is not skilled at working in a group, and group effort does detract from concentrating on the technical details of a problem. However, it is increasingly true that teamwork skills are valuable—even necessary—to the individual in developing software. The analogy "management is to engineering as teamwork is to individual work" breaks down for two interrelated reasons:

1. There is real technical substance to teamwork; unless engineers know how to do it, it can't be properly done.
2. Although the concerns of a team are somewhat different from those of an individual, they cannot be separated and assigned to someone else; teams are made up of individuals.

Thus engineers need to know about and practice teamwork.

However, this textbook contains little more about working in teams than it does about management issues. Part of the reason is that the skills required are based on psychology more than on mathematical science. Though we feel comfortable including an introductory section on (say) first-order logic, we cannot include a psych primer. The more important reason for omitting technical material on teams is that the skills are best learned by participation in a team itself. So a textbook being read by a person sitting alone is just the wrong vehicle for teaching those skills. There is one exception to our lack of coverage: software inspection is so important that we give an introduction in Section 5.3. Inspection illustrates the technical nature of team activities: the psychological aspect is important, but equally important is the engineering skill of the participants. A team could be assembled to do software inspection, trained in the dynamics of the activity but without engineering skills. They could do a classical, textbook-perfect job that would nevertheless be almost worthless because their work would miss the point of the inspection. It is the engineering that is being inspected, and only engineers can do the job. (We are not denying the necessity of psychology: engineers can also fail miserably at inspection for lack of this knowledge.)

There is one valid part to the management/teamwork analogy. A person may not want to work in a team any more than he or she wants to be a manager. Such a bias would dictate looking for employment in smaller organizations where teamwork is not valued. But even here, the analogy breaks down because even in a startup company with a handful of technical employees, teamwork like inspections can be immensely valuable. Thus someone who likes the idea of being part of a team is really not restricted to larger companies or projects.

1.1.3 Different Tasks—Development Phases

Finally, we come to the separation idea that is at the heart of software engineering. It is as useful to an individual as it is to a development group: the development task is arbitrarily split into several distinct tasks. These tasks are called "phases of the software life cycle." For example, the "design" phase is concerned with dividing the programming task into independent parts, which is quite separate from doing the programming in the "coding" phase. Some of the boundaries between life cycle phases are pretty arbitrary or fuzzy, particularly when an individual is doing the work rather than a group of people. But there is a principle for marking off the phases: each results in a self-contained "document" that encapsulates part of the effort of developing software. This document concisely captures all the work done up to a point (which defines the end of the phase); after that point the document is consulted without rethinking any of the decisions that went into it. For example, part of the "design document" describes the modules (subroutines) of the software. All the work of choosing appropriate modules and defining their interconnections is called "design" and captured in a "design document." Once the design phase ends and the "coding" phase starts, the module breakdown is accepted as gospel by the programmer. To question it would be to open up all the old issues and decisions again. Using the design document makes for efficient programming; the concerns have been separated and part of the problem solved.

Of course, it can happen that mistakes in one phase come to light only later on. It is in the nature of problem decomposition that ignoring all but one part blinds the developer to some information. When such mistakes are made, the decomposition may prove counterproductive. For example, if the interconnections of the module design mistakenly omit something, and this is only discovered near the end of the coding phase, then much work of both design and coding may have to be done over. In that case it would have been better not to separate the phases, but instead to deal with the whole design/coding problem at once. There is no guarantee that mistakes will not be made. But here is where the discipline of software engineering makes its contribution. The design/coding separation is not arbitrary, and engineers can learn to do a good job of design by studying its principles. Then in most cases mistakes will *not* be made, or at least lessons will be learned from mistakes so that they are not repeated, and the problem decomposition will usually work.

It is natural to describe software development by describing each phase in an ideal time-order of occurrence, and indeed that is the plan of this book. Real development seldom takes place in this ideal order, one phase neatly following another. But if it did, there is a name for the ideal process: "the waterfall model." It has been sensibly suggested that this nonexistent ideal is a great way to describe development, even if the development didn't work that way. Each phase has a distinct goal, and a distinct product that defines it, showing the separation of concerns involved.

However different the phases of development may be, they share many principles, important considerations that apply to software and its development in general. Rather than repeat these principles for each phase, we have collected them in Chapter 2. The principles express important ideas about making software, and in a sense the definition of a "life cycle" is an artificial means to create phases to which the principles apply.

1.2 Phases of the Software Life Cycle

The software engineering literature is inconsistent in naming the parts of software development. There is no real disagreement on what actions take place, but there is confusion about just how many distinct phases these actions should be broken into and what names to use for the phases. As usual in computer science, the same names have different meanings in different papers and books.

The first confusion arises in the name for the whole process. Some people call the complete construction of a software system "software development." Others refer to the process as software "design," "construction," or "building," or combinations of such words. Here we choose to use *development*. (And in particular, we do not call the whole process "design" because that will be our name for one part of development.) Together, the parts of development are also called the *software life cycle*.

A "phase" of software development is defined by the existence of a product (artifact, document, work product, etc.) that results from that phase. The goals and concerns of the phase are embodied in properties of that product. Once the phase is completed, its product serves as the basis of the subsequent phase(s). The whole point of dividing the task of development is to get intellectual control of the process by "separating concerns." That means part of the work is considered by itself, completed, and encoded in a document. Later, when other parts of the work are done, that document is consulted as a given—the earlier work is not reexamined or redone. For a small project, this rigid organization is a handicap—it is better to have all aspects of the work fluid and able to change as other aspects are considered. But for a large project, too much freedom is a curse: there are so many choices to be made, and so much interaction among the choices, that one must be arbitrary (and perhaps wrong) in making them and then must stick to early decisions, or the work will go round and round seeking the "best" solution, and never be finished.

There is another, less obvious advantage to be gained by separating development into distinct phases. People developing software *will* make mistakes. Working on a self-contained part of the process allows mistakes to be made (and discovered) as early as possible. Correcting a mistake is far easier at the beginning than at the end. Imagine that in the process of testing a software system, it is found to fail, and the failure is traced to a misunderstanding about what the software was supposed to do. Then the developer must go back to square one and do everything over, perhaps rewriting much of the code. If that same misunderstanding was discovered at the outset, there is almost no investment yet made, and it will be easy and cheap to correct.

The remainder of this section describes the processes that go into any software development, without giving them any definitive names, and then summarizes the life cycle that will be the basis of this book. Most of the difficulty about names comes at the beginning of the life cycle.

1.2.1 Information Exchange Between Developer and End User

The end user is the person for whom the software is to be developed. A classroom instructor might be the user (for an assigned project); the developer might also be the user (for a personal utility program). In commercial software the user is a customer who may be someone in the same organization as the developer (so-called in-house development); or people in a different organization that is contracting to have the software developed; or even an over-the-counter buyer (for so-called shrink-wrap software). In any case, the user needs to tell the developer what is wanted, and this is the first and probably most important phase of development. In the case of shrink-wrapped software, the real end user is not present in the discussion but only suggested by a marketing representative or by the developer's own personal idea of what will sell. Sometimes the product resulting from the user/developer dialogue is a binding contract signed by both parties—a contract to which the developer may later be held by law. However, it is more usual for the agreement between the parties to be less formal, only a nonbinding description of what is required. The common situation is one of good will on both sides: the user believes that the developer will try to do the right thing, and indeed this is the developer's intent. When things go wrong, it is more likely to be a mistake than a conspiracy.

▼ Never attribute to malice what can be explained by incompetence.

Perhaps the most common name for the product that results from user/developer interaction is the "requirements document." One of its most important characteristics is that in its entirety it should be comprehensible to the user.

1.2.2 Complete Problem Description (Developer Only)

Some aspects of what software must do are not of concern to the user, but only to the developer, and may be expressed in terms the user does not wish to master. These requirements therefore do not enter into the user/developer dialogue, or when they do, the user dismisses them as "don't care" conditions. The developer, however, must settle all such details before proceeding. Thus there may be additional "requirements" placed on the software, and a separate phase to create what is often called a "specification." Or the product may be called a "design," with adjectives like "architectural" or "high-level." The distinction between this and the previous task is that here the user is absent. However, often when the developer begins to add these "don't care" requirements, it is obvious that the user *will* care, so the case is re-presented to the user, with some specific choices.

Hence a developer-only specification may put itself out of business: part of it might be added to the user requirements dialogue, whereas the rest might be moved to a subsequent phase. The test for what should be in a specification is:

It is supposed to say exactly *what* the software is supposed to do, but to avoid as much as possible saying *how* that functionality will be attained.

The "how" belongs in subsequent tasks of development.

1.2.3 Break Down into Detailed Assignments for Programming

For a large, multiperson project, it is essential that the programming be done in parallel by people who need not talk to each other about the work; otherwise, the use of more people will result in less work getting done! Breaking the programming work into independent assignments is therefore the next task following functional specification. Even for one-person projects, however, this decomposition is important in keeping control of the work. If one is continually revising the pieces to take account of the other pieces and changes in them, nothing gets finished. In this breakdown phase, components are described, and each component has an interface to the others, which must also be described. The process is usually called "design," with adjectives like "low-level" or "detailed." The design process is concerned with the "how" of the software.

However, each component of a design must have a functional description, which brings the ideas of the previous phase (specification) into play at the level of components. The role of the user and developer are played, respectively, by the designer and the programmer. Because the designer is very knowledgeable about the programming to follow, the actual programmers who will implement the design may not be consulted, but only imagined by the designer.

1.2.4 Programming

From the component specifications and the design that interconnects the components, programming language code can be written. Insofar as the programmer assigned to this implementation has any questions or difficulties in deciding what is to be done, one of the earlier phases is at fault. Technically, when such a question arises, the development process should stop and the question should be settled (usually by consulting the end user). In practice, the ideal is realized only for "show stoppers"—problems so severe that no one can imagine just going forward. For less severe questions, the programmer must often make a decision and implement it. However, this decision *must* be communicated to the user. Putting a comment in the source code is entirely inadequate; at the very least the decision should get into the users' manual, and best of all, it should be described in a special notification to the user.

The product of the programming phase is, of course, a program executable on hardware. Often the source listing is taken as the product, but it is almost always assumed that high-level code has been compiled successfully. There is disagreement about whether the code should have been executed, but if the program is assumed to be tested, the testing is not extensive or necessarily well organized. Such testing as is done is rather like an extension of the syntax checking of compilation.

1.2.5 Testing

Once a component has been coded, it can be tried on examples in isolation. The components may be subroutines, data structures, header files, or combinations of pieces. The generic term *module* is used for complex components although this word also has a technical meaning as a particular kind of component called an "abstract data type." The term *unit* for an ill-defined component is often used, and component testing is almost universally called "unit testing."

When all components are ready, the composite system can be assembled and tried. If not all components are assembled, but only those that depend heavily on each other for some aspect of operation, the trials are sometimes called "subsystem testing." When the entire piece of software is tried, it is "system testing." Both of these aspects are covered by the term *integration testing* since units are integrated for the larger tests.

All parts of the testing phase include the computer-intensive aspect of executions. However, executions cannot be done without the input values for the components, the subsystems, or for the complete program. Furthermore, the executions are pointless unless the results are checked for correctness. These two tasks of generating test inputs and examining execution outputs usually fall to human beings, making use of the documents from earlier phases. Of course, results cannot be examined until the tests are actually performed, necessarily at the end of the development process. But finding test inputs can begin at the beginning of development. Each activity in development suggests tests, and if these are recorded along the way (in what is usually called a "test plan"), then testing can begin as soon as code is available.

The product of the testing phase is in one sense the tested software. But a better way to look at testing documentation is as an audit trail that establishes what was done. Thus the complete test plan (which has been growing throughout the previous parts of the life cycle) and a report of tests and their outcome are the testing "products." Reporting on tests means more than just listing them and giving the history of success and failure. The test report should seek to convince the reader that the tests conducted are meaningful, real evidence that hard work has been done and that the software was found to be of good quality.

1.2.6 Changing the Program

When a tested software system is delivered to its end user(s), it is more accurate to say that its life is beginning than that the life cycle is at an end. The user immediately discovers that what's wanted is something rather different from what's been delivered, or, serious deficiencies in performance or functionality are uncovered when the software is used for real work. Changes are required, and all such changes are lumped under the somewhat inaccurate term *maintenance.* The analogy is to the "maintenance" of physical equipment (e.g., automobiles), which refers to actions compensating for or preventing wear and tear. Software does not wear out, and its "maintenance" is more like "redesign." But the word *maintenance* is solidly established. It has been suggested that maintenance history describes how useful a piece of software is. If it has not been repeatedly changed, it simply is not being used.

Just as problems that arise in coding should ideally send development back to the first requirements/specification phase, so should most maintenance begin with user dialogue and proceed through an abbreviated version of the life cycle. In reality, maintenance is often viewed as a low-cost activity in which working code is "patched" to alter its properties, and specifications and designs are neither examined nor updated. Software that is maintained in this way soon becomes so fragile that it is impossible to alter because the accumulated undocumented changes interact with each other, and cause any new change to fail in some obscure, unsuspected way. When a system reaches this state, it is literally "unmaintainable" and *must* be redone from scratch. The economy of cheap maintenance is therefore thrown into doubt. In practice, unmaintainable software, if it can still be used and sold, is frozen, and an attempt is made to document all its existing deficiencies.

All existing bugs are hereby declared features. You may use them without fear that they will ever be corrected.

In a textbook for the individual, the "maintenance" phase is treated only briefly although it is of the utmost importance in real-world projects. In some organizations, software development is nothing more than maintenance because there is so much existing software that the resources for creating new programs are all taken up dealing with the old ones. Maintenance is less relevant for students in the classroom. Even in "project" courses like compiler writing, students do not typically keep or alter their own software—they turn in a completed assignment, and that's the end of it. In an industrial software development setting, this is usually referred to as "throwing the software over the wall"—the developer contracts to deliver the product, but not to maintain it. A cynic might say that by doing a poor job in the first place, the developer can hope for a lucrative follow-on contract for maintenance since no one else will be able to understand or fix the delivered software!

Maintenance has a hidden role throughout the life cycle. Since all useful software ends up being "maintained," many of the goals in all phases of development are really maintenance goals. Software should be constructed so that it can be changed easily. Furthermore, whenever mistakes are made within development, and it is necessary to return to an earlier development phase to correct them, the work being done is just like "maintenance." Many of the best ideas in software engineering have a dual role: (1) they help the developer stay in control of the project, and (2) they make it easier to return to the project later for maintenance. Thus maintenance will come up implicitly in the other phases.

1.2.7 Naming the Development Phases

In many cases of individual software development, the dialogue between user and developer is abbreviated. For example, a course instructor (the user) makes assignments (requirements) that students (the developers) are supposed to accept as perfect (although they seldom come close to perfection). Thus all the "what" about the software, its required functionality, is given by the assignment; in this case, the "requirements" are more like a "specification." For personally developed software, the "user" and "developer" are the same person, making the "requirements"/"specification" distinction unimportant.

When there is reason to keep the user-oriented problem description separate from the one the developer works with, we call the two activities *requirements* and *specification,* respectively, and talk about two separate documents. Often there is no distinction, but we still need to talk about "what the software is supposed to do," and for that we use either *requirements* or *specification* interchangeably, or sometimes even *requirements/specification.*

With or without user dialogue, the skills of constructing good requirements and specifications (and of criticizing poor ones!) are of great importance to individuals. To successfully develop software, it is essential to know what that software is required to do, and despite the best intentions, any requirements or specification document is almost certain to be deficient. Course instructors think hard about their assignments, but that is insufficient; to paraphrase the saying about representing yourself in court, "the developer who writes code for himself has a fool for a user." The sooner one can discover and correct deficiencies in requirements and specifications, the less work will be wasted.

Making a *test plan* is not a self-contained phase of development, but instead it goes on in parallel with the other phases, beginning as soon as work starts on the requirements/specification. Looking for tests that will exercise the required functions, as well as thinking about what outcome those tests should have, is one of the best ways to discover the deficiencies of a requirements/specification.

Our name for the "how" phase of software development, in which components and their interfaces are defined (and specifications given for each component), is *design*. Design includes more work on the test plan (to which component tests can now be added). The names *coding* for the programming itself (with more additions to the test plan), and *testing* where the test plan is used, are nearly universal. Finally, the tested program is delivered

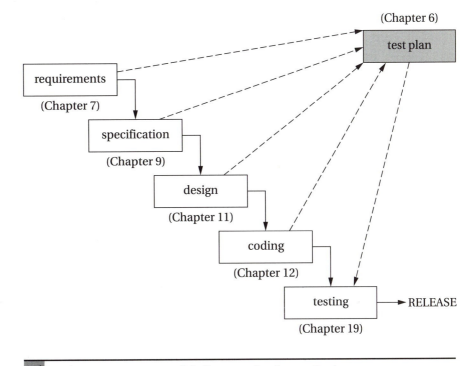

Figure 1.1   A waterfall diagram of software development.

and development is complete so long as everyone pretends that there will be no maintenance.

In talking about phases of software development, the name of the phase, say, "design," is technically an adjective: "design phase." But the name is commonly used alone, as a noun. Everyone says things like: "Design is taking longer than we expected." Unfortunately, the document that results has the same adjective: "design document," and the same abbreviated way of speaking is common: "The design didn't get updated to reflect those changes." So when you see "design" out of context, it might mean the phase, or it might mean the document, or (most likely) the person speaking or writing isn't paying attention, and it doesn't really mean much of anything.

Each phase of development is the subject of chapters to follow, as indicated in Figure 1.1, which shows the phases of development in what has come to be called a "waterfall" diagram. The name comes from imagining that work accumulates in each phase, to "spill over" into the next, in the form of a document capturing the earlier phase. The waterfall diagram fails to show the part of development where mistakes are made and corrected. This happens most frequently inside one phase, and often between adjacent phases. For example, testing uncovers a problem in the code, which

Our Names	Some Authors	Other Authors	Yet Other Authors
requirements	external requirements	requirements	specification
specification	internal requirements	architectural design	high-level design
design	design	detailed design	low-level design
code	code	code	implementation
test	test	test	test

▶ **Table 1.1**   Some names for phases of development.

must be fixed by returning to coding. (The usual name for that particular situation is "debugging.") Cross-phase feedback might be shown by arrows going "upstream" in the diagram (e.g., from testing to coding). The most serious mistakes are those whose correction requires retreating more than one phase. For example, a programmer might discover that the subroutine he is writing needs an additional parameter in order to handle some special condition, about which nothing is said in the design. Tracing the problem backward, it might happen that this special situation was never thought of, and it may be necessary to go all the way back and ask the end user what should be done. On the diagram, this could be shown as a feedback arrow from coding to requirements.

The worst mistakes that can be imagined in software development come to light only after the software has been delivered. In the classroom situation, they are the problems that flunk the student whose program doesn't work, problems of which the student was blissfully ignorant. "Maintenance" is the misnomer for changes made after delivery, but these could be captured as feedback from the "afterworld" of the released software. For example, "corrective maintenance," a fancy name for fixing a bug that wasn't caught during development, is feedback from release to coding. "Adaptive mainte-nance," a change to some feature of the software as delivered, is feedback from release to requirements/specification. There are potential feedback ar-rows connecting all the phases in the waterfall diagram, but they are not shown in Figure 1.1.

Perhaps the lack of standard-ization is the re-sult of using shal-low, poorly un-derstood, and imprecise ideas?

It is a measure of the youth of the software engineering discipline that the names for parts of development are not standardized. In this text, we will try to use the names from Figure 1.1 consistently, but the reader should be aware that in reading other books and papers a wide variety of names will be encountered. Table 1.1 gives a few of the possibilities, and the names in the table occur in combinations not shown as well.

There would be less disagreement about the names of the parts of soft-ware development if fewer distinctions were made. Most people could prob-ably agree on a waterfall diagram that looked more like Figure 1.2. The labels beneath the boxes refer to the parts of this book.

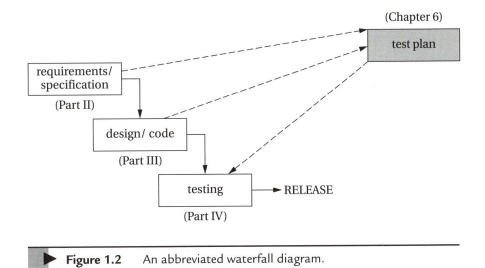

Figure 1.2   An abbreviated waterfall diagram.

1.3 The Business of Developing Software

Throughout this book, the development of software is treated as a technical problem, and the skills necessary to solve that technical problem are the book's subject. For what is so aptly called "an enthusiast," someone who loves to do the thing for its own sake, there is no more to software engineering than technical skill.

Computing has always had its share of enthusiasts—many people are fascinated by computers and what they can do. There is today an informal banding together of computer enthusiasts in what is called the "free software movement." "Free software" means that the end user of the software pays nothing for it, and anyone is free to modify the existing software and contribute to its development. The source is readily available to all users and developers, so there are a large number of people looking at the code. Although businesses can muster only small teams to develop and test their code, the entire world of enthusiasts and developers is available to write and test free software. Defects can be quickly and effectively resolved and distributed. (The other side of the coin is that chaos can ensue unless there is some control on changes made.)

Some businesses have embraced the idea of free software, but how is it possible for anyone to make money on free software? There are two ways: (1) A commercial organization can develop and sell software that runs "on top of" free software. The many enthusiasts using the free software are potential customers. (2) The pool of enthusiasts is a resource for a company that wants to contract for software development, for example, to support a specialized hardware device. There is far more expertise in the pool than any company could afford to keep in-house.

Free software proponents have formed organizations to advocate their ideas. The Open Source Foundation and the Free Software Foundation are consortia of developers and sometimes even businesses who fund, advance, and support the notion of open source software. The people who work for these organizations are paid something from fees that the members pay to belong.

The free software movement sometimes claims another kind of freedom for its members—a freedom more like anarchy. However, most software developers answer to some external authority—they work in a software business of some kind. Businesses are endlessly varied. To list a few common ones:

Garage.   The developer works informally and hopes to sell a product developed without any formal business structure. The extreme case is an enthusiast who plans to freely distribute the software, with no more than fame (or at least notoriety) as the reward.

Software startup.   A garage business can grow into a commercial enterprise that employs a few people and sells a small range of software products. However, there is little formality in the working arrangements, and all the principals in the company share all the business roles.

Microsoft.   Enough said.

Contractor.   Contract programming occurs in many ways, but the archetype is an independent consulting firm, whose employees are assigned to a software development project that the firm delivers under contract. Here there are two businesses clearly separated, the contractor and the customer. The contract situation is unique in that maintenance of the delivered product may very well be ignored or contracted out to a different company.

In-house.   In the early days of data processing using very expensive mainframe computers without much applications software in place, any computer system had to be written by those who wanted to use it. Data Processing Departments—now more often called management information systems (MIS) departments or information technology (IT) departments—were established to write and maintain the applications software the company needed. These in-house organizations are still around, more and more devoted only to maintaining the existing software. But organizations still have a need for tailored software, and any large company has its development staff, under whatever name.

Embedded-software developer.   Embedded software (and the computer hardware may be "embedded," too) is part of a larger product.

For example, the engine control computer and its software on a new car are a relatively small part of the car manufacturer's overall effort. Embedded software must interface smoothly with other, more conventional engineering systems designed by (say) mechanical engineers.

Each of these business types, and the myriad of variations on them, are concerned to a greater or lesser degree with issues "larger" than the technical ones of constructing the software. Except for the enthusiast, if these issues are neglected or mishandled, the business won't be around for long.

1.3.1 Time to Market

Software originates in the idea that a problem could be solved using a computer, and culminates in a working program that solves that problem. In a business, the program is in some way "delivered" to a customer. "Time to market" is a name for the interval between idea and delivery. For consumer software, it is the time that elapses before the product can be sold. The need to minimize time to market is a potent force controlling software development. It is said that customers always want delivery "yesterday," and they are not at all interested in the developer's difficulties in meeting that date.

It should be obvious that an artificially imposed development time limit may be impossible to meet, or if it is met, the delivered software might work badly, if at all. There is an engineering saw that in any product development it is possible to have any two of: schedule, budget, quality. (In complex enterprises like software development, however, increasing budget to meet a schedule but retain quality may not be an option. Fred Brooks is the author of a famous essay, "The Mythical Man-Month," that argues that adding personnel to a late project only makes it later. So perhaps one should say for software engineering it is possible to have one of: schedule, quality.) The only thing that can be done to hurry along a schedule without making a mess of the product is to shed features or performance. If overambitious plans are scaled back, it may be possible to deliver a good-quality product—just not the one originally planned—on time.

Time to market figures in even the least businesslike software development. An enthusiast working only for herself might rush things in order to get to the exciting part where the program is tried out. The compromises she accepts along the way may not matter—perhaps they could be revisited and mistakes corrected. But software bugs have a way of hiding where they cannot be found, and the rework could be so difficult that her project, once brought to premature completion and failure, is never finished.

A student working on a programming assignment has a fixed development time that ends on the assignment due date. The instructor who makes the assignment may or may not have allowed enough time; students have many things to do, and may not be able or willing to use the full period. (It is a rare student who then decides to begin at once and finish early.)

In a business, someone is responsible for selling the product, and the "marketers" are advocates for the shortest possible time to market. Engineers are usually opposed, asking for more time to do a better job. The two sides try to negotiate a compromise that will produce a good enough product in the shortest time. The conflict is a real one, but within a company everyone ought to be on the same side of trying to make the company prosper. It is one of a manager's toughest jobs to facilitate the discussion between engineering and marketing, and ultimately to be responsible for the decision that both will have to live with. Give the engineers too much and the excellent product they produce will not sell because competitors get there first; give marketing too much and the product will be so shoddy that it won't sell. Honesty on both sides is essential; all too easily the discussion can become a power struggle or a clash of ideologies. Engineering must be honest about the time required, and often the hardest part is asking for enough time—engineers are notable optimists, and always hopeful that they can perform miracles. Marketing must also be honest about how long the market will wait, and must not discount engineering concerns about quality by thinking: "We can sell anything if we just get it soon enough."

1.3.2 Perceived Software Quality

Like beauty, the quality of an engineered object is in the eye of its beholder (user). There are many dimensions to software, many characteristics that may or may not be important to different people. These characteristics are sometimes referred to as the "-lity"s because their names have that ending. Some of them are:

Functionality. What the software can do, its "features." In view of the all too prevalent possibility that software may fail to work, perhaps one should talk about its *advertised* features.

Reliability. The probability that software will not fail over a period of time. Reliability can be expressed as a "mean time to failure," how long on average it can be expected to work perfectly.

Dependability. The likelihood that the software will do what the user needs it to do. Dependability includes a weighting for the importance (to the user) of the task. Dependable software may fail, but not in a catastrophic way.

Usability. How easy the software is to use.

Interoperability. How well the software can be used with other software. Good interoperability means that input can easily be taken from other programs, and output can easily be sent to other programs. For example, a spreadsheet program should be able to send its output to a word processor program for inclusion in a report; a data collection program should be able to send data to a plotting program.

Maintainability. How easy the program is to change, both for fixing bugs and for adding to its functionality.

It is notable that "performance" of the software, in the sense of how quickly and efficiently it runs, is usually omitted from the list.

"Software quality" is elusive because it has so many dimensions. A user who needs interoperability may view a dependable program as poor quality when it can't be used with another as needed. Someone who finds all the functionality he needs will rate highly a program that another person thinks of as being of poor quality because it is difficult to maintain.

Software that excels in one quality dimension is likely to fail in another, just because every aspect of quality is different, and each takes time and trouble to attain. Time to market is the natural enemy of quality, and under time pressure, the development engineers may have to choose what can be accomplished and neglect something else. Furthermore, quality aspects interact in a pernicious way. To gain functionality increases complexity, which in turn tends to reduce maintainability and dependability.

Probably the most important dichotomy is dependability versus functionality. Some people don't want their software to let them down when they need it, and they don't care if it's a bit limited in what it can do; others are willing to put up with unstable software so long as it tries to handle everything, including the kitchen sink. It is reported that Microsoft's philosophy favors functionality over dependability; the overwhelming majority of service calls they receive are requesting not fixes for failures in their released software, but rather asking for new features. However, the advertising campaign for Microsoft Windows 2000 stresses its dependability, so the corporate vision (or at least the desired image) may be changing. A very similar tension occurs in the automobile market, and history there has shown that dependability can be sold, but only if features are not missing.

In every contest between an ugly, old-fashioned, dependable car, and a flashy one with poor dependability, the flashy one won.

Sometimes software applications dictate what kind of quality is needed. Microsoft seems to be right about its customers wanting functionality at the expense of dependability. Safety-critical applications like software embedded in medical equipment, on the other hand, demand dependability.

1.3.3 The Software Development Team

Software development is just one of the many human activities that must be organized to succeed—and it draws on the lessons of older cooperative enterprises. The two fundamental organizational paradigms are the "hierarchical" and the "distributed." In the former, people are placed in an organization chart that makes clear who is in charge of whom, and directives flow down the chart from the top in ever increasing detail. In the less common distributed organization, a group of people agrees to work together by consensus and cooperation, but each freely agrees to his or her assignment, and there is no reporting chain or supervisory relationship.

The essential psychological fact about human beings working together is that an effective working group cannot be too large. When more than a handful of people must cooperate, the overhead of mutual communication becomes so high that little else gets done. So if a project requires dozens of people, it will have to be organized hierarchically, with each small group reporting to a supervisor, a few supervisors reporting to a manager, and so on up to the project manager. IBM mainframe software was developed by such groups with hundreds of people; in its heyday, DEC software for minicomputers was developed by much smaller groups, almost in a distributed organization, reporting to a single layer of management. Microsoft uses an organization in which each application product (like the Excel spreadsheet) has its own team, probably run in a distributed fashion for small teams, but hierarchically for large ones.

The early phases of software development demand a few highly qualified people to handle requirements, specification, and design. Coding and testing can be spread over a larger staff. Design organizes the programming effort into independent units for assignment to programmers who work independently; testing is an inherently parallel activity that requires very little organizing effort to utilize hordes of testers.

1.3.4 Managing Development

The first decision that a software development manager (or the company for which the manager works) must make is the extent to which a formally defined and controlled process will be used in development. If there is to be control at this abstract level, the company has to spend considerable effort defining exactly what procedures will be followed, in training engineers to follow them, and in training managers to track the engineers' efforts. Passing from an organization in which there is no well-defined process used for development, to one in which all the steps are laid out and monitored, is a very large order. The Capability Maturity Model (CMM) described in Section 4.1.3 is a rough guide to five levels of organization that a software development operation might attain, and to pass from one level to the next is estimated to take on the order of two years. Most organizations are presently at or near the first level; many aspire to higher levels, but few to the highest ones—it is just too far to go.

Suppose then that something like the waterfall model, as an outline of the process to be followed, is in place in a company. What does management have to do as development proceeds?

Allocate resources.   Ideally, personnel can be assigned to development phases according to which ones can be done in parallel (test plan with design and coding, coding of independent modules), and staff can come and go on the project as they are needed. In practice, a fixed group of people is sometimes assigned for the duration of the project, and some of them may be under-utilized or overworked as it proceeds. Continuity in the group is important because there will be mistakes and feedback loops among the phases in which detailed knowledge, such as only an original team member possesses, will be essential.

Computing and staff support must also be allocated to the project, and there may be substantial lead times in obtaining them. For example, if a project is to use automated testing (Section 21.3), support software will have to be acquired and installed, and engineers must be trained to use it effectively.

Monitor progress.   A project manager lays out a detailed time-line for the work to be done, showing each activity and resource use as it is supposed to occur. Along the time-line, a manager wants to place as many "milestones" as possible—tangible items that the manager can use to monitor progress. The documents that end each phase of the waterfall life cycle are such milestones, and they are supplemented with interim reports.

Sometimes milestones are useful to engineers as well as managers although usually in a different way because their concerns are different. A completed test plan, for example, tells a manager that the requirements are good enough that later testing of the code can be carried out, and that the time-consuming testing phase has been prepared for in advance. Engineers are more interested in recording all the testing insights that can be gained from requirements before these are forgotten. But it is easy for management and engineering to be at loggerheads over a milestone—management insisting on it while engineering views it as unnecessary busywork. Both sides are right, according to their own concerns. Management needs to know how things are going. Engineering knows perhaps too well how things are going, and writing a report about it will take time that should be spent making progress. Engineering is at the mercy of management here, and the competence of a manager might be judged by how well he or she can evaluate progress without insisting on otherwise useless reports.

Assure quality.   Software development not only has to be completed (preferably ahead of schedule!), but in the end the software must work well enough to be useful. If the developer has carried out a sensible testing phase, this ultimate measure of quality is probably known, unfortunately too late to be of much use. (And of course, if the testing itself is of poor quality or has been eliminated because of a schedule crunch, nothing will be known until angry customers begin to be heard. The engineers, of course, will have a pretty good idea that all is not well, however little their managers know.)

What managers need as milestones throughout development are accurate indicators of how well the software to be finally delivered will perform. For example, what properties of a test plan, a milestone early in development, would point to a good final product or a poor one? There *are* ways to judge the quality of test plans and other development milestones, such as a design breakdown of code into modules. This book is devoted to explaining precisely what is known about good and bad software engineering. But unfortunately, the connection between doing good work along the way and getting a good result is a tenuous one. It is quite possible for engineers to go through all the right motions, their managers checking diligently all the way, yet still produce an unacceptable end product. For example, this could happen if a serious misunderstanding of the requirements occurs, or if a crucial design decision is wrong, or if code fails in some catastrophic way that testing did not detect. Everything in a modern software development process is designed to catch such mistakes, but no one believes that our best practices are good enough.

Furthermore, managers must rely almost exclusively on the good will of their technical engineering staff for any evaluation at all. Software development milestones like the test plan are complex and detailed, and although the people who made them usually know whether they are any good, it would be an unusual manager who would notice if his subordinates tried to cheat. Thus the force balancing the manager's ability to insist on a stupid report is the engineer's ability to fake the report without getting caught. An organization in which such games are played is in deep trouble. Under reasonable circumstances, engineers acknowledge the need for managers to know, and help all they can. Insofar as the whole development process works, and its documents and procedures are really useful to the engineers, the managerial overhead is small.

These management tasks are interrelated. If progress is not keeping up to the required schedule, more resources may have to be added to the project or shifted from one phase to another; or some features may have to be omitted from the software, or less time spent checking it.

The phases of the waterfall model are very useful to a manager because they provide self-contained checkpoints along the way to delivery. As each phase is completed, and with it the document describing that phase, a manager can examine these realizations in text of what has been done, and get a good picture of how well things are going. There is even a clever way to get expert help in assessing the test plan, requirements, specification, design, and code as they are produced, the "software inspection" described in Section 5.3. Without the waterfall phases, a manager is reduced to asking engineers to estimate how far along they are. The folklore is that whenever an engineer is asked this question, the preferred answer, independent of how things are really going, is, "I'm 95% done." A manager has no way to check such statements. Months after delivery was supposed to occur, it's still "95% done."

How Does It Fit?

(These questions at the end of each chapter explore ideas presented in each section. They do not necessarily emphasize the most important ideas of the section. A more pretentious name would be "thought questions," to help you see if you understand the presentation. Solutions and hints for some of the questions appear at the end of the book.)

From section 1.1

1. "Flashbacks" are a device often used to tell stories. Discuss the use of flashbacks from the standpoint of separation of concerns. How would you paraphrase Lewis Carroll's advice if the story is to be told mostly in flashbacks?

2. When people form into antagonistic groups, they find it very helpful to call each other derogatory names. Sometimes engineers are referred to as "nerds" in this way. And if a manager is pretentious enough, he might be called a "suit." If you have made up your mind which side you are or want to be on, write a paragraph on "What I hate most about suits (or nerds)." (If you haven't made up your mind, flip a coin to choose sides.) Then write a second paragraph in which you explain why it is right, proper, and good that suits (or nerds) are as you have portrayed them in your first paragraph. Which viewpoint is most true?

From section 1.2

3. The *products* of the development phases are not shown in Figure 1.1. Copy the figure and add them to it.

4. The waterfall model of the life cycle (Figure 1.1) suggests a river and a series of dams. The usual argument for dams is that they provide hydroelectric power, allow navigation, and control flooding. Opponents of dams say they interfere with the movements of fish, destroy the beauty of fast-flowing rivers and drown vast areas of the landscape, and when a large flood comes, they actually increase rather than limit the damage. Write a short essay in which you try to give analogies in waterfall software development to each positive and negative aspect of a series of dams on a river.

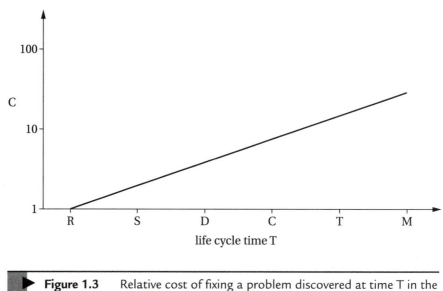

Figure 1.3   Relative cost of fixing a problem discovered at time T in the life cycle.

5. The curve in Figure 1.3 (after B. Boehm) shows the approximate relative cost C of fixing a problem discovered at time T in the development cycle. The rough positions of the phases are shown by their initial letters on the abscissa (e.g., "R" for Requirements). Notice that the relative cost scale is logarithmic. Thus, for example, if a problem found in the requirements phase cost $1000 to fix, it will instead cost about $10,000 to fix if not discovered until the coding phase.

   (a) Give an example of a requirements problem and explain the cost differential between discovery in requirements or discovery in coding.

   (b) Give a general explanation for why the graph has the shape it does (that is, why it is a straight line on semilog graph paper).

6. Suppose that someone invents a new phase of development called "bridge" that is supposed to go between "design" and "code." You are assigned to give a presentation about "bridge," but unfortunately you have only learned of this indirectly, and don't yet know just what is supposed to be done in "bridge." Nevertheless, you want to start preparing your talk.

   (a) In planning to be *critical* of "bridge," what kinds of arguments, based on general properties of the life cycle and the place of phases within it, might you use?

   (b) In planning to *support* the introduction of "bridge," what kinds of arguments would you use?

7. In Section 1.2.6, there is a cute saying about bugs and features. Give an example of a "bug" that a user might actually want to call a "feature," and explain why that is so.

8. Give a personal example of classroom "maintenance" of a piece of software, where you modified the results of one assignment to satisfy another, or changed an assignment's program to help with other work. Or, if you haven't done this, make up a plausible case where a student might do it.

9. Suppose that making the test plan *had* to be included as a separate phase in the waterfall model (Figure 1.1), connected as the other boxes are, not off to the side.

   (a) Where would be the best place to put it, and why?

   (b) Explain why making test planning a separate phase in the waterfall model is *not* a good idea.

10. A manager observes that the software engineers who work for him usually do not create test plans early enough in development. So he decides to force the creation of these plans by adding three new phases to the life cycle: (TP1) Test plan 1 is added between requirements and specification, (TP2) Test plan 2 between specification and design, and (TP3) Test plan 3 between design and coding. The inputs to these phases are the documents of the previous phase, and the outputs are three parts of a test plan. Explain what is wrong with the manager's idea.

From section 1.3

11. Does time to market figure as a force in contract programming? Explain how it does, or why it does not.

12. In the Challenger space-shuttle disaster, how did time to market enter, and who were the people analogous to "marketing" personnel?

13. Are power windows, seat adjustments, and outside mirror positioning in a car as dependable and maintainable as if these functions were done manually? Make an analogy to software.

14. Explain the difference between "reliability" and "dependability" by giving examples of a software system that would be considered dependable, but is not reliable, and vice versa.

15. Give some extreme examples of software that emphasizes one quality "-lity" at the expense of others. For example, how could it happen that a program is very easy to maintain, yet has poor functionality?

16. It is not easy to explain why performance is usually omitted from the "-lity" list. Other than its unfortunate spelling, can you think of reasons why?

17. Large hierarchically organized businesses have many "dead-end," low-skilled positions that small, decentrally organized ones do not. Comment on whether this has to be so.

18. Suppose that in reporting progress in the coding phase, an engineer says she is "95% done." Later on, when the code has been tested and released, a count of the lines of source code reveals that on her part of the work, 5200 lines were delivered, while at the time of the earlier report, she actually had 5300 lines. Was she telling her manager the truth?

19. When an engineer misspells "milestone" as "millstone," what might he be unconsciously thinking of?

20. Can you think of any instance in which an engineer might want to prepare a report that her manager did not request? Should she tell her manager about it?

Review Questions

(These review questions at the end of chapters are supposed to help with self-study. Their answers provide a rough outline of the chapter, and all major topics in the chapter are supposed to be covered by the questions.)

1. Name the phases of the waterfall life cycle to be used in the text, and briefly describe each in your own words.

2. The subsections of Section 1.2 do not give names to parts of the life cycle they describe. But names are given in Section 1.2.7. Make a list of which subsection(s) go with each name. A good way to display the answer would be to write the subsection numbers on Figure 1.1.

3. Contrast the manager's view of a software development project with an engineer's view.

Further Reading

(The list of readings at the end of each chapter includes two quite different kinds of citations, with brief descriptions of their content. One kind provides additional information, for example, in a standard textbook. The other kind of reference will take the reader far afield, and provide information about topics quite unlike software engineering. We note without comment that the latter references are usually more interesting than the former.)

The so-called software crisis in which the complexity of problems overwhelms software developers and makes their work late, over budget, and even inoperable is well described in a *Scientific American* article [Gib94].

Barry Boehm is often credited with inventing the name "software engineering." His seminal article on the subject [Boe76] makes very up-to-date reading, especially interesting in its predictions from 20 years ago.

Most textbooks on software engineering differ from this one in being concerned with the whole development process that involves an entire organization. This wider scope makes them thick books in which technical topics are not treated in depth. Perhaps the most used text is by Ian Sommerville [Som96].

A valuable collection of current readings is contained in a tutorial volume published by the IEEE (Institute of Electrical and Electronic Engineers, a professional association with a member Computer Society) [TD97].

Although he no longer considers himself a software engineer, Fred Brooks has excellent credentials: he was the manager of what may be the most complex computer system project ever undertaken, the IBM System/360. He writes with wit and common sense about the experience in *The Mythical Man-Month* [Bro75]. His more recent thoughts on software engineering (and the "software crisis") appear in a journal article [Bro87]. (And the two are available combined in an "anniversary" edition of the book.)

The Internet, and the World Wide Web that uses it, are becoming important sources of technical information, often rivaling libraries and journals. We have avoided making many references to Web sites in this text because the sites often change their name or disappear. But it is certainly appropriate to suggest that information about the free software movement be obtained from the Web, which is an important reason for free software's existence. So try the link `www.opensource.org` to learn more.

For learning about "what's *really* important" in software development, there are two excellent books by Weinberg [Wei99] and DeMarco and Lister [DL99].

References

[Boe76]   Barry W. Boehm. Software engineering. *IEEE Transactions on Computers*, pages 1226–1241, 1976.

[Bro75]   Fredrick P. Brooks. *The Mythical Man-Month*. Addison-Wesley, 1975.

[Bro87]   Fredrick P. Brooks. No silver bullet: essence and accidents of software engineering. *IEEE Computer*, pages 10–19, 1987.

[DL99]   Tom DeMarco and Timothy Lister. *Peopleware—Productive Projects and Teams*. Dorset House, 1999.

[Gib94]   W. Wayt Gibbs. Software's chronic crisis. *Scientific American*, pages 86–95, Sept 1994.

[Som96]   Ian Sommerville. *Software Engineering, 5th Ed.* Addison-Wesley, 1996.

[TD97]   Richard H. Thayer and Merlin Dorfman, editors. *Software Engineering*. IEEE Computer Society Press, 1997.

[Wei99]   Gerald Weinberg. *The Psychology of Computer Programming, silver anniversary ed.* Dorset House, 1999.

Some Principles of Software Development

I n the chapters to follow, we will consider each of the life cycle phases in turn, giving the rationale for its separate existence, and describing how to carry it out in practice. In this section, we present a number of general principles that will appear again and again as software development is described. These principles are behind the phases of the life cycle itself, and they arise in the mechanics of every phase.

2.1 Intellectual Control

Only complex software needs to be engineered. In simple cases, "craft" techniques are better. The analogy to mechanical engineering aptly describes the situation:

> When making a relatively simple tool or gadget, a craftsperson works by "fit and try" methods, shaping and adjusting the parts until they work properly together. Craft objects are often pieces of art when the craftsperson has talent for beauty as well as function. But for more complicated objects, craftsmanship fails. When there are too many parts, and too many interdependencies between parts, there must be an engineering plan to which a mechanic works. With luck and experience, fit-and-try methods can succeed, but they are wildly inefficient compared to engineering, because when the final parts do not fit, the whole must be done over. However, attempting to apply engineering techniques to simple objects is also inefficient, because the extra work is wasted; the object can be built in the time it would take to plan its building.

It is the same for software. A simple problem can and should be solved directly by programming—its "life cycle" consists of just coding and testing, with feedback between them when something doesn't "fit." Software engineering is for problems in which the craft method leads to extensive programming that must be done over and over because it never quite reaches its goal.

Students are usually taught to program in the "craft" style. They begin with simple problems and convert them directly into simple programs. Perhaps this is a good way to learn programming, but it establishes a false confidence that any problem can be solved directly. When a student has successfully completed a course in data structure programming, and has constructed programs of perhaps 2000 lines of code for somewhat contrived class assignments, he or she is ill prepared to tackle the development of small- to medium-scale software. Writing a compiler or an operating system kernel, which is expected of computer science undergraduates, *can* be done by many students without using software engineering. But some students find it impossible to "get it to work." We believe that some measure of software engineering will help, and that even those who don't need the engineering techniques will find them to be timesavers. As the problem grows, engineering becomes more and more valuable, until for "large" systems it is indispensable. It is simply impossible to build a commercial airplane without mechanical engineering; it is equally impossible to write the flight control programs for that plane without software engineering.

2.1.1 Complexity and Control

Problem complexity is the root of the problem of software development. When a human being attempts to solve a complex problem directly, failure comes from a loss of *intellectual control*. The person cannot see far enough ahead to know if decisions being made now will prove correct in the end, and thus may spend a long time and extensive effort pursuing a nonsolution. By the time the approach is seen to be inadequate, too much time and too many details have passed to be able to see exactly what went wrong, so the next try may be no more successful. In short, the person cannot fully grasp either problem or complete solution, and so gets it done only by good luck. Those who have worked in situations where they do not have intellectual control—where they *know* that their best work may be wasted—know how uncomfortable it is.

To gain intellectual control of a complex problem requires that the complexity be reduced. There is a respected minority of computing professionals who believe that this should be done by refusing to accept problems for software solution that are "beyond the state of the art." They are a minority because the forces that drive software development encourage grandiose projects. Software has handled "impossible" problems in the past, some-

A general in the
Reagan admin-
istration "star
wars" program is
reported to have
said that if scien-
tists believed the
project impossi-
ble, he could cer-
tainly find others
who would take
his money.

times with apparently magical results; it is our strongest, most flexible tool
for doing difficult things; the payoff can be immense, so why not try? Those
who believe that some problems are just too hard may be right. Some optimists have gone bankrupt trusting to software solutions that did not ma-
terialize on schedule. Some projects have spent a great deal of money with
nothing to show for it. Nevertheless, the majority position is that software
professionals do not choose the problems on which they work, and hence
complexity must be handled in some other way.

Intellectual control must be gained in spite of problems in which it
seems unattainable. The problem decomposition of the software life cycle
is itself an attempt to reduce complexity and gain intellectual control. And
within each phase, other decomposition techniques are used with the same
intent.

2.1.2 Language Betrays Us

In a famous interchange in *Through the Looking Glass*, Lewis Carroll explains the meaning of words:

> "I don't know what you mean by 'glory,' " Alice said.
>
> Humpty Dumpty smiled contemptuously. "Of course you don't—till
> I tell you. I mean 'there's a nice knock-down argument for you.' "
>
> "But 'glory' doesn't mean 'a nice knock-down argument,' " Alice
> objected.
>
> "When *I* use a word," Humpty Dumpty said, in rather a scornful
> tone, "it means just what I choose it to mean—neither more nor less."
>
> "The question is," said Alice, "whether you *can* make words mean
> so many different things."
>
> "The question is," said Humpty Dumpty, "which is to be master—
> that's all."

This is, of course, just what mathematicians do with language—steal its
words for their own purposes—and what programmers do with program
variables—make them mean what they want. But we are not used to natural
language words being treated that way, and we think as Alice does that words
like "glory" can't be messed with. Unfortunately, it is all too human to behave
just as Humpty Dumpty does, and take over words arbitrarily. There is even
a word for these words of which we are "master:" jargon. In a new discipline,
the jargon isn't well established or agreed upon, so the very tool that is best
at establishing intellectual control—our language—can betray us. We have
already seen this in the lack of agreement about names for the phases of
the software life cycle in Section 1.2.7. If two people are trying to talk about
software development, and one of them uses "specification" while the other
uses "(architectural) design" for the same idea, things quickly get out of

control. In Part IV, something similar will happen with the word *test*. It is used to mean at least these things: an input value that gets tried for a program; a pair of values (input, output) that describe what a program *should* do on one execution; a similar pair that is what the program actually *does* do; a collection of inputs to try, or pairs, etc. So when someone says, "the test failed," it's hard to know just what is meant.

It would be better if it were not so, but in talking about software engineering, watch out for words with shifting, imprecise meanings.

2.2 Divide and Conquer

The only general problem-solving technique for reducing complexity is to break a problem into pieces. Finding the right pieces is an art requiring talent and creativity. Without this talent, two bad things can happen:

Trap 1.   Solving the pieces may not solve the problem. It is essential that any decomposition plan include a way to put the pieces together into the desired solution.

Trap 2.   Some of the pieces may be as hard to solve as the original problem. A "decomposition" plan that hides essential difficulties in one of the parts, solves the other parts first, then again tries to decompose the difficult part, has merely wasted time by deferring the real problem.

The creative genius to decompose a complex problem so that the complexity is really reduced is art, not engineering technique. But there are a few guidelines to be used in seeking such breakdowns.

2.2.1 Independent Parts

It is the essence of decomposition that the parts must be independent. Intellectual control is not improved unless a person can concentrate on one part without thinking about the others.

2.2.2 7 ± 2 Rule

Human beings seem to operate psychologically according to a "7 ± 2" rule. We keep intellectual control of collections best when they contain five to nine parts. The first rule for divide and conquer is therefore that there should be only a few items in the decomposition. (There are five parts to the software life cycle!)

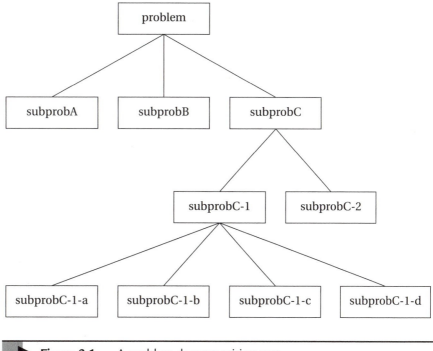

Figure 2.1   A problem decomposition tree.

2.2.3 Hierarchies

Breaking a large, complex problem into about seven parts guarantees that at least one of the parts will also be large and complex—the best one can hope for is to divide the complexity by 7, and if some of the parts are *not* large, others will have to be closer to the difficulty of the whole. To avoid falling into trap 2, it is necessary to continue by decomposing the parts, and the new parts in turn, until *all* parts are small and simple enough that their solution can be glimpsed.

The resulting problem decomposition can be drawn as a hierarchy tree—with the original problem at the root, under it the first-level break-down, and subsequent breakdowns under each part—the leaves of the tree being problems that are simple enough to require no further decomposition. In this tree, the nodes are the subproblems, and the arcs mean "is a subproblem of." For example, the decomposition tree shown in Figure 2.1 represents a problem broken into three parts: the first and second parts to be solved directly, and the third part further decomposed into two more levels.

Hierarchies have the virtue that they may contain a plethora of parts, yet no part of the structure is very complex. For example, a tree with seven levels, each part of each level decomposed sevenfold, can meet the criterion for good intellectual control of each part (the branches) and in the whole (the levels), yet may contain $7 \times 7 \times \ldots \times 7 = 7^8 = 5{,}764{,}801$ subproblem leaves (if the root level does not count as one of the seven). That is, our human abilities can be brought to bear on problems millions of times more difficult than we can handle directly, if a good decomposition can be found.

2.2.4 Know When to Stop

During the decomposition of large elements into smaller, more manageable elements, it is easy to get carried away. Since the technique of "divide and conquer" is targeted at making things more manageable, it becomes an abuse of the principle if the engineer generates so many smaller elements that they become unmanageable. It would be possible to generate specifications so detailed that they become unusable. In circumstances where it is necessary to generate large numbers of smaller elements, we must organize these elements under a larger but less detailed "umbrella" in order to have a manageable hierarchy.

Knowing when to stop may be the most difficult task of software engineering. The ultimate example is to stop before you begin, when software engineering itself is not needed for an easy problem. Once engineering is begun in the requirements phase, it is tempting to go beyond system requirements and begin to solve the problems they pose. For example, when discussing database requirements with an end user, an engineer might decide that linked lists are the storage mechanism to use. This decision is inappropriate—it mixes the concerns of the design phase into the requirements discussion where they are not necessary. "Knowing when to stop" can be thought of as making no decisions until absolutely necessary.

2.3 Identify the "Customers"

A basic tenet of producing quality goods of any kind is to keep in mind the needs of customers. In software development, there is a clear "customer" for the software, the user who met with the developer to work out the requirements. The user is also directly involved in the maintenance phase. But in between, in the details of the different life cycle phases, the user is not so clearly the customer. In the testing phase, for example, the engineering goal is to uncover problems in software. Of course, this is done so that the ultimate user will not encounter those problems, but the test engineer is not working only for this user. The test engineer's customer is also the programmer who must repair any mistakes uncovered.

In each of the software phases, it provides clear goals and focus to ask "for whom is this being done?" The answer is always the same. The primary customer for each phase is in the subsequent phase. Thus requirements are "bought" by a developer who writes specifications from them, and in turn "sells" these to a designer, whose customer is a coder, whose customer is a tester. In addition, the tester is a secondary customer for all the other phases although it is the test plan that is "bought." Another secondary customer lies in the previous phase (particularly for testing): having "bought" the previous phase work, feedback can be provided on its deficiencies, if any are found.

For an individual developing software, the designer, coder, and others are all rolled into one person. Nevertheless, to take advantage of the separation of concerns inherent in the phases of the software life cycle, that one person assumes different roles and works most efficiently by staying strictly "in character." The designer should not act like a programmer or tester, for example. But remembering who your customers are provides the necessary control on this role-playing.

The rule is: always try to put yourself in the place of your customers; when working for a customer, try to meet that customer's needs. The feedback corollary is: as a customer, demand that work done for you is what you need.

2.4 Fuzzy into Focus

The human mind has a capacity for abstraction that has served the human race very well since its beginnings. Early humans only had to be attacked by carnivores a few times before learning to be cautious around creatures with fangs. The ability to abstract allows humans to live in a world where cars come in different shapes and sizes, radios and televisions have controls in different locations, and stuffed animals with fangs are harmless.

However, though ability to abstract is arguably the human mind's greatest talent, it is also its greatest liability. Generalization leads to stereotyping, which can hinder our problem-solving ability. To illustrate this limiting concept, imagine a door with the door handle placed on the same side as the hinges: people entering the threshold would push against the door handle expecting it to swing out or in, but in fact it would be the *other* side of the door that would open. This would lead to a great deal of surprise, and a phenomenon known as cognitive dissonance (confusion).

In the arena of software development, abstraction has similar strengths and weaknesses. If we share a similar set of experiences, we tend to have similar ideas about the meaning of general concepts. For instance, if a software engineering team has built several payroll systems, they will probably share an idea of what is expected when a customer asks them to deliver "a payroll system." However, if this team is asked to build "a student registration system" (and they have never built such a system), the team members will probably have completely different ideas about what such a system is.

In the course of software development, a vague idea must be translated into thousands of lines of precise code. This work is the opposite of abstraction, and as such, runs contrary to what the mind is inclined to do. In trying to accomplish a task that is not well suited to the nature of the human mind, we find that problems we encounter are directly related to our tendency to abstract: sometimes important details are left out of our specifications and ambiguities creep in.

In conceiving a software system, it is not uncommon for the initial proposal to be a few vague diagrams drawn on a piece of paper. Translating this diagram to a completed, running system is what software development is all about: bringing a "fuzzy" idea into crystal-clear "focus." The ultimate focused system is what we want, but we have to start with the fuzzy diagrams because at the beginning they are the best we can do.

The idea of "fuzzy into focus" applies at all levels of software development. At the beginning, a good software engineer will take the initial diagram and develop clear, concise, and unambiguous specifications. These specifications have brought the initial diagram into better focus, but after all, specifications are not code. During the design phase, the specifications are brought into better focus by developing a general software system architecture to satisfy requirements. Then the requirements are partitioned into the architecture's subsystems; that is, each requirement is assigned to a particular part. More clarity has been introduced because now we know *where* each of the requirements will be fulfilled. Clarification continues until concrete code—that could not be less fuzzy—is reached. The next task is to let software engineers design each subsystem so that implementation engineers can then take the final step of translating the subsystem design into concrete code.

2.5 Document It!

A dangerous myth in software development is that work done well is "self-documenting." What "self-documenting" means to most people is that it is unnecessary to record anything outside the primary product being created. Thus self-documenting code needs no explanation; everything about it can be learned by reading it directly.

If all the products of a life cycle phase have been explicitly identified (as we identified a test plan in the requirements phase even though it is not the requirements document), *and* if no mistakes are ever made, then the "no documentation" of "self-documentation" may be all right. But the existence of a maintenance phase recognizes that there will be changes to software, mistakes at some level that must be corrected. Because of these changes, one of the secondary customers of a phase becomes the very person working on that phase. When change is required, it will be necessary to understand what was done *and why* in order to redo it. The explicit documents of the phase, whose customers are in other phases, are no help with changes in the phase itself. The most obvious illustration of this is in the coding phase, whose primary product is a precise program expressed in some programming language. Programs are notoriously hard to understand, and without comments describing what they intend, and how they accomplish it, most people (even their authors, when time has passed) simply cannot understand them.

2.5.1 Record It or It's Lost

Our inclusion of a test plan as part of the requirements, specification, design, and coding phases is in recognition of the truth that the most obvious information, once used but not written down, is lost forever. A programmer, coding some difficult algorithm, often "worries" about whether the code written is correct. At the time such a worry appears, the potential problem is glaring, and the programmer would love to conduct a test to see that all is well (or that all's not well, so it can be fixed). But the code is not complete and can't be tested—that lies in the next phase. The test must be recorded, along with the concern that gave rise to it, because weeks and hundreds of hours of programming later, it is almost certain that the programmer will not be able to recall the "worry," much less the specific test that would check it out.

2.5.2 Know What You've Assumed

Assumptions are an important part of developing software because assumptions are useful to constrain a problem to a reasonable and solvable domain. For instance, in writing a registration system for a community college with an enrollment of 2000 students, it is reasonable to assume a maximum capacity of 5000 students for the registration system. But suppose that the college intends (and intended all along) to sell this package to other universities to cover the development costs. If this information comes out only at the end of development, the assumption would be a disaster, since it will have dictated data structure design, storage capacity, system runtimes, and commercial support package selection (e.g., of a database management system).

If assumptions are documented at each stage of development, these assumptions are placed on public display for review by each person who reads the document. If any of the assumptions are incorrect, the odds of early discovery are improved.

2.5.3 Traceability

One documentation trick has proved particularly useful in relating each life cycle phase to the next. *Traceability* means being able to find the parts of the phases that go together. Consider how a software designer works from a requirements or specification document. Some small part of the document states *what* should be done to handle some special case. The designer of that part of the software is charged with stating *how* it should be done. Once that element of design is included in the whole, it will be hard to reconstruct where it came from and why. But if the parts of the requirements document are labeled, and those labels are carried as documentation on parts of the design, reconstruction will be easy. Similarly, design elements can be traced to the implementing code and to the test plan using the same label.

Any change can have repercussions in every phase of development, can affect all of the documents that exist and all the work that has been done before the change became necessary. Without traceability through requirements, specification, design, coding, and testing, the most minor change can turn into a nightmare of repeated work—work that is compromised because its integrity is lost and produces software no one can trust.

2.5.4 A (Document) Place for Everything and Everything in Its Place

Duplication of information conflicts with updating. If information is kept in more than one place, its copies may be changed to disagree with each other. Duplication of information results from poor organization of a document. The structures of the requirements, specification, and the design, which are repositories for vital information, should lend themselves to the tasks for which these documents will be used. If this structure is clear and concise, there will be one and only one logical and obvious place for each piece of information. Duplication of information can result when an important piece of information is inserted in the wrong place by a well-meaning engineer guessing at where it belongs. When other engineers go looking for this information in the document and can't find it, they may well "rediscover" the information by talking to a user or another engineer. Once they've got the information, they may put it in a different location in the document. Now that the information is in several places, there is a maintenance problem.

It is best to organize documents so that there is an obvious "place for everything," and if information is discovered to be in the wrong place, it should be moved to the correct location to put "everything in its place."

2.5.5 Documentation Isn't a Novel

Good writing style has characteristics that are *not appropriate* in documenting the complex process of software development. Here are three things that most of us like in fiction (and nonfiction), and why they should be avoided in documentation:

Cleverness. The best writing takes all of our intelligence to figure out—if it's too easy, we find it boring. But in documentation, clarity should come first. If a clever presentation loses even the most plodding reader, the document has failed in its purpose.

Varying terms. It's boring to refer to anything over and over using exactly the same word, and writers are taught to avoid this repetition. But in documentation, the reader is more interested in being sure of the subject than in variety. If it's a "garg," call it a "garg" and nothing else, even if "blorg" is a synonym.

Distributed ideas. Novels don't usually have an index, and if one did, each index entry would have many defining page citations, with information spread throughout the book. Documentation should be just the opposite, with every concept defined in exactly one place. It's hard to read straight through documentation, but it's easy to look things up.

> The great novels are those that are just slightly obscure so that readers cannot exactly be sure what they mean.

However, most of the rules of good writing apply to documentation. In particular, it's important to use parallel constructions, to use paragraphs appropriately, to keep to the subject, etc.

2.6 Input/Output Is the Essence of Software

The fundamental nature of software is to transform a set of inputs into a set of outputs. This seemingly simple concept (Figure 2.2) is a pervasive notion that needs to be remembered throughout the software life cycle. Much of the early effort in the software life cycle is directed toward:

- Identifying all the outputs from and inputs to the software. Sometimes these inputs and outputs are not apparent because they are hidden from view (e.g., system time and date, databases).
- Identifying the valid and invalid ranges of the inputs and outputs.
- Identifying particularly significant values of inputs and outputs. For example, checks are not issued for 0.00 even though a zero balance may occur.
- Identifying important combinations of the input and output values.

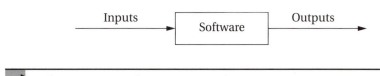

Figure 2.2 Software as a transform.

2.7 Too Much Engineering Is Not a Good Thing

Software engineering is a difficult and challenging profession. It requires discipline, hard work, and technical knowledge. It is a profession that involves constant learning that takes the engineer into fascinating areas of application and often to the leading edge of other technologies such as electronics, mechanical engineering, and mathematics. It is easy to lose sight of the primary purpose of software engineering: to produce software.

2.7.1 If It Ain't Broke Don't Fix It

A system can be "improved" to the point that it no longer works. Here are some examples of engineering a system to death:

- After the system has passed a majority of its tests, and is in the process of undergoing a final release, software engineers are sometimes tempted to completely rewrite a subsystem because it is convoluted or inefficient. This can introduce a whole new set of defects that can delay deployment of the system for a long time.
- The requirements, specification, and design processes are not the end result of the software process. However, the methods and structures that are to be used by these processes can be debated and discussed *at length* by obsessive engineers. This debate can set the project schedule back by an unacceptable margin. The phenomenon is sometimes called *analysis paralysis*.

2.7.2 The "Creeping Feature Creature"

Software developers must remember that the end user is not a software engineer, and is not using the software in a development environment. Instead, the end user may be trying to generate information quickly for a staff report, or generate payroll for a company, or trying to deal with a long line of irritated customers. The end user is supreme when feature sets and usability issues are concerned.

Software engineers are prone to discovery of "necessary," "useful," or "essential" functions at a late stage of software development. Often, engineers will install these features without discussion, hoping to surprise and delight the user. "Creeping features" have been known to destroy projects by delaying the development or deployment of features that the user had specified. The user is surprised by the delay of an essential software system, but seldom delighted. Sometimes extra features are indeed desired by the users, but the impact on delivery date must be presented to the user as an expense of having them installed.

It is not good engineering to deliver a luxury car when the end user wanted a basic truck.

2.8 Expect to Deal with Change

Although lip service is often paid to the desirability of novelty and change in our lives, few people really like upheavals in their world. When something fundamental changes in a software project, it is always a setback because work is wasted and must be redone.

2.8.1 Plan for It

Perhaps it is unnatural to plan for changes—why look for trouble? The question seems unanswerable in daily life, but for software the answer is: because trouble is bound to come, and planning for it can minimize the trauma that changes will cause, allowing them to be made routinely and correctly. Mistakes get made and must be corrected. New information is uncovered, and old assumptions prove false. And in software development, the most unpleasant changes are direct and common: the customer changes his mind.

2.8.2 Fix It Now

Once the need for change is clear, don't procrastinate. The implications of a change will not be known until it is accomplished, so making it should have first priority, however unsettling or difficult that may be.

2.9 Reuse Past Work

There is a large investment in a properly conducted, properly documented software project, in getting it right and keeping it right throughout development. When the project is complete, its organization will be a huge help in maintenance of the software. But a completed project has value beyond the life of its product because parts of it can be *reused*.

2.9.1 Previous Work Well Done Is Golden

One of the great inventions of the world goes under the trade name of Bisquick (Krusteaz is another brand). This stuff looks like white flour, and indeed it is mostly composed of flour, with powdered milk, baking powder, salt, and other ingredients of batters and doughs mixed in. Pulling the Bisquick off the shelf instead of mixing these ingredients from scratch saves a few minutes any time you want to make pancakes or biscuits. The story is that Bisquick was "invented" by someone who realized that if he mixed up a double batch of dry batter ingredients, it took no longer, but half would keep for next time. That's the principle of software reuse, only for software

We freely do-
nate the name
"BitQuick" to
anyone who
wants it. Be-
fore you use it, it
would be wise to
check that some-
one else hasn't
got there first.

"batters," which are more ideas than material stuff, one batch can be used over and over.

Software projects, or parts of projects, repeat themselves. To take a current example, screens full of icons, buttons, and menus occur in almost every PC product, and the requirements, specifications, designs, and even code and test plans for them are more similar than they are different from one another. When developing your twentieth PC product, you've done it all before. It seems a shame to do it all yet again, particularly because it's boring and error-prone, yet since the new product is not exactly the same as the old, you may have to. But if the common ingredients could be identified, they might be adapted to a new project with a great saving of time and a great improvement in quality.

Programmers have shared code from the start of the craft. Indeed, the IBM user organization has always been called SHARE, and it came into existence to pool subroutine libraries.

If code is the most obvious thing to reuse, it is not the only or even the best candidate. Each document starting with requirements may be easier to mine for its content and modify for a new project than it would be to repeat the phase that made the document. In the extreme, activity on a new project would be nothing more than modifying documents of an old one. The gain in time is substantial, and so is the potential for quality. The old project worked in the two senses that it was carried through to completion, and its code runs.

2.9.2 Create Software So that Reuse Is Possible

Software reuse doesn't just happen by looking back at old projects. The customers for reuse are the developers of future projects; unless their needs are thought of, they will find it very tough to get anything from the past. Planning for reuse means always trying to see present work outside the present context. When building part of a widget, an engineer is thinking, if only unconsciously, "what does a widget need here?" The (again, unconscious) rationale for a choice might be: "That's not important, widgets don't ever do that." In contrast, reuse thinking is: "What might get in the way of using this when it's *not* a widget, doing the very things widgets don't do?"

Always steal code
instead of writing
it anew. But don't
steal the wrong
code, and don't
steal code that
doesn't work.

Generality is important in making software parts that can be reused, but so is granularity and encapsulation. Chances are that what's needed in the future will be like a small part of what's being done now, not so much like the whole. The parts must not be inextricably woven together, and they must be small enough to recognize.

The final issue is one of quality. Work intended for reuse, since it may be placed in a context that is not imaginable when it was created, must be of much higher quality than work that is done quickly, fiddled with until it can be used in a limited context, and then discarded.

2.9.3 Don't Reinvent the Wheel

In medical research circles, the acronym NIH stands for the National Institutes of Health. In software development, it stands for a syndrome that is anything but healthy: Not Invented Here. What's wrong with someone else's work? Maybe nothing, just NIH.

"We could get those matrix routines from Stewart's textbook." "Nah, I'll write them myself."

Software people, since the day the first program was written, have felt that it is better to be in complete control, to "do it myself." There's some justification for this attitude—programmers who have tried to use someone else's code and found it to be riddled with subtle bugs, are determined not to be burned again in the same way. But this attitude is easily carried too far. In the 1960s, a lot was learned about operating systems for large mainframe computers. When minicomputers arrived in the 1970s, their operating systems were mostly reinvented from scratch. Their designers didn't read about the earlier work. In some cases, early lessons were embodied by programmers who worked just down the hall, as when the DEC PDP-11 systems group did not talk to the DEC PDP-10 systems group. When the microprocessor arrived in the 1980s, again its operating systems were invented from scratch. All this reinvention accounts for Microsoft systems that are far inferior to mainframe work done 40 years ago. The hardware designers did not make the same mistake: the CPU chip that those PC systems run on can do all the tricks that the 1960s' mainframes did (and do them far cheaper).

In other engineering disciplines, the first stop on a new project is the library, to see what's been learned in the past. A lot of education is "reading the classics," from Dickens for budding novelists, to ancient Roman highway construction for civil engineers. Software engineering has a long way to go.

2.10 Take Responsibility

Systematic procedures for getting things done, separating the concerns in different parts of the process, can be an excuse for blaming and finger-pointing instead of dealing with difficulties. For example, if during coding, an ambiguity in the design is encountered, the coder can think, "not my problem" and largely ignore what the designer failed to do. And if it manifestly *was* the coder's problem, because that same person did the design, then "can't deal with that now, fix it later," is the same kind of thinking. What the developer has to keep in mind during all phases of the development process is that he or she is directly and unremittingly responsible for the software. A myriad of things can go wrong, and if everyone involved has the attitude that any difficulty has to be examined with care and dealt with properly, then there is just a chance that all errors will be caught and the software will work properly.

In almost every kind of engineering, construction includes "safety factors," to account for unexpected or extreme conditions. For example, the girders of a bridge are made a bit stronger than calculations indicate is needed, just in case. Software engineers could use ideas like redundant code verifying a calculation, checksums, and other data-structure integrity mechanisms to try to protect against their own mistakes, but except in extremely critical applications, they do not use these devices. The reason probably lies in the myth that software is "logical" rather than physical, and hence can be perfect, not affected by forces of nature. It has long been known that human mistakes in software development are just as damaging (and occur far more frequently) than "acts of God" that bring down the structures of civil engineers. But for the foreseeable future, software safety rests with the care of human beings doing their best.

Procedures for developing software, like laws, have a "letter" and a "spirit." And like laws, the letter very imperfectly captures the spirit. Thus the people involved have to look beyond what they are "supposed to be doing" to what they are "supposed to achieve," and recognize that when the two don't match, it is the outcome, not the rule, that matters.

Flaws in all software have their source in the development process. To have seen the process going wrong and done nothing is irresponsible.

2.11 Summary of Software Engineering Principles

The subsection titles of this chapter can be woven together into advice for the software engineer:

> Take responsibility for the software you produce. Identify your customer and your customer's needs, and think of them in input/output terms. Research what has been done before. Stay in intellectual control of your efforts, and document what you do. When a problem is too difficult, divide it, always striving to bring more focus to initially fuzzy solutions. And when you've done everything perfectly, there will be changes, so be ready for them.

They will be ▶
marked like this

These principles will find application throughout this book.

How Does It Fit?

1. Group the principles of this chapter under three headings: (a) Of primary importance, (b) moderately important, and (c) peripherally important. List about the same number of principles in each group, and give a brief justification for putting each item in groups (a) and (c).

2. Pick two of the principles in this chapter. Give an example of each one, an example as far removed from software development as you can invent.

From section 2.1

3. The following formula was seen on a blackboard in the physics building of Cornell University in the 1960s:

$$\lim_{3 \to 4} \sqrt{3} = 2.$$

Relate this to Humpty Dumpty's idea about the meaning of words.

From section 2.2

4. Give an example from your own experience (not from software development if possible) of falling into divide-and-conquer trap 1.

5. Explain how a problem decomposition described by a sevenfold branching tree with seven levels after the root differs from decomposing the same problem into 7^8 arbitrary parts. How would you draw a tree for the latter decomposition?

From section 2.3

6. Explain why too much thinking about "customers," and what they want and need, can violate the principle of separation of concerns.

From section 2.4

7. What excuse can be given for bringing "fuzzy into focus" as opposed to working harder and never being "fuzzy" at all?

From section 2.5

8. Some people have an amazing memory for detail. They can recall the characters and plot of every novel they've read, for example, or rattle off textbook lists they mastered years ago. Suppose such a person is developing a piece of software. Does that person need documentation? Why or why not?

9. It has often been said that a writer (like a novelist or poet) must write for himself, never for his public. Why is this, and why doesn't the advice apply to software engineers writing code? Are there situations in which this advice doesn't apply to writers? Are there special software engineering situations to which it does apply?

From section 2.9

10. Comment on how hard it would be to steal code from an existing project as a function of its size, and on the worth of the effort. For subroutines of a few lines of code, it would be much easier to write them than to find, read, and understand existing ones. At the other extreme, it seems just as difficult to reuse a 100,000-line program than to write it. Where is the point at which reuse is worthwhile?

Review Questions

1. List the major principles described in this chapter and explain each briefly in your own words.

Further Reading

The authors of this text are not alone in collecting principles of software engineering. We have more than Boehm [Boe83] but fewer than Davis [Dav95].

The original work on "7 ± 2" appears in one of those articles that is worth reading just because everyone refers to it, but most have not read it [Mil56].

As an example of system requirements "beyond the state of the art," the so-called star wars system is considered in detail by Dave Parnas [Par85].

Anyone interested in writing of any kind, must read "the little book" [SW59], the collection of dogmatic grammar rules from William Strunk, Jr., and the wise thoughts of E. B. White on writing well.

References

[Boe83]   Barry W. Boehm. Seven basic principles of software engineering. *The Journal of Systems and Software*, 3:3–24, 1983.

[Dav95]   Alan M. Davis. *201 Principles of Software Development*. McGraw-Hill, 1995.

[Mil56]   J. Miller. The magical number seven, plus-or-minus two: Some limits on our capacity for processing information. *Psychological Rev.*, pages 81–97, 1956.

[Par85]   David L. Parnas. Software aspects of strategic defense systems. Technical report, University of Victoria, July 1985. DCS-47-IR.

[SW59]   William Strunk, Jr., and E. B. White. *The Elements of Style*. Macmillan, 1959.

chapter 3

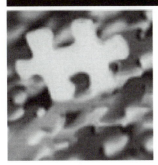

Is It Really Engineering?

M uch of the human activity of dealing with the objects in the world can be conveniently categorized as:

Art. The production or expression of what is beautiful, appealing, or of more than ordinary significance.

Craft. A trade or occupation requiring special skill, especially manual skill. Carries the shade of meaning that this skill is applied to bad purposes, as in "crafty devil."

Science. The systematic study of man and his environment based on the deductions and inferences that can be made, and the general laws that can be formulated, from reproducible observations and measurements of events and parameters within the universe.

Engineering. The art or science of making practical application of the knowledge of pure sciences; a profession.

(The definitions are taken, somewhat edited, from *The Macquarie Dictionary*. Most of the definitions include each other as special meanings. For example, *Art* is also defined to be "craft" or "science.")

Where does the making of software fall in this categorization?

Science seems the least appropriate since observations and measurements, not to speak of laws, are involved at most peripherally. *Art* may sometimes apply, but most software could hardly be called beautiful. Probably the best case today can be made for *craft* more than for *engineering*. Both are occupations of making things, but the engineer is a professional who applies scientific knowledge. This book is about the knowledge required to engineer software. (On *engineer* as a verb, the dictionary is a little more lenient: "to arrange or carry through by skillful or artful contrivance.") The reader must judge whether there is enough science here to take us beyond *craft*.

If program developers are to be "software engineers" and their activities are to be "software engineering," then it is worthwhile comparing the field to older, more established branches of engineering. In this comparison, there are three aspects to engineering:

1. The technical and scientific definition of the field.
2. The professional, organizational side.
3. The social responsibilities of the profession.

3.1 What's Different About Software?

Software development is different from other kinds of engineering because:

1. Computer hardware costs (almost) nothing and software can do (almost) anything. As a single example, a complete microprocessor can be installed in an appliance like a washing machine for roughly the same price as a conventional electromechanical switch, but the microprocessor can be used to make the washing machine appear extremely "smart" in its operation, and it will probably far outlast the switch.

2. Software is backed by "science" more like mathematics than like physics or chemistry. That is, it is artificial and logical, not tied to the physical world and its laws of nature. People invented both computers and their programs, and their creations are arbitrary. (Hardware operates within natural laws, but it is a good first approximation to assume that hardware answers only to an arbitrary, human design.)

3. Software is perhaps the most complex of human artifacts, both in itself and in the process that creates it; there is wide scope for human error.

4. Software development operates at a considerable remove from software use, so the consequences of developer actions are difficult or impossible to foresee. The more general a software solution is, the more likely that it will be used in ways the developers did not imagine.

5. The software industry is very young, and its explosive growth is unprecedented; hence many of the usual societal forces have not yet come to bear on it. At the same time, since software is growing ever more important in daily life, ethical issues do not wait for these institutions.

These differences make software very important in the world, yet not very well understood. The tried-and-true ideas in other branches of engineering may not work for software.

3.2 Artificial Science

The "scientific method" has as its fundamental idea a kind of contest between nature (or God for those who believe that nature is God's creation) and the human mind. The contest is an unequal one (even for those who do not believe in God) because nature is always right, and humans are usually wrong. In the contest, people try to figure out how the world works, according to some assumed rules. One of the rules is that nature plays fair by invariably repeating itself. The results of observations, if made carefully enough, can be trusted to be repeatable. Another rule is that the natural system is elegant and simple so that people have at least a chance of figuring it out. In the contest, people develop a theory to explain the mechanism by which a natural phenomenon operates. From this theory deductions are made about details of the phenomenon. An experiment is then performed to observe the details, and if it agrees with the predictions, the theory is "supported" (but theories are never "proved"). If the experiment disagrees with the theory, the theory is disproved.

> In Einstein's famous statement, he did not believe that God was "damn mean," only subtle in framing the laws of physics.

Engineering is based on science and constrained by it. The engineer tries to make things work but is unable to break natural laws. Thus, for example, theoretical physics has long supported (and experimental physics so far not disproved) the law of the conservation of energy. The mechanical engineer working within this law does not therefore expect to get something for nothing, like vehicles that require no fuel, or perpetual motion machines.

Software is in no sense a natural phenomenon. It has no laws but accidental ones that its human creators happened not to violate—and these are seldom elegant. Like mathematics, its "science" is no more than logical implication. As a mathematical example, if a real-valued function is continuous, then it has a Riemann integral. This theorem can be deduced from the definitions of the terms in it, and no one expects that it can possibly go wrong (say, by the discovery in Australia of some particularly nasty continuous real-valued function). In just the same way, if a program of length n is a member of a context-free language L, then it can be parsed in time $O(n^3)$ by a parser that properly recognizes all and only the programs of L. No one believes that counterexamples will be discovered on the hard disk of some PC in Tasmania. There might be a mistake in the proof of the theorem about Riemann integrals. There might be a mistake in a parser for L. Particular examples of functions and programs (respectively) might expose such mistakes. But the role of "experiments" with examples like these is completely unlike experimental physical science. In science, an experiment might disprove a theory and the theory would have to be discarded; in computer science, such an experiment serves only to expose a "bug" in human logical work. We continue to hold an unswerving belief in the theorem or the parser, which we fix up to handle the examples.

It is perhaps the most interesting thing about mathematics (and software) that despite its artificial, human-defined nature, it is subject to limitations. The software ones are better known than the mathematical ones (although they are of much the same character). For example, it is impossible, *in principle*, to find an algorithm to determine whether an arbitrary piece of software will ever abort with a runtime error, even if the particular input on which the software begins is given. (And this "runtime error problem" is of considerable interest to software engineers, who would certainly like to know if their programs are going to abort.)

These philosophical considerations have a profound effect on the way software research is done, and on the intellectual discipline of computer science. But most of the practical aspects (the *engineering* aspects) of software development arise in treating software as just another commercial product.

3.3 The Analogy to Other Professions

In other professional fields, tangible products are developed, and analogies exist between these products and pieces of software. The analogies are just that, though perhaps as often misleading as helpful. When information about software development is presented in the rest of this book, the reader may find it interesting to think about whether software is like a skyscraper, or an airplane, or a car, or a computer chip, or something else, and may want to look for lessons from the other fields.

3.3.1 Civil Engineering

Civil engineers design buildings and other large structures like bridges and dams. (The name of their discipline arose when it was necessary to distinguish them from the *military* engineers who do similar things for a different purpose. The U.S. Army Corps of Engineers is the best known modern group of military engineers.) The safety of these structures is of paramount importance. The science behind civil engineering is strength of materials, mechanics and hydraulics, on the grand scale referred to as "the forces of nature" (or "acts of God"). Newtonian physics provides elegant and accurate solutions to equations that describe how (say) a bridge will behave, and standardized components (like steel I-beams) are manufactured with well-understood qualities. The civil engineer can therefore predict how a design will behave when constructed and put out in the world; by adding "safety factors" that make the structure even stronger, a remarkable success record has been accumulated. (Not that there have not been also some spectacular failures, which have led to changes in materials and designs.)

3.3.2 Architecture

A civil engineer designs buildings only at a detailed level; it is an architect who does the high-level design. Architects are supposed to know enough science that they do not design buildings that are impossible to build safely, but their business is primarily fitting the building to its intended use and satisfying its human owners and occupants. Thus architecture is often taken as the model for the most difficult and creative part of software development, the overall concept within which a program is developed. Software engineers have even appropriated the name, calling the crucial first design ideas "software architecture."

3.3.3 Mechanical/Aeronautical Engineering

The industrial revolution of the 19th century was built on the application of the power sources of first, falling water, and then, steam. The engines drove all manner of gadgets that helped to make textiles and other consumer goods. Today, design of cars and airplanes is the apex of the mechanical engineering business. Both are relatively complex systems of cooperating parts, subject to wear and tear as well as to flaws in design or imperfect materials. It is said that a present-day commercial airplane cannot fly until the weight of paper design documentation is equal to the weight of the plane. "Maintenance" is a necessary part of the continued functioning of mechanical devices, including carefully conducted inspections to find and replace what is beginning to wear out. The components of cars and planes are assembled in hierarchies, where a component is built from other components, and in turn may be part of a larger component. Making these components work reliably together is a large part of design.

3.3.4 Computer (Hardware) Engineering

This subdiscipline of electrical engineering is the envy of all other fields today. The cost of computers has fallen repeatedly by orders of magnitude, whereas the capabilities and desirable characteristics (like speed, small size, and low power consumption) have improved even more dramatically. This progress is the result of massive integration of parts. Where the first computers were giants wired up by hand, a modern PC (which costs 1000 times less, and has 10000 times the speed) is built from a handful of semiconductor chips, each performing the functions of hundreds of thousands of separate parts. Thus the complexity of a computer is in its chipset, and chip design is the heart of computer engineering. A modern chip could not be designed without computer assistance, in the form of CAD (computer-aided design) programs. These help the designer lay out the circuits that will go on the chip, and the manufacturing process is heavily automated once the rather abstract design has been built in a CAD workstation.

The analogy to hardware engineering is naturally the most appealing for software, and has even given rise to something called CASE (computer-aided software engineering). But the dangers of analogy are also most evident here. Hardware at its most complex only begins to approach real software complexity. More important, hardware has constraints on its form that originate in the physics and materials science of its manufacture. These constraints paradoxically allow hardware designs to be under better human control. Software lacks all constraints, which tempts its human designers to construct software that is so crazily structured that it cannot work. The CAD program disciplines the hardware designer to stick to the tried-and-true; the CASE program can be only cosmetic help to the software designer, who is not prevented from trying crazy ideas.

3.3.5 Medicine

Medical doctors do not have a "product," at least not at the present stage of genetic knowledge, but they do diagnose and "repair" health problems that their patients experience, just as software problems sometimes fall to software engineers. The suggestive aspect of the medical analogy to software is that human medical problems are very complex and so variable that there seems to be only a little solid science behind treatment. Furthermore, doctors are consummate "professionals," and have been highly successful at controlling entrance to the profession and maintaining their incomes at a high level.

3.4 Responsibility of Software Developers

If software is a product made and sold like any other, most of the issues of engineering such products are well explored, if not always simple and clear. There is general agreement that anyone who sells a product bears some responsibility for it. The degree of responsibility turns on two points:

- Did the product do significant harm?
- Was its seller negligent?

It is agreed that real responsibility exists only when a user is seriously injured (otherwise nothing of consequence has occurred), and when the producer could and should have done better, but did not. The ambiguity in such a standard leaves wide latitude for interpretation, and the legal system exists to try to fill in the gaps.

A peculiar culture has grown up around software, perhaps as a consequence of its intangible, logical nature. Where software is involved, none of the normal human rules seems to have much force. Thus students who would never think of stealing a book will steal computer files and think nothing of it. People who would think it very wrong to read a letter addressed to a friend will snoop on the friend's e-mail without compunction. And people who would feel tremendous guilt over building a bookcase that falls down and hurts a friend have no problem giving someone software that crashes and causes considerable harm. The sociology of computing is just beginning to be studied, and such phenomena are striking but not very well understood. For software professionals, responsibility for the programs they develop is not an option, but an absolute necessity.

3.5 Engineering Institutions

Society has a need to control the interaction between people who produce a product and those who use it. A number of institutions exist for this purpose and have been used to good effect in a wide variety of circumstances.

3.5.1 Market Forces

People supposedly will not buy shoddy goods if they have a choice, and in a free market system, they should be able to choose a quality product and drive a dishonest producer out of business. The matter is complicated by price—people *will* buy shoddy goods if they are cheap enough, and will put up with them because they cannot afford better. In software, another complication is that users are not very good at evaluation—the goods may appear different than they are because software lacks the usual self-evident marks of quality. Further, software is quite discontinuous from one product (or release) to another, and users have no way of evaluating the quality of changes. Release 5.1 of what was an excellent program at 5.0, although it promises wonderful improvements, may turn out to be terrible.

Special commercial organizations exist to help sort out good products from bad (or safe from unsafe)—perhaps the best known in the United States is the Underwriters Laboratories (UL) dealing with electrical devices. For a fee, these organizations put their stamp of approval on a product after testing it to determine whether appropriate standards are met. However, it is a lot easier to certify a toaster than a word processing program, and although UL is beginning to venture into software, it may be difficult for any organization to acquire the public trust that is essential to such an operation.

3.5.2 The Legal System

Although ultimately it is the body of case law that determines the official societal position on any dispute about responsibility, the law moves very slowly, and works poorly in complicated situations. If professionals can't agree on what's right, how can they expect judges and juries to do better?

Existing case law applies to software in two quite different ways, depending on the view taken of the software itself. The precedents are in manufactured goods and informational services. If software is taken to be a product, comparable to a toaster, its sale carries clear responsibility for the manufacturer and sometimes for the seller. Should a customer be harmed and blame it on the software, a suit may be settled in favor of the customer, particularly if it is demonstrated that manufacturer or seller did not use proper care. On the other hand, if the software is taken to be an informational service, like a book, then the customer is expected to exercise common sense in taking "advice" from it, and if something goes wrong, cannot blame the maker or seller. "Strict liability in tort," although seldom applied to software, holds the maker responsible without excuse, providing that harm has been done.

3.5.3 Warranties

A warranty is an attempt to turn responsibility into a contract between producer and user, a contract that is part of the sales transaction. The producer agrees to some limited form of responsibility, and in return the user agrees not to hold the producer responsible beyond the limitation. Perhaps the "vacuous warranties" that we joke about in software are really producer attempts to realize the limitation aspect without giving anything in return. However, like all legal documents, warranties are not absolute. In the case of many products, producers have been held responsible even when the warranty explicitly denies responsibility. (In a similar way, many legal-appearing "releases" that we are all asked to sign have no real force if something bad enough happens or there is negligence.) Warranties also have a market function, in that users may be willing to pay for them, or to choose between competing products on the basis of warranties. Warranties provide a way for producers to add value to a so-so product by offering to replace it on warranty. Such a product may then successfully compete with one of better quality, its warranty making it equal.

WE PROMISE NOTHING. YOU ARE ON YOUR OWN!

Software warranties are more problematic than for most products because software does not wear out. An offer to replace software, for example, is not meaningful if the replacement is a copy with the same defect, or a new release with different unknown defects. To make a software warranty valuable, the producer would have to promise to fix problems. The complexity of software makes it doubtful that any meaningful warranty is believable. The producer probably cannot tell if software is adequate, and if it is not, may not be able to fix it.

3.5.4 Professional Organizations

Beginning with the craft guilds of the Middle Ages, the producers of any product or service have had an interest in controlling their own industry. The most important part of control is access to the profession itself. Professional organizations try to restrict the supply of people in their occupation, and thereby influence the price of their services. The American Medical Association is certainly the prime example of success in this control, with the American Bar Association a close second. Second, professional organizations try to police their membership. If some members behave irresponsibly, all those in the profession can be harmed. Professions are partly distinguished by having a generally accepted code of ethics to which their members subscribe willingly. However, it can happen that such codes are adopted more to avoid outside interference than because the "profession" truly accepts them. The dreaded outside interference usually takes the form of government regulation.

> ACM officials have several times tried to change the organization's name. The membership, however, always votes them down.

The software profession (if it is one) has two organizations. One, the Association for Computing Machinery (ACM), was formed just after the Second World War. The second organization is a subgroup of the Institute of Electrical and Electronic Engineers (IEEE), the IEEE Computer Society. The Computer Society is probably more concerned with hardware than is the ACM, but both groups have strong software, and software engineering, components.

3.5.5 Government Regulation

> A socialist would say that market forces *usually* run counter to the public interest and that the role of government should be much wider.

It is recognized that market forces can run counter to the public good, and that in such cases, government is the only entity with a broad enough scope to control abuses. A case in which this is clearly so is when a government grants a monopoly. Since it has by fiat removed the controlling force of competition, it is beholden to exercise control. Telephone and power companies are monopolies regulated by U.S. state and federal governments, which must approve substantial service changes and rates. Today's telephone companies are less monopolistic and less regulated than in the past, and the same "deregulation" is being applied to power. (What remains regulated are the hardwired distribution systems, since it is in the public interest not to duplicate them.) It is probably too soon to say whether deregulation itself is actually in the public interest. Another clear case for regulation occurs when it is demonstrated that competition is a force in the wrong direction—producers are led to make more and more dangerous products because they are in demand; government then steps in to protect the public (from itself!). Most drug laws, from the federal approval of over-the-counter products to criminalization of "recreational" drugs, are of this kind.

Governments generally do not approve of monopolies that they have not authorized and do not regulate. If commercial interests band together to control the market (or if one dominant company controls it by default), then the government may institute "antitrust" action to break up the "trust" organization and force competition. The theory of the "free" market has it that competition will lower the price and improve the service, which governments are supposed to favor for their citizens (and for themselves as buyers). The most famous antitrust action of recent years resulted in the breakup of the Bell Telephone empire of American Telephone and Telegraph. The U.S. Justice Department is currently following the same course with Microsoft Corporation, claiming that they have used their position as the de-facto supplier of most of the world's operating systems to unfairly compete with other software companies (notably, that Microsoft has conspired to deny hardware vendors their operating system unless they also accepted other software with it, to the detriment of companies trying to independently market such other software). A computer professional, listening to the technical claims being made in court in the Microsoft case, cannot help wondering if the legal system has any hope of coping with software issues.

There are at present only a few beginning attempts to regulate software, and these are part of ongoing regulatory activities. For example, the Federal Aviation Authority (FAA) necessarily deals with software because it is used in the aircraft they must approve for commercial use. The FAA's task is becoming much more difficult because the next generation of aircraft, beginning with the Airbus 320 and the Boeing 777, cannot fly without computer assistance, so the software *must* work. The Nuclear Regulatory Commission (NRC) is beginning to deal with nuclear power plant shutdown and control systems based on software, and hence to certify this software, as they have in the past certified other aspects of plant construction and operation. The Food and Drug Administration (FDA) is beginning to assume responsibility for medical products, both those used in treatment (like X-ray machines) and those prescribed (like heart pacemakers). These regulatory authorities have a far more difficult time dealing with software than with the other aspects of their domains because there is no agreement within the profession on standards and practices.

3.5.6 Professional Engineers and Accreditation

The engineering professions are unique in that their practitioners daily attempt public works that risk a vast liability should they fail. Civil engineers carry the greatest burden because the structures they design could potentially injure tens of thousands of people. To deal with this problem, a joint effort of government and professional engineering organizations has created the position of professional engineer (PE). To earn the PE title, an engineer has to be certified by government (a state in the United States). The certification involves training (approved by the professional association), work experience, and examinations designed by the professional association and administered by the government. On any substantial project, there must be a responsible PE, who signs off on each decision of the project. He is literally responsible because he can expect to lose his livelihood if anything subsequently goes wrong that can be traced to his lack of skill or foresight. Furthermore, engineering schools are accredited by a professional organization, and some projects will hire only graduates of an accredited program.

There have been a few attempts to introduce these engineering institutions into the software industry, but most have foundered on the difficulty of defining what a "software engineer" should know, and how to define the limitations of responsibility for a "software PE." There is a computer science accrediting body, the Computer Science Accreditation Board (CSAB), but its findings do not carry the weight of the ABET (Accreditation Board for Engineering and Technology) organization in the older engineering disciplines. It would be unthinkable for (say) an electrical engineering department at a major university to lose its ABET accreditation, but most of the top-ranked computer science departments disdain to even apply for CSAB accreditation. For the future, college programs explicitly in software engineering (as opposed to more general business or scientific computing) are coming into existence, and it may be appropriate for ABET to accredit such programs. The ABET and CSAB organizations are also talking about a possible future merger.

3.5.7 "Software Engineers" Are Legal Only in Texas

The differences between (say) mechanical engineers who design automobiles and "software engineers" who design programs are substantial, but there are similarities, too. The decision about whether there really is a profession called software engineering, however, is not at all in doubt. Engineering is a well-established profession, and like all professions, its members have taken steps to protect themselves from those who are "not in the club." In the United States (state by state) and in many other countries, laws regulate the use of the title "engineer" after a person's name in a business context. With some exceptions (people who drive trains and members of the U.S. Army Corps of Engineers, for example), these laws prohibit the use of "engineer" as a title unless the person has an appropriate degree from an ABET-accredited department and has passed a state licensing examination. The recognized fields of engineering are precisely defined, and though "sewage" is one of them, "software" is not. According to the legal definition, there can be no software engineers, and people have been prosecuted for

There are 470,000 electrical and computer engineers, but 860,000 programmers; there are 1.3 million engineers of all kinds. (U.S. Bureau of Labor Statistics, 1998)

calling themselves by that title. The state of Texas has, however, begun the first attempt to license software engineers. They began with the legal end of the stick, establishing the license. Now they have only to decide who is allowed to have that license and how that will be determined.

There are reasons why there may never be widespread recognition of "software engineering," not the least of which is far too many people are needed to practice in this field. Professions are by definition small, elite groups. Be that as it may, it is our contention that the ideals, standards, and technical character of software development can be modeled on the engineering profession, and we will use the words *software engineering* proudly, without the quotation marks, in the rest of this book. Let Texas do what it can.

How Does It Fit?

From section 3.1

1. In a discussion with a "real" engineer, say, in electrical power, it may carry the day to describe the way in which shrink-wrap software is sold and serviced—the customers are expected to pay for the developer's mistakes. The power engineer can appreciate the difference. Write a description under the title, "How it would be if toasters were like PC software," describing what would happen if a person bought a toaster that worked as badly as some software works, and tried to take it back to the store.

From section 3.2

2. From your experience in college courses, argue that mathematics, although it's been called the "queen of the sciences," is not a science at all. How do you suppose it got to be "queen"?

3. Building a perpetual motion machine, and finding an algorithm to determine whether software will abort at runtime, are both "impossible" problems. Identify as many differences between them as you can. In particular, if you had to choose which problem is not really impossible, and will someday be solved, which one would you pick, and why?

From section 3.3

4. What is the connection between salaries in a profession and its professional association controlling the number of people who are qualified to join the profession?

5. What if a software engineer behaved in professional life as a doctor behaves? What differences might there be in how the engineer would act? Describe some of the things a doctor-like engineer would and would not do.

From section 3.4

6. For each of the following situations, give a computer analogy, and decide the ethical thing to do, in the situation as described and in the analogous computer situation. If you wouldn't do the same thing, why not?

   (a) On a friend's desk you happen to see a receipt for a piece of jewelry, which you know was a present for a mutual friend. Do you look at the amount and tell the friend?

   (b) First-class mail addressed to someone you don't know is delivered to your house by mistake. Do you open it? Do you see to it that the letter is redirected?

   (c) In a restaurant you often frequent, you notice a mistake on the bill, in your favor. Do you call the waiter's attention to it and pay the extra?

   (d) A friend keeps his garage locked with a padlock. You are standing next to him when he opens it. Do you observe and remember the combination? Do you later go and explore the garage by yourself?

From section 3.5

7. Which of the institutions of this section is the strongest in controlling the harm that can be done by bad software? Answer for:

   (a) As things stand today

   (b) On the basis of potential for the future

   Justify your answers.

8. Do you think that a professional organization like the ACM should take a position on whether software engineers should develop software as their customers require, or sometimes refuse to do so because the software will cause harm? Justify your position in terms of:

   (a) What is good for the profession

   (b) What is good for society

9. If there are too many software developers to form an engineering profession, perhaps they could form a trade union. Discuss whether or not this would be a good idea.

Review Questions

1. Explain why software development is neither science nor art according to dictionary definitions.

2. What institutions are characteristic of an engineering profession? List them in what you consider to be the order of importance for "professionalism."

Further Reading

Philosophers of science have not yet begun to consider computer science, which is a discipline quite distinct from both the physical and social sciences. An exception is Herbert Simon's small book *The Sciences of the Artificial* [Sim96].

Harry Petrosky is a civil engineer very devoted to his profession and aware of its limitations as well as its joys. His *To Engineer Is Human* [Pet85] should be read by anyone aspiring to engineering, but particularly by budding software engineers. Nancy Leveson, an expert in the safety of systems that include software, has written a clever comparison between the dangers of exploding steam boilers in the industrial revolution and the dangers of software [Lev92].

Using any Web search engine, you can discover the site for a collection of reports called "Computer risks to the public," edited by Peter Neumann under the name "RISKS." The site has a good search engine of its own and can be used to explore detailed information on every sort of software and hardware problem imaginable, from malfunctioning of ATMs to airliner crashes. The information on the Ariane-5 rocket disaster in Chapter 10 came from the RISKS site.

Oliver Wendell Holmes wrote a famous poem about a perfect feat of mechanical engineering and what happened to it, "The Wonderful One-hoss Shay" [Hol76].

The ACM has an official code of ethics, which it has published in its membership magazine [ACM93]. Both ACM and IEEE routinely report on the evolving body of software law. A survey of basic legal issues and terms appears in reference [Sam93].

The U.S. Department of Justice is charged with bringing antitrust proceedings against corporations it judges to have monopolies not in the public interest. Its most famous recent case resulted in a court ordering the breakup of the Bell Telephone empire. The DoJ is now proceeding against Microsoft, with an outcome yet to be determined. However, at the same time, almost without publicity, a far-ranging revision of the Uniform Commercial Code (UCC), which governs the legal responsibilities of sellers, is in progress. Cem Kaner believes that the revision is a disaster, and it's hard not to agree with him. The Web address is `www.badsoftware.com`, where you will find links about the UCC.

References

[ACM93] ACM. ACM code of ethics and professional conduct. *Communications of the ACM*, pages 100–105, February 1993.

[Hol76] Oliver Wendell Holmes. The deacon's masterpiece, or the wonderful one-hoss shay. In Richard Ellmann, editor, *The Oxford Book of American Verse*. Oxford University Press, 1976.

[Lev92] Nancy Leveson. High-pressure steam engines and computer software. In *Proc. 14th Int. Conf. on Software Engineering*, 1992. Melbourne.

[Pet85]   H. Petroski. *To Engineer Is Human: The Role of Failure in Successful Design*. St. Martin's Press, New York, NY, 1985.

[Sam93]   Pamela Samuelson. Liability for defective electronic information. *Communications of the ACM*, pages 21–26, January 1993.

[Sim96]   Herbert Simon. *The Sciences of the Artificial*. MIT Press, 1996.

chapter 4

Management and Process

A ny enterprise small or large has a goal and expends its resources in the form of time, effort, and money to achieve this goal. When many people are involved, their efforts must be coordinated to keep their projects moving toward the goal. The people responsible for this coordination are the *management team*, and the path that a project follows is called its *process*. It's been said that management is the world's oldest profession— even hunters and foragers had to coordinate the hunt, assign territories for foraging, and keep track of food supplies. Since prehistory, management techniques have been developed into something like a science, and managers themselves have put down their weapons and devoted full time to coordination.

The managers who control the process, and the engineers who carry it out, are natural antagonists, but they have to cooperate for a project to succeed. Managers carry the responsibility for success, but they rely on engineers understanding what they have to do.

4.1 The Controversy over "Process"

At the turn of the last century, there arose within mechanical engineering (and its professional society, the American Society of Mechanical Engineers, ASME) a movement that eventually split the field. A similar situation appears to be threatening the software development community today, so it is worthwhile to look back at the historical situation.

4.1.1 Fred Taylor's Scientific Management

In the 1890s, a mechanical engineer named Frederick W. Taylor invented what he called "scientific management." Today, his ideas survive in part of what is called industrial engineering and, more popularly, as "time-and-motion study." Taylor's idea was that the *way* in which things are done is the key to better results. In the most famous and successful example, he studied the production of metal parts on lathes in machine shops. He found that huge increases in productivity could be obtained by:

1. Using better belting (in 1895, lathes were driven by central water or steam power, and each machine had a large leather belt that powered it off a central shaft).

2. Using harder steel for the cutting tools (Taylor "invented" what is now called high-speed steel, by accidental discovery while he was comparing different tools).

3. Changing the way lathe operators worked, to force them to use the fastest cuts and operations that the improved power and tools would allow, as determined by experiments.

Scientific management, or "Taylorism" as it was sometimes called, was then the discipline of hiring experts to perform the experiments and work out the efficient procedures (the forerunners of time-and-motion people of today), and of hiring shop managers who would use the experts' results to raise productivity.

Taylor's plan would not have been so interesting to business, nor would it have caused so much controversy, had it not had a "labor" component. The lathe operators had to work a good deal harder, under much more stress, to comply with the wishes of the scientific management. Only the best operators could carry out the demanding routines at all. Taylor proposed to solve the "labor problem" of unrest under sweatshop conditions by paying much better wages (as piece-rates in a complicated scheme) to workers who could and would follow his plans. Those who did not go along would be paid even less than they had been before, and the ideal was that these recalcitrant workers would quit, to be replaced by others better skilled or more compliant. It is not clear that Taylor was actually trying to improve the lot of the machine shop worker; he probably was not. It is clear that businesses that adopted his methods were enthusiastic about the productivity gains; they had no difficulty cutting wages for those who did not speed up but sometimes could not bring themselves to raise wages for those who did.

For the analogy to software development, the most interesting aspect of the scientific management movement was acted out in the ASME. Some of Taylor's fellow engineers were his supporters and disciples. But the larger group felt that his work was not really engineering but rather some kind of nontechnical hybrid that did not belong in the ASME. And eventually a competing "Taylor Society" was formed to which the scientific management advocates could switch.

4.1.2 Program Development as a Formal Process

Just as Fred Taylor noticed that 1890s' machine shops were not very efficient and could be better managed, so it has long been recognized that software development is too often a chaotic process, in which no one is in control. Indeed, software engineering as a discipline is thought by some managers to be no more than a collection of tricks for keeping technical workers in line. From the other side, those technical workers—software engineers—view this control as incompetent managers trying to run a project without a clue as to what's really involved. The latter view is daily put forth in Scott Adams's *Dilbert* comic strip.

It was a great insight to realize that the *process* of software development should be studied, formalized, and controlled by engineering techniques. The development process is just as much an artifact of human invention as the software itself. It is obvious that a documented, systematic development process is preferred over an intuitive, hit-or-miss one. A controlled process can be analyzed. It can be measured. It can be changed in response to what is learned about it. In short, improvement is possible only when working with a well-defined entity. There is no point in studying a haphazard development process because the next time it will be haphazardly different, and what might have been learned may not apply.

In Europe, the ISO 9000 standards (developed by the International Standards Organization) describe how business and manufacturing procedures should be documented, analyzed, and improved. ISO 9000 is used in the United States, but there is also a model developed explicitly for software development at the Software Engineering Institute, called the Capability Maturity Model (CMM). The CMM is described in Section 4.1.3.

The details of "software development as a process" are of only passing interest in this text. It should be clear that in any complex activity, organization is needed and useful, and that although those deeply involved in current chaos may fight to keep the status quo, it is certainly wise for managers to impose rational control if they can. However, just as Taylor split the ASME, a split is developing between technical and management software people over the importance of studying the software development process, as opposed to studying the software itself, the product, and the engineering techniques that produce it. The quick name for the controversy is "process vs. product." Something of the process-side argument has already been given: how can one expect to get things right if one does not even follow a recognizable development plan, a plan that can be analyzed and improved? The technical software engineer might respond that there are plans and plans, and plans directly concerned with the product should outweigh those concerned with organizing people. The engineer might say, "let's plan the software carefully, but planning how to plan, and writing reports on plans, is carrying things to a silly extreme."

Traditional engineering is based on the "product" orientation. It is the software engineer's job to know the technical skills needed to produce software, and to bring those to bear. No attention need be paid to just how that is done beyond following "standard practice." For software development, that standard could be the use of something like the waterfall development model. Just *how* the requirements analysis (say) is done is not very important. The engineer doing it knows what is to be accomplished, is trained in the techniques to use, and so should be left alone to do a good job. The engineer's manager may want to study how well it is working, but that's not engineering. Historically, this focus on product has been very successful. The argument is made that without technical skills, no bridges can be built, no matter how skilled the project managers may be. Without management skills, on the other hand, a project might go wrong, lose money, be late to completion, and so forth. But if badly managed engineers do build the bridge, the bridge can still be sound.

For software development, the record is mixed. There are many examples of projects in which no "bridge" was built at all—the project was abandoned before the software was completed. There are also examples in which a complete absence of management control resulted in superbly engineered, working software. There are case histories of a development team that repeatedly failed to complete difficult projects, and then became spectacularly successful through a change in management practices. In today's world of dangerous machines that are often under computer control, and the computer under software control, it isn't an academic question to ask how dependable software should be produced. Is a controlled process necessary? (Not in theory, but that's the way to bet.) Can a process be found that is sufficient? (Probably not.) Will better technical training for software engineers help? (Almost certainly.)

The controversy has been brought into sharp focus by Watts Humphrey's publication of a "Personal Software Process" (PSP). In a textbook and in training courses he proposes that software engineers do a kind of time-and-motion study on themselves, to learn to better control their own technical work, and to better estimate how long it will take them to do what they do. Humphrey's PSP is almost the logical complement of this book. Indeed, if there were time, it might be a good idea to use both the books together. This one would teach the technical material, and Humphrey would teach how an individual can use it most efficiently. But that's just the point: there isn't enough time. The engineering position is that it's hard enough to acquire and use the needed technical skills without having to clock them, too. The management position is that an engineer is in the best position to do the managing, and efficiency will be best served that way. Since software engineers are usually on salaried contracts, it seems rather like Taylor explaining to the lathe operators that they should work harder, only without the pay incentives.

4.1.3 Capability Maturity Model

Focus on software development processes has created a demand for evaluating the quality of an organization's process. Any extended discussion of software processes should be prefaced by a reminder that there is no necessary connection between process quality and product quality. Everyone believes that understanding and controlling the development process is a good thing, or at least that there is no harm in doing so. However, scientific validation is lacking for the hypothesis that a good process leads to a good product. To actually conduct the necessary experiments would be prohibitively expensive. So in evaluating a process, the product is mostly ignored except in rhetorical writing, such as: "How can a quality product come out of organizational chaos?" In evaluating an organization, no products are examined; the process is evaluated in its own terms.

The process description and evaluation system that most directly applies to software is the Capability Maturity Model (CMM), which assigns to a software development organization a level (1 to 5, low to high "maturity"). The model is not static; it views organizations as evolving toward higher levels. Some of the factors that go into defining the CMM levels are properties of the organization itself; most are properties of how its software projects are conducted. No specific project is used; it is assumed that all projects follow the same procedures. Thus it is quite possible for an organization to function at different levels for different projects. The evaluation of CMM level attempts to capture, from its established practices and goals, how an organization is likely to behave. But for each particular piece of software being developed, the organization may behave better or worse than its own procedures tell it to.

As might be expected from a subjective measure like the CMM, the level where an organization is placed on the scale depends a good deal on who is doing the evaluation. There is no certified, official CMM evaluation procedure. An organization may do a "self-evaluation" with the intent of finding and correcting organizational problems. An expert consultant can be hired to do a perhaps more objective evaluation. (But since consultants are paid by their clients, even the most rigorous professional standards are open to some question.) But all quibbles aside, an assessment of CMM level tells a good deal about an organization, and the factors that go into attaining the higher levels reflect general beliefs about the best way to develop software.

Critique of the CMM Levels

Most descriptions of the CMM levels are full of the hype of trying to sell the model to managers; our intention is more to warn engineers. We take the critical view that effort should not be spent on process at the expense of effort on product, unless there is a clear reason to believe that the product will benefit. The discussion will be organized around the names for the levels suggested by their originators.

Level 1: Initial.   An organization is described as being at level 1 when it pays no particular attention to its development process, which is thus haphazard.

Comments: It might be better to call this "level 0" since it has no description within the CMM. However, "level 0" could also be reserved for an organization which collectively says: "Process? What's a process?" A persistent problem with codifying subjective standards as the CMM does is that the standard does not easily apply unless things are done exactly in the order it assumes. Hence an organization that made use of many ideas from the CMM, but not in the order or the manner described in the formal levels, would likely be placed at level 1.

Why do engineers find zero a more useful number than businesspeople do?

Level 2: Repeatable.   At level 2, the organization's management can track the crucial development parameters of cost, schedule, and functionality, and can repeat past successes on new projects. However, this refers more to the *ability* to track than to the routine exercise of that ability.

Comments: Despite what might seem the modest requirements of this initial level, one persistent criticism of the CMM as a series of goals to attain is that the first step in the stair is too high. To reach level 2, an organization may have to devote so much time to examining its process that real work comes to a standstill. The only technical reference in the definition of level 2 is to configuration management (see Section 5.4.2). The management requirements are basic ones having nothing special to do with software development. (This lack of specificity is another persistent problem with the CMM. See Section 4.2.)

Level 3: Defined.   In a level-3 organization, the management practices of level 2 are formally defined and recorded. These are followed throughout the organization in a dependable way, even when things go wrong. There is a group within the organization, the "Software Engineering Process Group (SEPG)," that codifies practices. Thus the SEPG would (perhaps) decide that the organization will use the waterfall model of development and would describe how that will be carried out on projects. Software inspection (see Section 5.3) is introduced at level 3.

Comments: The distinction between level 2 and level 3 clearly shows the management (as opposed to a technical) basis of the CMM. A technical person would have been more concerned with defining sooner the way in which the engineering is done and would have moved this to level 2. The CMM authors argue that engineering procedures cannot be put into place until management is well enough organized to stick to them under the pressure of deadlines and emergencies. It seems that level 2 asks no more than routinely competent managers who understand such basics as the tradeoff between schedule and product quality. An engineer who behaved as badly as it is imagined that management behaves prior to level 2 would do things like use a compiler for the wrong language and not notice the outcome—he would be fired immediately.

Level 4: Managed. At level 4, the central concept is "measurement" of the development process and the software product. ("Product" is first mentioned at level 4.) Measurement means quantitative analysis for (management) understanding and for control of development. By quantifying each aspect of development defined at level 3, a manager is able to see exactly how the process is going and to fix problems quickly if they occur.

Comments: Although product measurements are finally mentioned at level 4, it is well to remember that these "products" are not primarily software that executes on a computer. The definition of an elaborate software development process creates many intermediate products, reports, and forms, each of which can be "measured." For example, it is a useful management measurement to know how many of a list of required meetings have taken place, but an engineer would not call this a product measurement. By its nature, real product measures of performance, reliability, and so on of the software itself must wait until near the end of the development process. These come too late to help manage the process, so most of the measurements the CMM imagines are really quantification of the process in its own terms, not of the final product.

Level 5: Optimizing. The highest CMM level introduces feedback into the process from the measurements of level 4. This process feedback is quite different from the control at level 4. For example, if a project is behind schedule in its design phase, a manager at level 4 will have measurements to show this, such as the fraction of requirements that have been covered by the design so far. The manager will try to correct matters in this misbehaving project, say by adjusting the schedule or staffing. However, at level 5, data from the delinquent project would be used to try to discover the root cause of the problem and to change the development process itself (in its future application to other projects) so that the problem does not occur again. Such a change might, for example, specify a different design formalism that is easier to use. "Defect analysis" is the name given to the level-5 process changes. Investigation of new technology might be undertaken to solve a process problem, but at level 5, new technologies are also explored in a proactive way to effect improvements even if no problems are experienced.

Comments: Comments made under level 4 about "products" that are not software itself apply also at level 5. When a process is measured in its own terms rather than by what it produces, adjustments based on those measurements may very well fail to improve the final product. The separation between measurement and feedback also seems foreign to an engineer—measurement has no engineering purpose *except* as the first part of a corrective feedback loop. For example, suppose that after software is released, it fails and a trouble report is generated. (Such a report is a crucial measurement of the real software product.) The failure must be traced to its source and eliminated, of course. But to an engineer it seems crucial to ask why it was not detected by the testing phase of development, and to see that this failure of testing will not happen again. In the same way, investigation of new technologies has such a small cost and so large a potential payoff that it should not be delayed until the last level.

To give the authors of the CMM their due, they acknowledge implicitly that levels 2 and 3, and similarly 4 and 5, are separated only so that they can be implemented in an orderly, systematic fashion.

It is a primary goal of higher CMM levels to introduce *predictability* into software development. A level-1 process can be very efficient and can produce impressive results, but does not do so with surety. Management would rather be sure, even if there is a penalty in the quality of the work.

When an engineer reads through a description of the CMM (particularly a critical one), many of the ideas presented seem to be good ones, albeit embedded in a managerial matrix that is unnecessary and overcontrolling. The engineer would perhaps pick and choose ideas from all the CMM levels (for example, preventing defects and investigating new technologies from level 5) and apply them to software development directly. The authors of the CMM caution against this (they call it "skipping CMM levels") on the grounds already alluded to. They say that without systematic management infrastructure in place, good ideas cannot be depended upon to work. There is some truth in their position. Because management is in charge, it can issue destructive and counterproductive orders that negate technical gains; it can also fail to act, allowing engineers to self-destruct. However, there is also truth on the other side. As an example, introduction of high-level programming languages and compiler technology as an alternative to assembly language programming was accomplished by organizations across the software development spectrum, most of them at level 1. There was no reason to wait for level 5 to investigate this new technology.

Using the CMM To Evaluate a Potential Employer

When an engineer is considering employment in some organization, knowledge of its CMM level (even from a somewhat unreliable self-assessment) is valuable data, but its meaning for the potential employee goes beyond the obvious. A company can be justly proud of being at CMM level 4, say. Its customers should be glad to know that things are well under control. An engineer might like working for a company that does a good job. But employees don't always like being controlled. Level 4 means that there is considerably more regimentation, less room for creative and exciting anarchy in the ranks than at (say) level 2. Many of the employees in a level-4 company will have rigid job descriptions and little scope for advancement. At the higher levels, exciting technical risks are not taken. Of course, a highly controlled organization also creates opportunities, but more often for managers than for engineers. So it behooves a prospective employee to look carefully at CMM level, at an engineer's place in the company's software process, and at his own temperament and goals. An engineer who rebels against the whole idea of the CMM might be better off working in a company that also dislikes the idea (and would probably be rated at a low level), where both employee and company can try to prove through the quality of their products that CMM doesn't mean much.

4.1.4 Process Management Isn't for Every Organization

At the two extremes of very small and very large software developments, there is agreement on the role "process" ideas should play. For a handful of people, process management is a waste of time. But a project employing hundreds of people, developing a multimillion-line piece of software over many years, will almost certainly founder without process management. The interesting cases lie between the extremes, where organizations have a choice about how things are done. For software whose development time is on the order of two years, about 200,000 lines of code, here are two possible arrangements:

Technical model. The organization can choose to hire on the order of eight senior engineers, who will work loosely together essentially without any management hierarchy. Their productivity to complete the job must be about 1200 lines of code per person per month (LOC/person–month).

Managed model. Or the organization can choose to hire 2 line managers and 16 junior engineers, the latter needing to produce only about 600 LOC/person–month, but if the managers are included, the productivity is only about 500 LOC/person–month.

The difference in productivity is accounted for by the overhead of managing the process (e.g., in meetings, inspections, and report writing), and by the lower skill level of the junior engineers. Perhaps the labor cost is roughly the same in both models because the junior engineers will work for lower wages. There is no question that it will be much harder to find and hire the senior staff. Most people believe that the product created under the technical model will be more innovative and that it will be more fun to work in that group.

In reality, the technical and managed models are combined in a variety of hybrids, for example, in which senior engineers start a project, and as the work builds up, a manager (perhaps one of the senior engineers) and junior staff are added.

4.2 Engineering Management

From the point of view of an engineer working under a manager, a good manager is one who provides state-of-the-art equipment, insulates engineers from nontechnical problems and demands, and successfully conveys engineering concerns up the management hierarchy. It is not surprising that the (upper) management view of line engineering managers is quite different. For the sake of written language, and without intending to address the very real gender issues of the workplace, consider the most common organization view of a good manager who happens to be a man:

▼

The presentation is facetious. In a reasonable organization, a manager might not face such contradictions.

1. He obeys orders and sees to it that those who work for him also obey orders.

2. He takes responsibility for what happens under his direction, even if he was just obeying orders.

3. He provides the information needed to accurately estimate schedule times, budget costs, and potential product quality and functionality. However, he is flexible when this information is questioned or ignored by his superiors.

4. He tracks work in progress, seeing to it that budgets and schedules are adhered to, but that quality is not sacrificed. Only in very exceptional cases does he request more money or time.

The technical component of a manager's job is thus involved with schedule, budget, and quality. (Recall from Section 1.3.1 that these are the three things out of which it is possible to control at most two.) To estimate budget and schedule for a product of adequate quality, a manager has no solid guide but experience and consultation with the engineers who work for him. Statistical models of the development process exist to predict costs and times required, described in Section 4.3, but estimating their parameters depends on knowing about similar projects from the past. Both the manager and engineers who are consulted have to decide how the game will be played. Should they ask for more than they really think is needed, or should they try to make accurate predictions? In an organization where respect and good communication are the rule, the truth is better since it will allow everyone to make valid decisions about what to attempt. But where management is arrogant or incompetent, it may be necessary to overestimate what is required in order to have some space to haggle. In the extreme case where only suspicion rules, projects too often are given impossible schedules or budgets, or inflated estimates cause the project to be abandoned as too expensive before it begins.

Once a project goes ahead, the manager's job switches from guessing what will be needed to monitoring progress and keeping the work on track. Again there is a "game" aspect for all concerned: if things are going better or worse than expected, should this be admitted or swept under the rug? In a well-run organization, truth should prevail, whereas in a dysfunctional one, it may be better to keep quiet and try to make up the shortfall, or to build in extra time in case something goes wrong later. It is not easy for a manager to learn how the project is actually progressing. Of course, it is wise to talk to the engineers working on the project, but without any quantifiable milestones, they may not themselves know how things are going. The only meaningful data comes from splitting the work into as many parts as possible, counting the parts completed, and comparing progress with similar past projects. The phases of development provide a very coarse division, and within each phase more detailed measures can be devised. For example, in the design phase, one task is defining and documenting the modules into which the system will be divided. A past project can be used to estimate the number of modules that will be required, and the fraction completed can be estimated. It is meaningful to say, "about 35% of the modules have been designed." The "task granularity" of what is counted is important. On a medium-sized project, the right things to count are ones that take about two person-days to accomplish.

Engineers naturally view estimation and tracking progress as nonengineering tasks, and indeed they are just that: they are management tasks. A good manager will learn how to do them accurately and without intruding into engineers' technical work. There are few enough good engineering managers, so engineers usually have to help. How much help to give, how much to do the manager's job for him, is a hard decision for an engineer. The only alternative to doing too much of your manager's job (or to trying to take his job away from him) may be to find a job in a different organization.

4.3 Metrics

Engineers can have the most impact on their job environment with the least investment by taking an active role in project scheduling. Even though a good engineering manager should create and accept only realistic schedules, what sometimes happens is this:

Someone in the organization makes what is called a "business case" for a new product by estimating the revenue that will be lost day by day if it is not available. Then they guess how long the business can stand the loss and come up with a schedule for developing the product—a schedule that bears no relation to what is actually required to develop it. Engineers are then told: meet this schedule.

It is natural to feel that there is no alternative. But engineers can respond and retain a measure of sanity in their working lives if the project goes ahead via an effective rebuttal to an extreme schedule. For a rebuttal to be effective, it must come from a knowledge of what is reasonable effort for a project.

The engineering case for a rational schedule is established in the same way that marketing or management made their business case. In the real world, no one can possibly know exactly how many widgets could be sold to customers each day (if only there were widgets to sell). The estimates that went into the business case are fundamentally guesses but founded on facts and experience. Engineers, too, have experience, with the hard facts of past schedules.

Damon Runyan: The race isn't always to the swift, nor the battle to the strong; but, that's the way to bet.

Think for a minute about a more commonplace question: is next week's Sunday newspaper going to be large? Experience says that every Sunday in the past five years, the paper has been large, so it's very, very likely the paper will be large next week. Even if someone has very good reasons for wanting or needing a thin paper, they don't carry much weight against all that experience. (When it comes to betting, before your desires run away with you, listen to P. T. Barnum: "There's a sucker born every minute.") The lesson in the fat Sunday paper is that when software engineers estimate schedules from past experience, they are very, very difficult to refute.

Consider the case where management has declared that the schedule for a project will be three months, with existing staff. Someone must ask the question: "Since our last project of that size took six months, what makes you think we can now do it in half the time?" Keeping the historical data to back up such a question can save an engineering team from three to six months of wasted effort, and can even save a company from bankruptcy. Business is not the place to make foolish bets.

Recorded history in software engineering has acquired the name *metrics*. The primary measurement is the size of a project, which can be used to compare it with others. There are differences of opinion on how to measure size, but lines of code (LOC) seems to be as good as more sophisticated metrics. Any metric can be criticized as inaccurate, but compared to wild guesses, almost any measurement is an improvement.

The historical record provides a link between LOC on a project and the resources needed to write that code in terms of:

1. People. How many people were used on the project, and during what period they used?

2. Time. How long was the entire schedule, and how long were the different phases?

3. Capital goods. How many computers, desks, work rooms, pizzas, and cups of coffee were needed?

4.3.1 Estimation Models

In the absence of your own historical data, it is still possible to provide estimates of effort using estimation models. Not many people will have personal experience with dozens of projects of all sizes, but the models have been constructed to summarize a great deal of experience in equations relating project size, schedule, and effort. They make it clear that the relationships are not linear: a 200000-LOC project takes more than twice the resources of a 100000-LOC project.

One popular estimation model is *COCOMO*, whose equations were derived from historical project data at TRW by Barry Boehm in the 1980s. Figure 4.1 illustrates the model. In the figure, some of the categories were renamed to match the names used in this book. "Requirements/specification" is what Boehm calls "product design" (including "plans and requirements"). "Design/code" is what Boehm calls "programming" (including "detailed design" and "code and unit test"). Figure 4.1 distills a lot of experience into a small space.

The first quantitative thing to notice in the figure is that the staffing level changes over the course of a project. It starts low, then rises through design/coding, then falls a bit during testing. The management jargon is that the project "ramps up" as it goes. The extra people coming onto a project represents the most important insight provided by the model: the effort that goes into software development is not linear in the schedule. For example, the time devoted to coding in Figure 4.1 is about 44% of the schedule, but coding required 55% of the effort. Even more striking is that although requirements/specification takes only 17% of the effort (the project is not yet ramped up), it consumes 27% of the schedule time.

When the project size changes, the model lets us see what happens. For a 300,000-LOC project otherwise similar to the one in Figure 4.1, it predicts a total effort of 1784 man-months, and a total schedule of 34.4 months. The distribution of effort and of schedule doesn't change very much. Design/coding takes a little less of the time (40%) and effort (52%), and the other phases take a bit more. But the nonlinearity is striking: for a project three times the size, the schedule is 34.4 / 22.3 = 1.54 times as long, and the effort is 1784 / 521 = 3.42 times as much.

Model mode: semidetached
Model size: large (100000 lines of code)
Total effort: 521.3 man-months, 152 man-hours/man-month
Total schedule: 22.3 months

Distributions:	Effort (Man-Months)		Schedule (Months)		Personnel On-Board
Requirements/specification:	(17%)	88.6	(27%)	6.0	14.7
Design/code:	(55%)	286.7	(44%)	9.8	29.2
Integration and test:	(28%)	146.0	(29%)	6.5	22.5

Programmer productivity during code and unit test phase:
619 delivered source instructions per month

Figure 4.1   Output from COCOMO for a 100,000-LOC project.

The data on which COCOMO is based represented different kinds of projects, and to model them required the model to have three types. The project type for Figure 4.1 is "semidetached" (i.e., software built for commercial applications to run on commercially available computers). The other two types are called "organic" development, such as tools for in-house use, and "embedded," for software that is part of a larger system such as avionics control software. Organic projects take the least resources, embedded projects take the most, and the semidetached are in the middle. For the 100,000-LOC project, the effort distribution over phases doesn't change much for different project types, nor do the schedule times change much. But the total effort is quite different, and so is the distribution of the schedule: an embedded project takes three times as much total effort as an organic one, spends more than twice as long on requirements/specification, and only 70% as much time on design/coding.

It's easy enough to remember a few facts from the COCOMO model. Projects in the range of 100,000 LOC take about two years to complete, and the required effort is about 20% for requirements/specification, 50% for design/coding, 30% for test. The staffing and the distribution of schedule depend more on the type of project but is about 500 man-months, distributed roughly 30:40:30% among the phases. Armed with these figures, an engineer is in a position to do battle with a proposed crazy schedule.

Imagine that you are an engineer in a meeting discussing your company's next project, the *hyperwidget,* the next generation of the previous *megawidget* project. The megawidget project took about 100,000 LOC, and it went through its life cycle very much as COCOMO predicted. The hyperwidget project, however, should bring in three times the revenue in one-quarter of the time because the feature set is better. The feature set for the hyperwidget is different enough that very little can be reused from the previous project. However, one thing is clear in the meeting: the revenue potentials are so great that the pressure is on to field the hyperwidget as quickly as possible. In fact, marketing claims that they could sell hyperwidgets today if they had them. Therefore, marketing argues, every day without hyperwidgets means a loss of $100,000 in revenue, not to mention market share that we could be taking away from our competitors. If we only had the hyperwidget! The tone is set. Since engineering can't deliver a product immediately, the general attitude seems to be that engineering is costing the company money. There may also be management "incentives" for quick delivery, bonuses promised for each month cut from the schedule. Perhaps marketing has already begun to promise hyperwidgets to important clients. The heat is on.

Excitement and enthusiasm in this imagined meeting have reached the point that the reasoning centers of everyone's brain are overwhelmed and shut down. Schedules are suggested with reckless abandon, and challenges are made. Finally, in the midst of the pandemonium, a consensus appears: this product shall be delivered in nine months, using only existing resources! There will be a product specification in four weeks, a complete implementation in three months; give it three months for test and a month to manufacture, and the *hyperwidgets* will be ready a full month before the announced date! This early ship date will be a stunning blow to the competition, who will be expecting more time to offer their competing product. A stroke of sheer genius!

At this point, the only hope for the engineering team is to offer vivid and illuminating arguments as to why this wonder simply can't be done. To start with, it takes about two years to deliver a product like this, not nine months. When this is offered to the excited project management team, the response is unanimous: *find a way to do it faster!* Faster, indeed—COCOMO to the rescue! The schedule will have to split roughly equally among the phases, three months on requirements/specification, not four weeks. In addition, 20% of the effort will have to be spent in that three months. Grabbing a piece of paper, an engineer quickly calculates: 20% of 500 is 100 man-months. This 100 man-months will have to be accomplished in three calendar months, so this will require more than 30 engineers. So to accomplish the (absurd) schedule, management will need to get 30 software engineers on board immediately, not the 15 they had on the last project. Further, 50% of the project is in the design/coding phase, which will require 250 man-months of work in three months, so during this phase the project will require more than 80 engineers. During the programming phase, management should be prepared to bring on an *additional* 50 engineers. Not only are the engineers required, but additional managers will have to be hired to manage them. At about 8 subordinates per manager, that translates to about 4 managers during requirements/specification, and 12 during design/coding, not to mention a second-level manager or two to manage the managers.

If anything can sober an overenthusiastic management team, it's facts from the last project. Furthermore, the back-of-the-envelope calculation counters the demand to "do it faster," bringing staffing home in terms of the *managers* required. Though it's a sad fact that many managers are not aware of the engineering complexities of large engineering teams, they are indeed aware of the management complexities of large *management* teams. Only such a well-founded "bucket of cold water" poured on the compelling business case can save the engineers (and the company) from an absurd and unachievable schedule.

4.3.2 Feedback from Metrics

Another benefit of a well-run metrics program is that it can provide simple reality checks for process improvement. Should an organization take up an effort to improve its process of building software, it should be prepared to record the result of process changes on code quality, production time and effort, and other indicators associated with software production. By comparing the changed process measurements with ones from the old established software process, we can determine whether the changes were beneficial or detrimental. This feedback is the essential feature of CMM level 5.

In the critique of CMM, it was noted that the model concentrates attention on the process itself, usually losing sight of the product that the process is producing. When metrics are applied to something other than what is really of interest, they are called *surrogate* measures. They are supposed to "stand in" for the real thing. For example, a real measure of code quality is the number and severity of trouble reports that come in from the field after the code is delivered. But process metrics may instead look at the average size of subroutines and the number of conditional statements in each subroutine. It is plausible that complex syntax will lead to field failures, but the syntax measure is clearly a surrogate. It is never really safe to use surrogates, but the real measurements are too difficult to make. In the example, the code syntax is easy to examine as soon as it is written; to get trouble report data requires a tracking system and the people to support it, which will not yield data until too late.

How Does It Fit?

From section 4.1

1. Find one of the Scott Adams *Dilbert* strips that expresses Adams's bias on the issue of software process.

2. Suppose a regulatory agency like the NRC must approve or disapprove the operation of a reactor that includes a software system that is supposed to shut the reactor down in case of an emergency. (In fact, the NRC is called upon to do just that.) Would a "process" argument that the software is adequate be better than a "product" argument?

3. It is standard practice in defending against a liability lawsuit to attempt to show that one has used a "reasonable standard of care," and thus, even though something went wrong and someone was harmed, the defendant is not liable. When trying to make such a case, is it easier to demonstrate that an acceptable standard of process, or of product, was in place? Why?

From section 4.3

4. Come up with an example from your own experience of something that it would not be wise to bet on, yet that a person might want or need desperately.

5. Extrapolate linearly from the COCOMO model given in Figure 4.1 to a piece of software of size 2000 LOC. Is the result plausible? How do the numbers compare with your own personal performance?

6. Give an example from real life (not from software engineering) of a surrogate measure that is used because no real measure is available.

Review Questions

1. Outline the conflict in software engineering between "process" and "product," making clear your personal view on which is the more important.

2. Describe the CMM levels in your own words, trying to keep all judgment about whether they are a good idea out of your answer.

3. What is a surrogate measure? Is COCOMO a surrogate?

Further Reading

Fred Taylor's famous book is *Scientific Management* [Tay47], but it was written long after the fact, and scholars have labeled it a distortion of some facts of Taylor's career and even his beliefs.

The best way to make up your mind about Watts Humphrey's PSP is to read his how-to book [Hum97].

The most interesting idea in the process vs. product controversy is an attempt to apply technical concepts and tools to the process, where those concepts are usually applied to the product. Leon Osterweil is the author of this idea, and his paper [Ost87] proposing the idea has been updated [Ost97] (on the occasion of its being awarded a prize).

Most of Scott Adams's books are funny; a particularly appropriate one for this chapter is *The Dilbert Principle* [Ada96].

Ed Yourdan has described software projects that are out of management control yet must continue under impossible conditions as "death-march" projects [You99].

Engineering management is a relatively new technical field. Reference [Tha92] is a basic text that defines it.

Software metrics is the subject of whole books. One of the best, which pays attention to the mistakes that can be made as well as the benefits to be gained, is by Fenton and Phleeger [FP98].

References

[Ada96]   Scott Adams. *The Dilbert Principle: A Cubicle's-eye View of Bosses, Meetings, Mangagement Fads and Other Workplace Afflictions*. Harper Collins, 1996.

[FP98]   Norman Fenton and Shari Pfleeger. *Software Metrics: A Rigorous and Practical Approach*. Thomson Learning, 1998.

[Hum97]   Watts S. Humphrey. *Introduction to the Personal Software Process*. Addison-Wesley, 1997.

[Ost87]   Leon Osterweil. Software processes are software, too. In *Proc. International Conference on Software Engineering*, pages 2–13, 1987. Monterey, CA.

[Ost97]   Leon Osterweil. Software processes are software, too (revisited). In *Proc. International Conference on Software Engineering*, pages 540–548, 1997. Boston, MA.

[Tay47]   Frederick Winslow Taylor. *Scientific Management*. Harper and Row, 1947.

[Tha92]   Hans Thamhain. *Engineering Management*. John Wiley and Sons, Inc., 1992.

[You99]   Edware Yourdon. *Death March: The Complete Software Developer's Guide to Surviving Implementation Projects*. Prentice-Hall, 1999.

chapter 5

The "Life Cycle" of Software

In Chapter 1, we introduced a collection of phases into which software development can be divided, phases that compose an idealized "life cycle" of a piece of software. Figure 5.1 repeats the diagram in Chapter 1, but shows one of the "maintenance" feedback cycles, in which testing uncovers a problem, which happens to require changes in design (and then subsequently code changes before retesting).

By separating development into "requirements," "specification," "design," "code," and "testing," the way is opened for placing the concerns of good software development into these arbitrarily named phases. Subsequent chapters will be organized along these lines, and it is generally agreed that these divisions are a good way to present many technical ideas of software engineering. However, real development is seldom so neatly compartmentalized, and the description of development as a "waterfall" in which the activities of each phase are nicely "dammed up" until the phase-defined document "spills over" into the next phase, never to return, is not realistic. The interaction and feedback between phases can be so important that what really happens during development looks nothing like the waterfall model.

Even if nicely separated phases are a fiction, they serve the purpose of describing technical software engineering activities and ideas because each phase draws to itself a body of goals and skills.

5.1 Alternatives to the Waterfall Model

The waterfall model was put forward by Barry Boehm in the mid-1970s. It profoundly affected software engineering (some would say that it was and is the basis of the field). Nevertheless, other models have been proposed.

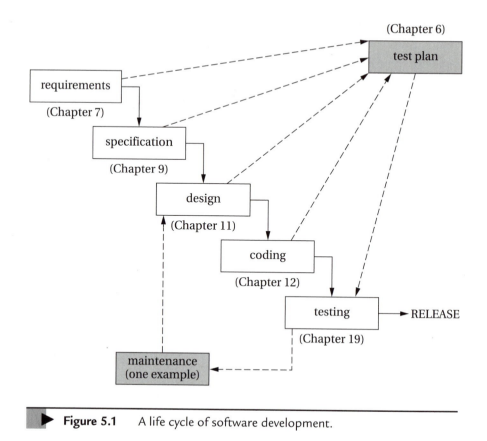

▶ **Figure 5.1**   A life cycle of software development.

5.1.1 The Spiral Model

Perhaps the most important variant of the waterfall life cycle comes from its inventor, Barry Boehm. He calls this variant a "spiral" model of software development because phases like those of the waterfall are used to develop software that is not necessarily the final product, and when that intermediate system is done, the project is evaluated to see if further development should be attempted. Development thus consists of one or more cycles following one another, and by representing these as turns of a spiral, a picture like Figure 5.2 emerges.

The model is driven by risk. In developing very large systems, or systems in which the developer is inexperienced, the risk of failure is high: it may not be known whether the system can be produced with the resources that can be brought to bear. So in the first turn of the spiral, the developers try to resolve this question. They may use simulation to investigate the feasibility of a design, or (as the figure shows) they may implement and test a prototype. After each turn of the spiral, new risks come to light, and a next turn is planned to resolve them. As the work proceeds, the software

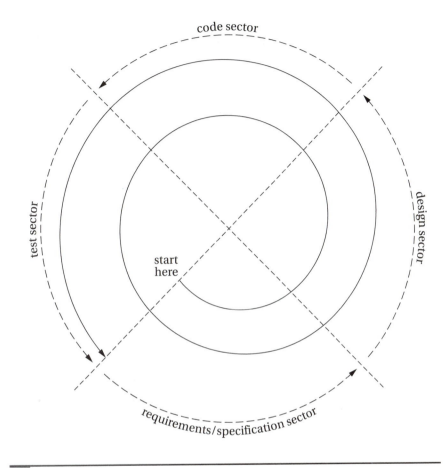

code sector

test sector

design sector

start
here

requirements/specification sector

Figure 5.2   A "spiral" model of software development.

prototypes produced begin to look more and more like finished products, and in the last turn of the spiral, the evaluation indicates that the results will solve the original problem. Along the way, the original requirements may well have been modified so that the final system includes only a portion of what was originally intended, that portion for which the risks of failure were overcome.

In any turn of the spiral, if the risks cannot be overcome (for example, the prototype does not perform as it should) then the project cannot succeed, and it is abandoned with a minimum of loss.

In Figure 5.2, the successive phases are shown as sectors of a counter-clockwise spiral laid down in successive layers. Two turns of the spiral are shown in the figure. The dividing line extending to the southwest is the evaluation point where the decision is made to abandon the project, to release the completed system, or take another turn. Figure 5.2 is a considerable simplification of any actual development process since quite different emphasis is placed on different aspects in the successive turns. In the first turn, requirements and design may dominate, and testing may be minimal; in the last turn, testing may dominate.

Evidently, study of the waterfall phases is directly applicable to the spiral model, where they are used repeatedly.

Although Boehm proposed this model to cover cases of the most complex development, it is directly applicable to an individual developing a novel system, or attempting a system more difficult than ever tried before. For example, students under time pressure in a course on (say) real-time software, who have never done real-time programming, have to identify what they do not understand and carry through a simple example or they will have little chance of completing the project. (For real-time, the problematic aspect is probably the concept of scheduled execution of polled or interrupt-driven tasks.)

5.1.2 Exploratory Programming

For some problems, notably small ones, especially when the problem is poorly defined, the early phases of requirements, specification, and design are simply a waste of time since the form of an implementation can be directly glimpsed, but it is not clear if the right program is being implemented. Then the right thing to do is get on with the coding. Because the software developer passes immediately from a vague problem idea to code to explore the problem, the name "exploratory programming" fits this method. Testing does follow coding but now only to discover just what the program does, not to compare its behavior to the standard that a requirements document would provide.

Exploratory programming might as well be no method at all, or be used to describe the chaotic development of software that software engineering methods were invented to control. Programming begins with no clear idea of the problem being solved and no design breakdown of programming tasks. Nevertheless, the "method" is valuable, not the least in the inner turns of the spiral method, where the problem to be solved may very well be whether or not code can be written, or whether code that can be written will perform well enough.

An unexpected danger of doing exploratory programming in a badly managed company is that a manager or marketing person who sees that code exists, however awful it is, may want to ship it!

5.1.3 Opportunistic Development

Bill Curtis used the adjective "opportunistic" for development that is driven by situations, the abilities and experience of the developers, and availability of resources. Both the spiral model and exploratory programming could be considered examples of opportunistic development. Bob Glass prefers to say "hardest-part-first" development.

5.2 The Phases of Development

The waterfall model contains the elements of many software process models. Its major components of requirements, specification, design, coding, and testing reflect processes that are intrinsic to software development. The waterfall model is well suited to the classroom since it has distinct lines of demarcation for each activity. In practice, these transitions from activity to activity are not so abrupt or so well defined as textbooks present them to be. It is not unusual for software engineers to be engaged in design activities while the requirements are being written. Two masters have to be simultaneously served:

Divide and conquer ▶

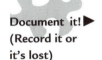

Document it! ▶
(Record it or it's lost)

1. Out-of-phase activities must be kept to a minimum.
2. Good ideas have to be captured, even if they are outside the requirements.

The waterfall model is a convenient fiction for organizing a textbook. It does not express the prevailing philosophy of software development. That philosophy would be better expressed as: there are many ways to engineer software. The necessary skills are present in the waterfall model, but what's important is that the software engineer possess the skills, not that they be used "according to the book."

Each of the activities reflected in the waterfall model uses the output of the previous activity as input, then in turn supplies its output as input for the next phase in the sequence. The best quality documents result when the document is written specifically for the use to which it will be put. While in the throes of the current phase, it may be hard to think of the "customers" in the next phase and what they will need, but that's what the engineer must try to do.

5.2.1 Requirements

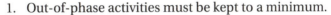

The requirements portion of the waterfall model is the phase in which engineers establish and document the user requirements for the system software. During this portion of the life cycle, the primary inputs come from the end user, and the output is a document that can be read and understood by both software designers and end users. The needs and activities of each group are different but equally important:

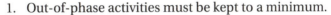

Identify the customers ▶

- *Software designers:* They will use the requirements document to lay out the organization of the software system. If there is a separate specification phase, it will start with the requirements document and add to it. If not, the requirements document will similarly serve as the source of high-level design.

- *End users:* They will use the requirements document to review the system requirements in order to understand what the proposed software is supposed to do. Often, end users will hypothesize a set of scenarios (sometimes called "use cases") and then walk through each scenario with the requirements to make sure that the system is specified to behave as needed. Consequently, end users need a requirements document that is easy to understand, clear, concise, and organized to help them find a requirement or set of requirements quickly, based on a particular input or set of inputs.

Both groups thus need a functional organization with individual requirements clearly identified. The difference is that the designer could make use of much more technical detail, which would overwhelm end users. That detail must wait for the design phase.

If the developer finds it difficult to stick to "what" in discussing requirements, the end user may find it even harder and may want to start talking about how the problem should be solved. To resist these premature solutions, the developer might be sarcastic: "Well, then, do it yourself!" But it may work better to say gently, "Tell me again what problem we need to be solving here?"

5.2.2 Specification

The specification phase of software development can be defined as a precise statement, for the developers' use only, of what the software is to do (not how it will do it). Thus specification is differentiated from the previous requirements phase (where the end user is first and foremost involved), and from the following design phase. Tidy definitions aside, specification is the hardest phase to separate from the others because there may not be very much "what" that hasn't been recorded, and it is a great temptation for engineers to begin to consider design issues, like what major subsystems will go to make up the system, and whether these should be constructed from scratch, or whether some existing or commercial packages can be used.

There are two gaps that specifications can fill, however:

Trusting user. The end user may be unwilling or unable to engage in a substantive requirements dialogue. The user might say, in effect: "Build me an accounting system for my office," and won't say much more than that (perhaps he is a busy doctor, not very interested in accounting, and used to just telling the nurses to use whatever sys-

The developer
would be foolish
not to talk to
those nurses . . .

tem appears). Then the developer will have to specify the system to be built, document it, and deliver. The difference between the specification document that results, and the requirements document that was never done, is that the specification will happily use computer jargon, skip over things that the designers consider obvious, and in general, be written for engineers to read.

Use of formalism. The developer may consider the system to be developed so complex and its correct operation so critical, that something beyond the requirements dialogue is essential. For example, it is easy enough for a user to say, "a safe interval will be maintained between the cars" (for a subway control program). But exactly what does that mean? Some considerable analysis may be required to learn if it is even possible to maintain a "safe interval" and still meet other requirements for the number of passengers to be transported at rush hours. This analysis is not of concern to the user (unless it shows that the system cannot be built), but the full details are of crucial importance to the developer. So a specification may be undertaken, particularly one involving mathematical analysis.

5.2.3 Design

Design is an "engineer-only" activity. Its primary input is the specification (or the requirements document), which will be translated into a design document, written by and for software engineers.

**Fuzzy into
focus**

Two distinct activities occur in the design phase, called "architecture" (or "high-level design") and "detailed design." The former is less precise than the latter. The software architecture is captured in a high-level diagram that shows the major subsystems and subsystem communications paths, and in a mapping from requirements to subsystems that documents which subsystems are responsible for fulfilling each requirement. This mapping connects requirements to design. The diagrams and traceability mapping are intended for use by the software designers and are pure engineer-to-engineer communication.

Document it! ▶
(Traceability)

Architecture diagrams and the traceability mapping are the schematics of software engineering—the blueprints of the system, to use analogous terms from electrical and mechanical engineering.

During detailed design, the design engineers use architecture diagrams, the traceability mapping, *and* the requirements or specification document to decompose each subsystem into a set of modules, each with a functional description. The module descriptions will be used by implementors to write the code for the system. Thus the output from the detailed design phase is aimed at coders. In many instances, the coders are the designers themselves, but the formal design document is important nonetheless since the designers need to maintain an acceptable level of intellectual control over each subsystem: they need to manage the complexity by writing everything down before starting to code.

As a side note, if the system design documentation is well organized and the subsystems decomposed to an appropriate level, it may be possible to save time by bringing in extra coders. The ideal detailed design document will present a coder with all the information necessary to code and test a small part of the system without the coder needing to understand anything else outside this module.

Divide and conquer ▶

5.2.4 Code

The line between the design phase and the coding phase is the least clear division in the waterfall life cycle. Depending on the effort put into design and the extent and detail in the design document, the coding task can itself be creative—almost like design—or so routine that it is almost mechanical. If the latter, it may be assigned to programmers who would be better labeled "code mechanics" than "software engineers." It is the common history of manufacturing that efficient processes attempt to divide the work into a creative part and a routine part, in order to concentrate scarce talent on the former, whereas the latter takes most of the effort. For example, in the automobile industry, there is a hierarchy ("pecking order" is another term for it) of designers, with the most experienced and creative mechanical engineers at the top, and assembly-line workers at the bottom. The coders of software development are closest to the assembly line. However, the software "line" is far more demanding than the ones in an auto assembly plant. Coders must use tools like a programming language and its compiler, and their assignments are more varied and extensive than repeating one small assembly operation over and over.

When important design decisions are left to coders, it is not surprising that coding takes the majority of time in the software life cycle. Perhaps it is surprising that even with coding reduced to the most mechanical elements, it still takes a long time. Program statements are crafted one by one, with constant attention to the data state of the program that each receives and modifies. The only prospect for large reductions in coding time seems to be the use of larger building blocks: program components that comprise many statements, manipulated by the coders as units unexamined internally. One buzzword for this component-based construction is "reuse" of software. But before code reuse is really a viable alternative to statement-by-statement programming, two difficult technical problems must be solved: (1) how to describe what an existing component does and what it assumes, so the designer can find it and believe it will work; and (2) how to certify the quality of components so that the designer can be sure they will not compromise the system to be built. For the present, real reuse remains limited to the use of modest "libraries" (for example, a collection of routines that manages the screens of a menu-driven inter-face).

Coding produces program units (subroutines, modules) that implement pieces of the design, units whose functionality has been described in the design document. These units can be combined into a complete system to meet the software's requirements. Both the units and the system can be tested.

5.2.5 Testing

If the line between design and coding is a faint one, and the line between specification and design comes only from separating "what" from "how" for intellectual control, the line between coding and testing is clear and necessary. Testing requires executable software, the output of the coding phase.

The testing phase is also unique in that much of the creative work can and should be done before the phase begins. This work is embodied in the test plan (see Chapter 6), whose construction can begin in parallel with analyzing the requirements, and continue through design and coding.

A final characteristic of the test phase is that it almost always leads to the feedback of maintenance. Figure 5.1 shows testing uncovering a failure that requires repair beginning with redesign. It is more common that the feedback goes only to the coding phase, and there is even a common name for test-to-code maintenance feedback: it is called "debugging."

Positioned as it is between coding, the last "constructive" activity of de-velopment, and release of what the developer hopes is good software, testing must serve two rather different masters. On the one hand, its purpose is to uncover execution failures so that they can be fixed. But eventually, testing puts itself out of the failure-finding business because its methods cease to discover any more failures. The last round of testing should therefore es-tablish confidence in the quality of the software that has passed its final tests. Unfortunately, as the proverb says, these two testing masters of find-ing failures and certifying quality are impossible to serve at the same time. In practice, the quality objective is too often neglected. The testing in a test plan that has been carefully accumulated throughout the development process is almost entirely directed toward catching mistakes or showing that a feared mistake is absent. As Chapter 21 will show, to measure software quality re-quires a completely different kind of testing.

5.3 Software Inspection

Everyone is familiar with the technique of "testing out" written material on a fresh audience unfamiliar with the work. The author of a document, especially a complex and technical document, gets to know the subject so well that he cannot distinguish what he meant to say but did not say from what he actually said. Nor can an author be expected to detect so-called errors of omission—they are by definition unknown. Authors are therefore poor critics of their own work. An outsider, even someone less experienced than the author, is in a much better position to find flaws in written material, so authors are well advised to get a critique from someone else. Copy editors perform this function for published books, and peer reviewers for journal articles. So long as the reviewer is unfamiliar with the actual material being reviewed, the more he or she knows about the subject the better.

Each phase of the software life cycle in the waterfall model ends with the production of a document, and the test plan is another document that cuts across phases. Each of these can be profitably reviewed. Unfortunately, reviewing is a boring job. A fledgling novelist can get his friends and relations to read a manuscript and perhaps tell the truth about it, but not so for software. An individual developing software is cut off from helpful feedback. In most classroom assignments, the other class members would make ideal, interested critics, but consulting them is usually defined as cheating on the assignment. Only when a class does software development with cooperative teams can there be useful reviewing.

Software reviewing has a number of names—"review" is one, "walkthrough" is another—and there are technical differences between what is done under the different names. For an individual, the idea behind a "walkthrough" is a good one. The author collars a listener and conducts a verbal tour through the document. Both people have the document in front of them, and where any question arises, they take notes. The surprising thing about a walkthrough is that the author is the one to discover most of the problems. In trying to explain, the author sees what's wrong. The listener may not even understand the issue.

In a software business, even a garage operation, review of the development documents can be made part of the job, and if it is sometimes tedious, it has been shown to be so valuable that people who want to produce quality software acknowledge that they must do it. The most elaborate formal reviewing process is called "software inspection;" it was invented by Michael Fagin in about 1978. Although a Fagin inspection is not something that an individual can do, it is worth describing briefly.

5.3.1 Inspection Works

Since its introduction in the 1970s, inspection has been used on a wide variety of software, on code (where it originated), and on all the other document products of the waterfall life cycle. Many of its users have become enthusiastic proponents of the method, but some who tried it had poor results. The only objective measure available comes in comparing inspection of code

---

Asking your mother or spouse to read and criticize your test plan or your C code simply won't work.

How about a 'walkthrough robot,' a mechanical listener that would utter phrases like, "Hmmmm, go on . . ." or "I don't understand . . . " at intervals?

modules with testing those modules. The evidence from a variety of studies making this comparison is conclusive: inspection finds most of the problems testing would find, and does so more efficiently. In fact, organizations that have wholeheartedly embraced inspection find that subsequent testing seldom finds any problems at all—the inspections have detected them and they have been removed prior to testing. (One organization reporting this effect is the CMM level-5 contractor responsible for the mission code on the U.S. Space Shuttle.)

5.3.2 The Participants and the Procedure

An inspection requires several participants, each with a required role to play. They are:

Author. The person who wrote the document being inspected is present to answer questions. The author is *not* to "defend" his or her work, but to help others understand it. An inspection could be conducted without the author, but since the author can't play any other role, he or she might as well answer questions.

Moderator. The moderator could also be called a "facilitator." The role is to run the inspection and to rigorously enforce its purpose, which is to discover deficiencies in the document being inspected. The moderator's job is mainly one of controlling bad behavior. In the inspection, people should not let their personalities enter; they should confine themselves to finding problems and avoid any attempt to suggest fixes; they should not go off on tangents but stick to a schedule. In some definitions of inspection, the moderator calls attention to each part of the document in turn, and thus paces its inspection. In others, there is a special participant called the **reader** who steps through the document.

Recorder. Whenever any problem is uncovered in the document being inspected, the recorder is charged with capturing its description in writing. At the end of the inspection, the recorder and moderator prepare an inspection report from the recorder's notes, which will be used to drive fixes for the problems found.

Inspectors. The inspectors give substance to the procedure. They are the ones who raise questions, suggest problems, and criticize the document. Just as the author does not defend, inspectors are not supposed to "attack." Everyone tries to focus on finding problems, not on placing blame. Each inspector comes with a different viewpoint. Some are technical experts, good at ferreting out problems (and without experts there is no substance to an inspection). Some may represent other groups in development, such as marketing or quality assurance. Everyone participating may act as an inspector, but the author, moderator, and recorder have to be careful not to get carried away from their primary roles.

When an inspection fails (and they do fail—practice is required to realize their substantial benefits), it is either because the rules were broken—the author and the inspectors got into an argument, for example—or because the inspectors did not probe deeply enough to find anything significant. The latter is the harder to correct.

All the participants are expected to study the document in advance. This is particularly crucial in the case of the technical expert inspectors, who must come into the inspection with detailed notes on issues to raise. None of the participants should be supervisor to any other participant, and nothing in the inspection should ever be used for employee evaluation.

Even a failed inspection, one that did not uncover any significant problems, is good for establishing communication within the development team, and for training new members of the team. However, these functions are byproducts of inspection, and there are more efficient ways to accomplish them.

Experienced inspectors find themselves probing the same issues over and over. They therefore can work from "checklists" of things to look for, lists to which they add as their experience accumulates. A checklist does depend on the document being inspected. The questions to be raised for requirements are obviously different from those to be raised for code.

5.3.3 Inspection Is Expensive

However well inspection works, it isn't cheap. Suppose there are five participants apart from the author, and that each one requires two hours of preparation. The inspection itself runs for (say) an hour. The recorder and moderator will have to spend perhaps two hours putting notes in order and preparing a final report. The total time involved is $5(2) + 6(1) + 2(2) = 20$ person-hours. In a small software system, there will be on the order of 100 code routines to be inspected, along with the other documents (which may perhaps take double or triple the estimated inspection time). This amounts to an overhead of about five weeks of the team's time, which is comparable to the length of one of the development phases itself. Code inspections are the primary expense. Since code can be execution tested, whereas other documents cannot, any inspection program should start with the other documents.

5.3.4 What Can an Individual Do?

Formal inspection requires a minimum of four people and is best with five to seven participants. In a small organization, the personnel don't exist to systematically carry it out. Not only are the time and staff not available, but everyone is too familiar with the details of all aspects of the company's software products to be good critics. But it is worth a hard look at the inspection process to see what an individual can learn from it, or what (say) two people could do. Two is, of course, much better than one since one of a pair can be a real outside critic. If two engineers work well together and can keep their egos under control, they can do a useful inspection with no moderator and the author acting as recorder.

Some lessons that individuals can learn from inspection, for looking at their own work, or for working with a colleague, are:

1. *Ego isn't appropriate:* Two friends can just as well fight over one's work as two business acquaintances—in fact, it is more likely they will, and the emotional damage will be worse. The minute a squabble begins, it's time to call off the "inspection." People who are not very self-aware would be advised not to begin. (But then, of course, they wouldn't be aware that they are not suited for it.) An individual working alone won't get into a fight, but putting ego aside will ease the problem of blindness to one's own mistakes.

2. *Find, don't fix:* A lot of the power of inspection lies in separating the different concerns of *finding* problems and attempting to *fix* them. A group loses focus and can get lost in potential solutions to a problem, and so can an individual.

3. *Be methodical:* It might seem unnecessary to have a "recorder" when only one or two people are involved, but it is essential. Writing down what is found guarantees that it will not be forgotten, but it also frees the mind(s) of the participant(s) to go on to the next problem without carrying any previous baggage. Later, when things are being changed to correct problems, the record is a good way to annotate what was done and make sure nothing has been missed.

An individual determined to realize some of the advantages of inspection, say, on a requirements document that she herself has just written, would sit down with the document, try hard to forget all the effort and energy that went into creating it, and methodically go through looking for problems, each of which she would carefully record for later action. It will help if some time has elapsed since the document was written, time to forget and achieve distance from the pride of authorship.

5.4 Maintenance Throughout the Life Cycle

Software "maintenance" is jargon for any software change that occurs after release. Here we also use the word to describe a change that occurs part way through development. The change requires "reworking" things that are in progress or already completed. Such changes are a fact of software life, perhaps the most fundamental fact. One source of change is that end users change their minds. Requirements analysis is a difficult, error-prone process, and it isn't surprising that users fail to communicate what they *really* want. But even if the requirements were to be carved in stone and never changed, even if it were ideal in its accuracy, completeness, and so on, maintenance would be necessary. People—and all software engineers are people—make mistakes. They particularly make mistakes when working at the edge of their competence, and software projects present a challenge that often skirts that edge.

The separation of development into life cycle phases is essential to solving hard problems, but it carries its own drawbacks. One is that a mistake can remain hidden for a long time, until brought to light in a subsequent phase. When this happens, there is an almost irresistible urge to do exactly the wrong things: (1) deny that there is a problem, and (2) try for a quick, local fix. It's natural (especially when things are already stretched near to breaking) to hope that problems will just go away, but of course they won't, and the sooner they are honestly recognized, the less additional work will be wasted. It's also natural to try to "patch" over a problem at the place where it is detected. In software, the "patch" almost always takes the form of a code change to fix something that showed up in testing. The reason such patches are usually the wrong thing to do is that they compromise the integrity of the entire development. Unless the requirements, the specification, and the design documentation are examined and changed to eliminate the problem, they will immediately be rendered outdated, and hence useless. Further work cannot trust them, and thus the benefits they are supposed to bring are lost. Worse, if the change does impact the requirements, the end user must be informed or consulted. Making only a code change is a prescription for disaster when the user runs afoul of it. And attaching a stern comment to the code won't help: users seldom read code.

Thus the essential rule in maintenance is: trace a required change to its source, and correct it there, even if that means extra rework to carry the change through several parts of the life cycle.

5.4.1 Debugging

If maintenance is never any fun, one kind has the virtue of being technically challenging and providing great scope for human ingenuity and creativity. *Debugging* is maintenance feedback from testing to coding: a test has failed, and the problem is to find and fix the erroneous code. Debugging is classic detective work, pitting the software Sherlock Holmes against the fiendish clues the program has not managed to destroy before it crashes. The worst bugs are intermittent—they are reported, but cannot be routinely repeated under controlled conditions, so the clues are misleading and contradictory.

The theory (not much!) and practice (too much!) of debugging are far beyond the scope of this book, but one principle is obvious: *finding* the trouble, and *fixing* it, can and should be separated. The debugger first seeks to understand exactly what went wrong, a process in which the design document is an invaluable aid. When that understanding is complete, it is time to contemplate changes. Fixes applied too soon, without real understanding, are likely to miss the point, to gloss over just some examples of the problem, and to further complicate a real correction.

5.4.2 Configuration Management

Introducing change—software maintenance—into a complex process—the development life cycle—is itself an error-prone process requiring documentation and discipline. When changes are made to an interrelated set of documents, particularly changes that may be tentative and have to be later revoked or modified, it is easy to lose track of the work and wind up repeating or redoing it. In the worst case, all control is lost, and no one knows whether a given change has been made or not, much less whether it was successful. An individual can get into this dreadful position, but for individual-sized projects, a little record keeping and creative use of computer file dating and comparison usually straightens things out. (Section 12.2 describes some of the tools that are helpful.) But in a large organization, there must be a set of procedures—called the *configuration-management* procedures—that describes how a change moves from identifying some problem, reviewing the necessary actions, reworking, checking to see that the problem has been solved, and documenting of the whole process. Sometimes configuration management (CM) is called "change management."

As a simple example of the technical problems that change introduces, consider debugging a program stored in multiple files, one subroutine per file. The debugger's analysis might first indicate that a subroutine in file XXXXX needs to be changed. But when that is done, the program still fails (likely in some new way!). Better analysis with this new failure data points to changes needed in file YYYYY instead. But after making those, the debugger might forget to restore XXXXX (or incorrectly restore it), and thus create new and even more wonderful failure symptoms, whose analysis and repair can waste a great deal of time. The tools explicitly designed to help keep track of multiple versions of a file ("version-control" software) are described in Section 12.2.8. These programs are usually overkill for an individual, and even for a small group they can be harder to use than the benefits they provide. However, there is no excuse for not "freezing" a set of files, making copies, and working only on the copies for debugging. (In the preceding example, it could otherwise happen that the original XXXXX was lost forever!)

5.5 Managing a Development Life Cycle

Structuring software development into distinct phases has two quite different purposes. As presented in Section 1.2, the purpose is technical, to separate concerns, divide and conquer a complex problem. But a management purpose is also served: the phases are milestones of development, which can be used to estimate schedule and budget, and then to track progress. Indeed, managers are the inventors of software engineering, and there are those who say that the technical case for distinct phases is not a strong one. The management case *is* compelling. Without milestones and well-defined work products, a manager is lost.

5.5.1 Progress Reports

It is tempting for a manager to further subdivide development with the sole purpose of monitoring it. Such a manager creates new milestones, and the documents that describe passing them, for engineers to complete. Sometimes the documents are called "progress reports." The data for some reports are created as a natural part of the engineering process, and their value is unquestioned. For example, in design, the completed modules and their documentation reside in disk directories; a "report" might be no more than a list of names of completed files. Similarly, module code, results of test cases, and so forth, have to exist for sufficient technical reasons and cannot be said to be busywork requested by a manager. A creative and competent manager can use such natural report data to monitor progress in a nonintrusive way. A weaker manager may need help from the engineers in the form of a formal report. However, such reports can often be mechanically generated from the raw data (such as disk directories) by clever engineers.

Given the dubious necessity of even the phases of the waterfall model, there seems no excuse for the creation of management milestones other than those that occur as a natural part of the engineering process, ones that require little or no extra engineering effort.

5.5.2 Dividing Effort Among the Phases

For the classical waterfall development model, data exist on the fraction of development effort that is spent in each phase. Section 4.3 discussed some of the parameters of these measurements in detail. The numbers are roughly:

Phase	Effort	Time
Requirements	15%	20%
Specification	5%	10%
Design	20%	20%
Coding	30%	20%
Testing	30%	30%

The maintenance phase is not included; if it were, it would amount to 80 to 90% of the whole for long-lasting software. Thus all effort breakdowns that do not include maintenance may have little meaning since the maintenance will dominate all efforts, and shifting (say) 10% effort among the other phases will make only a 1% change in the whole. Maintenance is not included in the figures, however, because there are projects in which it does not enter at all—for example, contract development of software where maintenance will be covered by a separate contract.

Even aside from the distortion introduced by ignoring maintenance, effort numbers are themselves suspect. They mostly come from projects where a waterfall development model was adopted by an organization that formerly included design as a part of coding and did very little requirements analysis or specification. Proponents of better requirements and specification argue that serious attention to the early phases of waterfall development will reduce the time required for later phases that depend on them and also reduce the total development time. Thus they speculate that if the effort on requirements and specification were (say) doubled, it would cut overall time by (say) 10%, the reductions occurring in the other phases being more than the increase in requirements and specification. (The most substantial reduction would probably be in the testing effort.) It is very difficult to acquire valid support for such conjectures since an experiment would involve repeating expensive projects with independent teams. But it does seem likely that the effort observed is partly a matter of choice. If the early phases of development are slighted, the latter ones will take longer, and vice versa. It is evidently possible to carry this idea too far, as well. One might invest excessive time in (say) design, time that does not benefit coding or testing, and thus only increases total development time.

 Divide and conquer (Know when to stop) ▶

Thus the decision of how to apportion schedule time among the development phases, and the details of work to be done in each phase, are the primary management choices that control software development.

How Does It Fit?

From section 5.1

1. Figure 5.2 is a very generalized, simplified view of the spiral development model. Draw and label a more accurate diagram that describes the following particular development:

The primary risk is that performance of the system may not be adequate. It is decided to check this by writing and testing a prototype system that has only a few of the features required of the final system. Performance of this prototype proves to be acceptable. The second risk identified is that staff resources will not permit the required functionality to be developed within the given schedule. A conventional waterfall cycle is instigated to find out, using a subset of the required features. This development is completed within the schedule constraints, but without enough remaining time to do a second waterfall cycle. So the user is consulted and a few additional features identified as crucial, features that will not change the design significantly. These are added to the previous implementation, which is tested, and the final product released.

From section 5.2

2. Suppose that on a software development project there are just two very clever programmers, cleverer in fact than the software designer. What kind of design is appropriate in this situation, and why?

From section 5.3

3. It is sometimes made a rule of inspections that the participants are not permitted any discussion. When a point is raised, the recorder notes it, and the moderator moves on. Give some arguments both pro and con about such a rule.

4. Suppose that an author *had* to play another role in an inspection. Which role would be the worst for the outcome and why? Which one would be the least troublesome and why?

5. Come up with an appropriate item for an inspection checklist to be used with:

   (a) a requirements document

   (b) a test plan

   (c) a code module

6. How can an individual overcome the blindness that intrinsically exists when reviewing his or her own work? Can you think of something creative that might help?

7. Explain why an inspection that finds nothing wrong should be considered a failure. Or should it?

8. It has been found that the best inspections involve six to eight people. Is this an example of the 7 ± 2 rule? Explain why or why not.

From section 5.4

9. The following are three general debugging techniques.

   When a test point x is tried and it fails (giving output y that is incorrect because the output should be $z \neq y$), then:

   (a) Add a statement just after the program input statement, testing the input variable for value x and when it is, outputting z and skipping all the existing code to continue after the result is printed.

   (b) Add a statement just before the existing output statement, testing the output for y and when it is, outputting z instead.

(c) Add a statement just before the existing output statement, testing the input variable for value x and when it is, outputting z.

Explain what, if anything, is wrong with each of these techniques.

From section 5.5

10. It has been observed that when a software development effort fails, it is because the phases of development before testing have been done so poorly that many tests fail. The code is reworked, but as many new problems are inserted as are fixed, so it fails again. This code/test/debug cycle does not end until the project schedule time runs out. Using the rough numbers on effort spent in each phase, consider a failed project that runs out of time after 1, 2, 3, ... code/test/debug cycles. What fraction of time will be spent in each phase on such projects?

Review Questions

1. If the waterfall model fails to capture what software developers actually do, what's the point of studying it?

2. During what phase(s) of development is inspection most valuable, and why?

Further Reading

Most software engineering textbooks devote a great deal of space to the life cycle. Three of the best are Ian Sommerville's [Som96] and Shari Pfleeger's [Pfl99] and Roger Pressman's [Pre97].

Barry Boehm's original article on the waterfall model [Boe76] and on the spiral model [Boe88] are among the classics of software engineering literature.

David Parnas is responsible for many of the best software engineering ideas and is a perceptive critic of the trendy or overblown. He has written a wonderful essay on why the ideal development life cycle is important, exactly when it is not followed in practice [PC86].

Bob Glass has for years edited the technical *Journal of Systems and Software*, in which he often publishes a thoughtful editorial column. He has both practical and academic credentials, so what he says is usually worth reading.

Inspections are sometimes called "Fagan inspections," after the person who invented the often-used procedure. His paper [Fag86] gives the rationale. A cookbook presentation of how to do a code inspection, including a checklist for the C language, is available from the Jet Propulsion Laboratory at satc.gsfc.nasa.gov/fi. For information on a kind of "poor-man's" inspection method, see a proposal by Bisant and Lyle [BL89].

References

[BL89]   David B. Bisant and James R. Lyle. A two-person inspection method to improve programming productivity. *IEEE Transactions on Software Engineering*, SE-15:1294–1304, 1989.

[Boe76]   Barry W. Boehm. Software engineering. *IEEE Transactions on Computers*, pages 1226–1241, 1976.

[Boe88]   B. W. Boehm. A spiral model of software development and enhancement. *IEEE Computer*, pages 61–72, 1988.

[Fag86]   Michael E. Fagan. Advances in software inspections. *IEEE Transactions on Software Engineering*, SE-12:744–751, 1986.

[PC86]   D. L. Parnas and P. C. Clements. A rational design process: how and why to fake it. *IEEE Transactions on Software Engineering*, pages 251–257, 1986.

[Pfl99]   Shari Pfleeger. *Software Engineering: Theory and Practice*. Prentice-Hall, 1999.

[Pre97]   Roger Pressman. *Software Engineering: A Practitioner's Approach, 4th Ed.* McGraw-Hill, 1997.

[Som96]   Ian Sommerville. *Software Engineering, 5th Ed.* Addison-Wesley, 1996.

c h a p t e r 6

The Test Plan

S oftware testing is a process that should begin when a software system is still only a "gleam in the eye," and ends with the success of a particular collection of executions of the system, whereupon the software is released. Of course, the executions must wait until an executable program has been brought into existence by specification, design, and coding. But each test execution has its *test point*—the program input that initiates the execution—and devising these inputs is a major part of the testing task. As soon as any ideas about the software are put forward, inputs for testing suggest themselves, and should be recorded. If the tests that arise naturally during development are not recorded on the spot, the developer will find that recalling them later is extremely difficult, and many important tests will have been forgotten.

A beneficial side effect of thinking about tests and recording them is that it sharpens the attention of the developer during other life cycle phases. A test gives a concrete example of what the software must do, and examples are useful, even necessary, in avoiding mistakes. The main purpose of recording tests for later use, and the side effect of focusing attention, come together when some difficult aspect of the software is brought forward. For example, a certain requirement may be complex, hard to understand, and hard to capture in writing. Thinking through an example (a test point) should help to make sense of it (or to see that the user must be called on to explain better). Furthermore, there may very well be trouble correctly implementing this aspect—it is an error-prone part of development. But if test points are recorded for it, they will be available later (when the difficulty may have been forgotten) to check that things have been done properly.

 Document it! ▶
(Record it or it's lost)

A test plan may be thought of as comprising two different aspects of testing, one the concrete form of the other. Any particular test points given in the plan are concrete; their abstraction is the principles used to obtain those test points. Some people prefer to confine the test plan to the principles and defer finding the concrete test points until the testing phase itself. In a large, complex development project, there may even be separate plans, one for the principles and one for the substance of the tests. The latter may be called the *test specification*. The abstract plan can be carried to the extreme of a purely management document: a test plan that is literally a description of what will be done, without any concrete tests. Two examples of testing principles have already been mentioned:

Record tests when they come up.   During development phases prior to testing, test points that suggest themselves should be added to the test plan.

Test error-prone parts of development.   Difficult parts of software construction should have test points that will, when executed successfully later, establish that the difficulties have been overcome.

To these should be added a statement of the purpose of testing as it is practiced:

Testing uncovers errors (defects) in the software.   Chapter 19 will explore the reasons for this purpose, but at the outset it should be clear that there will *be* errors, and that tests can find them.

For an individual, and for all but the most complex situations, the general plan is no more than: "Test cases will be devised and recorded throughout development, particularly in the requirements phase for system tests, and in the design phase for unit tests. Their purpose is to detect software failures."

In a technical test plan that contains the substance of work to be done in the final, testing phase of development, test points can be recorded without being detailed, concrete input values. A somewhat vague test plan might capture only a situation from which the actual test points can later be derived. For example, during design of a subroutine with an argument Ang that represents an angle, the following might be added to the test plan: "Test a negative value for Ang and values in each quadrant." Or "Test that Ang is expressed in radians, not degrees." Although recording such "meta tests" is better than nothing, it is all too easy to have done so little thinking about the test that too much is left until later. For example, just how will a radian/degrees test be constructed?

Two general techniques, of functional testing and fault-based testing, are particularly well adapted to generating test points before software is coded.

6.1 Functional Testing

The primary technique for testing software is called *functional testing*, or "specification-based," or "black-box" testing. The "functions" are tied to a requirements document, which contains many statements beginning,

> "The software shall . . . "

where the " . . . " describes some observable behavior that must occur. These behaviors are the software's "functions," and functional testing is the process of devising tests for them. It is possible to go systematically through a requirements document, making sure that there are test points that probe each requirement. This systematic effort can be invested while the requirements are being analyzed, or long after, but will be most beneficial if done as work proceeds. In many ways, testing is an adversarial process. A tester is trying to expose mistakes that a developer is trying not to make in the first place. It is a better adversary who is on the spot looking for trouble as the process unfolds.

Functional testing, like all testing, is a process that in principle need never end. It is always possible to find more functions, or more test points for the same function, without end. (The sole exception occurs when there are only a few possible test points for some function. Then "exhaustive testing" is possible, and there is nothing gained in repeating a test exactly. Software does not break from one execution to the next. But it may be hard to arrange for two tests to be "exactly the same.") In order to limit the number of test points, an arbitrary decision must be made about which functions will be tried, and the degree to which each will be explored. Too often, it is exhaustion, not exhaustive testing, that sets the limits. Testing up to time constraints is a dangerous game in software development because testing is the final phase before release. If something slips in earlier parts of development, it may eat into testing time so that almost no tests are performed. That's another argument for devising the test plan up front, as development proceeds. It's a lot easier to omit a phase for which no one is prepared than it is to discard a carefully made plan that has already seen a large time investment. Every student has experienced a shortage of testing time in projects that "took longer than I expected" or "didn't quite work," as the term ends.

"How much did you test?"

"Until I ran out of time."

6.1.1 System-Level Functional Testing

At the system level, the requirements and specification documents describe functions that can be tested only when the software is complete—system tests. System tests often try many functions at once if the functions are recorded at a low level of detail. For example, if software is required to respond within a certain time, then every test of any function checks this requirement. On the other hand, when there are distinct high-level commands to a system, each of them suggests tests that do not involve other commands, as well as tests of command sequences. "Error situations" are always a good source of tests: the test must check that the error is detected and properly handled. However, routine functions are also important, the more so the more likely it is that a user will invoke that function. At the system level, there really are no inputs that are "not allowed." Even if the specification "doesn't care" what happens in a certain case, there is an implication that the software will do something reasonable, in particular that it will not "crash" or destroy information if that case comes up.

The best specification-based tests come from considering usage "scenarios," or what are now called "use cases." These are sequences of inputs, sequences that end users try in their routine use of the system. For example, in a banking system, a teller does not "enter a check amount" (although that might be a particular input), but rather deals with a customer who is depositing the check, so the scenario includes identifying the customer, perhaps reading out the current balance, going into "deposit" mode, and only then entering the amount. "Modes" of the software, general situations where its actions address a particular part of the application (like "depositing" in the example), are good organizational units for testing, so the first part of the test case must put the system into the mode that is to be tested.

6.1.2 Functional Unit Testing

System requirements and specifications, since they are defined to be non-prescriptive and to avoid mention of how the software system will be decomposed into its structural parts, are no help at all in testing those parts, and the initial test plan can include no more than system tests. But during design, the parts are laid out, and each component has its specification—what it must do to fulfill its place in the system. When each unit specification is written in design, it is time to devise functional test points for it, then add them to the test plan. If the units are subroutines of some kind, their "inputs" and "outputs" are parameter values, not the actual input/output operations of the larger system.

The general plan of testing will be to first test the components, then combine them into the system for test. An obvious reason for this order is that components are coded one at a time, so unit testing is possible before the system can be assembled. But the more important reason for unit testing is that it organizes the testing problem. Each unit is small and well understood, and it will be possible to find and fix unit errors in isolation much more easily than to deduce their presence from strange system behavior.

Divide and conquer ▶

At the unit test level, the specifications are for components and interfaces between components. Both require functional testing. For components themselves, the same rules used at the system level apply, except that the component specifications of the design phase are used instead of the overall system specification. Components have an important additional way to treat errors, however. A specification for unit U may state that U does not handle certain cases, say, X, and hence U should not be tested on X. The justification is that other units of the system are required to protect U from encountering X. Here is an obvious example of something larger that must be tested although it is not easy to do so: how are tests to be devised that will assure that U does *not* receive X? (Answer: The tester goes looking for a way to force X to be sent to U. Some possibilities will be too difficult to analyze without trying them, and these are the basis for tests. But the tests are really fault based, as described in Section 6.2.) Another way of dealing with exceptions is to require that U detect receipt of X, but that it immediately return an error code of some kind, which is handled by the unit that called U. Now the functional test of U is clear: U must be sent X and must return properly. Perhaps it is less obvious that every unit that calls U must be tested (in *its* unit tests) to see that it properly deals with the returned code.

6.1.3 Normal vs. Exception Test Cases

Almost any specification at system or unit level distinguishes "exception" or "illegal" situations from normal processing. It's common that exceptions more easily suggest functional test cases. For example, exceptional inputs are often isolated: if (say) input 0 is illegal, then the exception test case is obvious. But if all the other, legal inputs are lumped together by the specification, how can they be broken up into functional test cases? Sometimes it goes the other way, and the error values are a large set all lumped together. For example, a program might be required to process only strings of 4000 characters or fewer—the vast majority of input strings would then be illegal. Again, what could be done to functionally test such a huge domain of possible problem strings?

One way to handle a large block of inputs is to divide them systematically into groups. For example, if there is no apparent distinction between all positive integer inputs between 0 and 1000, try every 10, say: 0, 10, 20, ..., 1000. (But it's a good idea to avoid such "round" numbers, so 0, 13, 27, 41, ..., 1000 might be better, and why not add -1, 1, and 999, 1001 to try around the boundaries?)

The second way to break up input blocks is to guess at what algorithms might be used to process them. (This is almost the same as "broken-box testing" that peeks at the code to see what the programmer has done. See Section 6.1.4.) For numerical values, this kind of guessing groups negative inputs and positive inputs, and tries each (and the boundary point 0) be-cause they may have to be treated differently by the program. Guesses may be wrong, of course. It's unclear if the groupings make sense for testing if the program does not make the distinction guessed at.

The easy part of functional testing is trying relatively isolated cases that will probably be handled by the program code in isolated ways. A special input (or a small class of inputs), which the program explicitly checks for and processes, has test points that are easy to find, and if the test points succeed, the tester correctly believes that the program is working properly in that functional case. The hard part of functional testing is cases in which there are no apparent specification or likely code distinctions.

Functional testing isn't a matter of convenience, unfortunately. The very input classes that are difficult to break down may be the important ones. And normal inputs must always be considered more important than exceptions. When a program fails on an exceptional point, the worst that can happen is that a phony computation ensues that misleads the user into thinking the input was valid (or, the program may crash). There are circumstances in which such erroneous behavior can cause a lot of trouble. But programs are typically used over and over to solve much the same problems, and exceptional points come up less and less frequently as the human beings become experienced with a program. The end users have work to do, and if the program can do the routine work (consisting of normal, nonexception cases), then it may be good enough to use even if it occasionally botches an invalid input. The lesson for the functional tester is clear: isolated exception cases may be the easiest to find and try, but the normal cases are the more important.

6.1.4 Broken-Box Testing

Instead of guessing at distinctions the program might make, a breakdown of an apparently monolithic specification into cases can be accomplished by studying the implementing code. Technically, looking at the code isn't "black-box" testing (Brian Marick has called it "broken-box" testing), but everyone does it. In the simplest case, the program really does treat a large group of inputs in the same way. For example, in the case of all strings of length greater than 4000 being illegal, there might be a statement:

```
if (length(InputString) > 4000)
    ErrorExitMessage("Illegal string -- too long");
```

in the program. Then the tester can just try one long string and be pretty sure that if the message appears and the program terminates (or whatever it's supposed to do for illegal input), then the whole huge class of too-long strings has been tested. (Whether or not the length() function is OK to handle them is another matter.)

But sometimes there is a program separation of cases. A common example is one in which memory is dynamically allocated, and although the specification does not distinguish cases that require different amounts of memory, the program does. Suppose the previous program example has static storage available for input strings of up to 200 characters, and for longer strings it dynamically allocates up to 4000 characters. Looking at the code, there are then three functional (in the broken-box sense) cases to be tested: 1-200 characters, 201-4000 characters, and more than 4000 characters. It would be a good idea to try the boundaries, namely, strings of exactly 1, 200, 201, 4000, and 4001 characters as well because that's where the program is likely to go wrong.

What about the null string of zero length? Does the specification cover it? Is it illegal?

Broken-box testing raises another problem: just looking at the results may not really test the program. For example, in the dynamic memory example, suppose the program has a bug that causes it to ignore the static storage and just allocate 4000 characters for all inputs. It may appear to be working, but the programmer's storage ideas (perhaps for speed on short inputs) aren't being carried out. It may be necessary to resort to low-level instrumentation, using a machine-level debugging program, for example, to see exactly what is happening on each test.

The danger in broken-box testing lies in recording the tests and reusing them after the program has been changed. This reuse, called *regression* testing, is usually a good idea that saves a lot of time. But suppose the tester has seen from the code (as in one example above) that there are several cases of input strings involving a boundary point at length 200, and has devised test cases accordingly. If the program subsequently changes, even by only adjusting the boundary to 100, these tests are invalidated. It is very likely that no one will notice, and false confidence will be placed in the regression testing, which may very well have never tried a short-string case.

6.2 Fault-Based Testing

Functional testing is systematic because the tester begins with a catalog of functions, and systematically finds tests for each one. Another systematic method is called *fault-based testing*. In fault-based testing, the tester tries to imagine what might go wrong (that is, a fault, or bug in the software), and tries to devise a test that will unambiguously determine if it *has* gone wrong (that is, if the fault exists). It is essential to this process that the fault be very well understood, and narrowly circumscribed. The principle listed earlier of seeking to test error-prone conditions is another description of fault-based testing.

Fault-based testing is more subtle than functional testing because its outcome must be unambiguous. When any test fails, the developer knows there is a problem and can begin to fix it. When a functional test succeeds, less is learned because the test is only a single probe into a "function" that may include many subcases and special conditions. It could happen that the one case tried was OK but that other cases of the same function (untried) might not be OK. But in fault-based testing, success of the test has more significance: when the test *succeeds*, it should establish that a particular fault is *not* present.

6.2.1 An Example

Suppose that in writing a specification, a software system is required to allow its user to interrupt and terminate printing by typing a special keyboard character (control-O). Suppose that the system is also required to allow its user to "type ahead" up to 256 characters while output is proceeding, with the type-ahead characters being saved and echoed at the conclusion of dumping the output. The alert analyst might worry about the following faults:

- Will type-ahead input be lost if the user types control-O after typing ahead?
- Is it possible that typing all 256 characters ahead will make control-O fail to work? (The analyst is probably thinking that the design may use a 256-character input buffer, and that same buffer must hold the control-O.)

(Of course, the time to check these issues with the user is during the specification phase. Perhaps the user *wants* type ahead to be discarded on control-O; however, it isn't likely that anyone wants control-O to fail because of type ahead.) A single fault-based test can be devised to investigate both faults: the software must be set to producing a lot of output (so that it can be counted on not to stop too soon), 256 characters should be typed ahead, then control-O typed. The outcome will tell if the faults are present. (Not, unfortunately, with absolute certainty. There may be timing problems that make the result dependent on exactly how fast the output is being generated, the speed of typing ahead, or even the position in a circular buffer that the control-O occupies.)

6.2.2 Interface Testing

A design describes not only the functional specifications of its components, but the interfaces between them. Interface testing can be an example of fault-based testing. Consider the simplest situation in which an interface between components is a subroutine call with all the information carried by parameters of the call. What can go wrong? How might the calling and called routines disagree about the interface?

- The number of parameters, or their types, may not be the same. (But most modern compilers should check for such a disagreement.)
- The order of parameters may be confused. (And if there is an accidental agreement of types, the best compiler will not catch this. However, by defining additional types that are apparently different, this case could be reduced to the one previously mentioned.)
- A parameter meaning (but not type) may be different. A common case is that units do not agree; for example, one routine provides a length in inches, but the other is expecting it in centimeters.
- The calling routine fails to observe restrictions on parameter values that the called routine is depending upon. For example, if the called routine divides by the parameter value, the interface specification may require that it be nonzero.

To write fault-based tests for interface conditions requires either direct examination of the values passed at the interface or deductions about what will happen to values as they are processed by the code and reach the interface from elsewhere. The latter is less sure; for example, one might start with a length of 1.0 inch, which is easy to distinguish from 1.0 centimeter, but if the program happens to divide this value by 1000 before passing it across the interface, and adds 10, keeping only a few significant digits, the value resulting from 1.0 will always look like 10.0, and success of the test will not preclude the inch/centimeter fault. A direct fault-based test at the interface requires observing the "output" there of the calling routine and considering what the called routine should do with this "input."

6.2.3 Boundary-Value Tests

It is a peculiar fact of human nature that we prefer the middle of the road. Perhaps in politics that's because the majority of people are precisely that—the majority—and hence in the middle of any kind of distribution. In programming, the middle of the road is the typical, normal case that must be processed, and of course, that's where programmers concentrate their efforts. It is where their algorithms are needed and where users are most often using the software. It is no surprise, then, that programs most often go wrong at the edges of the road, at boundaries that are the extremes of functional domains. A typical example is in string processing, where all too often the null string of zero length is forgotten, and when it occurs, the program does the wrong thing. (Commonly, it goes into an infinite loop, or acts as if the string had one character, perhaps left over from another string.) The null string error is a special case of setlike objects that have no members. Other examples are a list of files in which there happen to be no files, a linked list in memory from which the last member has just been removed, a loop counter that starts out at zero so the loop body should not be executed at all, and so

Almost any pro-
gram that gets
a number from
its command line
can be crashed
on a 32-bit ma-
chine by giving it
a 50-digit integer.

on. The other extreme is too large, out-of-range values, like the string whose length exceeds a restriction on which the programmer was counting.

Every functional test, system, or unit level, black or broken box, induces boundaries of its functional domain. It is *boundary value testing* to systematically try cases on and around those boundaries. Often, the boundary is a single point (e.g., 0 as the boundary between positive and negative integer values). That makes the testing particularly easy. Or the boundary may itself be a set of values, for example, the set of matrices that happen to be singular. Then the boundary set may itself have boundaries to test.

Boundary value testing has a wrinkle that is not so obvious as trying points on the boundary. One should also try points that are just on either side of it. For integer values, this means that along with a boundary point, say, 0, −1 and +1 should be tried. For floating point values, the either-side points would be the ones in which the mantissa changes in just the least significant bit. These "barely off-boundary" test points, if they fail, demonstrate that the program is using the wrong boundary definition, something more than merely failing on the boundary. The simplest example involves binary numerical comparisons in a program. A conditional test using, say, the != (C inequality) comparison, defines a boundary where the compared values are equal. But if the test should have been, say, > (strictly greater), the boundary value alone will not expose the mistake; either-side points will expose it.

That boundary value testing is the best way to find the most errors most easily is well established and seems a consequence of the way people think. It points out the distinction between fault-based testing (of which boundary value testing is such a good example) and regular functional testing, to imagine a test plan including *only* boundary value testing. A programmer who knew that this test plan would be used could write code that didn't handle the required problem at all—no algorithms, no data structures, and so forth, just a collection of special boundary case processing code. The tests would show up any errors in these cases, which when fixed would produce a program almost totally without value to its users. Functional testing in the middle of the road is important, too, and it's only because it is assumed to have been done that boundary value methods find most of the problems.

6.3 Test Plan Throughout the Life Cycle

Document it! ▶
(Record it or
it's lost)

The majority of contributions to the test plan are made before testing begins, primarily in the requirements phase (system black box tests) and in the design phase (fault-based and broken-box tests). There is every reason not to wait: devising tests early helps in development, and it is easier to do then.

In other phases, additions to the plan are less important. During specification, new test cases may handle the distinction made by sharpening a requirement. During coding, a programmer may be concerned about some aspect of the code being written, and might add a fault-based case to see that it hasn't gone wrong. During the testing phase itself, a test in the plan may expose a failure, and further tests are indicated to gain more information for debugging. Or a fault-based test may succeed, but the tester realizes that its success does not cover some exceptional case that was not imagined before. Just as it is foolish to think of test cases during specification and design and not record them, so these additional last-minute tests should be added to the plan.

6.3.1 Adding Systematic Testing to the Plan

That part of the test plan that is devised in advance of the test phase is devoted to peculiar scenarios that come to mind during development. There are, in addition, systematic methods that can be mandated by a general test plan, but whose actual test points cannot be added to the plan until the testing phase itself. One general class is the so-called structural coverage methods, in which test points are evaluated for how well they exercise textual parts of the program under test. Intuitively, these methods are a good way to excite failures. Chapter 20 discusses structural coverage and explains why it should be used with caution. Another method is "random testing" that requires tests selected without any dependence on each other. Random testing is the single technique that has significance in assessing the quality of tested software; it is described in Chapter 21.

Since systematic techniques have precise technical definitions, they can be included in a test plan by name (e.g., "Perform statement-coverage testing on all components during unit test" or "Perform random testing on the whole system using 10,000 test points").

6.3.2 After Testing

When the testing phase is done, and software has been released, its test plan has two important uses:

1. The test plan serves as a record of what was done, which is invaluable when trouble reports come in from users. When a user experiences difficulty, knowing that "we tried that" may mean that there is a communication problem rather than a real software failure. In any case, the conflict between "it worked when we tried it" and "it doesn't work for this user" is helpful in tracing the problem.

2. If any maintenance changes are made in the software, they will have to be tested. The most difficult part of this *regression testing* is deciding that things intended *not* to change have in fact remained stable. The original tests and their description in the plan are an invaluable aid in regression testing.

How Does It Fit?

From section 6.1

1. In a code inspection, it is very important that inspectors and author not get into an adversarial relationship. Why is this psychological pitfall less important for testers and programmers?

2. Give an example to show how a program, given input X and then given X again, might not produce the same result the second time. How could testing be conducted to be certain that there is no need to repeat any tests? Would it be a good idea?

3. Suppose a program processes ASCII character string inputs, where a string is defined to end with an ASCII LF (line-feed) character. The specification requires special treatment for strings of fewer than 16 characters.

    (a) How many ASCII strings are there of fewer than 16 characters? (The ASCII character set has 128 characters, of which LF is one.)

    (b) Explain why this special case cannot be exhaustively tested by trying all the strings of (a).

4. A rhetorical question about testing unit U for error case X is raised and answered at the end of the section.

    (a) Restate the answer that is given, now that you know what a fault-based test is.

    (b) Suppose that U is recursive. How should it be tested for X?

5. The text suggests that it is hard to test that a routine U has *not* been sent X, when the design states that U does not have to handle X. Why not have U check for X anyway, just in case? Wouldn't that fulfill any possible requirements for U? If X isn't sent, that's fine; if it is, then the check will catch it.

6. Give an example of a program and its use such that a failure to properly detect and process an invalid input could be disastrous.

7. Mathematical subroutines are often hard to test functionally because the normal cases have no apparent breakdown. For example, consider a routine whose specification is:

    > This routine computes the exponential function with accuracy 1 in 10^5 in the range $[-10^7, 10^7]$.

    > How would you go about finding functional tests for this routine, and what might they be?

8. The obvious functional classes for testing an implementation of the absolute value function seem to be negative, zero, positive. Comment on the usefulness of these for a program that is implementing the algorithm of taking the square root of the square of the input.

9. Suppose a program is delivered that works perfectly so long as no exception condition arises, but if there is any exception, the program just terminates. Is the program usable at all? Explain.

From section 6.2

10. In the fault-based test example, give details of the way that:

    (a) Type ahead might be lost.
    (b) Control-O might fail to work.

    for a particular (poor) buffering algorithm.

11. Give a brief argument that fault-based tests should never be executed; that instead they should be added to the checklists for code inspection.

12. Suppose that functional tests have been devised by guessing at distinctions that a programmer might make before the code is written. Later, broken-box analysis shows that in fact it was *not* written that way. Should the original test be discarded? Why or why not?

13. See how many UNIX system programs (like `grep`) you can make malfunction by giving them large command-line integers. (And why is 50 digits large for a 32-bit machine?) Remember that crashing is not the only way a program goes wrong—is the integer being used correctly? Does the specification indicate that there should be an error message for it being out of range, or that there even is a range?

From section 6.3

14. Some large organizations have special groups (usually called "Quality Assurance" or QA) that are in charge of testing, inspection, and other aspects of checking software. Suppose that a rule is made that only QA can make, modify, or use test plans. Is this a good or a bad rule, and why?

15. It has been said that if programmers know what tests will be applied to their code, it is more likely that those tests will not find any problems. Discuss.

Review Questions

1. If no test plan has been made during requirements, specification, design, and coding, what is the best way to make one at the last minute before testing begins? Why?

2. If a test plan made during requirements includes no actual test points, but only general descriptions of what is to be tested, during what phase will the actual test points be devised? Explain.

3. What is the difference between function testing and fault-based testing?

4. What kinds of tests are devised during requirements analysis as opposed to during design?

Further Reading

Test plans of the general, management-oriented variety are sometimes called "quality plans" instead, and they may also include procedures other than testing (notably, inspections). Books on "software quality" describe these plans. One whose name indicates it is more about testing is reference [Het88].

Although in a textbook the description of the test plan must come before the description of testing, in practice, people who make test plans are knowledgeable about testing, as they must be to do a good job. A student trying to cut through the muddle of when to study what aspect of testing could do no better than to read Glenford Myers' little book [Mye79]. The particular techniques it describes are dated, but the quality of the writing and the author's clear priorities recommend it.

One of the few articles in the literature that addresses the practical problem of devising functional tests is reference [OB88]. That there isn't a great deal of substance to say about functional testing hasn't stopped entire books being written on the subject [Bei95].

References

[Bei95]   Boris Beizer. *Black Box Testing: Techniques for Functional Testing of Software and Systems*. Wiley, 1995.

[Het88]   William Hetzel. *The Complete Guide to Software Testing*, 2nd Ed. Wiley-QED, 1988.

[Mye79]   G. J. Myers. *The Art of Software Testing*. Wiley-Interscience, New York, NY, 1979.

[OB88]   T. J. Ostrand and Marc J. Balcer. The category-partition method for specifying and generating functional tests. *Communications of the ACM*, 16: 676–686, 1988.

PART II

Requirements and Specification

▼

The beginning phases of the software lifecycle are devoted to capturing the problem to be solved: what is the software system supposed to do? In this process, the customer, the end user of the software to be developed, is king. To rework an old saw, the customer may not understand software, but he knows what he wants. It is the task of requirements analysis to find out "what he wants" and record it in such a way that development can then proceed without him.

After requirements are gathered and analyzed, it is sometimes appropriate to enter a second phase to refine the description of what the software must do, creating a more technical document called the specification. There is no reason to engage in this specification exercise unless the project is very large and complex, or unless special mathematical techniques are brought to bear. The latter case, which is most often seen in safety-critical software, has acquired the name "formal methods." Formal methods are hard to use and the subject of a current controversy: do they, can they, work? The formal methods we use for illustration are the fundamental ones: first-order predicate logic and its realization in the logic programming language Prolog.

Requirements

inding out what the software must do—requirements analysis—is *the* most important part of the development process. If the developer does not know precisely the problem to be solved, no useful solution is likely. If the customer for whom the software is intended is not heard and understood, he cannot possibly be happy with the result. But the need for a requirements document (or even for this phase of the life cycle) is less clear for an individual developing software alone. A student programming a class project receives the requirements as an assignment—there is often no give and take with the instructor. Someone writing a utility program for personal use is both user and developer—how could there be misunderstandings? Even a software engineer who enters a development project as a designer or programmer has the requirements as a given. Why do these people need to know about requirements?

The answer lies in the interconnection of phases in the life cycle. The requirements document is, of course, what directs the whole of development to follow, so all developers would be advised to understand it. What's more important is that requirements analysis never really ends, not with a document, not even if that phase is omitted entirely. Being clear about what the software must do is essential, and the best way to attain this clarity is for a developer to be explicitly concerned with requirements issues. If there is no actual requirements phase or document, these concerns will come up elsewhere in development. If there is a document, whenever a mistake is discovered in it (and identifying its mistakes, as well as knowing that they are in fact mistakes in gathering requirements, requires knowledge of that phase), the developer must return to consider the problem with eyes that see requirements issues. Imagine the (all too common) situation in which a requirements problem is discovered during coding:

A programmer (perhaps thinking about an ELSE for some conditional expression) discovers that there is no documentation for that case, and furthermore, it is not clear just what should be done there. What should he or she do? It is common to simply make a choice (code that ELSE!) and proceed, documenting with a code comment. From the requirements viewpoint, nothing could be more wrong-headed. Users will not read that comment, yet they are bound to be affected by the choices the programmer has made. What must be done is to communicate with the user, settle what is wanted, change the *user* documentation to reflect this decision, and propagate the change through any other affected documents.

Without taking the requirements view, developers are forever doomed to surprise the users with what's not wanted.

7.1 Exploring Requirements

Input/output ▶ is the essence of software.

Establishing requirements is the first and most important step of the journey from a fuzzy concept to a concrete implementation. But the task is difficult and confusing, so it is common for software engineers to suffer "writer's block"—no ideas, and no concept of where to start. Thinking of software as an input/output transform provides a few clues.

7.1.1 Requirements Describe a Software Transform

The transformation wanted from a software system is given in terms of inputs and outputs to the system, and here enters the first and most important property of good requirements. In the requirements document, it should be stated *what* set of inputs get transformed to *what* set of outputs. It is tempting to instead state *how* inputs get transformed into outputs, but this information belongs in the design document and not in the requirements document. The most important reason for separating *what* from *how* is intellectual control, to divide and conquer. The two can be separated, and to do so simplifies both aspects of recording the transform. *How* to do something is one way of describing *what* to do, but it drags in lots of unnecessary baggage. This baggage could be deferred to design, and if it is not, the hands of the designer are tied because the work has already been done.

There can be two distinct aspects of the "what" for software development: the *requirements* of this chapter, and the *specification* of Chapter 9 to follow. Unless a software project is very complex, or there are special circumstances as described in Chapter 9, the two phases will be combined, and the requirements aspect will dominate. After the customer and developer agree on what is wanted and codify this in a requirements document, the developer will begin to design the software, and there will be no separate specification phase.

It is surprisingly difficult to keep to the "what" away from the "how." It is somehow most natural for people to describe what should be accom-

Many mathematics texts define a *function* (that is, an input/output transform) as "a rule for associating an output with each input." This definition confuses the input/output *relationship* (what) with an algorithm (how) that realizes the relationship.

plished by explaining the steps to be taken. The distinction comes into play in programming language paradigms. So-called declarative programming (for example, in Prolog) is "what," whereas imperative programming (say, in C) is "how." Thus a language like C is not a good vehicle for capturing "what;" Prolog is better. (And so Prolog will be used for specification in Section 10.4.2 to follow.)

7.1.2 Identification of System Inputs and Output

The developer's requirements writer meets with the customer to discuss the inputs that are required to accomplish the task, and the outputs that are required for the users to accomplish their *next* tasks. When there is an existing system, people who use it know the inputs and outputs, and what the transform should be. The corresponding danger is that the existing system may in fact be doing the wrong thing, or doing it badly. Joseph Weizenbaum has said that automation is too often brought in to shore up a pernicious manual system, one that would (and should!) fall under its own weight if it were not for computer support. Perhaps it is asking too much of the software developer to find out what a user *really* wants when it is suggested that a manual system be automated. It might be hard to tell the user that what's being requested is to do something nasty to more people, faster.

In the process of identifying system inputs and outputs, it is useful to record a name, description, and value restrictions for these items. Sometimes, inputs are *aggregate*—that is, a composite of basic elements. Consider a simple payroll system for a moment. Certainly one of the inputs to a payroll system would be an employee timecard. A timecard is not a "simple" input since it contains several pieces of information, such as:

1. *Employee name.*
2. *Identification number.*
3. *Hours worked.*
4. *Sick hours.*

At the highest level, "*Employee Timecard*" is a system input, but several individual fields compose this record. In the requirements document, the input description might be recorded in a format that allows reference to either the entire record or to a field (very much like a data structure in a programming language):

- Timecard: Aggregate Structure: Employee information for payroll.

  - Timecard.Employee-Name: Alphanumeric field (80 characters): Employee name.

- Timecard.Id-No: Numeric field (9 digits): Employee identification number.
- Timecard.Hours-Worked: Numeric field (2 digits): Hours worked. Should be less than 80 hours.
- Timecard.Sick-Hours: Numeric field (2 digits): Sick hours. Should be less than or equal to 40 hours.

In this presentation, we are using a time-honored practice of displaying the technical input names in a type font different from the one used for prose. The primary purpose is to avoid confusion in talking about these names.

An experienced requirements analyst might pick up an important implicit assumption from the timecard input description. Apparently the restrictions on hour values are for a *weekly* payroll. There is nothing wrong with such an assumption, provided that the user is not thinking about changing it. If it might change, then probably the user believes that the change will be easy to make, which has implications for the way the software is designed and coded. In any case, *implicit* assumptions are always dangerous. The only good assumption is one that is written down and agreed to all around. Otherwise, the assumption is merely a hidden requirement that will rise later to bite the developer.

Document it! ▶
(Know what you've assumed)

System outputs can be described in the same way. Suppose that the accounting department wants the payroll report to contain the employee name, identification number, hours worked, sick hours, gross pay for the period, total deductions, and net pay. We could specify those outputs as follows:

- Payroll: Aggregate structure: Payroll report for accounting.

  - Payroll.Employee-Name: Alphanumeric field (80 characters): Employee name.
  - Payroll.Id-No: Numeric field (9 digits): Employee identification number.
  - Payroll.Hours-Worked: Numeric field (2 digits): Hours worked.
  - Payroll.Sick-Hours: Numeric field (2 digits): Sick hours.
  - Payroll.Gross-Pay: Currency field (5 digits before the decimal point, 2 digits after—abbreviated "5.2"): Total pay before deductions.
  - Payroll.Deductions: Currency field (5.2 digits): Total withheld from pay.
  - Payroll.Net-Pay: Currency field (5.2 digits): Pay after deductions. Issue check for this amount. Flag checks for more than $5000.00, for special hand processing. Do not issue checks for negative amounts or amounts less than $1.00.

These descriptions of inputs and outputs look so much like the typed "structures" of a programming language that it's tempting to write and maintain them in the language that is going to be used for implementation. COBOL is a particularly attractive language for such specifications because it has a number of pictorial notations for just this purpose. For example, a two-digit numeric field is described by "99." There is nothing wrong with falling into the programming language, but a good test to apply is: If the language of implementation were to change, would it still be a good idea to use the structures from the wrong language?

However they are expressed, at this point there is a catalog of system *inputs* and *outputs,* with some ideas as to what the values are.

7.1.3 Partitioning Inputs and Outputs

The notion of *value ranges* is natural to inputs and outputs. At the very least, users will have an idea of what constitutes valid and invalid values.

For example, in the inputs of the payroll example, the work hours listed on the employee timecard should be two digits and less than or equal to 80. This means that valid values for Hours-Worked are 00–80, inclusive. Some invalid values for this field are single digits, alphabetical characters, and numbers greater than 80. Thus input values are *partitioned* into valid and invalid values.

Divide and conquer ▶

Similarly, the range of output values can be partitioned. Consider the Net-Pay field, which has special provisions associated with the values $5000, $1, and negative values:

1. Values between $1.00 and $5000.00 inclusive.

2. Values between $0.00 and $0.99 inclusive.

3. Values less than $0.00 (negative amounts).

Only category 1 has valid inputs. The isolation of a "negative" range (as distinct from "less than $1.00") suggests something different about this case. Maybe the developer is thinking that category 2 represents work for which the check will be held over until the next pay period, while category 3 represents some error in the input data or the program's calculations. In any case, the reason for the categories should be recorded.

Although partitioning of the input and output values is peculiar to each software situation, the value ranges should be equivalence classes—that is, they must have empty intersections (the ranges are disjoint), and together the ranges must exhaust all possibilities.

7.1.4 Exploring Relationships Between Inputs and Outputs

The major themes that recur when exploring the input/output transform are:

- *Normal mode processing:* This is the central theme of requirements: What should the system do when all the inputs are valid and as expected?
- *Exceptions:* What should be done in situations that fall outside the range of normal processing?
- *Interdependencies:* Many times the way a particular input is handled depends on the value of a different input. What are these interdependencies?

The requirements writer should systematically consider how all values of all inputs affect the values of all outputs. This could be an exhausting task because there may be far too many values. However, when values are partitioned into range equivalence classes, it may be possible to treat all values in a range in the same way.

To illustrate requirements that evolve from partitions of just a single input and a single output, consider Hours-Worked and Net-Pay. The permutations of the equivalence classes are:

1. Valid Hours-Worked, valid Net-Pay.
2. Valid Hours-Worked, Net-Pay greater than $5000.00.
3. Valid Hours-Worked, Net-Pay $0.00 to $0.99 inclusive.
4. Valid Hours-Worked, Net-Pay less than $0.00.
5. Invalid Hours-Worked, valid Net-Pay.
6. Invalid Hours-Worked, Net-Pay greater than $5000.00.
7. Invalid Hours-Worked, Net-Pay $0.00 to $0.99 inclusive.
8. Invalid Hours-Worked, Net-Pay less than $0.00.

Requirements are generated by considering each of these possibilities in turn, and asking: "What should happen?" For instance, what should the system do if someone has a valid number of hours worked, but his or her pay computes to less than $1.00? This exercise might lead to the following requirements:

r1. If Hours-Worked is valid and Net-Pay is valid, the system shall generate a paycheck for the employee. (Case 1) r2. If Hours-Worked is valid and Net-Pay is greater than $5000, the system shall generate a message indicating that this paycheck is to be processed by hand. (Case 2)

r3. If Hours-Worked is valid and Net-Pay is $0.00 to $0.99, the system shall carry the amount forward to the next paycheck. (Case 3)

r4. If Hours-Worked is valid and Net-Pay is less than $0.00, the system shall carry forward the liability to the next paycheck. The system shall also issue a message indicating that there is a possible error in the timecard or in the calculation. (Case 4)

r5. If Hours-Worked is invalid, the system shall not process the timecard and shall issue a message indicating that the employee check has not been issued because the timecard is in error. (Cases 5–8)

Decisions have been made to clarify issues that weren't apparent at the outset. It has been decided to carry forward small amounts, and it has also been decided to carry forward liabilities (but to flag them as possible error cases). In many cases, without a systematic exploration of these input and output relationships, some of the subtle problems posed by unusual (valid or invalid) combinations of inputs and outputs may not be considered. Since there are too many combinations to handle easily, systematic evaluation and recording are needed, or some will be missed.

Divide and conquer (7 ± 2 rule) ▶

Considering unusual cases can also lead afield to quite different requirements. For example, in the requirements generated, there is a clear error case (**r5**) and another possible error case (**r4**). The employees (or the system operators) concerned may very well need to correct errors so that people can be paid on time. This suggests that there must be some special mechanism for processing exceptions outside the normal sequence, and it must be defined and specified. The most common mistake made in data processing systems is failure to provide for exceptional, corrective processing—it is the mistake that leads eventually to someone saying: "We can't do that because the computer doesn't allow it." Like most "It's the computer's fault" statements, what's really meant is that the requirements phase of the software development was badly done.

The degree to which all possibilities of inputs and outputs have been captured is called the *completeness* of a requirements document. Engineers seldom see requirements that are 100% complete, but systematic exploration using partitions is a way to work toward completeness.

7.1.5 From Requirements to the Test Plan

Cases defined by considering partitions of input and output are precisely those needed to functionally test software (Section 6.1). Each of the previous eight cases is a distinct "function" to test, and as such can go directly into the test plan. The corresponding requirement **r1–r5** tells the tester what should happen when the test is run. For example, case 1 is the normal-processing function in which a check should be issued; case 3 is the function of too little pay, which is to be forwarded, and so on.

The functional test classes, unfortunately, are not described solely by the input partition, so test data cannot be directly recorded to try the software in each class. For example, although it requires a valid Hours-Worked to get into case 3, that case does not arise from every value of Hours-Worked. So in the testing phase it will be necessary to find test inputs that fall in the functional class of case 3.

Document it! ▶
(Record it or
it's lost)

It should be clear that if the test plan does not record the eight functional test classes, it is unlikely that they will be tried in the testing phase. It is certain that the most efficient way to test these classes is to save the results of the analysis rather than to repeat it in the testing phase.

7.2 Example: Printing Trees

The payroll example given in Section 7.1.2 is so straightforward that it doesn't entirely capture how difficult the requirements phase of software development can be. As a more complex case, consider a problem faced by those who are trying to write prose about the data structure called a tree. Such people include the authors of textbooks (like this one), programmers who want to document the use of trees, and so forth. The customer in this example is therefore a writer, who comes to a software developer with the problem of drawing diagrams using a computer. This customer may be computer literate, at least in the sense of using a sophisticated word processing package, and may even be the same person who must write the software. But the customer could also be a buyer for a publisher of textbooks whose employees need to draw trees and have asked the relatively uninformed buyer to acquire software to do it. The following presentation inclines toward the case of a knowledgeable user.

The first cut at a statement of requirements might be:

I want to draw trees along with word processor text.

That is enough to proceed, but not with anything that could be called software engineering. Software engineering demands that detailed requirements be recorded at the outset as to what the software must do. Without an analysis of requirements, most of what the user will see as the functionality of the developed software will be invented in the process of designing and coding, a process that the user may not understand very well. It is likely that when the tree-drawing program is done, the user will say, "That's not what I had in mind." It is to forestall such an outcome that the customer/developer dialogue should take place.

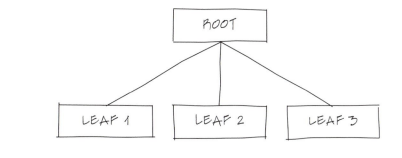

▶ **Figure 7.1** A user's first indication of a tree.

The developer must direct the dialogue because only the developer knows what is not yet on the table. The magic words are input and output: what the user must say is what will be given to the software to tell it which tree to draw and what the resulting picture will look like. Let's start with the output.

7.2.1 Pinning Down the Output Format

The user can probably sketch a few examples of trees that are desired. From these, the developer has to abstract generalities about all the trees that might be drawn and question the user about details, limitations, and exceptional cases that might arise. For example, suppose the user sketches a tree like Fig. 7.1. The developer has to find out whether all the trees have exactly this form (labeled boxes of fixed size for the nodes, a root, and three leaves), or if the user had more generality in mind. Likely as not, it's the latter. So let us imagine that the user says, "Oh, of course, there might be more levels and the order of branching might be anything." It will help a good deal whenever user and developer can agree on standard definitions. Here it will be important that they are both thinking of the same mathematical abstraction for "tree," and they could settle that easily by agreeing on a published definition, say, in a textbook. Consulting a textbook immediately brings up the question of order in the descendents of a node; trees are usually ordered, and probably our user's are, too. With agreement on a mathematical source, words like "root," "branching order," and so on, become well defined. Both parties may still not understand the same thing by a tree, but if later a dispute or question arises, they have agreed on where to look to settle it, and the textbook will be the arbiter of who is right.

Reuse past work (Don't reinvent the wheel) ▶

Now that a potential infinity of trees might be drawn, it is time to consider limitations. Although a larger and larger page would allow any size tree to be drawn, this isn't likely to be what the user wants; more likely, the trees are to be of some uniform size, and the lines and boxes of some minimum size, which leads to limitations on the trees that can be drawn. So let's suppose that the tree has to fit within a 7-by-9.5-inch rectangular space, such as would be centered on a standard U.S. page of paper with $\frac{3}{4}$-inch margins. Suppose also that the boxes are to be drawn as large as possible, in one of three sizes (height × width, inches): $1 \times 1\frac{1}{2}$, $\frac{1}{2} \times 1$, and $\frac{3}{8} \times \frac{3}{4}$. At this point, the prudent developer had better check if all the boxes in one tree are to be the same size! Let us hope that one of the participants—developer or user—remembers to clear up the point about what might or might not appear in the boxes, and let us suppose that it is a single line of text, which must fit in the box using the largest Times Roman type size possible between 6 pt and 12 pt. At this point, the participants may need to agree on a reference book about typography.

What are appropriate limitations about the size and shape of trees? Probably the user wants them to "look good" on the page, but "looking good" is not that easy to define. Let's say that the user is willing to go no further than to say that boxes must not tilt; it must be clear which node is above which; all the arcs must be straight lines; all arcs leave the bottom center of the upper box and enter the top center of the lower box; and no arcs or boxes may cross. (Developer: "Can arcs and/or boxes just touch, without crossing?" User: "Of course not!" What question does this interchange leave unanswered?) The developer would be wise to suggest consideration of the example of a set of ten descendents from one node, which can be accommodated under the rules thus far only if they are not put on the same level (why?)—is that OK? The user might answer that it would be better to keep all descendents on the same horizontal level, but that if they won't fit, then it's OK do something like Fig. 7.2. It is in the developer's interest to forbid this staggered appearance because it complicates the question of what can possibly be drawn. When a box like L2 is squeezed between and above two others like L4 and L5 in Fig. 7.2, it forces L4 and L5 apart, and it can limit the number of L2 descendents whose input arcs can be squeezed between L4 and L5.

This extended discussion of the output format suggests a lot of example trees that the user and developer could examine and argue about—the user to get the most versatile program, the developer to make the software as simple as possible. The user should win most of these arguments, but it could happen that the developer decides along the way that perhaps someone else was meant to develop this software. Each example that is brought up and agreed upon should immediately find its way into the developer's test plan. The user is likely to try them later and to remember the agreement to get them right.

Document it! ▶
(Record it or it's lost)

7.2.2 The Input Format

No matter how well the output format has been captured, the usefulness of the program will largely depend on its input: how is the user to inform the

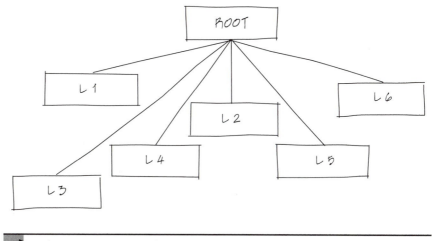

Figure 7.2   A tree that's OK, but not preferred.

program of the tree to draw? There are many quite different possibilities, ranging from the completely graphical (which might be like programs for drawing on the screen using the mouse) to noninteractive batch formats in which the input is some textual description of the tree. Graphical inputs are much in vogue, but the serious user with lots of trees to draw will probably prefer a textual interface. Drawing one tree with a lot of pointing and clicking is easy, and the best way to do the job; drawing dozens gets tedious. Major advantages of the textual format are that it can be easily edited with a regular text editor, and it can be generated by a program. Perhaps the user imagines some kind of "graphical editor" that is to be part of the software. But in that case, the developer might withdraw because the job has grown to a state-of-the-art research project. For better or for worse, our example will use textual input.

The mathematical definition of a tree is a good place to start on an input format. A tree is a special case of a directed graph, which is a pair of sets—the nodes and edges. (Technically, the user wants *labeled* directed ordered acyclic graphs—the labels are the text in the boxes—but let's put that aside for now.) The nodes and edges could simply be given as sets. For example, the user's first example in Fig. 7.1 is the graph

$$(\{b, r, s, t\}, \{((b, r), (b, s), (b, t))\}).$$

Note that the edges are ordered to show left-to-right order of the subtree. The node names are arbitrary;

$$(\{1, 2, 3, 4\}, \{((1, 2), (1, 3), (1, 4))\})$$

would do as well. One pitfall of the general notation is that it can perfectly well describe nontrees, such as $(\{o\}, \{(o, o)\})$, or even nongraphs, as
in $(\{x\}, \{(y, z)\})$, or nonsense, as in $(\{\{\{\}\})$. These problems could be handled
by a requirement that the software check the input for "treeness" and issue an error message when that does not obtain. The node labels could be
incorporated by pairing them with the node names, as in

$$(\{(b, \text{root}), (r, \text{leaf1}), (s, \text{leaf2}), (t, \text{leaf3})\}, \{((b, r), (b, s), (b, t))\})$$

for Fig. 7.1. Let us suppose that the mathematical notation is to be used.
It has the great virtue of being defined in standard textbooks. Again, it is
essential that the developer capture examples—particularly examples of
erroneous inputs—and add them to the test plan. It is remarkably easy
to jot down the essence of such examples as a discussion proceeds, and
remarkably difficult to remember them a few hours (much less months)
later. The quality of testing is very much a matter of thinking ahead.

   The user, however, is certain to be impatient with all those commas and
brackets, and the developer had best anticipate this impatience, even if in
their common enthusiasm for the conciseness of the mathematical notation
they seem to agree on it. The developer might note that they are going to be
cumbersome to parse, too. The notation is also redundant in that the node
set (but not its labels) can be induced from the edge set. To make a long story
short, suppose that the participants agree on an input notation consisting
of node labels in lists (one label per line) in which the first label has those
following as direct descendents from left to right, and a blank line separates
lists. Labels must appear as descendents before they appear first in a list,
with the exception of the root label, which must head the first list. Thus the
user's first example (Fig. 7.1) might come from the input:

```
root
leaf1
leaf2
leaf3
```

As another example,

```
r
m
n

m
x
```

would be input for the tree shown in Fig. 7.3. (In the remaining examples,
the attempt to make the trees look hand drawn is abandoned.)

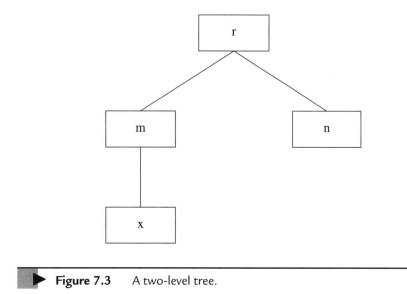

▶ **Figure 7.3**   A two-level tree.

If the tree has nodes with duplicate labels, the same label may appear in different lists with different meanings, which the software is to keep straight by associating a subsequent list with the so far unassociated list item that is farthest above it. For example,

```
r
a
b

a
b
b

b
x

b
y

b
z
```

has the 4th occurrence of b associated with the 1st, and the 5th with the 2nd, and the 6th with the 3rd, and so is the correct input for the tree shown in Fig. 7.4.

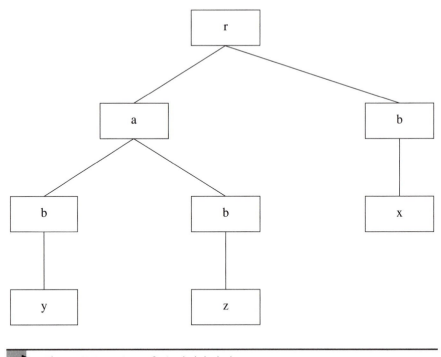

▶ **Figure 7.4**   A confusingly labeled tree.

How likely is it that the user notices that this concise input notation makes it impossible for the software to draw a tree with *unlabeled* boxes?

7.2.3 Specifications That Are Not of Concern to the User

In discussing tree output, nothing was said about the actual printing device that should be used, nor how this device will be used. In one sense, this omission is of no consequence—the input and the trees have been described. However, the user who possesses only a typewriter-style printer will want quite different software than will a user with a laser printer, or one who wants to preview the results on a screen. The issue can be finessed by relying on standard output packages, and their existing implementations for a variety of output devices. For example, the language Postscript can be used to drive a variety of printers and displays, and by choosing to produce Postscript output, the developer can satisfy just about any user. Postscript also has a published standard description—a big advantage.

Furthermore, there are a variety of "little languages" used to draw pictures, with processors to translate into Postscript; one such language in the public domain is pic, which has commands for drawing and connecting labeled boxes, commands that would make it very attractive to the developer.

If the user is unconcerned about this discussion, the whole issue would simply be left to the developer, who would fill in the details as a part of design. But such a user is probably unwise; there are advantages in specifying that (say) `pic` be used, not the least being that `pic` format can be read by a human being when the printing device is busy or broken. The example trees in this section were in fact first drawn using `pic` (even the ones like Fig. 7.1). The `pic` program to draw Fig. 7.3 follows:

```
define grid #$4: box "$1" at ($2,-$3)#
define darc #line from $1.s to $2.n#
boxwid=.75; boxht=.375
grid(r,3,0,B1)
grid(m,2,1,B2)
grid(n,4,1,B3)
grid(x,2,2,B4)
darc(B1,B2)
darc(B1,B3)
darc(B2,B4)
```

The two macro definitions (`define...`) are hard to read, but evidently `grid()` places a box and `darc()` connects two boxes. Given the macros, the drawing of a tree is a matter of finding a set of positions at which to place the boxes (the 2nd and 3rd arguments to `grid()`). With these positions in hand, generating the `pic` text is trivial. However, the requirements that are being constructed are properly nonprescriptive (Section 8.2). They give no hint whatsoever about *how* the set of box positions will be figured out—that is the central problem of writing the tree-drawing software, and it is left to the design phase.

7.2.4 Commentary on the Example

This brief sketch of a dialogue between user and developer has only hinted at the difficulties that may arise in even so simple a set of software requirements. Here are a few more issues that might have arisen along the way:

- Is it possible to have "errors" in the input notation that was agreed upon? That is, can one write inputs whose form is close to correct, but in fact describe no tree at all? (Of course one can!) Error cases must be defined, with appropriate messages when they arise, and some error-detection test cases should go into the test plan.
- Consider the tree in Fig. 7.5. Does this tree suggest any new difficulty or test cases?
- What would have to be done to the requirements document so that it can handle unlabeled trees? What misunderstandings might arise between developer and user over unlabeled trees?

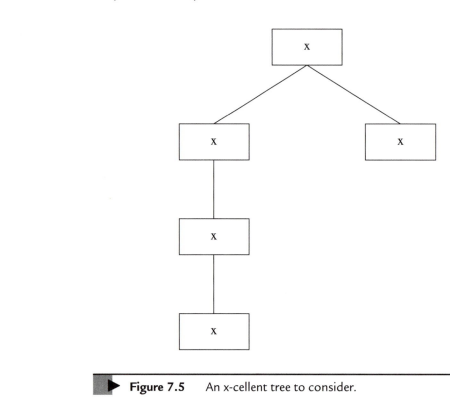

Figure 7.5   An x-cellent tree to consider.

7.3 Software "Modes"

Although the two examples presented are too simple to illustrate it, there is an idea in requirements analysis that is very useful in grouping requirements and decomposing the problem of describing what software must do. For problems that require interactive software to solve, certain input sequences are supposed to force the program to behave in a special way. For a trivial example, in using a point-and-click word processor program, there is an icon on the screen for changing the font, say, to boldface. When the user clicks on the boldface icon, it is supposed to throw the program into "boldface mode," where input characters are displayed differently (in boldface, of course), and the calculation of line lengths, and so forth, is unique to this mode. By identifying such modes, the requirements analyst can separate out the inputs that cause entry and exit from the mode, and the special behavior therein. It is common for the required behavior to be different for the same input, when in different modes. In the example, the result of the user typing (say) an X character is supposed to be one thing in boldface mode and quite another in the regular mode. If the requirements are organized first by mode, and second by actions within the mode, it is much clearer than introducing the mode as a qualifier on each input.

One of the most common modes in practice is some variant of "error mode." While the software is executing, something goes wrong and subsequent actions are required to be unlike normal operation. The best way to describe the situation in a requirements document is to separate out the actions required in error mode (including the return to normal operation) and to list the ways in which error mode can arise. For example, an editor may be able to recover a file that was being processed when the system on which it was running goes down. Starting the editor in this situation puts it into "recovery mode," where all its commands are different (and not available normally) until the recovery is completed.

7.4 Rapid Prototyping

The twin problems of software development have been described as:

1. Getting the right software.
2. Getting the software right.

The reference in (1) is to an adequate dialogue between user and developer, while (2) refers to the rest of the process. It is unfortunate that (2) takes so long because mistakes in (1) come to light only when the user can execute the released program.

There is a practical way to avoid developing the wrong software, called *rapid prototyping*. Rapid prototyping attempts to hurry the process of creating a program that can be tested, and does so at the expense of getting the software right. The developer tries to get something that the user can see right away and cuts every possible corner to do it. Some of the techniques used are discussed in the chapters on design and coding in Part III to follow, notably the use of iterative enhancement (Section 11.2.1) and special programming languages and operating system commands (Chapter 13). The developer tries to concentrate on quickly implementing particular features that may be misunderstood and pays no attention to efficiency, proper data structures, or even the platform that the user will eventually use. It could be called an extreme form of rapid prototyping to have the user sit at a keyboard that is not connected to a computer at all, but rather gets its response from a hidden engineer who works things out by hand.

Users are notorious for "not knowing what they want" until they see something, and then that is exactly what they don't want. This rejection most frequently involves the format and sequencing of input and output. For example:

- The report format is wrong—those columns should be switched, and an additional column is needed.
- The wrong information is requested on the input screen—some of the items on the second screen should be on the first and vice versa.
- There is no need to request that input and then to check it—the program can just generate the correct value.
- That menu should pop up, not be pulled down, and it should be in the middle of the screen.
- The background color is too dark.

And so on. These requests for changes are mostly superficial—it's no harder to do what's wanted than what's not wanted—but what's wanted isn't known until too late. It is therefore not surprising that special-purpose software development tools have been constructed to deal with input/output requirements of fickle users.

The most general tools are special-purpose languages, often called "visual" versions of regular programming languages (for example, "Visual Basic"). These languages include as extension features large support packages for putting things on a screen and for getting input through menus and screen-pointing devices like the mouse. The programmer can pass directly from a sketch of what the screen should look like to a program that implements it. The visual languages are no better then regular languages at making the *calculations* that the user wants, so the rapid-prototyping programmer may fake the calculations. The inputs are actually discarded, and the results are dummies. The user is told to ignore the actual values and pay attention to the format.

It is not very far from the visual languages to tools that involve no programming at all, but use just a description of input/output formats. These tools then generate programs (often in a visual language) to implement the format described. Users may themselves be able to make use of these "interface simulators" to take over part of the developer's work in "getting the right software."

7.5 Managing the Requirements Phase

The requirements document that results from and ends this phase of software development is unique in being shared with the user for whom the software will be developed. The software manager must see to it that this document will serve its purpose in guiding the specification or design phase to follow (as all such ending documents guide the next phase); however, it is also crucial that the user is satisfied with the document, and that the user has not been misled about what the software is going to do. As the person who will be held responsible if the wrong software is produced, the development manager must answer not only to the engineers and others in his own organization, but to the user. An enlightened user will understand that communication can fail in many ways and will be helpful in trying to make clear what is required. But users who do not understand that it is in their own best interests to be involved and demanding may not be very interested in a difficult process of requirements analysis, and the software manager may have to look out for interests that rightly belong to someone else.

As in every technical activity with a business aspect, the trick in requirements analysis is to spend enough time getting it right, but no more. Controlling the time spent is a manager's responsibility. Depending on their personalities, engineers may want to go into far too much detail with the user; or, they may want to end the dialogue prematurely, send the user home, and move on to specification or design.

Someone has to write the actual requirements document. The user may have a draft or be interested in producing one, which makes an ideal starting point. But only the software engineers involved know what is needed for them to subsequently design, code, and test the software, so they have to write much of the final document. Once a draft exists, the inspection process (Section 5.3) is an ideal way to review and improve it. The two main players—the user and the engineers—should be represented at the inspection, but other parts of the software development organization (such as marketing) might also supply inspectors. The rule that managers should not participate in an inspection of their employees' work might be relaxed because by participating the engineering manager can be assured that the requirements document is adequate. The dangers of manager-as-inspector are so difficult to avoid, however, that the manager would be wise to send a trusted engineer.

How Does It Fit?

From section 7.1

1. Translate each of the following "how" descriptions into a possible "what" description. Include a description of inputs and outputs.

   (a) (To a student:) Take out a piece of paper, put your name in the upper right-hand corner, and make a grid below this labeled with the days of the week at the top and times of the day on the left side. Fill in the grid by shading in the times you are not in class.

   (b) Scan the list of names, and find the one that comes last alphabetically. Write it at the bottom of a blank sheet of paper, and cross it off the list. Now repeatedly do the following until no names remain on the list: find the name that is not crossed off that comes last alphabetically, write it immediately above the top name on the other sheet, and cross it off. If while you are doing this, the sheet of paper you are using fills up, get a new sheet and continue at the bottom. Stack the sheets so that the last one you did is on the bottom.

2. Any "what" description can have many "how" descriptions—the "how" is not unique. Is this true the other way around? Given a "how" description, is there just one "what" that it might have come from? Explain.

3. In the timecard example, suppose the record had been defined as:

   - Timecard: Aggregate Structure: Employee information for payroll.
     - Timecard.E-Nam: Alphanumeric field (80 characters): Employee name.
     - Timecard.I-N: Numeric field (9 digits): Employee identification number.
     - Timecard.Whrs: Numeric field (2 digits): Hours worked. Should be less than 80 hours.
     - Timecard.Shrs: Numeric field (2 digits): Sick hours. Should be less than or equal to 40 hours.

   Explore what difference this would make in the requirements document and in talking about it, as in Section 7.1.2.

4. In Section 7.1.3, it was suggested that input and output values be partitioned into equivalence classes. Explain the problems that come up if the classes do *not* form a partition because:

   (a) The classes overlap.
   (b) The classes do not exhaust all possibilities; that is, they don't cover some inputs.

5. In the eight cases identified for payroll system requirements in Section 7.1.4, explain what will have to be done to find a system input that will test (say) case 7 after the software is actually available for execution. Why can't this input value be put into the test plan as soon as the partitions are identified in the requirements analysis?

6. Explain how the 7 ± 2 principle is involved in the necessity for writing down and evaluating situations with more than about seven possibilities.

7. Give an example from your personal experience of being told by someone in an organization or business that something was impossible "because of the computer."

   (a) Describe the problem from the point of view of a requirements mistake.
   (b) Write a sample letter to a manager, vice-president, or the owner of the organization involved, complaining about how you were treated and suggesting what could be done better in the future. Do you think such a letter would be understood and acted upon?

From section 7.2

8. In the discussion illustrated by Fig. 7.2, several questions were left hanging. Answer with explanations:

   (a) What is left unanswered in the interchange about whether boxes can touch?

   (b) Why should ten descendents be considered? And why does the figure show only six?

   (c) Give as many reasons as you can why the developer should be against vertically staggering the nodes of a subtree.

   (d) Write a description of exactly how descendent nodes may appear if the developer should win the argument.

9. Why doesn't Fig. 7.3 meet the requirements?

10. Write down a concise list of requirements that captures what the user and the developer discussed about drawing trees. Use TBD (To Be Decided) where there is doubt about what is required.

11. Give some of the test plan information (say, covering two situations) that should have been recorded during the discussion between user and developer about drawing trees. Record not only the information for test, but why that test is needed and what it will establish. Are the tests recorded functional or fault based?

12. Define one clear "error case" in the input format agreed upon for drawing trees (Section 7.2.2). Give a description of the case, an appropriate error message that the software should give, and a test case that should produce this message.

13. Fig. 7.5 is presented as an example worth looking at.

   (a) What difficulty does this tree pose?

   (b) Find a way around the difficulty of (a) that requires minimal change to the input format.

   (c) Comment on why this is a particularly good test case to try.

14. Discuss the case of unlabeled trees, assuming that a requirements document has been written without considering them.

From section 7.3

15. Consider the "recovery mode" in an editor.

   (a) How can an editor know that it is being asked to edit a file for which an edit was in progress at the time of a previous system crash, and how can recovery be effected so that the previous work is not lost?

   (b) Explain why some editors do not have this feature, expressed as a failure to properly analyze requirements.

   (c) Make up a set of requirements for what a simple editor should do when in recovery mode. Be careful not to make use of any of the "how" expressed in part (a). What should happen in recovery mode if the editor's user tries to use regular editing commands?

From section 7.4

16. If you are familiar with Milne's *Winnie the Pooh* books, an example of a user who claims to know what he wants but when shown a series of prototypes likes none of them, should come immediately to mind.

17. Describe a case in which an input/output simulation written quickly in a visual language would not find out what the user didn't want.

18. Is a user who learns to use an interface simulator actually doing part of his own software development? Explain.

Review Questions

1. A set of requirements, a specification, and a design can all be documents in English that describe the same software. What general rule can you give for telling the three apart?

2. How does the requirements writer get started in finding out what a customer wants?

3. Why is incompleteness the most common failing of a requirements document?

Further Reading

Joseph Weizenbaum is an articulate critic of computing. His book *Computer Power and Human Reason* [Wei76] makes compelling reading for anyone who develops software, and its lessons could be taken to apply to the requirements phase. He is also the author of one of the most intriguing computer programs ever written, ELIZA, which with its "doctor" script attempts to convince its user that it is a human disciple of Carl Rogers, not a LISP program.

Donald Knuth is one of the most respected names in computer science. He is writing a series of books *The Art of Computer Programming*, of which three volumes have so far appeared. Volume 1 is subtitled *Fundamental Algorithms* [Knu68], and it is well worth the careful study it requires. It is a textbook that could serve as the authority in Section 7.2. It is probably true that more volumes of Knuth's planned series would have been released had he not taken a substantial detour into writing text-processing software. But the authors of this book (and many other authors) are very glad that he did. His TeX software was used to produce this book.

Speaking of text software (and detours), the reader interested in computer displays can learn about Postscript in its reference guide [Inc85]. It is a "machine language" that is fun to use (if you like that sort of thing) because its "machine" is a printer and programs make printed pages.

The pic processor was originally part of the UNIX text-processing package, and Jon Bentley gives a nice introduction to it [Ben86]. Bentley talks of "little languages" that are a very clever way to accomplish difficult but limited tasks efficiently (something that software engineers often need to do). The input format for describing trees

Divide and conquer

in Section 7.2 is itself an example of a little language, and using a series of them is a way to decompose and solve a hard problem.

The IEEE professional organization publishes tutorial collections of current research papers. Reference [TD90] is the one on requirements.

A group at the Naval Research Laboratory under Dave Parnas is responsible for an impressive example of sticking to "what" in requirements analysis. The lessons they learned by writing a requirements document for the Navy A-7 aircraft are briefly described by Heninger [Hen80].

References

[Ben86]   Jon Bentley. *Programming Pearls*. Addison-Wesley, 1986.

[Hen80]   K. L. Heninger. Specifying software requirements for complex systems: new techniques and their applications. *IEEE Transactions on Software Engineering*, 6:2–13, 1980.

[Inc85]   Adobe Systems Inc. *Postscript Language Reference Manual*. Addison-Wesley, 1985.

[Knu68]   Donald E. Knuth. *The Art of Computer Programming*, volume 1. Addison-Wesley, 1968.

[TD90]   Richard H. Thayer and Merlin Dorfman, editors. *System and Software Requirements Engineering*. IEEE Computer Society Press, 1990.

[Wei76]   Joseph Weizenbaum. *Computer Power and Human Reason*. W. H. Freeman, 1976.

chapter 8

Properties of Good Requirements

G ood requirements are characterized by qualities that contribute directly to splitting off user communication in a separate phase of software development. These qualities help to keep the work self-contained and make the requirements document maximally useful in other phases.

In short, good requirements are:

- Understandable by end users
- Nonprescriptive
- Correct
- Complete
- Concise (succinct)
- Precise
- Clear
- Unambiguous
- Consistent
- Traceable
- Modifiable
- Testable (verifiable)
- Feasible

Each of these properties will be discussed, with (mostly bad) examples, in the sections to follow.

8.1 Understandable by End Users

Specifications are a contract, real or informal, between end users and software developers. For this contract to be effective, the end users must be able to comprehend what has been written. Consider the following "requirement:"

> To ensure predictable operation, the system shall not employ nondeterministic methods.

Though a software engineer may understand what the jargon "nondeterministic" means (it refers to concurrent processing, which has the potential to lead to race conditions so that the software might not produce the same results on two apparently identical runs), an end user will probably be less sure of what is intended. In this example, there are really two requirements: a primary requirement and a derived one. The end user is concerned with the primary requirement:

> System operation shall be predictable and repeatable.

The derived requirement is:

> The system shall not employ nondeterministic methods.

Requirements that are derived from the primary requirements are usually of consequence only to the development team and most often appear in the specification or the design documents. Remember the reason for life cycle phases: intellectual control comes from separating concerns. Just as the user may have trouble with "nondeterministic," so he cannot be expected to know about the considerable controversy about whether use of concurrent processing actually favors or inhibits predictable operation. This is a choice that the developer must make in design, and if concurrency is allowed, perhaps special efforts must be made to see that it does not introduce unpredictability—but the whole point of separating out a requirements phase is to defer making such decisions. Thus derived requirements should usually be omitted or separately recorded as suggestions for the design to follow.

8.2 Nonprescriptive

The purpose of the requirements document is to describe *what* the software will do, not *how* it will do it. The reason for making this distinction is that when it is made, a self-contained document results, concerned only with characteristics of the software that can be observed from its external workings. The wrong side of the "what/how" distinction is illustrated by the following "requirement:"

> The software shall employ B-trees for storage of information kept in memory.

This describes how information in the program is accessed and maintained. Although it might be deduced or derived from other requirements, for example, because B-trees are the only storage mechanism that would satisfy some other requirement, it does not describe the behavior of the system from an external point of view.

A useful rule of thumb is that any discussion of algorithms or data structures belong in the design document, not in the requirements document.

8.3 Correct

A requirement is defective if it is not correct. The user is the sole judge of correctness. If the user's intent is misrepresented, the requirements document is plain wrong. Consider the following:

> The system shall accept operator input from up to and including 29 consoles.

If the customer means to later connect more consoles to the system, even if the number is not known now, this incorrect requirement can be catastrophic. If, on the other hand, the customer intends to connect only five consoles to the system, the development team may put time, energy, and money into designing a system that far exceeds the customer's needs. The user cannot be expected to know which decisions are crucial to cost and capabilities, and which are trivial to change. The developer must point out the importance of each.

8.4 Complete

There are two ways of looking at the "completeness" of requirements. One is to determine whether any necessary requirement is missing. It is, of course, impossible to illustrate a missing requirement without providing the reader with an entire requirements document. Completeness can be thought of as one aspect of a correct requirements document—nothing the user needed was omitted.

The second aspect of "complete" deals with each individual requirement. If information is missing from the requirement, the requirement itself becomes a hazard:

> The system shall provide the operator with the information needed to safely shut down the controlled machinery when an exception occurs.

This is an example of what may be called a "blanket" requirement: the writer is trying to cover a great deal of ground with a single statement. Perhaps all that is really intended is:

> The system shall provide the operator with time-stamped messages describing system exceptions.

Then all the questions about what actions the operator should take and what is "safe" can be relegated to operator training and a shut-down manual, not to the software being developed.

In many instances, the exact nature of a requirement may be unknown. It is best to flag missing information with the letters TBD so that at the end of the requirements writing phase, incomplete requirements can be located and completed. Thus the following might be best in this case:

> The system shall provide the operator with time-stamped messages describing system exceptions (list of exceptions TBD). The messages shall not lag more than TBD seconds behind the exceptions they describe.

Document it! ▶
(Record it or it's lost)

It may seem little different to leave out what isn't known, or to put in a TBD that says nothing. But the *location* and *subject* of the TBD are themselves important information to record.

8.5 Concise (Succinct)

Requirements should deal with the issues at hand and avoid rambling prose that does not contribute directly to the description of what the software must do. Consider the following requirement:

> We feel that good systems provide the end user with good value. Because of this, we think that the system should provide adequate performance with a 2 Gb disk, since this is the least expensive disk that we may purchase from the designated vendor. Of course, the user may elect to configure the system with a larger disk, and we recommend this, but we have attempted to come to grips with most of the problems raised by use of the smaller disk, and we feel that they can be, by and large, satisfactorily resolved.

This is hardly a concise requirement—it contains a great deal of extra prose. Here is one way to make this requirement succinct and eliminate the abbreviation "Gb:"

> The system shall fulfill all specified functions when configured with a 2-gigabyte disk.

Identify the customers ▶

The problem with rambling prose has to do with information access. When people are looking for the actual requirement, they have to read a great deal of other text before they find it. By hiding the information in unnecessary text, the writer contributes to the risk that readers may pass over the information they seek.

8.6 Precise

It seems obvious that a requirement must say exactly what it means to say so that it is difficult to misinterpret. The opposite of "precise" is vague—one cannot understand exactly what is being said.

Consider the following requirement:

> The system shall accept valid employee ID numbers from 1 to 9999.

At first glance, this seems perfectly sensible. But on closer examination, several questions could be asked about this requirement. Are all numbers from 1 to 9999 valid ID numbers, or is it just that numbers outside this range are invalid? Is 1 a valid ID number? How about 9999? Does the representation of the numbers matter? For example, if 2 is OK, how about 0002—or in fact must all the representations be exactly four characters long?

To remove the vagueness, this requirement could be rewritten as follows:

> The system shall accept only valid ID numbers as defined elsewhere. No otherwise valid number will be accepted unless it is an integer between 1 and 9999 inclusive, represented without leading zeroes.

Thus 02 is not accepted, nor is 734 if it happens to be invalid (and "valid" must be defined by some other requirement).

"Elegance" is a word sometimes used to describe precision that is esthetically pleasing to human beings. The rules of Backus normal form for describing programming language syntax are elegant.

8.7 Clear

Requirements need to be clear. "Succinct" or "precise" is not always clear. A famous example is Alan Turing's manual for an early computer. The machine actually calculated using base-32 arithmetic in reverse, so Turing chose to present the examples in the manual in this form. They were perfectly precise (and more succinct than base-10 would have been!), but most people had a difficult time understanding them.

Here's another deficient requirement:

> The items in tab-separated columns and underscore-separated rows of the output may refer to each other, but no item in (row,column) position (i, j) may refer to another in position (p, q) unless $p < i$, or if $i = p, q < j$.

It's not always safe to presume that the end user has an extensive command of the English language. Nor is it reasonable to assume that the user's concentration and appetite for detail is as strong as that of a software expert who has been studying the situation day and night for an extended period. In general, it is best to write requirements at an elementary school level, using short, declarative sentences. When the writer separates out as many ideas as possible, it is harder for the reader to miss one. The preceding might be better as:

> The output consists of rows and columns. Items across each row are separated by tabs. There is an underscore between rows. When item X refers to item Y, Y must either be in a row above X, or if they are in the same row, Y must be in a column to the left of X. An item may not refer to itself.

It can be helpful to give examples or to draw a picture illustrating the point about items referring to each other. Faced with a requirement that is difficult to understand, both user and developer will naturally resort to examples for clarification. The developer might say something like this:

> Let me see if I understand what you want here. If I had two items in different rows (sketches picture), then the bottom one can refer to the top one, but not the other way around, right?

This communication through examples is valuable and desirable, but it has limitations, and it should not substitute for best attempts to capture the general situation. Any collection of examples can be misleading because it relies on the participants "talking them through" to get the idea. Later on, looking at those same examples may not call up the same idea. Since a requirements document is going to be the central repository of information throughout development, it is essential that it capture the idea itself, not just some examples of it.

These inequalities were reversed (relative to the more intuitive description given later) in several drafts of this text. Hundreds of students and five instructors failed to notice.

8.8 Unambiguous

Ambiguity is a major problem in stating requirements. If it is not entirely clear what the system is supposed to do, it certainly cannot be tested when done. The distinction between vagueness and ambiguity is that a vague requirement doesn't seem to have any clear meaning, whereas an ambiguous one has a small number of different, incompatible meanings.

A notorious example of ambiguity in specifying the format of computer data is the "separator/terminator" distinction. It is often necessary to describe sequences of items that have some delimiter "between" or "after" them. The words in a text file have space(s) between them; sentences in traditional touch-typing exercises are to end with two spaces after the period; parameters passed to a programming language subroutine are separated by commas; and so on. But what of the last item in such a sequence? Does it have the delimiter or doesn't it? If the case isn't explicitly covered, the requirement describing it is ambiguous.

This sentence is guilty of what it is talking about. So is this note.

Pronouns are another source of confusion. The pronoun is a wonderful thing because it can refer to a very complex idea, and instead of repeating the description, it can be called "it." But this ability to refer is also a curse since it may not be clear what the reference is. Which complex idea does the "it" point back to? The same thing happens with the use of "this" and "that"—to avoid repeating, an author starts a sentence with "This is a good idea . . . "—but exactly what idea is being talked about? It is usually possible to fix such ambiguous references by replacing the "it" or the "this" with an explicit noun or phrase, the same phrase that occurred previously. The result is very stilted sounding, but not ambiguous.

The worst case of ambiguity arises when there are two different interpretations of a requirement. The user thinks it means one thing, the developer thinks it means another, and neither can imagine the other's interpretation, and so neither thinks that there is any difficulty.

8.9 Consistent

A set of requirements is inconsistent when two parts of it contradict each other or fail to fit together in some way. Inconsistency can result from a problem so complicated that human beings cannot keep track of all the interrelationships between different requirements.

Inconsistency can also be created late in the requirements phase, when one part of the requirements document changes but other parts that deal with similar information aren't changed. Consider the following:

The system shall track detected airborne objects traveling at speeds from 200 to 400 miles per hour inclusive.

Many pages later, there is another requirement:

> The system shall flag all detected airborne objects traveling at speeds from 300 to 500 miles per hour inclusive.

There might be nothing wrong with this combination, but it does require the system to flag some objects that it is not required to track. Before the developers start to consider how this wonder may be done, it would be wise to see if the first requirement did not originally read " . . . from 200 to 500 . . . " and was changed. As they stand, these requirements are probably inconsistent.

Typically, this problem arises when system parameters change, and the engineer who is updating the requirements document updates only a single requirement, not realizing that the information is contained in several places. If requirements are easily modified (see Section 8.11), they do not so easily lose consistency. But for complex sets of requirements, it remains hard to obtain consistency in the first place.

8.10 Traceable

Since the requirements document is to direct all the subsequent software development work, it is important to be able to connect its details to the details in subsequent documents: designs, test plans, and code. The first step in this traceability of requirements is to uniquely identify each part of the document.

When requirements are reviewed, changes are noted that must be communicated to the requirements writer in an efficient manner. In the course of a review meeting, it is not uncommon to hear remarks like: "Do you see the fourth paragraph from the top? No, I mean the fourth *complete* paragraph. Good. Now, the third line down, halfway through, see the sentence that begins 'The system shall . . . '? Great. That requirement seems untestable to me because . . . " (But don't most requirements begin with "The system shall . . . "? Is the speaker sure that listeners are looking in the right place?) Unique identifiers make it easy to efficiently locate requirements. Since requirements documents are often divided into numbered sections, the section numbers can be incorporated. Hence a requirement might be numbered [4.1.13] if it were the 13th to occur in section 4.1.

With unique identifiers, the preceding conversation is reduced to the following: "Requirement 4.1.13 seems untestable to me because . . . " If it is necessary to record the discussion, the number clearly identifies the subject. When it is easier to locate a requirement, discussions can be concerned with the requirements and not how to find the requirement.

In the other phases of development, references to the requirements document can be made by unique identification. For example, in the design phase, requirement numbers can be inserted into the design documents to locate where in the design a particular requirement is being satisfied. In the test plan, a test can be marked as verifying that a particular requirement holds, and so on.

Reverse traceability is also an issue, since changes in the design may affect the fulfillment of a requirement. In other words, if the designers change a portion of a design, they will need to know what requirements were satisfied by that portion of the design in order to check that they are still satisfied. Similarly, if a test is changed, the test writer needs the requirement identification to check that the source of this test in a requirement is still being properly verified.

Traceability is an issue that affects a large part of the software engineering process. It is an essential part of the unifying philosophy of information collection and organization.

8.11 Modifiable

Good requirements are easy to modify. Recall the example of inconsistency (now with identifiers) from Section 8.9:

> [**4.1.5**]. The system shall track detected airborne objects traveling at speeds from 200 to 400 miles per hour inclusive.

and

> [**8.1.6**]. The system shall flag all detected airborne objects traveling at speeds from 300 to 500 miles per hour inclusive.

Let us suppose that this inconsistency arose from replacing "500" in 4.1.5 with "400" and neglecting to change 8.1.6.

This problem is best avoided by keeping information in a single place. Consider the following approach:

> [**1.1.1**]. The normal operational range is 200 to 500 miles per hour, inclusive.

> [**1.1.2**]. Airborne objects are called "exceptional" if they are traveling at speeds of more than 100 miles per hour above the floor of the normal operational range.
> ⋮

> [**4.1.5**]. The system shall only track airborne objects traveling in the normal operational range.
> ⋮

> [**8.1.6**]. The system shall flag all exceptional objects.

Changing the upper limit to 400 in 1.1.1 now causes no inconsistency. There are more requirements in this form, but it is easier to maintain the entire collection since they rely upon terms and information that is given in a single place.

8.12 Testable (Verifiable)

Too often requirements are placed on a system that are not testable. Consider the following all-too-typical requirement:

The software shall operate on a PC for 5000 hours without failure.

Here the testers have a tremendous testing problem. Unless they test *every* PC hardware configuration under *every* possible set of circumstances for 5000 hours, they will never really know if the software meets this requirement.

Epistemology (the study of truth) is apparently of vital interest to software engineers. Suppose for a moment that it were possible to acquire the resources to try this software in every kind of PC system (surely there must be a finite number of such configurations at any given time) for 5000 hours. The test writers would still have to ask themselves, "what are all the possible circumstances?" How would they know that every possibility had been cataloged?

This kind of reliability requirement is the sweetheart of almost every marketing and customer representative on the planet. To be able to tell every customer that life and limb can be staked on the first 5000 hours of a product's operation is too attractive to pass up.

Unfortunately, it won't help much to insert adjectives in such a requirement: "standard PC configuration" isn't much improvement over "a PC" (does that include a fax card?). And qualifying the 5000 hours as (say) being "under normal conditions" just raises the hopeless question of what is "normal" (a book dropped on the keyboard while the software was waiting for input?).

Another way to describe untestable requirements is that they are "vague." If the terms used are not quantified, it is a matter of opinion as to whether the software does what it should. For this reason words like "fast response" (just how fast is that? one millisecond? one hour?) or "efficient storage" (fits in exactly how many megabytes?) must be avoided. Whenever a requirement cannot be checked by some particular test, and the software seen to clearly pass or fail, that requirement is not testable. A requirement that is not vague is also called *precise*, but testability goes beyond precision to insist that a verifying experiment can actually be carried out.

While the developer is trying to make requirements testable is the ideal time to be adding to a test plan.

8.13 Feasible

All requirements should provide a sound basis for design. Consider the following (absurd) set of requirements:

> **[1.1].** The software shall operate on a 100 megahertz 486 system.
>
> **[1.2].** The software shall respond to any critical event within 1 pico-second.

It is infeasible to specify a software response time that exceeds the machine cycle time of the processor.

The following occurred in a class project assignment:

> **P9.** The required software is a C main program that links with an arbitrary collection of user-supplied subroutines.
> ⋮
> **P34.** An error message will be issued if the main program should try to call a nonexistent user subroutine.

As several students immediately pointed out, a main program that attempts to call a nonexistent user subroutine cannot be successfully linked because the linker will complain about the missing entry point. So the program can never get into execution to issue the required message!

These two example difficulties could also be classed as inconsistencies; when two requirements contradict each other, the system cannot satisfy both.

There are also many problems known to be impossible to solve (so-called undecidable problems), for example, the problem of deciding before it executes if a program will abort with a subscript out of bounds. Therefore, it is infeasible to specify that a compiler will give a syntax error message to cover this case in general.

Other problems have no known algorithm to solve them in practical amounts of time. The theoretical position is not so clear with these "in-tractable" problems, whose only known solution technique is brute-force search of a space that grows exponentially with the size of the problem. No one has succeeded in proving that no algorithm other than the brute-force one exists; however despite a great deal of work by clever people, no one has found the magic algorithm to do better. If a requirement calls for search of a large space, and there is a time constraint, it should be a red flag that the requirements together may be infeasible, and very difficult theoretical analysis may be required to resolve the question.

8.14 Summary: How to Write Requirements?

A catalog of good properties (or bad examples) is not much help in actually writing a requirements document. The properties help to criticize but not to create. Trial and error is the way people gain experience in an art like requirements writing. A novice begins with a draft describing the software, without regard to good properties. Then the list of good properties is applied to this draft, and corrections made. For example, every time the draft slips into saying *how* things are to be done, it must be corrected to say *what* must be done instead, according to the nonprescriptive property of Section 8.2. Every time someone finds something that the spec does not seem to cover, it has been demonstrated to be incomplete (Section 8.4), and the user and developer must fill in the gap.

How Does It Fit?

1. Copy the properties of good requirements in this chapter, but place them in what you think is the order of importance. For the first three items in your list, explain why they are the most important. Also explain why the last two items are not so important.

2. Give an example and draw the picture suggested at the end of Section 8.7.

3. At the end of Section 8.7, the requirements writer is cautioned that examples may fail to capture a general idea. Give an illustration in which the same set of examples could come from two different ideas.

4. When user and developer attempt with good will to hammer out an agreement on requirements, as is illustrated in the problem of printing trees in Section 7.2, which property of good requirements in this chapter is most likely to be violated, and why?

5. For each misunderstanding or difficulty that arose in the attempt to establish requirements for printing trees in Section 7.2, one or more of the properties of good requirements in this chapter was involved. List two of these difficulties, with the properties involved.

6. The principle of documentation that puts each piece of information in just one place could be realized by a property that a good set of requirements is not *redundant*. What combination of properties in this chapter best covers this? Do you think eliminating all redundancy is a good idea?

7. Some of the properties of good requirements overlap. Pick two properties that you think are the most similar, choose just one of the two, and rewrite the description of both under the one heading. How well did it work?

8. Some properties of good requirements are stated positively and some negatively. Choose one of the negatively stated ones, and rewrite it in an entirely positive fashion.

9. In Section 8.11, requirement [1.1.2] uses "normal operating range" from [1.1.1] to avoid using a constant as in [8.1.6]. Improve the example further to eliminate the "100 MPH" constant in [1.1.2].

10. This question is about "multiple correct results" in a requirement. Some people think that it is necessary to require exactly one output for each input. Others think that it is all right to permit any one of several possible outputs for a single input, all correct. The latter view is the more common because it allows the user to have "don't care" cases, for example, in the exact wording of error messages. Assume that "multiple correct results" are therefore OK in a requirement.

   (a) Reconcile this property with the undesirability of inconsistency.

   (b) Repeat (a) for ambiguity.

Review Questions

1. List two properties of good requirements, and explain each in your own words, but without using an example.

2. Why is it impossible to *guarantee* that a given requirements document is correct?

3. Why is it better in a requirements document to use TBD with no other information than to put nothing at all?

Further Reading

The commonsense properties of this chapter occur implicitly in most surveys of software engineering (e.g., Sommerville's [Som96]), and in practical treatments of the development process [BO88].

The study of what is *impossible* to program is of great intellectual interest to those whose daily work is programming (which may seem impossible at times!). Two senses of "intellectual" are intended: the work is abstract and has real depth, and it isn't of immediate practical use. Hofstadter's book [Hof79] that was written for the "popular" market is an unorthodox, self-contained presentation of the ideas behind unsolvable problems, but it is not to everyone's taste. A wonderful collection of the original source papers by Alan Turing, Emil Post, Alonzo Church, and others has been assembled by Martin Davis [Dav65]. Garey and Johnson [GJ79] is a standard textbook on "intractable" problems.

References

[BO88]   N. D. Birrell and Martyn A. Ould. *A Practical Handbook for Software Development*. Cambridge University Press, 1988.

[Dav65]   Martin Davis, editor. *The Undecidable*. Raven Press, 1965.

[GJ79]   M. R. Garey and D. S. Johnson. *Computers and Intractability: A Guide to the Theory of NP-Completeness*. W. H. Freeman, 1979.

[Hof79]   Douglas R. Hofstadter. *Gödel, Escher, Bach: An Eternal Golden Braid*. Basic Books, 1979.

[Som96]   Ian Sommerville. *Software Engineering, 5th Ed.* Addison-Wesley, 1996.

Specification

There is a tension among the properties of good requirements given in Chapter 8 because the primary property of requirements is that they be understandable by end users. Yet several of the other properties are difficult to achieve if that first one is observed. In particular, the very language that makes the requirements document understandable to nonsoftware people will introduce ambiguities, compromise precision, and interfere with checking that properties like completeness have been attained. This tension is what motivates an additional requirements-like phase of "specification" in software development. The specification phase is "requirements without the user." A specification document should have all the same properties given in Chapter 8, *except* that it is for the developer alone, and so end users need not be considered. This additional separation of concerns does carry its burden, however: the developer must see to it that the specification does not do violence to the requirements document. If a distortion is introduced, it is a mistake, and cannot be justified to the user. Another way of saying this crucial property of specifications is to alter the "correctness" property for specifications: a specification being correct means that it agrees with the requirements as the user sees them.

9.1 Customers and Their Needs

In order for the requirements and specification documents to be useful, they must meet the needs of their primary customers:

- *End users:* The end users of the system will use the documents as if they were a contract for work to be performed (which, in a sense, they are). From this perspective, it is important that the requirements be correct, complete, and easy to understand. The specification is unlikely to be consulted.

- *Designers:* The design engineers will use the documents to define subsystems that carry out specific functions, and so they need a specification that is correct, concise, complete, and easy to decompose into functions. They can work from the requirements if a separate specification document is not produced.

- *Testers:* The test engineers will first use the documents to find test cases for a test plan. The requirements are their primary resource, and requirements must be testable and easy to analyze for input/output cases. During testing itself, they will need to know what result is expected for each test, for which a more precise specification is best. It must be unambiguous, consistent, complete, and correct.

The practical decision about whether or not to construct a separate specification document turns on how well it would serve the designers and testers. If it is work they would have to do anyway to sharpen the requirements, better to have a separate specification phase and document. If they could just as well work with the requirements document as it exists, let them get on with design.

The most important questions in deciding whether to build a specification are:

Precision and organization.   Is any information missing or obscured on what the software is to do?

Formalism.   How much formalism is needed, and how much can be used?

Completeness and consistency.   To what degree can these important properties be analyzed?

How much formalism is used depends not only on the need, but on the culture where the specification is built. Typically, formalism has to be introduced into an organization in small, incremental steps. Some projects might use "formal natural language," as described in Section 9.3.1, and later ones would progress to a more mathematical formalism. If mathematical formalism is introduced, tools to analyze the specification are a big help in justifying the extra effort involved.

Completeness is by far the most important property of requirements and specifications and the least often achieved. Here a specification document can help, and the more formalism used, the more that can be learned and the more that tools can do. Mathematical formalisms may permit automatic checks of a specification for completeness and consistency.

Organization and formalism (and the specification that embodies them) are not ends in themselves: if they are not valuable to the designers and testers, then time spent on them is wasted.

9.2 Sharpening Requirements into Specifications

Everyone acknowledges that the requirements phase of software development is at once (1) the most important and difficult in the whole process, and (2) the most imprecise, the least "technical."

The importance of requirements is obvious because it is here that communication between user/customer and developer takes place (until the software is delivered, when it's too late for communication to do anyone any good). Mistakes made in the beginning will prove the most costly later. The imprecision of the process follows from the use of a natural language. Languages like English are well adapted for people gossiping with each other ("Where did he get that *tie*?"), for important business transactions ("I want a large pizza with the works but hold the anchovies."), for giving warnings ("Watch out! That guy just lost a wheel!"), for expressing emotions ("I love you."), among other things. But they are seldom used for precise, explicit descriptions, and when people try to use a natural language precisely (for example, in writing legal documents), the result is not very satisfactory. Requirements are a kind of legalese since they serve as a contract between user and developer.

In addition, dialogue between user and developer carries an extra burden: the two participants don't really speak the same language. Although both may be fluent in English, the user is a "domain expert"—that is, the user possesses and uses a specialized vocabulary that is the jargon of the limited world in which the computer application will be used. This world has many arcane details, with which the user is intimately familiar, and many hidden assumptions that are well known, even second nature, to the people who work in that world. But the software developer does not speak the language of the user's domain. On the other side, the developer knows a great deal about software, again with a specialized vocabulary and a forest of interlocking facts and assumptions, of which the user is ignorant. When they try to communicate, there is bound to be trouble. With the best will in the world, they can agree that they will avoid jargon on both sides and try to carefully define and explore any concepts that either one finds foreign, but there are certain to be problems that slip through. One large difficulty is the common practice of taking over regular words and giving them restricted, special meanings on both sides. The developer says "list," meaning a particular data structure with particular properties (for example, locating an item is normally slow using a linear search). The user hears "list," meaning some items written on a piece of paper, from which an item can be instantly picked out by eye. They think they have communicated, but later on, the software will be too slow because a random access array was needed, not a list data structure. (And in a domain of radio transmission, "array" probably refers to an antenna configuration!)

A useful specification document can be constructed by starting with the requirements document and making modifications or adding details wherever they seem needed, paying no attention to whether these are understandable to the end user. Often these details might come from notes taken during the requirements dialogue, when the developer thought of clarifications and issues that could be expressed only in technical language.

Fuzzy into focus ▶

9.2.1 When the End User "Doesn't Care"

Software developers, who themselves are users of computer software, find it hard to understand why an end user might not care about some facet of a system the user wants developed. But perhaps the user cares more about the business he or she is in, not software, which is viewed as a necessary evil. Even if the user doesn't particularly trust the developer, trusting may be preferable to having to sit through long discussions of requirements. If the end user is represented by an executive who will not actually use the software to be developed, not caring comes naturally. Later on the workers will be ordered to use whatever is delivered. Perhaps this fact of life in large institutions accounts for more software that is ill-suited to what it must do than any other. And even the most involved end user, who knows the importance of getting the requirements recorded and understood, gets tired or impatient and stops caring.

Filling in "don't care" situations can be a major specification phase activity. The developer, of course, must fill them in since execution programs have to take exact, specific actions and are not permitted to be as vague as users. If the work isn't done for a specification document, it will have to be done in design or in coding, and the farther away from the requirements phase the developer gets, the harder it will be to make sure that every case has been filled in, and the harder it will be to check with the user about problems where the user ought to have cared.

One example will show the virtues of handling "don't care" conditions all at once in a specification document. It is very common for users not to care about the exact text of software messages, particularly error messages. Naturally, users are thinking of the normal cases and of using the software productively, not of the error cases where things go wrong. The exact text of messages hardly seems to matter. Users are probably foolish to neglect this aspect of software because messages can be very important in saving past work when something goes wrong, to name just one of their uses. Be that as it may, often a requirements document contains only brief descriptions of messages, leaving the exact text up to the developer. It will save the developer time to consider all the messages at once rather than as each comes up in later design or coding. The people doing the work will become temporary experts at message content, and they will see to it that a consistent form is used and that the messages themselves are not conflicting. Most important, considering all the system messages at the same time will be an

No one loves a system that displays, "Enter the date (MMDDYYYY):" and then when it's entered, displays, "Correct date format is DDMMYY, try again," and even worse, then repeats the first message.

opportunity to check that proper actions have been specified before and after each message and will batch together whatever questions arise for the
end user.

9.2.2 Internal ("System") Errors

Programs interact with the computer environment in which they run, and in
embedded software, that environment includes electrical and mechanical
devices that are part of a wider system, like an automobile. When the program requests something from the system or environment, there is always
the possibility that the request will not be honored. The archetype examples are a program requesting additional memory (in C, calling `malloc()`),
and a program reading or writing an external device (such as a disk drive,
or a sensor or actuator in the wider system). These operations can fail (because the memory is exhausted or the device is broken), and the program
receives some sort of "error return" on its call. Programmers are trained not
to ignore these returns for the obvious reason that something *must* be done
immediately to deal with the error. It may be possible to retry and succeed,
or to switch to another device, and then the program can recover. But what
action should the program take when a permanent "system error" occurs?
Requirements seldom provide the answer. End users are not in the business
of memory allocation or device failure.

The response to system errors certainly matters a good deal. The programmer always has the option to abort the processing, but that is seldom
acceptable. For just two examples, consider: (1) a database update program
that is in the midst of a complex locking operation—if it aborts without
"cleaning up," the files may be left in an unusable condition; (2) a program
controlling a car's braking system when it is applying the brakes.

The specification phase is a good time to make a systematic study of
system errors and what to do about them. This study begins by listing the
system errors that can occur (out of memory, read failure on disk, sensor
reading impossible, and so on). The list is partly obtained from the developer's knowledge of problems that any computer may have, and partly induced from the requirements document, because there will be indications
there of all the special devices involved in the problem. Next, the various processing "modes" are considered—general situations in which the software
may find itself because of the sequence of inputs it has received. (For the car
example, "applying the brakes" would be one mode.) Then the specification
makers have to think about each system error in each mode and invent the
best recovery actions they can. It may well be that the end user must be consulted. As with the example of system messages, the analysis will be better
because it is a focused activity ranging over the whole set of requirements,
and the user will be bothered only once to resolve the collection of problems
uncovered.

9.2.3 Using a Specification as a Test Oracle

The specification has an important role to play in the testing phase of software development even though that phase is far away when a specification is being constructed. When an executable program is being tested, it is essential to know whether the tests are coming out right. It is pointless to try a program without being able to judge the outcome. (The program might, of course "blow up" in some way, and then it could be seen to be wrong no matter what it was supposed to do, but crashing certainly is not the only way, nor even the most common way, that programs go wrong.) It is the task of the specification to make the right or wrong judgment. Testing requires an *oracle*, a means of judging one input/output pair. A test point is the input, the program delivers an output, and the oracle decides if it's right.

The cases that went into exploring requirements (a timecard example was given in Section 7.1.4), and that should have found their way into the test plan, are easily made into a partial oracle. For example, in one timecard case, an invalid input value for "hours worked" required an error message to be issued. So in the test for this case, the program is run with an invalid "hours worked" input, the program does something, and the oracle says "OK" if what it does is issue the error message; otherwise, the oracle says "no good." Of course, it is really a human being, reading the requirements and the specification, who acts as the oracle. There is nothing hard in principle about being a human oracle, but in practice it's a tedious business. People make mistakes, particularly when faced with boring tasks such as checking over voluminous program output. "Find and print the smallest value in the table" is easy to program, but to determine whether it's being done correctly, a person has to examine the whole table or contrive to know which value is smallest. In some cases, although the designer has figured out how to construct the software, there is no easy way for a person to decide independently whether a result is correct. The calculations required to get the answer may be so time consuming that it is impossible to do them "by hand."

A requirements document can serve as a test oracle, but the greater precision and attention to more detail in a specification makes it a better one.

9.2.4 Writing a Specification Only to Discard It

After a specification has been created, the developer may discover that development would profit from eliminating the document that has just been created. Some of the information in the specification should be moved to the requirements document, namely, those things that clarify and sharpen requirements. It may be difficult to state these clarifications so that end users can understand them, but if the effort is not made, the specification runs a risk of being incorrect. Most information that users cannot be made to care about concerns not what the software should do, but decisions on how it will do it, and therefore belongs in the design document. After the specification is mined for information that is really requirements, and information that is really design, there may be almost nothing left.

The size, difficulty, and importance of the software problem, and the size of the organization doing the development, are often the determining factors in whether or not to use an explicit specification phase and a specification document. When the problem and organization are relatively small, it is hard to justify the extra effort of two "requirements" phases. When specific users are particularly important (for example, in writing software to contract), a single document that looks more like "requirements" will be produced. When users are less in evidence (for shrink-wrap software, for example), the one document will look more like a "specification."

There is one case in which a specification serves a wholly new purpose that can't be moved into another phase: when the specification is written to introduce formalism.

9.3 The Uses of Formalism

The most technical specification in English, concentrating on software development issues and perhaps incomprehensible to a user, is still in English. "Formalism" is the short name given to methods of expression that are better for stating what software must do and for analyzing the statement than is natural language. Every branch of engineering has its formalism; a well-known example is the mechanical drawings ("blueprints") of mechanical engineering. In formalism, precision is the goal because it brings with it the power to mechanically detect mistakes. The payment is in clarity because precise statements are hard to understand.

Formalism is 100$ pure jargon.

9.3.1 Informal Formalism

Engineers are rightly concerned about the quantity of information in a set of requirements—a seemingly simple desktop color printer can easily have over 2600 requirements. Many requirements seem to have an "evil twin:" While one requirement describes what the system is to do when things are going well, there is another requirement describing what the system needs to do when things go wrong. This phenomenon causes the number of requirements to almost double. The expression of so much information is bound to contain mistakes, and the most common is that the document is incomplete. By altering the form, the developer may be able to effect an improvement.

Consider a system that is a project time manager, a "time clock" that will allow employees to record when they start and stop work on a particular project. The system will keep a list of projects and clock people in and out on "registered" projects. The system would certainly have a requirement stating that projects must be registered. However, what happens when things go wrong? If the employee makes a mistake in entering a project name, the system should catch it. The requirement might be written:

> **1.1.**   The system shall check to see if the project name is registered.

This requirement is straight to the point, but it does not say what the system is supposed to do. For instance, if a user types an unregistered name, the system might issue an error message or could register that project.

It would have been better if the requirement had been written as:

> **1.1′.**   **If** *the project name is not registered*, **then** *the system shall issue an error message and request another project name.*

Requirement 1.1′ takes a form that reflects software as transforming inputs into outputs. Its form is:

> **if** *condition* **then** *response*.

The first part specifies *what inputs are present,* and the second part specifies *what outputs are required or affected.* Such a form for requirements addresses in its syntax the issue of missing system responses, and a mechanical analyzer could flag requirements not in the correct form. A specification can be forced to adopt such a rigid form. Of course, the requirements document itself can also be held to a form. But users will be impatient with the time required to see that this is done and unhappy with the stilted form the document would take. In a specification phase, these are not such important considerations.

It would be possible to insist on even more form, for example, that *condition* be similar to the Boolean expressions of programming languages. The end result of being completely formal could be the definition of a *specification language*, which would look a lot like a programming language. The *condition* would be expressed in terms of input values. The *response* would be expressed in terms of output values. The example of the time clock shows that the hard part is to keep from imperative "programming" in the *response*. If the specification is to remain nonprescriptive, it is improper to give the steps of *how* the software will handle *condition*. However, *response* can be kept to *what* the software should do, with the result that there is a large gain in precision and more ability to check for mistakes.

(As an aside, when *response* is allowed to include the *how,* the result is called *pseudocode,* a very useful, semiformal design technique described in Chapter 13.)

9.3.2 The Opportunity to Verify

The separation of software development into phases is done primarily to concentrate on one aspect at a time, and thus keep intellectual control of the process. But at each phase after the first, the opportunity for *verification* arises, an opportunity to approach the development from a new angle, and perhaps uncover problems that previous viewpoints could not see. Specification, as a different look at requirements, is the first place where verification comes into play.

Verification is defined as checking that two independent representations of the same thing are consistent in describing it. The "thing" is the software to be developed, and the two representations are a requirements document and a specification document. Their consistency can be described by insisting that the specification be correct—it must agree with the requirements document. Both must describe the same cases, and there must be no case where there is disagreement about what the software is to do. Verification is a burden placed on those who make a second description of what has already been described. Here this burden is placed on the specifiers. As development proceeds, the verification burden is next placed on the designers, not to do violence to the specification in their design, then finally on the coders, not to distort the design.

Verification can be a blessing as well as a burden. When people rethink a problem in new terms, and then check that their work is the same as previous work, it often uncovers a mistake that one or the other has made. For example, when a specification effort analyzes system errors and what to do about them, it may well uncover deficiencies in the requirements. Or it may find that an apparently sensible scheme for handling these errors is incorrect because the requirements prescribe different results. Comparing the two documents leads to better understanding.

9.4 Formal Specification and Design Methods

As the requirements phase of software development has been presented in Chapter 7, it is a process that relies heavily on intuitive understanding by the developer of the problem to be solved for the end user. Everyone involved in the requirements dialogue must "internalize" what the software is to do, form a precise mental image, and check their understanding with the others involved. Despite everyone's best efforts, this process may go wrong because the developer's understanding of the user's problem may be vague and because the user's understanding of software issues may be equally poor. When there is a failure to communicate, the developer produces software that is not what the user expected—it does not solve the user's problem. The specification phase improves matters only a little, and only if the developer is careful to keep the user informed about what is learned in the exercise. (And, of course, many users will not be willing to listen.)

"Formal methods" are a name for a kind of mathematical specification activity intended to really make a difference in the developer's understanding of the problem to be solved by software. Chapter 10 explains the basis of these methods and their potential benefits. But as Section 9.3.1 indicated, there are more practical "formal methods" a developer can use. In this book, we have chosen to present practical formal methods as a part of design and to describe them in Part III, Chapters 13 through 17, not as part of requirements and specifications. The first, and more important, reason we have chosen to place formal methods under design is that these methods are not confined to dealing with "what" the software is to do. They naturally spill over into "how" it will be done and into the decomposition of the software, which both clearly belong in design. A second reason for organizing this book as we have is that for most of today's software engineers, formal methods *are* part of design. It is an unusual organization that holds up development until a complete formal specification has been constructed and analyzed, and its insights checked with the end user. In practice, the formal methods are just the first part of design, and no attempt is made to avoid design issues. On the contrary, the most popular methods are those that apply to design issues such as how to divide the software into modules.

The "ideal" software development process, and the part played in it by formal methods, has not been agreed upon, nor is the future likely to bring agreement. Different problems are best solved in different ways, and a rigid set of development phases is more a device for organizing technical material than a prescription for carrying out the work. However, phases of development are defined by the documentation that is produced to separate them, so choices of what to include where are not without significance. The developer makes decisions at the outset about what will happen in each phase, and those decisions link the phases. It is important to make the separations, but it would be silly to ignore what everyone knows will follow. For example, if the developer knows that the C programming language will be used in coding, then it makes sense to allow some C ideas to intrude into design, for example, by using C procedure headers to describe the interfaces between modules. Similarly, if the developer knows that an object-oriented design will be used, ideas about objects can be introduced into the specification, even into the requirements phase. For example, the developer can have in mind a central object for the design and can ask thinly veiled questions of the end user about the required behavior of that object.

The line between software development phases is arbitrary, and where it falls is determined by the tension between needing to keep concerns separated for intellectual control and needing to avoid duplication of effort for efficiency. Three of the formal methods to be described in Part III are particularly suited for crossover into the specification phase.

9.4.1 Finite State Machine Design

For details of finite state machine design, see Chapter 14.

Viewed as a technical specification, a finite state machine (FSM) design describes what should happen if the software system is in a certain "state," and a certain "event" occurs. The state diagram of the FSM is a precise description of all such possibilities. The intuitive idea that corresponds to an FSM state is often called a software "mode." When in a particular mode, the software is to respond in ways peculiar to that mode. When the required behavior is being discussed with the end user, it can be very helpful to talk in terms of modes because this divides the software actions in a natural way. For example, many interactive systems have an "edit" mode in which text is manipulated and stored, and a "run" mode in which command actions are taken. The "edit" mode may be further decomposed into "input" mode where all the characters are simply accepted and stored, and "control" mode in which characters have editing functions. If the end user is comfortable talking in terms of modes, it may be much easier to get detailed information about what is supposed to happen. In particular, the conditions and events that are supposed to cause the system to change from one mode to another are important.

FSMs are particularly good at describing the interaction between independent computer software systems. Each system may have a number of modes, sending to and receiving from the other systems accordingly.

A FSM design may entirely determine the software implementation because implementation techniques exist for translating the formalism directly into code (see Section 14.2). The precision and accuracy of FSM design and implementation, coupled with a user's ability to discuss corresponding intuitive modes, make FSMs a powerful specification and design method. However, like many formalisms, FSMs introduce their own special problems. One of the worst is that the developer may believe that a technical FSM state exactly corresponds to an intuitive mode on which the user has provided information. If the correspondence is a bit off, the software will do the wrong thing in ways that are very difficult to envision and track down. As an example, an aircraft control program might have a mode for "takeoff" in which a certain switch is to retract the landing gear. If somehow "takeoff" is translated into an FSM state that by a mistake in the design can be entered (or not exited!) when the plane is on the ground, the software would allow the wheels to retract on the runway, not at all what the end user had in mind. When a person has tried to translate a precise design into precise code, it is somehow very difficult to conceive of anything going wrong.

9.4.2 Object-Oriented Design

For details of object-oriented design, see Chapter 16.

The object-oriented (O-O) view of a software system is as a collection of entities (the "objects"), each of which maintains an internal state and can perform for each other a list of services. When object P requests that object Q do something, it is said that P "invokes a method" of Q. One way of looking at O-O design is as a generalization of FSM design. For an FSM, the number of states and events are both finite, and there is a single simple rule of transition between states. For an O-O design, the number of objects and methods are finite, but the internal states of objects may be of unlimited complexity, and the actions taken by objects and their methods are not limited. Another way of looking at an O-O design is as a collection of procedures, each with its own private storage (its state) and with a number of entry points (its methods). Neither of these views really captures the intuitive idea of object orientation, however.

Objects and their methods can be helpful in communicating with users about problems to be solved by software. Often there are actual physical entities that the user understands well that can be cast as objects. For example, in an inventory control problem, the database that records the location and quantity of stock on hand can be thought of as an object whose methods record a location, change a quantity on hand, and so forth. The manufacturers who supply the stock can be thought of as an object whose methods "order" and "deliver" items, whereas the warehouse itself is an object with methods that check items in and out. The interaction between these objects can be described in detail in terms of their methods.

O-O design is particularly appropriate for embedded programs that control physical devices—the devices and their parts are natural objects. It is also appropriate for simulation software, in which the objects are the components of the physical system being simulated.

In combination with an object-oriented programming language like C++, O-O design is very prescriptive. The classes defined in the software, and the access functions within each class (to use the C++ terminology) are the objects and methods so that the user talking about them is really discussing design details.

9.4.3 Design with Data Flow Diagrams

For details about data flow diagrams (DFDs), see Chapter 17.

DFDs are part of a method called *structured analysis and design* (SA/SD). SA/SD was one of the first approaches to formal analysis and design and probably the first to gain acceptance in the software engineering community. This approach uses diagrams and design rules to achieve a level of formality that produces a model that can be mechanically converted to a design, and finally, an implementation.

Input/output ▶ is the essence of software

The basic element of a DFD is the data transform, which is nothing more than taking data as input and producing an output. A problem is broken down into a series of data transforms, which when taken together solve it.

When software developers first see the data flow approach, they wonder how to represent control functions in DFDs. The problem here is that often developers want to focus on a "what next" approach to software design, probably because they are so familiar with imperative programming languages. Data flow diagrams ignore order of execution, and this can be difficult for programmers-turned-designers to understand. DFDs are best used for systems where "response" does not need to be modeled—systems that are not "reactive." Instead, batch systems are those most commonly modeled using DFDs for data processing applications such as payroll and accounting systems.

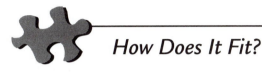

How Does It Fit?

From section 9.1

1. If a requirements document is like a contract, then the two sides making this contract have their own interests, which they might like to see protected. Explain how this need would adversely influence the quality of the requirements document. Would a specification document suffer in the same way? Explain.

2. Explain why testers find it easiest to use a requirements document for devising test cases but might prefer a specification document when actually carrying out tests.

From section 9.2

3. For each of the examples of natural language given at the beginning of the section (for example, for ordering pizza), explain why (A) the statement *is* imprecise, ambiguous, and so on, and (B) why this is or is not actually desirable in the given situation.

4. Pick a "software term" and find two completely different meanings for it that might be misunderstood by two end users because of the particular domains in which they work.

5. Suppose that a requirements document did cover what should be done for internal "system" errors. What properties of good requirements is it likely to violate?

6. Suppose a natural language (informal) specification S is used as an oracle, with a person interpreting the meaning of S.

   (a) If S is inconsistent, what could go wrong?

   (b) If S is incomplete, what could go wrong?

From section 9.3

7. Suppose that a specification is given in the **if** *condition* **then** *response* form. What analysis could be done on the set of all the *condition*s to preclude the case that something has been left out (the specification is incomplete)?

From section 9.4

8. If you are familiar with object-oriented software development techniques, take a position that this process is really part of (choose one) {requirements, specification, design, coding}, and argue for your position in a short essay.

Review Questions

1. Write out the list of properties of good requirements in Chapter 8, noting for each property any changes that would be required to make it apply to good specifications.

2. What can be specified about software response to "system" errors? To what extent is the end user involved in deciding what to do?

3. What is the primary reason for introducing formalism into the specification process?

Further Reading

Alan Davis wrote a paper [Dav88] about the example of giving the requirements for a telephone system. His book [Dav90] is probably the closest to the approach presented in this chapter.

In looking for information about a specification phase that is really only a more technical requirements phase, the many names used for parts of the software engineering life cycle are a definite handicap. The material is likely to be found under "requirements" or under "high-level design." Older papers are less likely to be devoted to selling the author's favorite formalism. Gannon, Purtilo, and Zelkowitz have little patience for inflated claims and maintain a balance between practice and theory [GPZ93]. Wiegers [Wie99] is more interested in the specification process than in its technical details.

References

[Dav88]   Alan M. Davis. Comparison of techniques for specification of external system behavior. *Communications of the ACM*, pages 1098–1115, 1988.

[Dav90]   Alan M. Davis. *Software Requirements: Analysis and Specification*. Prentice-Hall, 1990.

[GPZ93]   John Gannon, James Purtilo, and Marvin Zelkowitz. *Software Specification: A Comparison of Formal Methods*. Intellect, 1993.

[Wie99]   Karl E. Wiegers. *Software Requirements (Dv-Best Practices)*. Microsoft Press, 1999.

chapter 10

Formal Methods

For software developers working in what have been called "the trenches" of real software projects with real requirements and real deadlines, "formal methods" are seen as fighting words. Some people in the industry are there because they have a fascination with building things but lack the mathematical training needed for the more established kinds of engineering. But software problems are the most difficult ones human beings have ever attempted to solve, and mathematics is the single most powerful intellectual discipline for problem solving. So it seems inevitable that the two will come together.

10.1 Specification Languages

Communication between end user and developer seems to be *the* problem of software development. The solution to communication problems could be the invention of a special language, an artificial ("unnatural!") language, to be used for specification. The analogy to programming languages is apt. A programming language serves to bridge a gap even wider than that between user and developer: programming languages communicate from human being to machine. The precision of programming languages is admirable (and terrible!)—one can (must!) say *exactly* what is meant, and there is never any argument about this meaning.

But the analogy also raises an important question: in programming, people have learned to speak the machine's language. If we devise a specification language, will it be the user or the developer who has to go back to school? The answer is that both will have things to learn, but more on the computer side. Domain experts do communicate in their specialized jargon, but it differs from one application to another, and it lacks the needed precision. (In the analogy, both humans and the IBM 701 had to learn FOR-TRAN, but it was really the machine's language because the machine needed only an automatic compiler to "learn" it.) So the developer will learn the new specification language(s).

The precision needed for specifications can come only from mathematics. A useful specification language must rely on mathematical concepts, particularly two mathematical ideas: that of a *function* (mapping between inputs and outputs), and that of *logic* (making symbolic assertions about something in order to define it). These ideas are very much present in programming languages, whose syntax is very similar to the "well-formed formulas" of symbolic logic, and whose semantics can best be described using input/output functions.

Unfortunately, users/customers will not learn a new language, most particularly not any kind of mathematics. For a few applications, were there a standard specification language, it would be worthwhile for some domain experts to learn it. These experts would then serve as consultants in important negotiations involving software requirements. They would be the translators who could help the two sides to talk to each other. But for the vast majority of applications, the experts would not exist or would be too expensive to bring in.

On the software developers' side, learning new mathematics is not a free ride. Although the mathematics of specification are not too different from formal programming languages, developers might also need special experts to translate. This raises the specter of a requirements session involving four parties: the user, the user's specification expert (to translate from the domain version of natural language to specification language), the developer's specification expert (to translate from specification language to the software version of natural language), and the developer. Perhaps the result would be positive. More likely the two specification experts might understand each other—but there would be misunderstandings between them and the others, not really an improvement over the user and developer doing their own misunderstanding directly.

Specification languages must be viewed as an extreme, opposed to the other extreme of natural language. Trying to create good specifications without introducing conventions and special vocabulary and form (that is, going to the natural language extreme) is doomed to failure. Going to the other extreme, using only a precise mathematical language, will also fail because people will not be able to effectively employ it. (But there might be a way out, suggested by "compiling" a specification language into an executable program; see Section 10.5.5.) Probably the answer lies somewhere between the extremes, using some mathematical ideas and some natural language ideas. The "formal" sneaks in as we attempt to gain precision in natural language specifications.

The experiment with "new math" in the 1960s taught us a lot about learning. Children didn't have too much trouble with new math, but the "old math" teachers and parents had a terrible time.

10.1.1 Enabling Human Talent

The principles of software engineering presented in Chapter 2 all fall under the heading of "commonsense organization." They are not necessarily obvious to someone who has not worked in software development, but once presented, there could hardly be an objection to these ideas. To use them is just a matter of getting organized. Organization may not come naturally to some people, and not everyone enjoys being organized, but everyone admits that when faced with a complex task, organization will help to get it done. However, the principle:

Use a formal, mathematical model for problem analysis.

was not among those presented in Chapter 2 because it goes beyond commonsense organization. Nevertheless, formal models for analysis are powerful tools, which are in the ascendency in software engineering. Indeed, it has been said that the existence of mathematical analysis is what characterizes a full-fledged branch of engineering. For example, it is the electrical engineer's ability to calculate the instantaneous currents and voltages in circuits, and the structural engineer's ability to calculate the interplay of forces among the girders of a bridge, that allow them to practice as professionals.

Formal, mathematical analysis is valuable because it amplifies the power of the human intellect, and in hands that have mastered it, allows the solution of problems that would baffle a genius who lacked the mathematics. Some problems can be solved directly, at a stroke, by an experienced person using a poorly understood "intuition" about what to do. But mathematics extends the range of human ability beyond what intuition can do. A simple example comes from elementary algebra. So-called word problems are almost impossible to tackle intuitively (although some people can do them intuitively), but algebra makes their solution trivial and available to everyone. An easy example:

A man is 2 years older than his wife. His age is now twice that of their son. Last year their ages added up to 100. How old is everyone? (42, 40, and 21.)

Calculus and differential equations can be used to solve problems that seem even more impossible. Here's the famous "snowplow problem" posed by R. P. Agnew:

One day it started snowing at a heavy and steady rate. A snowplow started out at noon, going two miles the first hour and one mile the second hour. What time did it start snowing? (11:46; the solution requires an assumption about why the plow slowed down.)

The snowplow problem is a good example of the kind of analysis used in physics. A differential equation is set up to describe a physical situation, and its solution answers questions about that situation that could never be "intuited" without the mathematics. Newtonian mechanics, which underlies all structural and mechanical engineering, has many triumphs of just this character to its credit. One is the prediction, from observations of the motions of inner planets of our solar system, that there must be an additional planet (Neptune) and precisely where to look for it in the skies. Another is the kinetic gas theory, which quantitatively predicts the thermodynamic properties of gases (such as pressure) from assumed microscopic motions and collisions of their molecules.

All branches of engineering, and many branches of science, aspire to the power and precision of mathematical analysis that physics boasts, and software engineering is no exception. Software engineers tackle some of the most complex problems the world has ever known; where is the mathematics that will help them? Abstract algebra and mathematical logic have been proposed rather than differential equations, and although mathematical formalism is not universally accepted, there are no other suggestions for a revolutionary technique of software analysis. When talented people want to do their best to solve difficult problems, they welcome any means that could help.

Harlan Mills was a strong proponent of mathematics in software development, and he believed that mathematical training is always useful, even when the direct application of mathematics is apparently not relevant. A long career at IBM had convinced him that no matter what the difficult problem to be solved, those who successfully attacked it were people whose training included mathematics. His unashamed position was that mathematics is good for you, independent of how much you directly apply your training.

10.1.2 Hard-to-Use Mathematics

Software is a new phenomenon, invented and developed only within the last 40 years. In older branches of engineering, mathematical methods are available to engineers as well-developed "cookbook" techniques. A good example occurs in electrical engineering, for electronic circuit analysis. The physical situation in an electronic circuit in the steady state is described by a linear differential equation expressed in time as the independent variable, and a mathematician can easily solve this equation. But over a period of more than 100 years, engineers and mathematicians have found rules for circuit analysis based on transformations of the circuit equations to domains other than time (Fourier and Laplace transforms), rules that reduce circuit analysis to solving simple algebraic equations. Every electrical engineer is taught these techniques and can use them routinely for circuit problems. If the techniques had not been invented, the circuit problems could still be solved but would require time and mathematical talent that are beyond the average engineer's training.

Software engineering is still at the stage where its mathematics is hard to use and beyond the reach of the average engineer. (Indeed, there is still argument about what constitutes the proper mathematics.) In most software development, there is neither the talent nor the time available to apply mathematical methods. The alternative is to "just do it"—to construct software without really understanding its properties, hope it will work properly, and if it does not, make adjustments (again without real knowledge) to try to improve it. The same thing can be done with electronic circuits—they can be built by trial and error. But such methods are chancy, and the results do not always pass the "smoke test"—when power is applied, a jury-rigged circuit may explode. The existence of mathematical methods for software, even if they have not been developed to the point that engineers can routinely use them, offers an option when the stakes are high. If software *must* work, then applying talent, time, and mathematics can improve the chances that it does.

Take responsibility ▶

After an example of formalism, and computer support for it, are presented in the next two sections, the discussion of whether formal methods are a good idea continues in Section 10.5.

10.2 First-Order Predicate Logic

Many specification languages have been proposed, languages at the formal extreme, and languages that lie closer to natural language. The common background for most of these languages is symbolic logic. The logic most often used for requirements is "first-order predicate logic." This is essentially the language invented in the 1930s by Bertrand Russell and Alfred North Whitehead for expressing with precision the reasoning that mathematicians use in doing mathematics.

The syntax of predicate logic includes:

Constants. Our examples will be only integers: $\ldots, -2, -1, 0, 1, 2, \ldots$;

Variables. The usual x, y, U, V, n, i, and so on, sometimes with subscripts.

Function names. The name perhaps followed by an argument list, the allowed forms being defined recursively in a familiar way.

Predicate names. In particular, binary relational predicates like $=$, $\leq$, and so on, which are written in the usual infix form. If in prefix form, a predicate may look like a variable or a programming language identifier and may be followed by an argument list.

Logical connectives.　These are: and $\wedge$, or $\vee$, not $\neg$, implies $\implies$, equivalence $\equiv$.

Quantifiers.　Just two: for all $\forall$, and there exists $\exists$, which may only apply to the variables, hence the "first order."

First-order logic has a carefully defined syntax, which is familiar to programmers because it has many similarities to the syntax of program statements. A syntactically correct string is called a *well-formed formula* or *WFF*. A WFF is intended to have the meaning of an *assertion*, a statement that may be true or false. For example, the WFF

$$\neg(1 = 1 \wedge 1 = 2) \implies (\neg(1 = 1) \vee \neg(1 = 2))$$

is true (it is part of DeMorgan's law), by the definition of the operators used. That is, the particular arithmetic statements from which the WFF is constructed are immaterial to its truth. Another WFF that is true because of its form only is

$$\neg(\neg(P)) \equiv P$$

for any P.

But many WFFs are neither true nor false. For example,

$$x = y$$

might be either true or false, depending on the values of the variables. Quantifiers force such WFFs to take a truth value, and in this case,

$$\exists x \forall y (x = y)$$

is false, whereas

$$\forall x \exists y (x = y)$$

is true. The quantifiers are related as follows:

$$\exists x P(X) \equiv \neg \forall x (\neg P(x)).$$

In these examples, we are really using not a "pure" first-order logic but one that includes some unstated axioms about equality and about integers so that

$$1 \geq 2$$

is false, for example, and so is

$$\exists x (x > 1 \wedge x < 2),$$

whereas

$$0 = 0$$

and

$$\forall x \exists y (y > x)$$

are true.

Beginning courses in logic force students to practice translating natural language assertions into WFFs, a process that is difficult at best and often leads to as much contention as would the original ambiguous assertions. This translation process, however, is just what is done to convert intuitive natural language requirements into a formal specification in logic. An extended example (sorting) will be presented in the next section.

This brief introduction to logic ends with translation of a counterculture bumper sticker, taken from J. R. R. Tolkien, which reads:

Not all who wander are lost.

Its translation will require two predicate names with the intuitive meanings:

$W(x)$: x wanders
$L(x)$: x is lost

Then the bumper sticker asserts:

$$\neg(\forall x (W(x) \implies L(x))).$$

Using the relationship between the universal and existential quantifiers, this is equivalent to:

$$\exists x (\neg(W(x) \implies L(x))).$$

By definition of the connectives, this is also:

$$\exists x (W(x) \wedge \neg L(x)).$$

Presumably the person whose car displays the bumper sticker believes that he or she is the x in question, wandering but not lost.

On the other hand, the bumper sticker did not read:

All who wander are not lost.

The literal logic translation of that is:

$$\forall x (W(x) \implies \neg L(x)),$$

or equivalently:

$$\neg(\exists x (W(x) \wedge L(x))).$$

The meanings are quite different; in the second one, there are no lost wanderers.

10.3 Example: Sorting

As an example of using logic for precise specification and the pitfalls of doing so, a very simple problem will do. Consider specifying software to sort integers. In natural language, the requirement is very easy to give:

> The software will take a finite sequence of integers as input and will produce as output the sequence sorted in ascending order.

The reason the natural language requirement is so straightforward is that it uses the word "sorted." If indeed this word is understood between user and developer, then there is no need for more precision. But it is instructive to express this idea in logic.

10.3.1 A First Try

It is a virtue of logic that it naturally expresses "what" and using logic it is very awkward to express "how," so logic specifications are naturally non-prescriptive. The essence of sorting is that an order is imposed, and most people would express this in logic in the same way.

Given an input tuple of integers

$$X = (x_1, x_2, \ldots, x_n),$$

the output tuple of integers

$$Y = (y_1, y_2, \ldots, y_n)$$

is *sorted* (this is the definition) if and only if

$$\forall i (1 \leq i \leq n - 1 \Longrightarrow y_i \leq y_{i+1})$$

Notice that the length of X and Y are the same. We could have let Y have last element y_m and then asserted that $n = m$, but it is more elegant to do it implicitly by just giving them both the same symbol. Often elegance in a specification could as well be called a lack of clarity; here using two distinct subscripts and explicitly stating that they have to have the same value would call attention to this requirement and might be clearer.

The implication in the definition is a way of limiting the universal quantification. It is shorter to write this in a form called "restricted quantification":

$$\forall i \in [1, n-1](y_i \le y_{i+1}).$$

Another way to look at this is that we are defining a binary predicate $sorted(X, Y)$, namely,

$$sorted(X, Y) \equiv \forall i \in [1, n-1](y_i \le y_{i+1}).$$

Strictly speaking, we should put the relationship between X and Y and the tuples of x_is and y_is in the formula because otherwise the righthand side uses symbols not on the lefthand side, bad form in a definition. Thus:

$$sorted(X, Y) \equiv X = (x_1, x_2, \ldots, x_n) \wedge Y = (y_1, y_2, \ldots, y_n)$$
$$\wedge \; \forall i \in [1, n-1](y_i \le y_{i+1}).$$

We also ought to include the assertion that the elements of X and Y are integers, but this is not really the essence of sorting, nor is it needed in the definition, except to justify the use of the $\le$ symbol with the elements of Y, so we leave it out.

This definition of sorting has been given many times (informally and in technical journals), and it is quite wrong. (Technically, in terms of properties of good specifications, it is very precise, but it is incomplete.) What it fails to say is illustrated by the example:

$$X_b = (1, -1, 3),$$
$$Y_b = (0, 0, 1).$$

You can easily check that $sorted(X_b, Y_b)$, but intuitively the mark has been missed. Nothing in the formal statement says that the elements of Y have to be the same elements as in X.

A common "correction" is to add the conjunct

$$\forall i \in [1, n](\exists j \in [1, n](y_i = x_j))$$

to the definition of $sorted$. This certainly fixes the example given before, but it fails for

$$X_c = (1, 2, 3),$$
$$Y_c = (1, 1, 1).$$

Perhaps now it is obvious that all the elements of X should also be in Y, that is, for the two *sets* (not sequences) of elements to be the same. This means adding the further conjunct

$$\forall i \in [1, n](\exists j \in [1, n](x_i = y_j))$$

to *sorted*:

$$sorted(X, Y) \equiv X = (x_1, x_2, \ldots, x_n) \wedge Y = (y_1, y_2, \ldots, y_n)$$
$$\wedge \, \forall i \in [1, n](\exists j \in [1, n](y_i = x_j))$$
$$\wedge \, \forall i \in [1, n](\exists j \in [1, n](x_i = y_j))$$
$$\wedge \, \forall i \in [1, n - 1](y_i \leq y_{i+1}).$$

This augmented definition handles all the examples suggested so far, and it might be accepted as capturing the idea of "sorted." But it does not, as shown by the example:

$$X_d = (1, 1, 5, 3),$$
$$Y_d = (1, 3, 3, 5).$$

(Check to see that indeed $sorted(X_d, Y_d)$ holds.)

Before we struggle to correct this flaw, it might be easier to negotiate with the user.

10.3.2 Restricting the Input

The example using X_d and Y_d raises a situation in which there are duplicate values in the input and shows this to be a difficult case to specify. Duplicates also raise the harder question of how to require something that in English would be said:

The order of duplicate inputs shall be preserved.

This idea makes no particular sense for sorting integers, but when a sort routine is given a *key* on which to sort, a key that is only a part of the whole data item, it is important to state whether the initial order is preserved on duplicate keys or the full record brought into play in a secondary sort. Unless this issue is addressed in the basic definition of sorting, a sort program might be written, and later modified to be used as a key sort, that is not what the user expects. Something of this kind happened with the UNIX sort command, which often surprises its users.

The developer faced with handling input tuples containing repeated values might go back to the user to see if these in fact may occur in the application. If not, the matter is easily dealt with. The specification can simply state that there are no repeated values in the input sequence:

$$\forall i, j \in [1, n](x_i = x_j \Longrightarrow i = j).$$

Another way to say the same thing more elegantly (less clearly?) is:

$$| \{x_i \mid i \in [1, n]\} | = n.$$

Perhaps there is no part of a specification where precision is more important than the part that describes what the software is *not* going to handle.

10.3.3 Second Try

Let us suppose that the user does *not* agree to the restriction of no repeated values in the input sequence. There are pedestrian solutions to the problem, ones in which the case of duplicate values is explicitly described, for example, by insisting that the number of repetitions of each value be the same in input and output. However, it is usual to attempt a more elegant solution, based on the definition of a *permutation* of a sequence, intuitively, another sequence that contains the same elements, but not necessarily in the same order. Let $perm(X, Y)$ be a predicate expressing that Y is a permutation of X. An inductive definition might be:

$$perm((), ()) \equiv \text{true},$$

$$perm((x_1, \ldots, x_n), (y_1, \ldots, y_n)) \equiv \exists k \in [1, n]$$
$$(perm((x_1, \ldots, x_{k-1}, x_{k+1} \ldots, x_n),$$
$$(y_1, \ldots, y_{n-1})) \wedge x_k = y_n).$$

Both of these formulas should be universally quantified over the integers for all variables that appear in them; we have adopted the usual (almost universal!) convention of omitting this quantification. The first condition says that the empty list is a permutation of itself, and the second defines an n-long permutation in terms of an element added to a shorter permutation. Then our definition becomes:

$$sorted(X, Y) \equiv X = (x_1, x_2, \ldots, x_n) \wedge Y = (y_1, y_2, \ldots, y_n)$$
$$\wedge \, perm(X, Y) \wedge \forall i \in [1, n-1](y_i \leq y_{i+1}).$$

This definition successfully handles all the preceding examples.

10.4 "Programming" a Specification

Most of the specification languages in use today have been constructed explicitly for this purpose and sometimes for writing a specification for a particular project. However, there exists a general-purpose programming style called "logic programming" that ought to be in every software engineer's bag of tricks. Logic programs are formal specifications.

Reading this brief section won't teach you logic programming, but it should allow you to see how clever the idea is and how computer support can be used in formal specification.

10.4.1 Prolog: A Quick Introduction

Prolog is the best known logic programming language. The name is a contraction for "PROgramming in LOGic." Prolog supports a restricted version of first-order predicate logic (Section 10.2) and can mechanically compute the truth value of some WFFs. Even better, when the WFF correctly asserts that something exists, Prolog can actually find such an object—that is, it can compute unknown values.

Prolog Terms

Prolog provides a means of stating facts and describing logical relationships between *terms*. A *term* is a fact, logical relationship, or a symbol representing a fact or a logical relationship. This means that terms can be placeholders for other logical relationships. In Prolog a *term* is:

- A constant
- A variable symbol
- A compound

Prolog provides for simple, straightforward *constants* (*atoms*). Constants may be numbers or symbolic constants. Symbolic constants *must* begin with a lowercase letter. The following are examples of Prolog constants:

- Numbers: 1, 2, 100
- Symbolic constants: `rain`, `oregon`, `joe`, `tbd`

Variable symbols are placeholders for terms. Variable symbols must begin with a capital letter. Examples of variables are:

- `Weather`
- `STATE`
- `N`

Variable symbols can take on values of terms, a process called *instantiation*.

Compounds are terms formed from other terms, using functions with terms as arguments in the usual recursive way. Most useful examples involve built-in infix functions like arithmetic operations (for example, +), and the special list notation to be described. For example, X + 3 is a term.

Prolog Predicates

The main building blocks of Prolog programs are its version of first-order logic assertions. *Predicate symbols* have the same form as symbolic constants (strings of lowercase letters), but are followed by arguments (sequences of terms) in parentheses. Examples:

- `position(3,2)`
- `sentence(nowisthetimeforallgoodmen)`
- `big(X+3)`
- `bigger(X+10,X)`

A few built-in predicates are in infix form, like =< (for ≤).

Prolog Facts

A Prolog predicate with arguments that are all constants or terms constructed only from constants, when terminated with a period, is the simplest example of the Prolog program part called a *clause*. These simplest clauses are called *facts*, and collections of facts make up the simplest programs. Here is a program using only the predicate knows(), which has seven facts:

```
knows(joe,c).
knows(joe,fortran).
knows(jan,fortran).
knows(harry,c).
knows(jan,c).
knows(joe,prolog).
knows(harry,prolog).
```

A fact program of this kind is also called a *Prolog database* because its meaning is to make knows() true for the various arguments it has been given (and no others). In a conventional imperative language, knows() would be defined elsewhere, and this program would "call" the definition. In logic programming, things are quite different. This program *implicitly defines* knows().

Prolog is given programs only by placing them in a file, so suppose that the preceding program is in file profacts. In execution, Prolog is expecting input *queries*, for which it prompts with:

```
| ?-
```

Queries can be thought of as questions or commands. To give Prolog the program in profacts requires the command:

```
| ?- [profacts].
yes
```

The Prolog response yes indicates that the database program has been successfully processed. Then questions can be asked about the facts in the database. For example, to ask "Does Joe know C?" means asking Prolog if it can match the fact knows(joe,c) with any facts in that database. The query and response would look like this:

```
| ?- knows(joe,c).
yes
```

When there is no match, Prolog answers as in the following query:

```
| ?- knows(jan,prolog).
no
```

More Complicated Queries

It is possible to use *conjunctions* to build clauses that are more complex. A conjunction is represented by a comma. So, if a user wanted to know if Joe knows C and Prolog, the query would be:

```
| ?- knows(joe,c), knows(joe,prolog).
yes
```

Prolog "computes" beyond the matching of facts when it is given variables in queries. Suppose that a user wants to ask if there is *any* programming language that Joe and Jan *both* know. The first-order logic WFF is:

$$\exists X (knows(joe, X) \land knows(jan, X)),$$

which is true when there is a common language X. But Prolog goes beyond a yes/no answer to *find* an X that establishes the truth of the query (because in fact it is true):

```
| ?- knows(joe,X), knows(jan,X).
X = c ?
```

Prolog has found a match c for X. (The ? after the Prolog response will be explained shortly.)

One way to understand Prolog programs is to go through the process that most implementations use. Recall the fact base, in which the facts have been numbered by comments:

```
/* Fact 1 */  knows(joe,c).
/* Fact 2 */  knows(joe,fortran).
/* Fact 3 */  knows(jan,fortran).
/* Fact 4 */  knows(harry,c).
```

```
/* Fact 5 */  knows(jan,c).
/* Fact 6 */  knows(joe,prolog).
/* Fact 7 */  knows(harry,prolog).
```

Prolog looks at the first clause of the query knows(joe,X), and tries to unify that term with the Fact 1 of the database knows(joe,c). Since the variable symbol X has not been previously instantiated, X is instantiated to c. With this instantiation, Prolog has a solution for the first clause in the query, and that solution is X = c.

Now Prolog tries to unify the second clause of the query knows(jan,X) with the database. But X has already been instantiated to c, so it is really knows(jan,c) that must unify with the database. Unification with Facts 1 and 2 fails because joe is not equal to jan. However, unification of knows(jan,c) with Fact 3 gets a little further since the first arguments are equal. But c fails to unify with fortran, so the attempt to unify proceeds to Fact 4, which also fails. But Fact 5 is a perfect match. Thus Prolog has matched both clauses of the query with the database, and prints the solution X = c.

Prolog also prints a question mark to ask what action should be taken next. If the user types a carriage return, it signifies that the solution is sufficient, and Prolog prompts for a new query.

However, if at the ? prompt the user types a semicolon, it is a request for further solutions. Prolog remembers that the last point at which X was instantiated was in its examination of Fact 1, for the solution of the first clause of the query knows(joe,X). Prolog will *backtrack* to this point in the program, uninstantiate X and unify with Fact 2, knows(joe,fortran). Thus X is instantiated to the value fortran. Since the first query clause has been matched again, Prolog continues with the second query clause, and tries to unify knows(jan, fortran) with the database. After several comparisons, it succeeds at Fact 3, and now the session looks like:

```
| ?- knows(joe,X), knows(jan,X).
X = c ? ;
X = fortran ?
```

An additional solution (fortran) to the query has been found.

Of course, there may be no further solutions, and if the user continues to ask for them, Prolog will eventually run out of facts to try no matter how it backtracks:

```
| ?- knows(joe,X), knows(jan,X).
X = c ? ;
X = fortran ? ;
no
```

Horn Clauses

Prolog programs can assert more complicated logical relationships than facts, in more complex clauses. However, logic programming cannot handle arbitrary first-order logical assertions. Only a restricted form of first-order WFF called a *Horn clause* can be used. Horn clauses define one predicate on the left side of the operator : – in terms of a conjunction of other predicates on the right.

For instance, for the preceding fact base it could be useful to know if there is a universal language that all the programmers know. If the predicate asserting that they all know a language is *commonlang* (), in first-order logic, the definition would be:

$$\exists X (knows(joe, X) \wedge knows(jan, X) \wedge knows(harry, X) \Longrightarrow commonlang(X))$$

The Prolog form is:

```
commonlang(X) :- knows(joe,X), knows(jan,X),
                 knows(harry,X).
```

If this clause is added to the Prolog program in `profacts` the updated file can be passed to Prolog:

```
knows(joe,c).
knows(joe,fortran).
knows(jan,fortran).
knows(harry,c).
knows(jan,c).
knows(joe,prolog).
knows(harry,prolog).
commonlang(X) :- knows(joe,X), knows(jan,X),
                 knows(harry,X).
```

Using the newly defined predicate, it is easier to ask the question about a common language:

```
| ?- [profacts].
yes
| ?- commonlang(Com).
Com = c ? ;
no
```

After the first solution c was found, a request for additional solutions failed. So C is the only common language.

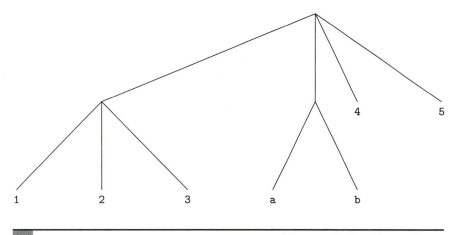

Figure 10.1 A representation of the list `[[1,2,3],[a,b],4,5]`.

Lists

As a language that supports symbolic computation, Prolog provides a mechanism for describing collections of symbols: the list. Prolog lists are built from atoms or other lists using the constructors `[` and `]`, for example:

- Null list: `[ ]`
- An atom or list: `[programmer]` or `[[b]]`
- A sequence of lists or atoms: `[[1,2,3],[a,b],4,5]`

A list can be visualized as a tree. For example, the last list would appear as in Figure 10.1.

Prolog has a built-in (infix) function `|` that combines an atom or list (the "head") and a list (the "tail") to form a new list. For example, the lists

```
a | [x,1]
[a, x, 1]
```

are the same, but

```
[a, [x,1]]
```

is different from these, but the same as

```
[a | [[x,1]]]
```

The head/tail operator is almost magically useful when its arguments are variables. Here is how the preceding programmer database might be represented as a list of lists:

```
knows([
        [joe,c],
        [joe,fortran],
        [jan,fortran],
        [harry,c],
        [jan,c],
        [joe,prolog],
        [harry,prolog]
      ]).
```

If the file profacts contains this single fact, the list can be queried using the head/tail operator. The head of this list is a list whose head in turn is an atom:

```
| ?- [profacts].
yes
| ?- knows([[N|L]|T]).
N = joe,
L = [c],
T = [[joe,fortran],[jan,fortran],[harry,c],[jan,c],
     [joe,prolog],[harry,prolog]] ?
yes
```

The query asks to match the knows list to a structure with an initial list [N|L] and a remainder T, with the result shown. Notice that the tail of that first-matched list L, as a tail, must be a list and so is shown in square brackets ([c] in the example), whereas its head N is an atom (joe in the example).

Defining Predicates

The computational power of Prolog comes from defining predicates that are more than just facts. Horn clauses for recursive predicates allow definitions that are very similar to the powerful inductive/definition mechanism of mathematics.

For example, consider a sequence of n items $S = s_1, s_2, \ldots, s_n$, and inductively defining whether a particular item is a member of the sequence. The usual definition is:

> x is a member of S if it is s_1 (Base case)
>
> x is a member of S if it is a member of the "tail sequence" $s_2, \ldots, s_n$ (Inductive case)

In Prolog, this is expressed using the list notation in the definition:

```
memb([H|T],H).
memb([H|T],X) :- memb(T,X).
```

Predicate memb() is typical of recursive list processing in Prolog. Its first clause asserts that the head of any list is a member of that list. Its second clause asserts that if X is a member of a list T, then it is also a member of the list formed by adding any head H to T. The trick in writing these predicates is to:

- Find a base case, a situation in which some simplest objects (here a list T and its head H) have the desired property, and to assert that as a fact.
- Write an inductive implication (which in Prolog has the hypothesis on the right side and the conclusion on the left side) of the form:

  If the desired property holds of a *shorter list*, then it holds of a *longer list*,

  where *longer list* is a simple modification of *shorter list*. In the easiest cases like memb(), this modification is to add a head to *shorter list*.

With these clauses, any complex object that has the defined property can be built up starting at the base case, then using the inductive clause to repeatedly make a larger object. Most Prolog systems work in the other direction: they determine whether a complex object has the defined property by repeatedly using the inductive clause to reduce a query to one about a shorter list, until the list of the base case is reached.

Although it isn't very helpful in figuring out how to write a definition, working an example can help in checking a trial definition. Consider the query:

```
| ?- memb([7,9,1,1],9).
```

A typical Prolog implementation would begin by trying the clauses in order, with subsequent failures and backtracking, as described in Section 10.4.1. But as human beings, we can cut straight to the "top down" sequence that Prolog would eventually find, as follows:

memb([9,1,1],9) by the first clause, with H = 9 and T = [1,1]. Then memb([7,9,1,1],9) holds by the second clause, with H = 7, T = [9,1,1], and X = 9.

Here is a more complicated example, the append() predicate of three arguments. Intuitively, append(x,y,z) is true if and only if z is a list containing the members of list x in order, followed by the members of y in order.

```
append([],L,L).
append([H|L1], L2, [H|L3]) :- append(L1, L2, L3).
```

The base clause is easy: adding any list L to the empty list should produce L. The inductive clause asserts that if L3 is formed from L1 and L2, then any item added at the head of L1 must also be added at the head of L3 to preserve the relationship.

10.4.2 Prolog as a Specification Language

We revisit the sorting specification of Section 10.3 in Prolog. The following predicates are needed:

Predicate	Meaning
memb(L,X)	X is on the list L
allmemb(L1,L2)	every item on L2 is also on L1
ord(L)	the list L is in ascending order
samelen(L1,L2)	the lists L1 and L2 are the same length
sorted(L1,L2)	L2 is the "sorted" version of L1

A Prolog program defining them is:

```
memb([H|T],H).
memb([H|T],X) :- memb(T,X).

allmemb(X,[]).
allmemb(X,[H|T]) :- memb(X,H),allmemb(X,T).

ord([]).
ord([X]).
ord([H|[F|T]]) :- ord([F|T]),H=<F.

samelen([],[]).
samelen([A|X],[B|Y]) :- samelen(X,Y).

sorted(X,Y) :- samelen(X,Y),allmemb(X,Y),
               allmemb(Y,X),ord(Y).
```

The predicates allmemb(), ord(), and samelen() are recursively defined in much the same way as memb() in the previous section, and studying them should help to make the pattern of inductive definition clear.

The predicate sorted() captures the specification of Section 10.3 that did not deal properly with repetitions in the input. It insists only that the input and output lists have the same elements as sets. Supposing that Prolog has been given the preceding program, it can be executed in a number of ways:

```
| ?- sorted([5,9,0,1],[0,1,5,9]).
```

```
yes

| ?- sorted([5,9,0,1],[1,0,5,9]).
no

| ?- sorted([5,9,0,1],S).
S = [0,1,5,9] ? ;
no
```

But the program also shows the deficiency of the specification:

```
| ?- sorted([5,0,1,0,3],Y).
Y = [0,0,1,3,5] ? ;
Y = [0,1,1,3,5] ? ;
Y = [0,1,3,3,5] ? ;
Y = [0,1,3,5,5] ? ;
no
```

Four lists are solutions to the formal requirements; only the first is wanted. Thus (as we already know from Section 10.3), this version of sorted() isn't what most people mean by "sorted."

To use a better formal specification requires a predicate defining L2 as a permutation of L1, perm(L1,L2):

```
append([],L,L).
append([H|L1], L2, [H|L3]) :- append(L1, L2, L3).

perm([],[]).
perm(X,[HY|TY]) :- append(F,[HY|B],X),
                   append(F,B,XT),perm(XT,TY).
```

The new definition of sorted() is:

```
sorted(X,Y) :- perm(X,Y),ord(Y).
```

In this definition, the auxiliary predicate append() was explained at the end of Section 10.4.1. The recursive definition of the predicate perm() starts with the base case: the first clause asserts that the empty list is a permutation of itself. The inductive clause asserts that when TY is a permutation of XT, then the list with head HY and tail TY is a permutation of X, where XT can be split into a head F and a tail B, and X has HY inserted between F and B, following the form of the first-order inductive definition at the end of Section 10.3.

Executing the new code:

```
| ?- sorted([5,0,1,0,3],Y).
Y = [0,0,1,3,5] ? ;
no
```

and the formal specification translated into Prolog correctly handles this example.

10.4.3 Prolog and First-Order Logic—Correct Specifications

Identify the customers ▶

▼

Trusting sorted() means trusting the typist of the Prolog program file, and the person who types in the queries and examines the answers, and the team of designers and programmers who specified and implemented the Prolog programming system, and those who did the operating system on which it runs, and the computer vendor who designed and manufactured the hardware, and the chip designers and fabricators of its CPU . . . .

Is the final version of the sorting specification (Section 10.3) correct? That is, does the formal version capture what the user really wanted as "sorting"? The first point, of primary importance, and the one that software developers too easily forget, is that *the user* is the absolute authority on correctness. The software engineer who has been working long and hard on an abstract version of the specification in Prolog can easily substitute his own intuition for the user's. He knows what's wanted! But intuition resides only in the mind, and two minds may disagree without either of them being aware of it. So every time the question, "Is this correct?" comes up, the engineer should think of the user, and if the case being considered is unique or difficult, a consultation is in order.

Two quite different paths are available for finding out whether a specification is correct. First, one might carefully study the logic of Section 10.3 and come to believe that it is "obviously" correct. This path is of dubious worth when one considers the historical record of mistakes made in arriving at the final WFF *sorted*(). Second, one might test the WFF through its Prolog implementation, trusting that in fact the Prolog predicate sorted() captures the WFF exactly. But trusting Prolog is not the real drawback of taking the second, testing path. Which tests are sufficient to guarantee that sorted() is correct? If one test should fail, that establishes *incorrectness*, but there are an infinity of potentially correct cases. The difficulty is a fundamental one, which will be further considered in Section 10.5.6 on drawbacks of formal methods, and in Chapter 19 on testing.

It was almost effortless to translate the first-order sorting specification into Prolog, but things do not always go so well. First-order logic is an *undecidable* system; that is, there is no mechanical way to check whether an arbitrary WFF is in fact true. Prolog is a mechanical system for checking truth, so there must be a discrepancy. Prolog avoids most first-order undecidable questions because Horn clauses are not the general form of first-order WFFs. In particular, Horn clauses cannot express *negative* requirements, that something does *not* exist, nor do they have universal quantification. Prolog also retains some very inefficient ways of dealing with quantifiers. For example, there are many Prolog constructions that are executed essentially by trying the natural numbers 0,1,2,3, . . . in order until a predicate is satisfied. One must be careful of these inefficiencies, or a specification that can be executed in principle becomes one that is too slow to be used in practice. Nevertheless, Prolog is an attractive way to try out first-order logic specifications, a kind of "computer-aided requirements exploration" (CARE, to coin an acronym).

10.5 The Controversy over "Formal Methods"

"Formal methods" isn't a very descriptive name for the use of mathematical techniques for writing precise software specifications, but that's today's jargon for it. Sometimes its advocates are called the "Formal Methodists" to hint that their advocacy has a fervor that resembles religion. Most formal methods lie close to the "artificial" end of the language spectrum. It is agreed that formal methods are the business of the software developer alone; the user is not expected (or allowed?) to use them. Thus formal methods are used to make a "shadow" specification that the user cannot understand. The Formal Methodists argue that this is a gain because the software developer's understanding is much improved, and this understanding can be communicated to the user (using natural language, examples, whatever is appropriate) for the user's approval.

The process works by user and developer engaging in a natural language dialogue, augmented by the user's domain-specific language. Perhaps they produce a natural language requirements document as best they can. Then the developer goes into hiding with the formal methods and produces the *real* (that is, formal) specification, in all its mathematical glory. In the process of using the formalism, difficulties in the natural language requirements will come to light. These are brought to the user's attention and clarified to agree with the formal specification. Once the formal specification is finished, and all issues it has raised have been checked, it alone is used in developing the software. The developer keeps the formalism hidden.

Formal methods are used today only in safety-critical applications. The cost of software failure may be so high that it justifies a large investment in getting things right. In most cases, it is a government regulatory agency that is the driving force. Regulation requires stringent product testing, and regulators insist that the developer present a convincing case that the product has been made as carefully as possible. The use of mathematics carries weight in making this case, and developers believe that mathematical analysis improves the real chance that software will pass its tests.

"Software safety" is the name given to an emerging branch of computer science, concerned with investigating why software fails, and how failures can be prevented or controlled. In engineering products that involve risk to the public, it is usual to employ a "safety engineer," a person who is wholly concerned with those risks and how to mitigate them. Software has been the ugly duckling among all engineering disciplines involved in such a project. The other engineers have been able to analyze their contributions and to estimate the chance that a failure will result. For software, no such analysis has been available, and the safety engineer has traditionally taken the failure probability of the software component to be zero, that is, to assume that the software is perfect and cannot fail. (Chapter 21 is an introduction to the probabilistic treatment of software failure.)

Nancy Leveson says that the historical record best supports taking any software failure probability to be 1.0.

The use of formal methods in development is a first step toward making software safety a science.

10.5.1 Dangerous Software

G. H. Hardy, in a famous essay on pure mathematics, proudly stated that none of his work had ever been "useful"—that is, it had not been applied to any practical purpose. (He was, of course, wrong about this, as pointed out by people who had found applications of his results in real analysis.) Although software is something like mathematics as an intellectual exercise, and the programs that software developers "build" are intangible—not physical objects that can explode or be dropped on your foot—software has never been able to claim that it was "safe" because it was not applied. Indeed, digital computers were originally developed at the end of WWII to calculate ballistics tables for field artillery. This military tradition continues into the present, not least in massive support for computing research from the U.S. Defense Advanced Projects Research Administration (DARPA), whose most famous project is the ARPA net, the basis for the World Wide Web, but originally intended for military command and control.

Any engineering project can go wrong in two distinct ways. First, it can fail to do what it was supposed to do, and by this inaction, harm may be done. Second, it can do something it was not meant to do, something directly harmful. (Somehow engineers don't like to think about a third important case where the project does harm that is precisely the harm it was intended to do.) The distinctions can be illustrated by the development of the atomic bomb in WWII. The motivation for the project was to avoid the first kind of harm: scientists like Einstein feared that Hitler would develop the bomb and win the war. So the project needed to succeed to prevent Hitler's victory. The second kind of harm was a distinct possibility because not enough was known about chain reactions: setting off an atomic explosion might have caused the uranium in the earth's crust to fission, destroying the planet. (In a lesser evil, bomb tests did cause an increase in cancer deaths worldwide because of the radiation from the unexpected fallout.) And the harm that the successfully developed bombs did to two Japanese cities and their people was put aside to trouble the scientists' consciences later.

Take responsibility ▶

Software projects, particularly when they form part of a larger engineering project (so-called embedded software), are subject to these same risks, and the list of dangerous software applications is growing daily. Here are a few examples:

> **Transportation.**   The Airbus 320 was the first commercial airplane fully dependent on its flight-control software for its ability to fly. The programs sense pilot control and actuate the control surfaces of the aircraft. They also restrict what the pilot can do—for example, they will

not allow maneuvers that might damage the airframe, such as rapid engine speedup and climb. There are two obvious dangers: (1) if the programs crash, so will the plane since it will not respond to the pilot; (2) in extreme situations, computer control will not allow the pilot to attempt what may be an essential (but dangerous) action. For example, if an obstacle appears unexpectedly, it may be necessary to pull up rapidly even if it endangers the airframe—the alternative is to crash. (Later versions of the Airbus software have mitigated danger (2) by giving the pilot an emergency override. The Boeing 777 and subsequent computer-controlled aircraft include this feature.) Although the Airbus 320 has a somewhat poorer safety record than older aircraft, there have been no spectacular accidents that could be directly blamed on software failure.

Railway lines can be computer controlled to avoid collisions yet make maximum use of the trackage. This is carried to an extreme in urban mass-transit lines, where by scheduling the cars close to each other and using computer control of the cars themselves, far more passengers can be carried on a fixed set of tracks than would be possible with signals and human drivers. The Paris subway system is about to adopt such a completely automatic control. The dangers of software failure are obvious—cars would crash into each other. Many subway failures (for example, on the BART line in the San Francisco Bay area) have involved computer problems, but as yet no serious accidents have been directly traced to software.

It has been suggested that automobiles could operate in a way similar to subways, and by giving control to computers in each car and on a highway, cars could move in close formation at high speed without traffic jams. Such "smart cars" are not yet a serious possibility, but every modern car includes dozens of small computers and their software to control engine performance, braking, and so on. A computer failure in a car moving at high speed in traffic might seem no worse than a mechanical failure under the same circumstances; however, most mechanical problems (say in the braking system) result in only partial loss of stopping power, whereas complete software control has the potential for immediate and total loss. But there have been no well-publicized accidents blamed on software.

Computers and their software are used in transportation for sound engineering reasons: computer control of an engine can result in better fuel economy, for example. In some cases, the computer is essential. U.S. military aircraft have been computerized for years, and control of supersonic fighters requires that the pilot relinquish control to software. The Paris subway will not be able to handle the demand without adding impossibly expensive trackage unless software is put in control.

Medical. Perhaps the first well-documented case of dangerous software failure occurred in a medical radiation machine called the Therac 25. Over several years, this machine was responsible for overdosing six patients so seriously that they received burns, and some received lethal doses. The manufacturer at first refused to acknowledge that there was any problem with the machine, in the time-honored tradition of a corporation denying liability for health risks. When the evidence finally forced a moratorium on use of the Therac 25, a careful analysis found clear software errors (involving timing of operator actions and the movement of the parts of the machine) responsible for the overdoses.

The U.S. Food and Drug Administration (FDA) is responsible for approving new medical devices (as well as new drugs and food additives) using clinical trials of safety. A device currently in the approval process is an adaptation of a heart pacemaker that attempts to control heart arrythmia by sensing that the heartbeat is irregular and applying an electric pulse to correct it. Patients with arrythmia might welcome such a device (the manufacturers are betting a very considerable development cost that they will), but not if the software fails and kills them.

Space exploration. It is striking that when a patient was burned by the Therac 25, there was a thorough *medical* inquiry, but little *software* investigation. The conclusion was that the patient had indeed been harmed, but that the cause was uncertain. On the contrary, a well-publicized failure of an Ariane-5 rocket test firing received an immediate and thorough analysis, which showed that the software specification and design were to blame. The European rocket was valued at about $6 billion; it carried a satellite valued at about $750 million. The software was developed with extreme care by a U.S. company. The root cause was the use of code that had been employed and tested in the earlier Ariane-4 rocket—code that failed with the more powerful booster.

A pundit said that the Ariane-5 failure was the most expensive imaginable in the measure of loss per line of software changed: no lines were changed because the code was reused; loss: $6.75 billion.

The full details of the failure analysis make fascinating reading. A routine from the Ariane-4 was called that was not needed for the Ariane-5; this prevented needed data from being delivered to a routine in the inertial guidance system because the CPU was overloaded. The missing data in turn led to an out-of-range value that caused a software exception; an error code was taken to be the value of a horizontal velocity. That particular variable could have been protected by exception-handling code, but a design decision determined that protection was unnecessary. There were two independent computer systems, but since both were running the same software, both failed within .05 second of each other. The computer shutdown caused the guidance system to drive the rocket off course so violently that there were structural failures that in turn triggered auto-destruction. The final mistake was in the software process: although engineers requested that the reused code be tested in an Ariane-5 simulator, their request was denied "for budgetary reasons." Later simulation showed that had the test been run, it would have detected the problem.

The Ariane-5 is a successful commercial rocket used to launch satellites. It was estimated that the test failure would simply add a few percent to the cost of each subsequent launch. But the software technology used is the same as (or better than!) that used in rocket weapons systems. The obvious danger in military software is that it will not work when needed, and its nation will thereby lose a war. The other side of that coin is that weapon rockets will go astray and hit "friendly" targets. (The Ariane-5 seems to have handled the second possibility all right, in that its self-destruction mechanism worked; the human beings tracking it also pressed the "destruct" button.)

Simulation.   One of the things that computers do best is simulation. Instead of trying an actual test of some physical system, software is written to mimic the real-world conditions and give "what-if" results that can often accurately show what the physical system would have done. (The Ariane-5 simulator does just this—it presents the control program with data that it would see if the rocket were fired, and then keeps track of how the program's responses would interact with the forces of the real world. Simulators can be used to train aircraft pilots by giving them a virtual airplane to "fly.")

Commercial airliners are a major success for simulation. The airframe can be simulated before it is ever built, making it much more likely that the prototype aircraft will fly instead of crash. Apart from reducing life insurance rates for test pilots, such simulation has made financially possible the construction of planes since the Boeing 747. No company could afford to "throw away" several billion dollars worth of real airplane to iron out the inevitable problems with a new design.

Simulation can also be used in a variety of "games" in which complex, interacting factors are programmed to play out their relationships in a computer rather than setting the actual events into motion. "War games" are the name given to trying multiple possibilities to see how an actual war would take place on the ground. Financial simulations are less complex than war games; they explore the potential results of various business decisions.

Software failure in a simulation program takes the form of an erroneous outcome: the program and the real world do not agree. Unfortunately, the real world is always right. If there is a mistake in the stress calculation in the 747 airframe, the prototype may crash after all. If the war game fails to take into account some important factor, it may predict early, easy victory in, say, Viet Nam. The most reliable simulators represent real-world forces by differential equations, and are used by engineers who often have a good "feel" for a mistaken result, which they may be able to check by some independent means. (Models in wind tunnels provide a rough check on airframe design, for example.) The least reliable simulations handle complex, imponderable human situations, and may very well be used by high-level administrators (generals, in the military) who have no way of evaluating the predictions.

In some cases, the danger introduced by software in these projects is gratuitous—engineers made a conscious choice to use software when other choices were available. The driving force may be economic (because computer hardware is cheap and getting cheaper, and software is often thought of as free), or engineers may be seduced by the clever things software allows them to do without thinking of the safety implications. For example, many of the computers used in automobiles are cosmetic rather than strictly necessary. However, most of the dangerous applications of software are not optional. Without software, the project cannot be done at all. (Of course, this raises the larger question of whether it *should* be done, the question that many engineers don't like to think about.) A good example would be medical radiation treatment machines. Without their computer software, these machines could not produce the precise radiation patterns that stand the best chance of killing a tumor without killing the patient. So to fail to build software-controlled machines is to let a certain number of patients die of cancer. The harm that will certainly be done if the software is *not* written has to be balanced against the possible harm that will be done if it goes wrong.

10.5.2 Can Formal Methods Make Software Safe?

It shows the immaturity of existing formal methods that they are used only in extreme circumstance such as under the whip of regulation requirements. If the methods were universally acknowledged to be sound, they would be universally taught to students of software development and universally used (to a greater or lesser extent as the application warrants). In fact, they are seldom taught and seldom used.

Three arguments are marshaled against formal methods by software developers:

Formal methods are hard to use. The "formal" component of most formal methods is based on mathematics like symbolic logic or abstract algebra. It is well documented that talent for abstract mathematics is relatively rare in human beings. In some ways, engineering as a discipline concerned with concrete objects is the antithesis of formal mathematics. Whatever the cause, most software engineers do not believe they can "do" formal methods. Even experts, researchers who invented the formal techniques, acknowledge that formal analysis takes at least as much time as writing a program and is more difficult.

Formal methods are not certain to work.   Like any mathematics, formal methods involve human activity and so are necessarily subject to error. It is an important advantage of formalism that even its most difficult statements and results can be checked. It is a serious drawback that this checking must be done by a different person from the one who originally did the work and that the process is slow and laborious. Published mathematical proofs are notorious for their minor technical errors. It is usually not the theorem that is wrong, nor is the idea of the proof wrong. What usually happens is that the author makes mistakes so that a proof is incorrect, but a colleague finds it very difficult to understand the proof with the mistakes in it and can correct it only with great difficulty. In the case of formal methods, technical mathematical errors can completely invalidate any particular application. For example, if it is formally proved that some problem cannot occur with a piece of software, but the proof is in error, what has been gained?

Fuzzy into focus ▶

Formal methods miss the point.   All software begins with somewhat vague ideas about how to solve a problem using a computer. But a computer program that is the final result of software development is not at all vague: it does precisely defined things. The program is a solution to some problem; the difficulty comes when it does not solve the right problem. When formal methods are not used, development can drift away from the desired intuitive solution in the design and coding phases. The use of precise mathematics helps to keep design and coding under control, to check that the software being developed corresponds exactly to a formal description of what's wanted. But there's the rub: how does one know that a formal description embodied in some formal method is what's wanted? There is still a translation needed, from the intuitive ideas to the formalism. Critics of formal methods say that the two factors previously mentioned— that formal methods are hard to use and subject to minor mistakes that are hard to find—make formal methods the worst vehicle for capturing what software is supposed to do. It is all too likely that the formal work will *not* correspond to what's wanted, with the result that the developer will expend a great deal of energy doing precisely the wrong thing.

With the possible exception of "hard to use," these arguments could be used against any engineering technique in any branch of engineering. No matter what an engineer does formally, he or she is still a person and can still make mistakes. As an extreme example, some kind of formal checking might be carried out, and the result might be that a software system is "NOT SAFE." A stressed-out person can neglect to examine the result, or can even read it as "NOW SAFE." That mistakes can be made is not a reason not to use methods that work when mistakes are not made. The negative argument is stronger if the formal method itself sometimes goes wrong and gives misleading results about safety. However, even an imperfect method may be worth using with caution—after all, it may not go wrong. The argument that formalism merely displaces the problem of misunderstanding, and hence misses the point, is also suspect. It is the power of abstraction that formal, abstract understanding is *not* the same as direct, hands-on reality. Reality is always to the point; unfortunately, it is also often incomprehensible. Abstractions that can be understood and analyzed always pose the danger of being false, of being not close enough to reality to give the right answers. But analysis of even a poor abstraction can reveal aspects of reality that would otherwise go unnoticed.

In the more established branches of engineering, the difficulties of making mistakes and of analyzing an unreal abstraction are taken into account. Experience shows the engineer when to be extra careful and when to distrust the correspondence between the abstract and the real. We can only hope that a similar "engineering judgment" will develop for software formal methods.

The argument that current formal methods are hard to learn and hard to use may also yield to time—as the field matures, better ways to teach formal methods will be discovered, and the methods themselves will be simplified and refined. However, this historical record of acceptance of formal methods in other branches of engineering may not be replicated for software. Nothing so complicated has ever before been attempted, nor has any other engineering been so cut off from the limiting and constraining pressure of the laws of the physical world. It could be that in inventing software, human beings have simply gone beyond their capabilities, and that useful formal methods will always be too difficult for the average engineer to use. If that's the case, it will have to happen that society cuts back its appetite for software solutions to problems. We will have to pick and choose the cutting-edge problems we try to solve, to bring the demand for difficult software into line with the supply of extremely clever people who can use hard formal methods. The rest of software will be the "cheap stuff" that isn't expected to work very well.

10.5.3 Mathematical Precision for Its Own Sake

The Formal Methodists argue that there are two distinct advantages in using mathematical ideas behind the user's back. These two advantages dictate somewhat different formal methods.

Formal Methodists of the "notation" school advocate the use of mathematics as an end in itself. They argue that using a precise notation is of great value in sharpening the developer's understanding of the problem and in exposing properties that might be hidden in the ambiguities of a natural language specification. The "notation" Formal Methodists advocate precision because it is good for you, giving the developer better intellectual control and a good feeling about having that control.

Harlan Mills said: "Programmers can write correct code, and know that they have done so."

10.5.4 Mathematical Precision for Proof

The second advantage claimed for introducing formal methods is the possibility of computer-assisted proofs in analyzing a specification. A specification in first-order predicate logic is a definition of software behavior that contains as seeds *all* the possible things the software may be seen to do. Many of the behaviors that are logical consequences of the definition are not at all apparent. But logical consequences can be investigated using a mechanical theorem prover. Any statement that can be made about the possible behavior of software meeting the specification can in principle be proved or disproved with a theorem prover. The Formal Methodists of the "proof" school believe that without this ability to prove software properties, formal methods have little value. They argue that modern theorem provers are very good at establishing exactly the kind of tedious, error-prone proofs that the developer needs to investigate in order to bring unsuspected cases to the attention of the user for clarification.

10.5.5 The Formal Methodists' Dream

Today's Formal Methodists have a grand plan in mind.

Going back to the analogy between a specification language and a programming language, it has occurred to many people that once complete formality is attained in a specification language, it *is* a sort of very-high-level programming language. Suppose that instead of people implementing the specification in a lower-level language (that is, translating the specification language "program" into, say, a C program that can be compiled and executed), the specification could be compiled and run directly. Then the criticism that a "shadow" specification is inappropriate is answered: it is not a hidden specification, but the software itself, which is properly the province of the developer. But a specification "program" is much better than the usual software because it is written at a level closer to the user's requirements, and hence there will be less misunderstanding.

The reason that compiling specification languages remains a dream can be illustrated by the case of a first-order predicate-logic specification language. Quantifiers play an important role in this language, and they will occur in every specification. Universal quantifiers must be used to assert that something must always happen, and existential quantifiers to describe searches for special objects (often the output values). The logical formalism is more than 50 years old, and mathematicians have always been interested in "programming" with it. (They call this "proving theorems.") But it was early proved (in a field now called "metamathematics," mathematics that is the study of mathematics itself) that powerful logics just don't work this way: if a logic can express everything needed for software, then its operations (notably the quantifiers) *cannot* be mechanically carried out. The metamathematical proofs are not simple, but there is a plausible argument: how would one "compute" a universal quantifier except by trying an infinity of cases? And how to "compute" an existential quantifier except by searching through an infinite set? Prolog illustrates these points—it has no universal quantifier, and its existential quantifier may be forced to work by brute-force search.

The Formal Methodists' dream remains alive today because it is not certain that the full power of first-order predicate logic is needed in specifications, and by reducing the expressive power (as in Prolog), it *is* possible to "compile" the language.

10.5.6 The "Agnostic" Position

Those who are not Formal Methodists do not share the dream of a specification language that is also a programming language, for two quite distinct reasons:

Practical. A useful specification language will always have programs that run too slowly. So long as the language is good for specification (hence it avoids the "how"), it must be inefficient.

Theoretical. The Formal Methodists' dream is irrelevant to the essential problem of software development, which is the communication between user and developer. So long as this gap exists (and it must exist), the language a developer uses is immaterial: when the user's requirements are not understood, the wrong program will be produced.

The practical objection has not been met, but Formal Methodists are hard at work trying to meet it, and the jury is still out on whether they can succeed.

Formal Methodists are quite aware of the theoretical objection, but they argue that a specification language gets the developer closer to the user's world, and that it short-circuits much of the existing development cycle so that the user sees results more quickly (to know that they are not what's wanted).

In practice, formal methods are not often used in software development today because they are too expensive: the human effort required is on the order of the complete development cost without formal methods. However, there is one situation in which this cost (or perhaps any cost) is justified: when the software will be used in extreme safety-critical applications, such as the emergency shutdown program for a nuclear reactor.

10.5.7 Formal Specifications as Automatic Oracles

Software testing, when a formal specification is part of the development process, moves from being the final phase to part of the user/developer requirements dialog. In the Formal Methodists' dream world, tests are examples for which the formalism supplies results, which are then used to query the user about obscure or difficult cases. Once the formal specification is done (in the dream world), it need not be tested because it will be mechanically compiled. It will therefore do exactly what it states, with no room for human error. The agnostic would say that if an extensive test were conducted along the lines of conventional testing, and the user were to act as oracle, it is almost certain that the results would *not* be accepted, and the specification (that is, the software) would have to be done over.

Where all can agree is that if the specification is *not* executed as the final software system, but if instead a conventional design and implementation is carried out, then the specification can serve to test the implementation. This testing does not suffer from the inefficiencies the practical agnostic sees.

For example, in the Prolog specification of sorting (Section 10.4.2), the queries

```
| ?- sorted([5,0,1,0,3],[0,0,1,3,5]).
yes

| ?- sorted([5,0,1,0,3],[0,1,1,3,5]).
no
```

are efficiently executed. When given both input (from a test) and output (from the execution of software written conventionally), Prolog can determine whether the test succeeded (yes) or failed (no); that is, the Prolog program is an automatic oracle.

It is a telling advantage of using a formal specification as test oracle that the specification *must* then be kept up to date. If the software is changed and the documentation (specification) is not updated, then the changed code will fail to pass the unchanged oracle. Since the specification must thus be maintained along with the code, it encourages doing things right, namely, considering specification changes first, then following an abbreviated version of the development life cycle to implement them.

How Does It Fit?

From section 10.1

1. Between what two groups of people in the world would you say there is the largest communication gap? Do you think a special language would help them communicate?

From section 10.2

2. Translate the two WFFs derived in Section 10.2 from the bumper sticker:

$$\exists x(W(x) \wedge \neg L(x))$$

and

$$\neg(\exists x(W(x) \wedge L(x)))$$

into idiomatic English.

3. Find out whether the UNIX `sort(1)` command preserves the order of inputs in a key sort.

From section 10.3

4. Is it just as difficult to describe inputs that do not contain duplicates as it is to describe that inputs and outputs have the same exact duplicates?

5. Show that $perm(X_d, Y_d)$ is false, directly from the definition of $perm()$.

6. As an alternative to the definition of the predicate $perm()$, suppose a predicate $countdup(L, x, v)$ has been defined, which is true when x appears in the sequence L exactly v times.

   (a) Rewrite the final definition of $sorted()$ to use $countdup()$ instead of $perm()$.
   (b) Give an inductive definition of $countdup()$.

7. Explain why it is impossible to be absolutely certain that a WFF like the one that ends this section is correct.

From section 10.4

8. In the brief introduction to Prolog in Section 10.4.1, a good deal is left out. Viewed as a specification of the language, it does not, for example, cover terms such as `1xx`, `n0t`, `ab5`.

   (a) What property of good specifications is being violated here?
   (b) Give an example to show that the same property is violated in defining predicates.

9. Why are all the facts in the people/languages database of Section 10.4.1 in all lowercase (`jan`, `c`, and so on)?

10. Section 10.4.1 gives an example of defining an existential quantifier WFF as a Horn clause for the predicate `commonlang()`.

    (a) The WFF

    $$\forall P \exists X \,(knows(P, X))$$

    could also be used to define `commonlang()`, but this WFF cannot be put in the form of a Horn clause. Explain why.

    (b) Can you think of a way to "program" the examining of all the people named in the database rather than naming them explicitly in `common-lang()`?

11. At the end of Section 10.4.1, a query `knows([[N|L]|T])` is given.

    (a) Why does Prolog end its response with `yes`?

    (b) How would you change the query so that L comes out as an atom rather than as a list?

12. Explain the definition of `ord()` in Section 10.4.2 in a way similar to that in which `memb()` is explained.

13. In the context of Section 10.4.2, consider the specification:

    ```
    sort(X,Y) :- ord(X), ord(Y).
    ```

    In English, what is specified by this clause if X is taken to be the input, and Y the output?

14. Would the predicate `append()` in Section 10.4.2 still work if its base clause were `append(L,[],L).`? Explain.

15. The final form of the predicate developed in Section 10.4.2 is

    ```
    sorted(X,Y) :- perm(X,Y),ord(Y).
    ```

    Would it make a difference if this were written

    ```
    sorted(X,Y) :- ord(Y),perm(X,Y).
    ```

    instead? Why?

16. A marginal note in Section 10.4.3 includes a catalog of things that must be trusted if tests using a Prolog program are to be meaningful. Drawing on the predicates defined in Section 10.4.2, give an example in which things go wrong because

    (a) There is a typo in the Prolog program.

    (b) The Prolog system fails to interpret the program correctly.

    (c) The operating system fails to execute the Prolog system correctly.

17. Prolog lacks a way to do universal quantification, but it does have a way to do existential quantification. Why can't the Prolog programmer use the relationship between ∀ and ∃ to get the effect of universal quantification?

From section 10.5

18. Suppose that a specification is expressed in Prolog. Discuss the question of whether it can be "wrong."

19. Suppose a formal specification is inconsistent.

    (a) If the specification language were Prolog, what form might the inconsistency take?
    (b) Repeat (a) for first-order predicate logic.

20. Suppose a formal specification is incomplete.

    (a) If the specification language were Prolog, what form might the incompleteness take?
    (b) Repeat (a) for first-order predicate logic.

21. One property of sorting that a user of any sorting program needs is that the result is unique—there is only one outcome from a sort. This can be expressed formally by saying that

$$sorted(X, Y) \land sorted(X, Z) \Longrightarrow Y = Z.$$

    (a) Prove this property from the formal definition of *sorted* that ended Section 10.3.
    (b) Prove that the formal version of *sorted* that does not properly handle duplicates does not have this property.
    (c) What would a Formal Methodist of the "proof" school say to someone who claimed that the proof of (a) was a waste of time because sorting *has* to be unique by definition?

22. Consider a Prolog specification in which some queries lead to multiple answers (when ; is used at the prompt). Discuss whether or not this will be a problem if the specification is used as an automatic oracle.

Review Questions

1. Why is it inadequate in specifying sorting to require only that the output items be in the correct order?

2. In what ways is Prolog a weaker language than first-order predicate logic? Could the deficiencies of Prolog be eliminated in some other executable programming language?

3. What is a test oracle, and what properties are desirable in an oracle?

4. What is the strongest argument *for* use of formal methods in software development? What is the strongest argument *against* their use?

Further Reading

Kurt Vonnegut has written (in his first novel) a very perceptive account of a world in which people are fascinated with engineering but are unable to work in the field because it is virtually all mechanized, and the few jobs available require more training and talent than most people possess [KV99].

There are many specification languages, but even the best of them is so cluttered with peculiar details that it seems far inferior to Prolog. Prolog has the advantage of being based on first-order logic, which has been studied and refined for over 50 years. A standard textbook describing Prolog [CM84] is the best way to learn that language. Many examples are needed since logic programming is a way of thinking quite unlike programming in imperative languages.

Of the many symbolic logic texts, Mendelson's [Men64] is accepted as a reliable standard, but it is pitched at the graduate mathematics level. Whitehead and Russell's *Principia Mathematica* is one of those books that are always cited and seldom read. If you look at it in a library, you'll see why. (You can have your own copy of *Principia*, which is back in print [WR62]. But it costs about $600.)

Hein's text [Hei95] contains a presentation of logic tailored to the beginning computer science student. The reader interested in learning *about* symbolic logic, but not in learning symbolic logic itself, should look at James R. Newman's wonderful four-volume collection *The World of Mathematics* [New56]. It contains popular essays on the history and significance of logic. The essay on a city council's attempt to draft an ordinance restricting dogs in the park [Nag] is a clever presentation of the problems and joys of translating English into logic. Newman's book also contains Hardy's famous *A Mathematician's Apology*.

Formal methods are the hottest controversy in software engineering today. The lines are quite clearly drawn between theoretical computer science academics and practical working engineers; it's easy to guess which ones favor mathematical formalism. Gerhart and Yelowitz collected a number of examples in which use of formalism went wrong (for example, in specifying sorting) [GY76]. Nevertheless, there seems no practical alternative to the use of mathematics if we want software to work, and for safety-critical projects, we do indeed. First-order logic is the basis for any formalism in which proof is involved.

Probably Z [Spi89] is the most-used formal language today, but it began as formalism for its own sake, without any proof component. The PVS proof system [COR⁺95] is clearly in the other camp of formalism to enable proof, yet it is surprising how similar the PVS and Z notations are.

An impartial study of successes and failures in actually using formal methods [GCR95] makes fascinating reading.

References

[CM84]   W. Clockson and C. Mellish. *Programming in Prolog*. Springer, 1984.

[COR⁺95] Judy Crow, Same Owre, John Rushby, Natarajan Shankar, and Mandayam Srivas. A tutorial introduction to PVS. In *Proc. WIFT '95*, 1995.

[GCR95]   S. Gerhart, D. Craigen, and T. Ralston. Observations on industrial prac-
           tice using formal methods. In *15th International Conference on Software
           Engineering*, pages 24–33, 1995.

[GY76]   S. Gerhart and L. Yelowitz. Observations of fallability in applications of
           modern programming methodologies. *IEEE Transactions on Software En-
           gineering*, pages 195–207, 1976.

[Hei95]   James L. Hein. *Discrete Structures, Logic, and Computability*. Jones and
           Bartlett, 1995.

[KV99]   Kurt Vonnegut Jr. *Player Piano*. Delta, 1999.

[Men64]   Elliott Mendelson. *Introduction to Mathematical Logic*. D. Van Nostrand,
           1964.

[Nag]   Ernest Nagel. Symbolic notation, haddocks' eyes and the dog-walking
           ordinance. In James R. Newman, editor, *The World of Mathematics*, pages
           1889–1893.

[New56]   James R. Newman, editor. *The World of Mathematics*. Simon and Schuster,
           1956.

[Spi89]   J. M. Spivy. *The Z Notation: A Reference Manual*. Prentice-Hall, 1989.

[WR62]   Alfred North Whitehead and Bertrand Russell. *Principia Mathematica*.
           Cambridge University Press, 1962.

PART III

Design and Coding

▼

The aphorism has it that "real software engineers don't do requirements," with the implication that what they *do* do is code and perhaps design a bit if absolutely necessary. There's some truth in the "code is everything" position, however much the subject of software engineering correctly emphasizes the phases "up front" as important. With the best of requirements and specification, you have empty words on paper; with the worst of code, the software really exists and can be run. No wonder there is the strong temptation to get on with the programming as soon as possible.

In this part of the text, we present a case that there is much more to writing code than just "hacking it out" without much of a plan. But the burden of proof rests with those who are trying to prove that a systematic approach to design is really a help in getting a software system to run. If the reader is not convinced that the methods presented here are worth trying, then he or she will continue to just hack it out, and we will have failed to make our case.

This part begins with two introductory chapters, one on design and the other on coding, presenting these subjects in the most practical possible light. The following chapters go into detail about several particular design notations or methods, each with an example of its use, complete through coding. We hope that these sections will introduce the beginner to useful techniques and later serve as models should the reader actually want to try the methods.

chapter 11

Software Design

I t is in design that the fundamental art of software development flourishes. Of course, the requirements and specification phases are of primary importance—one cannot begin the technical task of writing software without the clearest possible understanding of what that software must accomplish. But in requirements analysis the customer or user is in control, the application domain is all-important, and the technical expertise of the software experts is kept in the background. There may be no separate specification phase, so it is in design that the real work begins. This feeling that design is the heart and soul of the process accounts for the common practice of calling the whole software development process "design." When Fred Brooks speaks of "great designers," he isn't talking about those who manage the whole process (as he managed development of IBM's System/360), or about those who are skilled at negotiating with users about requirements, nor yet about routine coders or testers. He means those who design.

The line between requirements/specification and design is clearly drawn by the shift of emphasis from understanding the problem—"what" must be done—to solving it—"how" to do it. It is harder to draw clear lines between parts of the solution process, parts variously called "architectural design," "abstract design," "external/internal design," "detailed design," and so forth. In fact, even the line between "design" and "coding" is not a clear one, particularly for the individual. One kind of "design" is writing so-called pseudocode, a kind of semiprogramming notation that looks like program control structure around comments on what to do. Here is a simple example describing how parameters for a run will be set:

```
Read the number of parameters from the terminal.
FOR each parameter
  Read the value from the terminal.
  Check the valid range.
  IF not valid
    THEN retry until valid.
```

```
      FI
      Store in the parameter data structure.
ROF
Print the value of all parameters.
```

(More on pseudocode can be found in Chapter 13.)

When the designer writes pseudocode, isn't it really just coding? Some of the acknowledged great designers (notably Nicklaus Wirth) have treated the whole of design as a part of programming, each design decision being treated as a programming step. A final argument for lumping coding with design is that some problems are too straightforward to need anything more than a program written directly from the requirements.

Despite the similarities between the processes of designing and coding, there is one tremendous distinction between the end results: code can be executed on hardware—a design cannot. Thus *testing* must wait for code to be completed. The *test plan* must *not* wait—design is a place to record test cases, particularly broken-box and fault-based test cases for the system, and functional tests for each of the program units of the design.

For most projects, the design will have some formally recorded diagrams or tables of information, but perhaps no explicit narrative description. For large projects, a formal narrative document is essential. It is part of being a good designer to know what kind of design is appropriate. Section 18.2.1 describes properties a design must have when it is finished; unfortunately, that isn't much help in the process of creating one.

11.1 Purposes of Design

Design has two paramount purposes, both concerned with "how" the software will solve the problem described in the requirements or specification.

The basic algorithm. It is the essential creative part of design to get over the barrier of how to solve the problem, which a nonprescriptive specification has carefully avoided. Once the designer sees the germ of how it can be accomplished, the remainder of the process is relatively cut-and-dried. But no one has any real advice to help discover that germ. For example, in the problem of drawing trees considered in Section 7.2, the central design problem is how to position the boxes so that the tree fits on the page. Furthermore, some ideas for solving the problem will prove much better than others. A good design will be easier to correctly convert into a program, and this program will be more efficient and fail less often than for a poor design. A good design's program will be easy to change. After the whole process is complete, it isn't too difficult to see that a design was poor. It is the great designer who can see in advance and can unerringly find a good design.

One technique that is some help in finding basic algorithms is to simplify the problem being attacked. In "iterative enhancement" (see Section 11.2.1), the designer looks for the "core" of the problem, and discarding all else, designs, implements, and tests a program to solve this core. With a working program in hand, the larger problem is reexamined, and the core design is modified so that it includes additional features. Iterative enhancement may take several steps to reach a design for the complete original problem.

Decomposition.   One of the best methods for converting the germ of an idea—the basic algorithm—for solving a problem into a full-fledged design is called "top-down design," or "step-wise refinement" (see Section 11.2.2). The "how" of problem solution is broken down into subproblems, and these in turn are broken down again, until the steps to be taken are so simple that the program nearly writes itself. The only trouble with this method for problem solution is that it gives no clues as to what these steps should be—that is still part of the creative process.

The purpose of decomposition is to gain and hold intellectual control of the problem solution. However, decomposition has another important purpose in the typical multiperson, parallel-effort software engineering project. Programming itself is an activity that many people can perform simultaneously *if their tasks are separate and independent.* A design decomposes the programming task, and

Divide and conquer (independent parts) ▶

once the design is complete, assignments can be made to many programmers who can work without consulting each other. For individually produced software, this cooperative feature seems of no importance. But the very properties that make a design implementable in parallel make it easier for a single person to code because the design has done its job of separating out and solving part of the problem. If the pieces are independent, each can be coded without thinking about the others.

11.1.1 What Is a Design?

A design is the bridge between specification and coding. The primary quality on which it must be judged is that programmers can work from it without having to rethink decisions already made. Unfortunately, there is no simple linguistic touchstone (like the "what–how" distinction separating requirements/specification from design) to separate design from code. In a real sense, code is just the lowest level of design, the final step in step-wise refinement (Section 11.2.2). The best separation is one based on the level of

Identify the customers ▶

competence of the programmers who will work from the design decomposition. If they are themselves skilled in the creative art of algorithms and data structures, then more can be left out of the design; however, if they are little more than technicians with a good knowledge of a programming language, then everything had better be spelled out for translation. When the designer and programmer are the same person, as in an individually created piece of software, the border line is of no importance. For simple enough programs, design may be no more than diagrams and documentation used as part of coding. Even in this extreme case, however, it is important to *record* the design as it evolves and not discard it for the seamless version of the code that finally results. If anything goes wrong later, the intellectual control that a design gives will be invaluable.

Document it! ▶

A bare minimum for design is a decomposition of the software into relatively small components (also called units, modules, or subroutines), with a careful description of each. It is commonly stated (although without much evidence) that no subroutine should be larger than about 50 lines of code. The best justification for such a limit is that code is far easier to read if it fits on a page or a screen.

Separation and independence of units requires that their interfaces be given precisely, that is, in the programming language to be used. Subroutine "headers" are appropriate because they provide the declaration information needed to call the subroutine. A complete collection of such headers is half of the syntax of a design. The other half is a precise description of any shared data structures, which should also be in the programming language syntax. (For low-skilled programmers, algorithms and data structures internal to the components may also have to be given.)

But headers and data structures are not enough for even the best of programmers to code from. The semantics must also be given: what is each subroutine to do? What does the stored data mean? It is usual to answer these questions in natural language prose, which then constitutes exactly a mini-specification for each component. It is in recording these mini-specifications that designers most often fail. There is a natural tendency to rush into writing code and a feeling that the code will be "self-documenting" so that writing *about* it is a waste of time. But component specifications are crucially important because they are needed in writing the *other* routines that will use each component. They are also essential for testing components. The properties that characterize good requirements (Chapter 8) hold for component specifications, after changing them to account for the "user" being the designer and the "developer" being the programmer (and perhaps them being one and the same).

11.2 General Design Ideas

Because the essence of design is creation of the software algorithms and structures that will solve a problem, the subject is like any problem-solving activity and cannot be taught or learned by rote. The best one can do is practice and hope to "pick it up." The general ideas in this section may help the designer to cope with the complexity of a nontrivial problem.

11.2.1 Iterative Enhancement

The complexity of large software systems is overwhelming. Their specifications easily run to reams of paper, and even a description "in 25 words or less" indicates serious difficulty. For example, a modern operating system is responsible for "running" a complex hardware system, interfacing it to programs that must cooperate with each other, dealing with human terminal users, handling files and network communications, and so on. Such a system cannot be easy to design. Another measure of complexity is the volume of implementing code. Operating systems, for example, are typically programs of more than 100,000 lines in a language like C. (Some are *much* larger.) That translates into thousands of routines and data structures.

Divide and conquer (independent parts) ▶ The only known way for human beings to deal with overwhelming complexity is by decomposition. Large problems *cannot* be solved, except by turning them into smaller ones. Each of the small problems will be solved independently. The iterative enhancement scheme is both simple and vague: to design a complex system, put its specification aside, and instead specify and design an easier system. The vagueness comes in because to be useful, the easier problem must be related to the one originally given. There must be some clear way to "enhance" the easy design to become what was originally wanted. (Enhancement may involve several systems of increasing complexity, hence the "iterative" of the name.) One hopes, and it often proves to be the case, that the way ahead will become clear after each easy design is done. Finding easier problems, such that their solution and enhancement of their designs solves the original problem, remains part of the designer's art.

It is an essential part of the iterative enhancement scheme that each design be implemented and tested, as if it were the final system. The reason for this requirement lies in the difficulty of even the simplest, "core" system. If the implementation were not carried through, the designer might be fooled into thinking that successive problems have been solved, where in fact each carries a fatal flaw that will not be seen until the whole (badly designed!) system is completed. The operating system example is particularly apt here. It is arguable that the essence of an operating system is its treatment of applications programs and the way they are interfaced to the hardware and to each other. A core operating system to just run programs (no user commands, no files, no communications, and so on), if completely implemented, will check out all the designer's ideas in this basic area. An unworkable assumption, a performance problem, an inconsistency, will be exposed in the first iteration.

Iterative enhancement has been used since the beginning of programming large systems; it was named and described in the 1970s in a compiler development project. The compiler was first implemented for a typeless language, then types (and eventually data abstractions) were added to the language, and to the compiler as enhancements. Iterative enhancement worked well except that the original compiler symbol table had to be redesigned several times. This illustrates a fundamental drawback of the technique: if the problem to be solved is too difficult, isolating a core may be helpful, but in designing the core, mistakes are bound to be made, mistakes that will be expensive to correct as the design is extended. Problems with data structures may be mitigated by using information hiding, as described in Section 11.2.3 and Chapter 15.

11.2.2 Step-Wise Refinement

Nicklaus Wirth entitled a book on programming *Programs* = *Algorithms* + *Data Structures*, and he was describing what is now called "design." His presentation (as well as that of others like Harlan Mills) treats design as a process of implementation. Beginning with a specification, it carries through to executable code, and the examples are given largely in coding form. However, it cannot be emphasized too strongly that even when the designer passes quickly to code in the programming language, the design must be recorded before it becomes submerged in an interwoven program text. The decomposition into components must be saved, with a precise description of interfaces and communication data structures, and functional specifications must be given for each component, along with component tests derived from these specifications.

Wirth's systematic advice about the design process is another version of the problem-solving strategy divide and conquer, and might be paraphrased as follows:

Divide and ►
conquer (7 ± 2)

Proceed top-down in a hierarchy of stages. The first (top) stage is given by the specification: *solve this problem*. The designer then needs to advance to the second stage: to find a handful of steps that *will* solve the problem. This initial handful may of course be quite vague and imprecise, not at all like a program, but rather at a much more abstract level. They are often expressed in a natural language, or in pseudocode: "First, do this. Next, if this is so, do that, otherwise do the other. Now keep doing the following until this happens . . . ," and so on. It is necessary to limit the steps to a few (and hence to make them very "high level") because people cannot keep intellectual control of more than a few ideas at one time. If the details of any step were filled in immediately, the other steps would be driven from the designer's mind and lost. Once the second stage is complete, the designer selects one of its high-level steps, and breaks it down into a handful of steps, then similarly with the next high-level step, and so on. Eventually, the process ends because the last refinements leave steps so simple that there is nothing more to break down.

Step-wise refinement fits naturally with decomposition. At some stage of refinement, the steps are of the right size for subroutines, and further refinements can be viewed as the design of those subroutines (which might be omitted if the programmers are competent to make them). Another factor that dictates that some step become a subroutine is that the step occurs in several places in the design. Or if the same step does not occur, perhaps a common subroutine can be used if it is given parameters to modify its actions for slightly different steps.

Data structures may enter the design when the level of steps is detailed enough to require them, or when steps need to say, "Save this value . . . ." However, data structures can also come first in a design. Knowing that storage will be required, and from the basic algorithm something about how storage will be used, the designer may think through the necessary qualities of the storage and pin down detailed data structures at the outset. It is more common to leave storage structures as vague as the algorithmic steps in the early stages of top-down design, and sharpen them as the algorithms develop by refinement.

Fuzzy into focus ▶

11.2.3 Information Hiding

Information hiding is not so much an idea in aid of design, as it is an additional dimension of the design problem itself. Sad experience has shown that useful software, however well it works, is never left alone. Its users want improvements and modifications, and the software is changed to accommodate them—it is "maintained." If it is possible to effect a change in behavior by altering just one small part of a large software system—one "module"—then the task is relatively easy. The maintenance programmer needs to study only the one module, and the change is less likely to have hidden interactions with other parts that are not understood. In the extreme opposite case—when a change cannot be made without studying and involving the whole of the existing system—maintenance is literally impossible. It therefore behooves the designer to think carefully about the modular structure of a system, and to design for change. David Parnas suggested the guiding principle of *information hiding:* each module should have "secrets," which it "hides" from all other modules. These secrets are information required for the complete software system to function correctly, and, by localizing each piece of information, changes to that information are also localized.

Expect to deal with change (plan for it) ▶

For example, an operating system program is required to service hardware devices such as printers connected to a computer. Data will be sent to the printer from many parts of the operating system, and a naive design would handle all the complications of printing (for example, printer out of paper, font selection, and end of line) at each place where printing is done. An information-hiding design would collect all the things to be done in a single module, which would be invoked whenever printing is required. In fact, in this case information hiding *is* universally used in operating systems; the modules that handle hardware devices are called "device drivers." When a new printer is installed, it is the device driver that controls it.

At this writing (2000 A.D.), a textbook example of a situation in which information hiding should have been used has been much in the news. Businesses and governments spent literally billions of dollars to solve the so-called Y2K problem, sometimes called the "millennium bug." In many existing software systems, dates were stored as two-digit values, assuming that they fall in the 20th century. Thus 1964 was stored as 64. In the 21st century, such dates do not compare correctly. For example, the year 2000 (stored as 0) would appear to come before 1964 since $0 < 64$. These programs had to be changed; otherwise, in the years after 1999, subscriptions would expire, interest would be miscalculated, and people would be thought not to be born yet when their pensions come due, to name a few potential problems in these systems. If date calculations and storage had been made the secret of a module, changing that one module would solve the Y2K problem. As it is, the information was not hidden, and programmers found that to fix the millennium bug required studying an entire system, a daunting and error-prone task.

11.2.4 Adding to the Test Plan in Design

As the primary creative activity in software development, design is full of decisions and information. As the decisions are made and the information recorded, each idea naturally suggests tests to be applied to the software that will eventually emerge. Just as in requirements analysis, if these test opportunities are not recorded, they will be lost.

The design activity of creating functional specifications for the modules that comprise the software breakdown is quite similar to the specification of the whole system, but in miniature. The same opportunities arise for recording test cases for each module, cases called its *unit* tests.

Design is also the place to refine some of the system-level functional tests that arose during requirements analysis. Once the designer knows a little about *how* the required functions will be carried out, "black box" tests can be augmented by "broken-box" tests. The most obvious example involves the fragmentation of data. The requirements state only that there will *be* certain data of varying size, say, some text strings. In the design, it is decided to handle these strings by allocating a circular input buffer of length 1024 characters. There is nothing special about the 1024 length except that the designer must pick some buffer length. Once it is chosen, it establishes a special case for testing—evidently it will be important to try strings of length 1024 and 1025 since they will overlap the buffer boundary.

11.3 The Designer's Art

In practice, design is the art of turning requirements or a specification into program code, or into something so close to code that only a routine programming job remains. It is essential to understand both ends of this process well: a designer must know exactly what problem is to be solved, and must also be expert in how programs solve problems. But the connection remains an essentially creative step, difficult to describe much better than: "The experienced designer knows what to do." When formal notations can be used (see Section 11.6 and Chapters 13–17 to follow), they enter the design process to solve hard problems that arise along the way; they are aids, not the process itself. In this section, we outline what to do in practical terms.

11.3.1 By Engineers for Engineers

Even during the requirements phase, it is difficult for experienced engineers to contain their urge to begin discussing algorithms and data structures. They begin to see the system architecture emerge in the mind's eye as requirements are discussed. Certain requirements will rule out certain design options and cause the system to take on a particular structure. For instance, if high-processing speed is a primary requirement of the system under construction, static data structures are dictated since dynamic structures such as linked lists will be too slow.

Two principles govern the transition to design and the conduct of the design phase itself:

> **Form follows function.**   A system's function as described in its requirements might dictate one and only one form for the system. But the limited software knowledge of the end user usually means that in the universe of all possible computer programs, *many* programs fulfill the user's needs, and these programs may work in quite different ways. The requirements document is good enough when it allows us to distinguish a program that will fulfill the end user's needs from a program that will not. Adding requirements to come closer to a unique system satisfying them, may hamper a designer's ability to create the best design. That unique system may be harder to develop, harder to test, and so forth, than if the designer had more freedom. This leads to the second principle:
>
> **Don't make any decisions before they are necessary.**   Every time a decision about system form can be deferred, it increases the chances that when choices *are* finally forced, there will be enough degrees of freedom left.

When the time for design arrives, an "engineering mentality" becomes the primary mode of thinking for everyone concerned. The design phase is exciting for engineers because it is the point at which theory is brought to bear on a real problem. Furthermore, design involves peer interaction, or "engineer-to-engineer" discussions and work. The unsophisticated end users are gone.

It is this engineer-to-engineer interaction that sets the tone for design. The design is written *by* engineers *for* engineers, and allows the use of technical terms, code snippets, mathematics, algorithm analysis, data structures, and arcane diagrams, all with a minimal amount of explanation. It is easy to see why this phase is particularly pleasing to engineers.

11.3.2 From Requirements to Design

The hardest part of design is getting started, and here the requirements document can help. Design can be thought of as the task of pulling it apart, but into pieces quite unlike the separate requirements of which it is composed. The designer's first task is a systematic exploration of the requirements document, in order to:

- Become intimately familiar with each requirement.
- Distill from the requirements a set of common, needed "functions" that must be provided for the system to work.
- Catalog the major data structures needed.
- Identify unique or important algorithms required.

During the course of design, the engineers may become more familiar with the requirements than the user or the requirements writer.

11.3.3 Common, Needed Functions

It is the business of design to devise a collection of actions, abilities that the software should have, that it could use to satisfy all the requirements in an economical way. This collection of "needed functions" is the one that will be implemented.

In the requirements document, every statement that something must be done is a clue that the "something" may be a needed function. When requirements are expressed in the form given in Section 9.3.1:

if *condition* **then** *response*,

then *condition* is also a candidate for a needed function. For instance, if many requirements include something like: "Print a failure message on the console," then a needed function that must be implemented is "print failure message on console." Or if many requirements begin: "If hours worked are . . . ," then the design must have a facility to check the hours worked.

However, a needed function is indicated only if the action or condition is frequently mentioned. If something comes up only once or twice, it isn't "common" enough to qualify.

Disparate actions can be handled by a single "function" that abstracts their common features. For example, many kinds of messages (failure, warning, informational, and so on) can all be printed with one "print message" common function. The differences can be thought of as the value of a parameter supplied to the common function.

A good collection of common functions is as small as possible, but it does not confuse distinct functionality.

11.3.4 Major Data Structures

Systematic examination of the requirements and specification documents will also reveal some needed major data structures, although most data structures are best left open as long as possible. Data structures can be placed in categories based on data longevity:

- *Permanent:* These data structures will exist after the system has run to completion, and will be used again the next time the system is run. They are usually implemented as databases or permanent files.
- *Temporary:* Transient data structures are created and used only while the system is running. The information is lost when the run is complete. Temporary structures may take any form, but memory-resident data is preferred for processing speed.

Permanent data structures deserve more thought and care, just because they have an external existence, and their definitions may be passed on to other systems, and outlive the program for which they were designed.

A data structure may be forced on the design because the input information comes from the output of other systems, or its output is to be used as input for other systems. It is always possible to convert from or into external structures, but if the structures are well designed, they often represent the best choice, and the work has been done by others.

Whenever a data structure is "dictated," the designer should be aware of the possibility that this is nothing more than an overly prescriptive requirement—there may be no compelling need for this particular structure. The process of changing the requirements to gain the necessary freedom is not an easy one, but it can mean the difference between a sound design and one that just won't work.

11.3.5 Major Algorithms

In the initial stages of design, it is not appropriate to pin down most algorithms, and the requirements do not dictate algorithms. Straightforward processing usually arises naturally from the data structures and functions that have been identified and should be left to more detailed design to follow. But where there are severe constraints on time or space, or the choice of algorithms requires specialist knowledge, the requirements may suggest that the designer deal with some algorithms at the top level.

11.4 High-Level ("Architectural") Design

Some philosophers think that intuitive flashes come because of hard thinking done in the past. There are even reported cases where the flash came in a dream.

The essential creative invention that underlies a software design goes on largely in the designer's mind, either in an intuitive "flash" where the essential ideas seem to jump out of nowhere, or from long, hard thought about how the application problem can be solved. But most of the actual day-by-day effort goes into devising the parts of the software, the decomposition aspect of design.

At the outset, decomposition means inventing major subsystems of the application, describing the interfaces between them, and defining the system interface to its environment. This section describes these activities in practice and includes some "rules" from design lore. Neither the descriptions nor the rules capture very well what experienced designers do; anyone who wants to become a professional designer must serve as an apprentice to someone actually doing this work.

11.4.1 Designing Major Subsystems

Divide and ▶
conquer (7 ± 2)

A high-level design comprises a handful of parts—its subsystems—each of which may be thought of as a miniature system with a specification, to be further refined during detailed design. What should the subsystems be? About the only guide comes from experience with the application domain, and the construction of previous systems.

Reuse past ▶
work

Using previously designed subsystems is not a new or radical idea, but under the buzzword "reuse," it is currently a hot topic. Designers may be working in a particular application domain, say, payroll systems, and have a body of previous subsystems on hand. On rare occasions, an application may be designed by connecting existing subsystems and library routines, with little or no new code. More frequently, identification of subsystems that are available will define by exclusion the new subsystems needed.

The two compelling arguments for reuse apply well to subsystems:

1. Reuse saves an immense amount of effort, not least the creative effort of inventing and describing the subsystem. No one could deny that this is beneficial.

2. It improves software quality to use existing code that has been tested and certified by use. Here the benefit is more problematic because the

quality of a subsystem that is reused may be in doubt, and misunderstandings about what it does may later cause subtle and unexpected failures.

Some common existing subsystems are:

- I/O subsystems and device drivers. (Included in the operating system.)
- Mathematical libraries. (Often accompany a compiler.)
- Application-specific libraries. (May be available from earlier, similar systems.)
- Graphics packages.
- Database management systems.

The needed common functions that were identified in the specification are helpful both in selecting existing subsystems to reuse and in inventing new subsystems.

Each subsystem of the high-level design must be described in sufficient detail to allow it later to be further broken down into parts. However, in many cases, the description can simply refer to the requirements or specification documents, which will be used throughout the design process.

One subsystem is present in almost every design and deserves special attention at the highest level: the error-handling subsystem. A software engineer can fall into "normal-mode thinking," paying attention only to what the system must do when no exceptions arise and nothing goes wrong. Normal mode versus exception mode can be a good separation of concerns, but exceptions must not be forgotten or left to detailed design as a jumble of special cases. The error-handling subsystem has the responsibility for the exceptions that are spelled out in the specification, which (if it is not incomplete) must state what should be done when each exception occurs. It must also handle errors that arise within the system code itself, as a result of some limitation or mistake. Calls to the operating system may fail; dynamic memory may be exhausted or an internal table may be full; a data structure may have somehow been corrupted; and so on. Designing an error-handling subsystem at the outset results in a system wide consistency in dealing with errors.

There may also be a "diagnostic" subsystem related to error handling. In the simplest case, this function is part of the error-handling subsystem and takes care of the generation and routing of error messages (and there are always error messages). In a large system, more elaborate aids are needed, and the diagnostic subsystem may provide for snapshot and postmortem dumps, or even for data collection within an internal table that may be dumped on command. These facilities are invaluable debugging aids (and there is always debugging), but they also come into play when something unexpected happens in production use of the system. Having a diagnostic subsystem in place from the beginning of design can save an immense amount of time later since the design, implementation, and testing of other subsystems can make use of it.

High-level design of subsystems is a trial-and-error process. After trial subsystems have been invented, the designer checks the requirements document to determine if each requirement can be satisfied by the subsystems. If not, the designer tries again. As more and more of the requirements are satisfied, it gets easier to invent the remaining subsystems. However, an elegant design is one that does not require too much tinkering because subsystems added to fix omissions are likely to be the least general and most intricate.

Divide and conquer ▶

Some rules from design lore about subsystems:

Expect to deal with change ▶

Document it! ▶

- Make subsystems independent of each other so that they can be worked on in parallel. Keep the number of subsystems to a minimum. They will be further decomposed in detailed design. Organize subsystems in a hierarchy to maintain intellectual control. For example, break error handling down into classes defined by the error type and its severity.

- Minimize the coupling (connectivity) between subsystems so that if one has to change, the others are not affected.

- Describe the error-handling and diagnostic subsystems so that detailed design and implementation can easily use them.

11.4.2 Traceability Matrices

As a part of checking that each requirement can be fulfilled by one of the subsystems of a high-level design, "traceability matrices" are helpful; they are invaluable in adapting the design if the requirements change and in testing when code changes.

The primary traceability matrix is organized by requirement, listing the subsystems responsible for realizing that requirement. For example, if requirements were hierarchically numbered, as in:

[**1.5.3**]:   The system shall be capable of processing input from 128 terminals.

Then this and other requirements might be realized by subsystems as indicated in Table 11.1, where we have made up some suggestive subsystem names.

If requirement [1.5.3] were to change to:

[**1.5.3**]:   The system shall be capable of processing input from 512 terminals.

Requirement	Subsystems
⋮	
[1.5.1]	I/O, DBMS, Math
[1.5.2]	I/O, Session-handler, Math, Error-handler
[1.5.3]	I/O, Session-handler, Scheduler, Error-handler
[1.5.4]	I/O, Session-handler, Reactor-scram, Error-handler
⋮	
[2.3.1]	DBMS, Error-handler
[2.3.2]	Math, Reactor-scram
⋮	

▶ **Table 11.1**   Sample traceability matrix.

the design must be checked to see if any subsystem has limitations that would make it impossible to support 512 terminals. The traceability matrix of Table 11.1 shows at a glance that the I/O subsystem, Session-handler subsystem, Scheduler subsystem, and the Error-handling subsystem need to be examined.

A second traceability matrix can be mechanically generated from the primary one. It is inverted—organized by subsystem, showing what requirements each subsystem supports. Part of the inverted matrix that corresponds to Table 11.1 is shown in Table 11.2. The inverted matrix helps in testing when the code is modified. For example, Table 11.2 shows that if the Reactor-scram subsystem is modified, it would be prudent to run the functional tests for requirements [1.5.4] and [2.3.2].

A rule from design lore about design traceability:

Document it! ▶

- Assign each requirement to as few subsystems as possible. Difficult requirements can be decomposed into multiple requirements that can then be assigned to only a few subsystems.

11.4.3 Subsystem Interfaces

Having identified the individual subsystems in the architecture, the designer must next work out which subsystems need to communicate, and the primary traceability matrix is the starting point. Subsystems that do not appear together in the matrix should not have to communicate; often, subsystems that help to implement the same requirement do need communication. In the traceability matrix of Table 11.1, requirement [1.5.3] involves the I/O subsystem, the Session-handler subsystem, the Scheduler subsystem, and

⋮

Reactor-scram subsystem

[1.5.4]

[2.3.2]

I/O subsystem

[1.5.1]

[1.5.2]

[1.5.3]

[1.5.4]

⋮

▶ **Table 11.2**   Sample inverted traceability matrix.

the Error-handler subsystem, so these subsystems are candidates for communication.

It is information within subsystems that establishes communication needs between them. The designer needs to ask questions like: "Is there any data the Scheduler subsystem *has* that the I/O subsystem *needs* in order to fulfill requirement [1.5.3]?" The answer to this question establishes or eliminates a need for communication between the Scheduler and the I/O subsystem based on [1.5.3]. Communication paths are directional, so each such question must be asked both ways. For example, the Error-handling subsystem always needs information from the other subsystems, but it less frequently supplies information to them.

Mechanical support can be a big help in design. Some software engineers consider a database management system the most valuable software tool in their repertoire. Databases can be used to store and retrieve requirements, tag requirements with their assigned subsystems (thus recording the traceability matrix), and can be queried about which requirements are assigned to a particular subsystem. Sometimes when a database system is configured to manage requirements, it is called a "requirement oracle" suggesting that information retrieval is so good that it seems almost mystical.

Some rules from design lore about interfaces:

Divide and conquer ▶

- Provide functionality at just one point. "One required function, one interface" is the rule. Minimize the number of ways to invoke or call a subsystem. The programmer who needs the subsystem must keep the interfaces in mind when writing code.

Identify the customers ▶

- Know who will be calling the subsystem and why. This will define data needed from the calling routine and the data that must be returned.

Document it! ▶

Expect to ▶
deal with change

- Record restrictions on interface usage. If calls must be made in a certain order, or one requires another, be sure these constraints are indicated. (Better yet, is there some way to make it *impossible* to violate the restrictions?)

- Keep complex, hard-to-change data structures out of the interfaces.

11.4.4 Environment Interface

Help-wanted ad: "Experienced X11 [a popular workstation graphical environment] engineer with 3–5 years experience to start immediately."

Interfaces with the operating system and libraries are usually not a part of high-level design. These are so much a part of the programming system that will be used, and so pervasive, that they may not be considered part of design at all. However, the system interface to its users is another matter. That interface may have an elaborate set of requirements and certainly has a number of needed common functions. Modern programming languages and screen-handling packages free the designer from inventing the user-interface subsystems. It is expected that the designer knows the facilities available in a particular environment package, which can be quite complex, and that the package will do most of what's needed. Understanding the particular environment that a system uses can be the most important factor in design.

11.5 Detailed Design

"Architecture" is a name given to the first, high-level stage of design. The work continues with what is usually called "detailed design," providing enough information for implementation to begin. The line between detailed design and coding is not clearly drawn. For simpler systems with fewer people involved, coding starts sooner; in large-scale efforts, the design may be carried to an extreme that reduces coding to a low-skilled activity.

Detailed design must identify and define "modules" (units) of the software implementation in enough detail that (1) they can be coded, and (2) they can be tested individually. ("Module" is one of those words about whose meaning program developers disagree, and we use it here only as a nontechnical synonym for a unit of code. The generic term *component* is also used.) A module can be defined as a portion of code that:

- Can be implemented by a single programmer.
- Fulfills the requirements of a logical or functional part of a subsystem.
- Is independent of the rest of the system except for defined interfaces.

11.5.1 Decomposition of Subsystems into Modules

The decomposition of a subsystem into components is similar to the one outlined for high-level design in Section 11.3 and 11.4:

1. Invent the major modules of the subsystem.
2. Define the module interfaces.
3. Specify the function each module is to perform.

   The process is still a creative one for which descriptions and rules are inadequate, but since the subsystems are less complex than the system itself, the intuitive "flash" comes more easily to more people. For design engineers who are aspiring system architects, designing a subsystem is a stepping stone to bigger things.

Reuse past work ▶

   A standard subsystem, like an error-handling or diagnostic subsystem, may be incorporated in its entirety and will not require any detailed design or subsequent implementation.

11.5.2 Designing Major Modules of a Subsystem

In addition to the specification of the subsystem, the designer has the inverted traceability matrix for the subsystem, which lists the requirements it must satisfy. The interface to the subsystem defines its inputs and outputs. There may be major algorithms that this subsystem is required to use. This collection of information may be enough to suggest the necessary modules.

   It is also helpful to look at verb–noun combinations in the requirements allocated to this subsystem. A designer might see that a requirement like the following appears in the inverted traceability matrix for this subsystem:

[**1.8.1**]:   The system shall determine the radiation level every 200 milliseconds. If the radiation level exceeds the critical value, then the system shall activate the criticality alarm.

The following verb–noun phrases occur:

- "Determine the radiation level"
- "Exceeds the critical value"
- "Activate the criticality alarm"

The verb–noun phrases can be taken as the names of modules to fulfill these requirements:

```
determine_radiation_level
exceeds_critical_value
activate_criticality_alarm
```

Proceeding through the subsystem requirements, writing down all the verb–noun phrases defines a list of possible modules whose names indicate roughly what they must do. This list can be pruned by looking for common subfunctions and grouping trivial actions. The result is a list of potential subsystem components.

Once the components have been identified, there may be some support modules to be written. For instance, if it becomes apparent that the system must deal extensively with strings, the developer may want to find or develop a library of string-handling functions.

Some rules from design lore about detailed module design:

Divide and conquer ▶

- Keep the modules independent. Information hiding (details are in Chapter 15) is a way of assuring independence. Keep the number of modules in a subsystem to a minimum. Don't overdesign modules. Allow the implementors to make decisions appropriate to the programming task.

Identify the customers ▶

- Provide a design that is appropriate to the skills and resources of the implementors.

Document it! ▶

- Link each module back to its subsystem, which is in turn linked to requirements.

11.5.3 Defining Module Interfaces

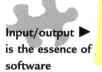

Input/output is the essence of software ▶

With the subsystem modules identified, interfaces need to be provided between communicating modules. An interface defines in detail the data that is being passed to and returned by each individual module. The syntax of a programming language is appropriate for recording the module interfaces and their parameters. The information that a compiler needs to deal with a module declaration is exactly the information a person needs to use the interface. Sometimes a comment that goes beyond syntax is needed for a parameter, but the parameter type information and a well-chosen name are often enough.

Here is a simple example of C syntax used to describe an interface:

```
/* Func determines the action to take */
/* Table may be changed through the pointer */
void UpdateTable(int Func, Idx Locator, TabForm *Table)
```

It is evident that this routine is called to change information pointed at by the parameter Table, in one of several ways depending on the value of Func, and that a position Locator in the table is involved. Further information is provided by the type definitions for the second and third parameters, which are to be given elsewhere. Sometimes the module function is also captured by a comment, but it is unwise to be cryptic because this information is often complex, and understanding it is crucial. In the preceding example,

```
/* Update the table */
```

would not be at all useful.

11.5.4 Specifying the Module Functions

In specifying what each module must do, there is less likelihood of misunderstanding than in the requirements dialogue with an end user. The designer and implementor are both software engineers who speak the same language. The module interface has been precisely described, perhaps as a subroutine header in the programming language that will be used for coding. It is often enough to give a brief English description of the module's function, perhaps augmented with a formal design notation such as those listed in Section 11.6.2. The description must be sufficient for the programming and testing to follow.

Identify the customers ►

Error handling is an aspect of each module's functionality that must not be neglected. At the module level, errors are local and specific, for example:

- *Data range errors:* Data is out of acceptable range.
- *System errors:* Operating system or library calls fail.
- *Internal failures:* Corrupt internal data structures are detected.

A rule from design lore about module specification:

Take responsibility ►

- It may be that error handling is not required of a particular module, but if there is the slightest doubt, find out and see to it that errors are dealt with properly.

11.5.5 Module Documentation

The final step of detailed design is to prepare the subsystem documentation for implementation by the programmers and as specification information to be used in unit testing. Module documentation should contain:

Document it (traceability) ►

- The name of the module and description of its parameters (subroutine header).
- The name of the file containing the module.
- Description of global or external inputs and outputs for the module in addition to its parameters.

- Functional description (specification) of the module, including error handling.
- Additional assumptions to be checked by the module's caller.

Many corporations have standards for module documentation as part of their software development procedures.

11.6 Formal Notations for Design

It has been said that a good notation for expressing problems is half their solution. Software designers use a combination of diagrams and text in several different formal ways to express algorithms for solving a problem and problem decomposition. Although there is clearly no one "best" notation for software design, a range of possibilities is given in chapters to follow.

Every branch of engineering uses diagrammatic notations. The best known are probably the "blueprints" of mechanical engineering. Blueprints are diagrams of mechanical parts, drawn using a set of conventions such that the diagram contains enough information to guide a skilled machinist in making the parts. Much is left out of a blueprint, but it concisely captures all dimensions and spatial relationships. Freed of other details, the mechanical engineer can concentrate on these and get them right.

Intellectual control ▶ The primary reason for using formal design notations is that, like all good notations, they help us think and stay in control of a complex problem. But a secondary advantage of using a formal notation is that formal description is the first step toward automation. The machinist works from the blueprint, but programmed automatic machine tools can also work from it. Without blueprints, clever machinists may be able to make parts from vague verbal descriptions—but automatic machine tools are lost. Automation may not be planned when a formal notation is adopted, but it often follows.

Just as a mechanical engineer uses blueprints to design, so a software engineer makes use of a variety of formal notations. From a blueprint, the machinist crafts the parts; from a software formal design, the programmer crafts a program.

11.6.1 Architectural Diagrams

Throughout the process of design, "block diagrams" are indispensable for recording ideas about how the system will work. Proverbially, such diagrams are sketched on napkins in restaurants or on the back of discarded envelopes. There is no standardized form for a block diagram, but it usually appears as a bunch of interconnected, labeled boxes, circles, and the like.

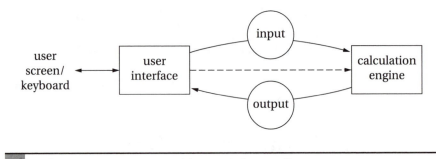

Figure 11.1   Arcane architectural diagram for a system.

The boxes represent system parts, and the lines between them have something to do with information flow. The whole thing is very vague and very useful.

For example, something like Figure 11.1 might be sketched to capture an idea for a system in which there is a user interface subsystem and a calculation subsystem that exchange information through textual files, with the interface subsystem having the overall system control. (This is a particularly good basic design for independently implementing the two subsystems since the text files can be created by hand and examined independently for testing.) To the person making this sketch, a box represents a subsystem, a circle represents a file, a solid arrow is a data path, a dashed arrow is a control path, and it wasn't clear how to fit in the "user screen/keyboard." Another person will not necessarily use the same conventions, so without explanation a diagram like Figure 11.1 is worthless as documentation, but to its author, in the short term, it is very helpful.

Fuzzy into focus ▶

11.6.2 Design Formalisms

The five chapters to follow (Chapter 13 on pseudocode, Chapter 14 on finite state machines, Chapter 15 on abstract data types, Chapter 16 on object-oriented design, and Chapter 17 on data flow diagrams) describe important design techniques. These methods are "formal" in the sense that they make use of diagrams and/or internally consistent technical abstractions. Working with a formal method, the designer is in an unreal world, a world simpler than the real one of the problem to be solved. The compensation for this unreality is that the artificial world focuses attention on some aspect of the problem and makes it easier to solve. These notations are not the only ones software engineers use, but they are good examples. Probably the most commonly used design method is more informal: the engineer uses a combination of code fragments and comments, tables, and sketches to record technical information, and natural language to describe the overall design.

By the time a design formalism comes into play, the programming language for the coding to follow has been chosen. It is then a great advantage to use that language whenever possible in design, but without losing the abstraction advantages of formalism. That is, where the programming language can express something that is clearly part of design, it should be used instead of a special design notation. But the direction should be taken from design—don't start programming too soon. For example, a design includes a list of components from which the final program is to be made, and a description of their interfaces. If the components are going to wind up as subroutines, declaration headers of the programming language are an ideal way to describe them. A programming language comment can be attached to the header to give design information the component. But don't write any more of the code!

Divide and conquer (know when to stop) ▶

How Does It Fit?

From section 11.1

1. Discuss the "rule" that no subroutine should be longer than 50 lines, with reference to the principles given in Chapter 2. Include intuitive arguments both in favor of such a rule and against it.

2. Consider each property of a good specification listed in Chapter 8 as instead a property of a good component specification created during detailed design.

   (a) Make a list of the properties that apply essentially without any change.
   (b) List properties that can be made to apply by making changes in the description, and give the necessary changes for each.
   (c) Are there properties that do not apply, even with changes in the description?

From section 11.2

3. Compare and contrast design using iterative enhancement with development using Boehm's spiral model (Section 5.1.1).

4. Find as many general principles of good software development (Chapter 2) as you can that iterative enhancement embodies, and explain why each one applies.

5. Which is likely to lead to more tests recorded during design, broken-box additions to the functional system tests or unit tests for the modules? Why?

6. Why wouldn't it solve the Y2K problem to simply modify all the programs involved to declare date variables as large enough to hold four digits and replace the existing programs with these? (How hard would it be to locate all the "date variables"?)

From section 11.3

7. Why shouldn't the designers becoming "intimately familiar with each requirement" happen as a part of the specification phase?

8. Why shouldn't *every* function identified in the requirements be treated as a "common" function?

From section 11.4

9. If a diagnostic subsystem is part of a design, there are reasons why it should be designed and implemented first.

   (a) Why would this be wise both in high-level design and in detailed design? Why is it unnecessary to do the detailed design of the diagnostic subsystem before the high-level design of the other subsystems?

   (b) Looking ahead to coding, think about the situation of a programmer who encounters a difficult debugging problem with some module. What might this person do if the diagnostic system is or is not already coded?

10. How well does the sample traceability matrix of Table 11.1 live up to the rule from design lore given at the end of its section?

11. Consider the rule that subsystems appearing together in the traceability matrix are likely to communicate.

    (a) Give an example where this is clearly correct.

    (b) Give an example where the rule is wrong.

From section 11.5

12. Exploring the intuitive definition of a "module":

    (a) Why would individual lines of code not fit the definition?

    (b) Why would the whole system not be a "module"?

13. In the lore about detailed module design, there are several rules flagged with the Divide and Conquer principle. Assign subsections of Section 2.2 to each part of these rules to better characterize the parts.

14. What would be wrong with *not* pruning the list of potential modules obtained from verb–noun phrases in the requirements?

15. Which part of module documentation will be the most extensive, and why?

From section 11.6

16. Make a "Key" for Figure 11.1 that identifies the symbols used in the figure. In the process, you might find a way to improve the figure now that it has a key.

17. The differential calculus was independently invented by Newton, who wrote the derivative of x with respect to t as $\dot{x}$, and $\ddot{x}$ for the second derivative, and so on; and by Leibniz, who used the notation $\frac{dx}{dt}$, $\frac{d^2x}{dt}$, and

so on. Can you think of a problem that Leibniz's notation "solves" that Newton's notation doesn't?

18. What are the advantages of using elements of the programming language destined for coding in design? What are the possible pitfalls?

Review Questions

1. What are the two main purposes of design?

2. Why is decomposition into independent program units important even when a single person does both design and coding?

3. What distinguishes "high level" from "detailed" design? What steps are common to both?

4. What kinds of tests are most likely to be added to the test plan during design? Why?

Further Reading

The literature on software design began as part of the "programming" literature, and some of the best advice for the individual is phrased in terms of a programming language as the design vehicle. Nicklaus Wirth is one of the great designers (both of languages like Pascal, and other software). His article on step-wise refinement [Wir71] is classic, and his book on design [Wir76] is a reference that does not stay on the shelf. The "structured programming" revolution [DDH72, Mil86] (which in its day enjoyed a higher buzzword status than even "object oriented" does today) really did make a difference in design using code. Jon Bentley is one of today's most articulate proponents of the programmer's craft [Ben86], a viewpoint that is often opposed to the more pedestrian one of software engineering. It may be that a programmers' backlash to too much separate design is developing, and the name "extreme programming" is attached to this movement [Bec99].

It is hard to find information on design in general. Available books seem to suffer from one or more of the following deficiencies:

1. They are really about programming or really about requirements.

2. They are too narrow in subject, being only about (say) *database* design.

3. They assume a particular design method ("object oriented" is today's fad) and spend all of their time on details of that method, these details differing substantially from author to author.

Basili and Turner [BT75] coined the name *iterative enhancement,* but are seldom credited with the invention because the idea was well known, its origin lost in the mists of common practice.

If one person had to be selected as the source of today's best ideas in software engineering, a good case could be made for choosing David Parnas. He has an uncanny way of looking at hard problems and finding novel solutions. He is the inventor of information hiding [Par72]. He has even found something profound to say about the lowly system block diagram [Par74]. His paper on "software aging" [Par94] is an insightful look at why we get into messes like the Y2K problem.

References

[Bec99]   Kent Beck. *Extreme Programming Explained: Embrace Change*. Addison-Wesley, 1999.

[Ben86]   Jon Bentley. *Programming Pearls*. Addison-Wesley, 1986.

[BT75]   V. Basili and A. J. Turner. Iterative enhancement: a practical technique for software development. *IEEE Transactions on Software Engineering*, pages 390–396, 1975.

[DDH72]   O-J. Dahl, E. Dijkstra, and C. A. R. Hoare. *Structured Programming*. Academic Press, 1972.

[Mil86]   Harlan D. Mills. Structured programming: Retrospect and prospect. *IEEE Software*, pages 58–66, 1986.

[Par72]   David L. Parnas. On the criteria to be used in decomposing systems into modules. *Communications of the ACM*, December 1972.

[Par74]   David L. Parnas. On a "buzzword:" hierarchical structure. In *Proc. IFIP Congress '74*, pages 336–339, 1974.

[Par94]   David L. Parnas. Software aging. In *Proc. International Conference on Software Engineering*, pages 279–287, 1994.

[Wir71]   N. Wirth. Program development by stepwise refinement. *Communications of the ACM*, 14:221–227, 1971.

[Wir76]   Nicklaus Wirth. *Algorithms + Data Structures = Programs*. Prentice-Hall, 1976.

chapter 12

Coding

M ost software developers understand coding very well indeed. If the system design provides a reasonable specification for some subroutine, its coding is straightforward. But like any discipline, coding has its tricks and traps that are not covered in basic textbooks but picked up in practice.

12.1 Programming Languages

Intellectual control ▶

Modern programming languages have been influenced by the needs of software engineers, needs that lie mostly in the direction of controlling the program being developed. However, *power* in a programming language—that is, the ability to do whatever the programmer wishes, even if the result is incomprehensible—is still the name of the programming language game. So a discussion of language features for software engineering includes both helpful features and pitfalls. Every language has both, but C will be used as our example. In UNIX environments, C provides the programmer with access to the lowest level of system services, notably real dynamic memory allocation, concurrent execution of processes and interprocess communication, and control of keyboard functions and interrupts. These powerful language features are important in solving some problems, but C can also help the programmer keep control of the coding phase of software development (or lose control!).

C has been called "the best high-level assembly language."

Most of the "control" features of languages (as opposed to "power") involve the idea of data typing.

12.1.1 Strong Typing

Strong typing refers to the important property of a programming language that it is forbidden to use values or variables of the language in improper contexts. Three important examples of errors that strong typing would not permit appear in the C code:

```
char
Next(int What)
{
   struct S {int a; int *b;};
   struct S anS;
   float x;
   scanf("%d", x);
   anS = x;
   return('*');
}

main()
{
.
.
.
   Next("abcxyz", 2);
.
.
.
}
```

The type errors are first that `scanf()` requires a pointer second argument (the programmer probably meant to use &x); second that `anS` and `x` are not of the same type, so assigning one to the other makes no sense; and third, that the call on `Next()` in `main()` doesn't agree with the declaration of `Next()` in the number and type of parameters, nor in the returned value. (This third error is most common when the routines involved are separately compiled.) These errors are all "static" in that the types are known at compile time.

Programmers probably never mean to make type errors, but do in fact make them frequently, either because they forget what type is required or because they have been lied to (by out-of-date documentation, for example) about types. With a strongly typed language, the damage lies can cause is minimized because the compiler catches type errors.

It's unfortunate that C is not strongly typed! Other languages (for example, Pascal and Ada—Ada even catches interface type errors across separate compilations) are better, but some are far worse (FORTRAN, PL/1—PL/1 technically allows *any* type to be assigned to any other, mostly with unknown effect). Type agreement is confused by the issue of "coercion" of types, in which arithmetical operations are expected to work properly despite differences among their arguments. For example, if / is an operator taking two real parameters, then one does not want to have to be careful to write (say)

1.0/2.0 to get the fractional value 0.5, but can write 1/2 as is natural. Only ALGOL 68, a language with a very small user community, really got strong typing right. In ALGOL 68, it is a type error to (for example) pass a procedure as an argument if that procedure has a different parameter structure than the called routine expects of its parameter procedure. ALGOL 68 is the source of much of the vocabulary about types and agreement—for example, it is the source for "coercion" and "casting" of types.

Faced with a language that lacks strong typing, the programmer would be well advised to use a separate syntax analyzer of some kind that explicitly checks for type errors. (For an example, see Section 12.2.1.)

12.1.2 User-defined Types

Type definitions (C typedef . . .) are a kind of encapsulation that hide the details of a type within a single declaration. Type definitions are important in adding clarity to a design because they allow abstraction from the details ("the bits") of machine storage. Types are even more important in allowing a programmer to check agreement between different parts of the design. Many inconsistencies result from assuming one type in one component, another type in another component, yet the two are supposed to be the same. Types can even help to control agreement of units. For example, suppose that in a subroutine header:

```
float
StallComputation(float Angle)
{
  .
  .
  .
   if (Angle == 90) ...
}
```

the implementation is assuming the argument expressed in degrees, while a caller might assume radians:

```
float theta, beta = 3.14159265;
  .
  .
  .
theta = StallComputation(beta/2.0);
  .
  .
  .
```

These two routines are evidently not going to work together correctly.

Things are much better (although success is not guaranteed) with:

```
typedef float DegreeAngle; /* Angles must be degrees! */
.
.
.
DegreeAngle
StallComputation(DegreeAngle Angle)
{
.
.
.
  if (Angle == 90) ...
}
.
.
.
DegreeAngle theta, beta = 180;
.
.
.
theta = StallComputation(beta/2.0);
.
.
.
```

If any of the quantities are declared float instead of DegreeAngle, a type error results. Unfortunately, without strong typing that applies to user-defined types, the programmer is deprived of the compiler's aid in detecting inconsistency.

12.1.3 Encapsulation for Data Abstractions

The definition of "objects" in a programming language can be thought of as an extension of the type definition facility. Real support for objects requires some facility for encapsulating data abstractions, in the sense that information hiding is enforced: outside the object's code, its secrets are literally unavailable. To access hidden data structures from outside the object is a syntax error. C lacks some of the necessary encapsulation ability, and the language C++ was invented to remedy this deficiency. Ada has perhaps the best data encapsulation capability of any widespread language because proper support for information hiding was one of Ada's primary design goals. Even without much encapsulation support, information hiding is an important design idea, and there are programs to check for transgressions apart from the compiler. (See Section 12.2.1.)

12.1.4 Run-Time Checking

The concept of type, even with encapsulation, does not cover all the mistakes that people never mean to make in programming. A class of mistakes usually called "run-time errors" is as foolish as type disagreement, and just as common. The archetype run-time error is a bounds violation of a data structure; that is, the subscript indexing an array goes outside the array's defined limits. (And what is more natural than that if the subscript is advancing through the array in a loop?) Or a pointer intended to be following a linked list is improperly set and points off into the wild blue yonder where the list isn't. Or input that was supposed to fit into a buffer happens to be longer than expected and overruns it.

Programs cannot be allowed to commit such transgressions when they execute because the out-of-bounds memory references can destroy data structures and code that are stored where they should have been safe. In a computer memory holding more than one program, what is destroyed may not be part of the application that runs amuck. Most computers of the 1960s had no hardware defense against bounds violations, and when a program went incomprehensibly wrong, the first place to look was at the array subscripts. Unfortunately, the evidence of transgression is usually far removed from the cause, and debugging bounds violations crashes is very difficult. However, not all machines were so badly designed. So-called capability architectures could pinpoint the violation just as it was about to occur, notify the operating system, and prevent damage. In combination with a high-level language, such a system would terminate an offending program with a message like:

```
Subscript 1001 is out of bounds for array Arr4[1000]
at program statement 35 in subroutine Calc.
```

The programmers who worked on such a system loved it, but the systems were not a commercial success. The hardware checking made them slower than their competitors at a time when there was not much speed to spare.

Today's popular machine architectures are not capability based, and there was a spectacular failure with a capability design in the 1980s. But today's machines do include some bounds-checking hardware to keep different programs from trashing each other. About ten years after this hardware was ubiquitous, the most popular operating systems are beginning to use it. Perhaps there is hope that in the future bounds checking will advance to where it was in 1960. It can be argued that to continue to permit programs to run wild is irresponsible behavior that would not be condoned in any other engineering profession.

Take responsibility ▶

Bounds violations are not the only run-time errors although they are the most catastrophic. Another common difficulty is illegal hardware operations, such as the attempt to divide by zero, or to add to an integer that already is at the maximum value a storage word can hold. Again, no one means to make such a mistake, but they happen frequently. Early computers were good at detecting such "overflow" conditions, and before operating systems existed, the hardware would simply halt and display an error light.

One hopes the bank's customer, the airplane passenger, or the patient being X-rayed, doesn't mind the answer being wrong.

In this area there has been negative progress—in the interests of speed, some modern machines do not have any hardware mechanism for detecting overflow. Of course, overflow is not catastrophic—the program doesn't crash; it just gets the wrong answer.

It was early recognized by those whose hardware or operating system failed to detect and forbid the occurrence of run-time errors that a programming language compiler could do the job instead. A compiler can surround any code that might go wrong with instructions to check first, and issue run-time messages. It would be as if every C programmer who wanted to write

```
Arr[Index] = ...
```

for an array with bounds [LB..UB] had to write instead:

```
if (Index < LB || Index > UB)
  {
    printf("Out of bounds...");
    exit(1);
  }
else
    Arr[Index] = ...
```

except that the compiler would add the checking code automatically. This "debugging option" on a compiler produces programs that run much more slowly than programs similarly checked using hardware support. A capability architecture incurs a penalty of a few percent on each store instruction; a debugging compiler slows down by a *factor* of about five. But the hardware and the operating system don't need to cooperate to make a debugging compiler work.

With their high run-time overheads, debugging compilers always provide a way to turn off the checking code, and programmers almost universally turn it off when they think they are done debugging. Thus when it matters, in real use, there is no check on run-time errors. There has never been a successful commercial system in which checking was required as a part of the language design—until now. The Java programming language requires checks for run-time errors, and requires them to be permanently in place. If Java continues its rapid rise to the top, it may put pressure on operating systems, and ultimately on hardware design, to get us systems that are just a bit slower, but ever so much safer.

It is unfortunate that there is no general solution to dealing with run-time errors. One of the triumphs of computability theory is to show that they *cannot*, in principle, be prevented or detected except when they occur in execution. If we insist on using pointers, or dividing, and so on, then the pointers can go out of bounds, and the divisor can be zero, and there is nothing to be done to prevent or detect this in programming language design or at compile time. An operating system in cooperation with computer hardware, or an interpreter, or a debugging option on a compiler can detect run-time errors at run time. But it always costs something in execution speed.

12.1.5 Program Redundancy Checking

The idea of run-time checking as a hedge against mistakes no one means to make but that get made anyway can be extended to encompass any and all unexpected things that might go wrong with a program. Everyone has encountered cases in which data structures "got messed up" for unknown reasons. One doesn't know exactly what went wrong, but somehow the linked list pointers got destroyed, or the array index stored in the table was trashed, and so forth. It is an extreme kind of "defensive programming" to put redundant, "checking" code into a program to try to catch arbitrary mistakes. Some examples will indicate the possibilities:

Data structures. A check for unexpected damage, by recording extra information, can be completed. Checksums can be used to detect bad values. Any pointer can be checked by keeping a back pointer at its destination. Once such mechanisms are in place, special code can be invoked to made a rudimentary check on the integrity of data. A *really* careful programmer makes the checking code a separate process, which includes a timeout parameter to catch checking attempts that themselves would go wrong if the structure is badly damaged. For example, it is unsafe to check a linked list that might have become circular.

Multiversion programming (MVP). This is a name given to coding a solution to a problem more than once. Of course, there isn't any use in writing a routine to do some calculation, calling it twice, and comparing the results. But suppose two routines were written using different algorithms for the same calculation. Then one might very well serve as a check on the other.

Impossible conditions. These conditions are often exploited by programmers to save a few cycles. The programmer *knows* that there are only a few possibilities for a data value, so having tested for all but one of the values assumes the value to be the one remaining. It's safer to make all the tests explicit, and always include an ELSE case to cover the "impossible" situation that the value is *none* of the expected ones.

Take responsibility ▶

It takes a different mindset to always be asking, "How can I explicitly check that nothing has gone wrong?" But it has proven to be much superior to the head-in-the-sand, "How could anything go wrong?"

12.1.6 Assertions

The assertion is a specific kind of run-time check, expressed in the values of program variables at a particular point in the program. The name comes from "asserting" that some formula takes some value at this point. Assertions come into their own when a calculation is difficult or error prone, but there exists a simple way to verify that the result is correct. Then coding the result check at the end of the calculation is a perfect way to be sure it has come out correctly. Most of us used this idea when we were forced to check long division problems by hand. It is far easier to multiply the quotient by the dividend than to repeat the division. (It has been suggested that had Intel used a multiplication check on their division algorithm, it would have found the famous "Pentium bug.")

Any run-time check can be viewed as an assertion. Running through a table looking at checksums, for example, is asserting that nothing is amiss in the table; checking a subscript before using it is asserting that it is not out of bounds, and so on. However, assertions are more usually placed just following some calculation, with the narrow task of verifying that result. Thus it is more the character of an assertion to examine one checksum just as each item is put in the table, or to look at a subscript as it is being stored for later use. Such assertions have the advantage that when they are violated, the violation is pinpointed. More diffuse run-time checks show that something has gone wrong, but the source of the problem may still be hard to trace.

Here is a simple example of assertion code, to be placed just after array A[LB..UB] is sorted into ascending order:

```
for (tmpi = LB; tmpi < UB; tmpi++)
  {
    if (A[tmpi] > A[tmpi+1])
      { /* Assertion failure! */
      printf("Array A not sorted at %d.\n", tmpi);
      exit(1);
      }
  }
```

12.1.7 And When a Problem Is Caught—What Then?

Perhaps the reason that programmers are reluctant to use run-time checks, and hardware and operating system designers are reluctant to support them, is that no one really wants such a check to succeed in detecting a problem. If the check "fires" when the program is being executed, what is there to do? This is an immediate dilemma for the programmer who codes the check as an IF statement and is then faced with filling in the actions that should follow. Somehow it seems better to hope that nothing will go wrong, save checking code and its execution time, and not be faced with that open { after the IF. There is a psychological name for this common state of mind: denial. But programs do fail, programmers do make mistakes, and "I'd rather not know . . . " isn't OK.

Take responsibility ▶

There are a few cases in which there is something unexceptionable to do when a run-time check fails. For example, it is common practice in numerical analysis routines to treat a floating-point underflow or overflow by scaling the data and repeating the calculation until it does not fail, then hoping that continuing calculations will bring the value back into floating-point range so the scale factor can be removed. Occasionally, a corrupted data structure can be reconstructed from the original source or from a backup copy. As a third example, if MVP is being used, it makes sense to code using *three* algorithms, and when there is disagreement, accept any result on which two agree.

However, it is the nature of unexpected or "impossible" errors that in general no satisfactory correction is possible. A subscript bounds violation, for example, cannot be fixed. An impossible condition cannot be "handled" by definition. There is one general course of action a programmer can take: the code can put everything in the best state possible, save as much information as seems useful, log a message describing the problem, and then halt or restart. Something will always be lost, of course. Engaging in an interactive dialog with the program user may be useful in deciding how much to save and just how to abort, but mostly the user can't help. In some cases, aborting is exactly the right thing to do. A miscalculated radiation dose in a cancer treatment X-ray machine, calls for shutting the machine off. That will cause some trouble in rescheduling the treatment, restarting the machine, and so on, but the patient and the hospital should prefer this to a lethal dose being administered. The big advantages in aborting for run-time failure are two: (1) the damage is likely to be minimized (compared to compounding the problem by treating bad data as good and likely corrupting everything more and more as the program executes), and (2) the saved information makes it much easier to fix the problem (compared to examining the mess after corruption has spread). Assertions are particularly good in realizing these advantages.

People who don't like run-time checks are fond of posing situations in which it is *not* acceptable to abort. If the program is controlling the flight of an aircraft that will plunge to earth without that control, then what? There is no answer except that perhaps the aircraft designers should have thought of that before building a plane so dependent on software.

12.1.8 Macro Capability

Many programming languages include a compile-time macro capability. The programmer can define an identifier that will be replaced by an arbitrary string, as a way to centralize and control repeated usages. In C, the macro facility is invoked by the #define construction. In its simplest form, #define can be used to establish symbolic names for constants of a programs placing the defined value in a single textual location for easy location and change. A very common usage is illustrated by:

```
#define BUFSIZ 1023
 .
 .
 .
char buffer[BUFSIZ+1];
```

Macros are even more useful when used with parameters, much like procedure calls. The difference between a real procedure call and a macro invocation is that the latter is expanded into the #defined text at compile time so that the macro "call" incurs no run-time overhead. Macros with parameters have many clever uses. One of the most important occurs in information hiding, in making efficient references to hidden data. Suppose that a module has as its secret that a global array HideIt is being used to hold information, and that there is to be an access function PutItIn(x) to store item x (in the array, but no one knows that except PutItIn). Also suppose that the sequential subscript for the next item is stored in HideIt[0]. Instead of writing an actual function, using a macro:

```
#define PutItIn(x) (HideIt[HideIt[0]++]=(x))
```

will use the array directly in the most efficient manner. Parentheses are recommended around macro arguments because one does not know the values that may be substituted, nor the context of substitution.

When a language lacks a macro capability, it may be worthwhile considering the use of a separate preprocessor to take programs containing macros and expand the macro before invoking the compiler. (In fact, this is how C #define works in UNIX systems.)

12.1.9 Programming-Language Libraries

A programmer uses procedures in a language like C to collect the statements for common functions and avoid repeating their code. The language itself uses procedures as the mechanism of the *C library*, a large collection of useful predefined functions. Library routines are so frequently used that most people consider them part of the C language, a part that just happens to be implemented by a different mechanism from the language statements that are not compiled into library calls. Perhaps the most commonly used C statement is in fact a library routine call: printf().

It is well worth surveying the library of your programming language. You may find that substantial difficult parts of your coding are already done and available in efficient and correct library code. It can even happen that the compiler actually replaces an apparent library routine with in-line code, for example, where some special machine instruction is available to perform the work directly.

Here is a small sample, selected haphazardly to show the power of the C library:

Mathematical routines. C has the usual elementary functions like `exp()`, `cos()`, and a great variety of others. The algorithms used for these functions are well known, but more often to numerical analysts than to software engineers. A case in point is the high-quality random number generator `random()`.

Input/output conversions. The much-used `scanf()` and `printf()` are very complicated routines that we can all be thankful are given. Perhaps less well known are a plethora of conversion routines that extract internal quantities from ASCII strings, such as `atol()`, which converts a character string of digits to the internal `long int` format. The ultimate in this kind of processing, which is used when the programmer wants complete control over the input, is `sscanf()`, which works from a string in memory rather than an input device.

String processing. C doesn't really have strings, but its zero-terminated character arrays are used for strings (and called by that name, however wrongly), and there are library routines to work with them. For example, `index()` finds a character within a string, and `memmem()` finds a substring. Library routines are not always what they should be; according to the GNU documentation, `memmem()` has some nasty bugs. Library routines have restrictions that are an essential part of their use. For example, `strcat()`, which appends one string to another, requires that the strings not overlap in memory.

Document it! ▶
(Know what you've assumed)

Operating system calls. C has complete access to the collection of UNIX low-level system calls that give the language as much control over the environment as any program is allowed. The list of system calls is worth of study along with the C library. (Each has an entry `intro()` in the on-line manual that gives general information.) Among many examples, `execve()` allows one program to execute another, and `sigvec()` gives access to the interrupt facilities.

Miscellaneous. Some library routines are so elaborate and special purpose that they are more like programs or even systems. The documentation can be so hard to read that it hardly seems worth the trouble. An exception is `profil()`, which allows a program to time its internal parts to discover which of them is using what fraction of the execution time.

In object-oriented languages like Smalltalk or Java, the "object" construction of the language allows even more complex and useful libraries than in C. It is no overstatement to say that in most applications, knowledge of the object-oriented class library is more important than the whole rest of the programming language.

12.1.10 Error-Prone Programming Language Constructions

Every programming language has "features" that are obviously (seen in retrospect, of course) error prone, constructions that experienced programmers learn to avoid or to check with extra care. Programming language design is an art that is imperfectly understood, and the best intentions of designers go astray. Often, a small amount of programmer discipline can compensate for a language's problems. For example, it has been observed that people are not very good at grasping the order of a complex sequence of operations whose grouping is not explicitly indicated. Yet most programming languages include a default "precedence" that allows expressions to be written whose meaning is opaque to people. C, with its plethora of low-level operations like ++, and <<, and its inclusion of the assignment operator in expressions, is particularly dangerous. Yet the programmer can simply establish the rule that parentheses will always be used, and thereby avoid trouble.

> Pascal attempts to control one precedence abuse. Its syntax *requires* parentheses in compound logical expressions.

By far the most common deficiency in common languages (including C) is a failure to enforce type agreement, especially across subroutine parameter interfaces.

Programming language syntax might be viewed as unimportant since it must be consistent and well defined for compilers to work, and hence questions can always be accurately answered by reading the manual. But syntax, like all notation, does matter, and there are many pitfalls for the language designer. COBOL, for example, is too wordy—the programmer is likely to develop carpal tunnel syndrome trying to type a simple arithmetic assignment. FORTRAN does not use reserved words, so the programmer is allowed to choose (perhaps by mistake) variable names like IF at the cost of considerable confusion.

> FORTRAN has = for assignment, but it uses .EQ., .LT., and so on for comparisons. So its users never make mistakes with =, whereas C users, with better comparison operators, do.

C has a somewhat antiquated syntax that combines some of the worst features of the ALGOL languages with arcane bits from languages out of the mainstream. No C "feature" is so nasty as the use of == for equality and = for assignment. C's pointer syntax is also particularly confusing, partly because the precedence conventions are not easy to remember. The pointer declaration is put on the variable instead of the type, and C does not distinguish between marking a pointer and the operation of "pointing to." Pascal is much better in this regard; contrast the two blocks of code:

```
Pascal                      C
  ⋮                           ⋮
var pI: ↑integer;           int *pI;
  ⋮                           ⋮
NEW(pI);                    pI = (int *)malloc (sizeof (int));
pI↑ := 99;                  *pI = 99;
  ⋮                           ⋮
```

Some of the peculiarities of programming languages can be attributed to the paucity of symbols available on keyboards, a lack that was much more pronounced in the days of upper case-only keypunch machines. To this day, we lack a standard keyboard containing the character ← (an ideal assignment operator), and standard comparison operations like ≤, not to mention the universal symbol for multiplication ×. It would also be desirable if we could use sub- and superscripts in programs although there seems no good way to type them.

> It is a characteristic illiteracy of programmers to outside a program use * when they mean ×.

12.1.11 Choosing a Programming Language

The choice of programming language is usually made on grounds other than its appropriateness for software engineering. Hardware may be dictated for which only some languages are implemented (for example, Ada is not well supported on PCs). Or the particular application may need special support libraries that are easiest to find for special languages (for example, the "visual" languages provide support for point-and-click applications). Or it may be desirable to copy components from an existing system, so the language of that system must be used.

If such overriding real constraints were not present, which is the best language to use in developing software using the principles of software engineering? Probably the contenders are Ada, C++, and Java because they have support for information hiding. There is certainly no agreement on *the* software engineering language, although C++ is more popular in private industry and Ada in government, particularly for the U.S. Department of Defense, which defined Ada and mandates its use.

A student of the history of programming languages can't help being disappointed by the "progress" that has been made in mainstream language design since FORTRAN was invented in 1953. The ALGOL family of languages was a significant achievement, but its penetration into commercial use was never strong (perhaps because these languages were more difficult to compile, and early compilers were often terrible, if they existed at all). Its Pascal variant was once universally taught in universities, but the information-hiding language of the line (Modula) never saw much use even in classrooms. Ada is Pascal based, but it is a complex language designed by committee for the military, and that's at least three strikes against it.

> C. A. R. Hoare: "ALGOL 60 was a vast improvement over most of its successors."

Engineers used (and still use) FORTRAN, probably largely because IBM promoted and supported the language in the days when computers and IBM meant pretty much the same thing. When engineers needed a language for writing nonnumerical software, they turned to C. Among many reasons, perhaps the most important were that C provided direct access to most hardware and operating system features (for example, in memory allocation and interrupt service), and C was simple enough that good compilers were not difficult to write. (Those were among C's design goals.) There was a snowball effect: in a world of diverse computers, the most widely available language becomes a universal language, just because a universal language is needed. In writing this book, the authors felt that only C knowledge could be assumed in the typical reader. C++ is probably the most widely taught object-oriented language, but far more people know C. One can't escape the feeling that C (and FORTRAN) will go on forever, as other languages come and go. And both of these languages are far inferior to the best of the competitors they outlasted.

However, there is a new language now growing rapidly in popularity, and it's a pretty good language: Java. Section 16.5.3 gives a brief introduction to Java, but here it suffices to say that in a comparison with C, Java comes out far ahead. Its features are:

1. Java supports information hiding.
2. Java has extensive reusable "object" libraries.
3. Java is strongly typed.
4. Java catches run-time errors.
5. Java provides automatic memory management (through "garbage collection").
6. Java code is portable.

C still has some strengths Java doesn't though:

1. C is compiled, whereas Java is interpreted, so C code is faster.
2. C directly uses hardware features for speed (notably pointers) that Java lacks.
3. C uses preprocessing to implement #define and conditional compilation; Java doesn't have these.

That Java is a pretty good language comes in a distant 6th as a reason for its success.

If Java succeeds in making real inroads on C usage, it will probably be because (1) its code is portable, and (2) modern hardware is so fast (and getting faster all the time) that C's better performance doesn't count. (3) Existing Java object libraries are large and growing all the time. Java also has (4) the advantage of being supported as an adjunct to browsers on the Internet, and of (5) having a successful commercial promoter (Sun Microsystems).

12.1.12 Languages for Rapid Prototyping

Rapid prototyping is really an idea that belongs in the requirements, specification, or design phases, not in coding. The reasons for constructing a prototype quickly might be to let a potential user experiment with its human–computer interface or with its functionality, or to investigate a risky aspect of the requirements (in the spiral development model, say), or an aspect of a possible design (in an early stage of iterative enhancement, say). Coding must be used to realize an executable prototype, but it is coding unlike what follows a careful, detailed design. When the full design has been done, there is no reason for a prototype; instead, the real thing is coded. Prototype coding is likely to be "quick and dirty" to realize computer execution without too much time or effort taken; when the final code is crafted, "dirty" is unacceptable, and that precludes "quick."

For prototype coding, there are special languages, often themselves with a "quick and dirty" character. For example, most prototyping languages are interpreted, not compiled, as befits code that is written only to throw away. At the same time, prototyping languages are very "high level," or they could not serve at all. Prolog is certainly such a language, and if the specification takes the form of some kind of logic, Prolog can be very easy to use early on, as exemplified in Section 10.4.2. A pseudocode design language can also be precisely defined, and implemented as a programming language, to really produce executable programs.

Because the human–computer interface is of much concern to the users of a proposed system, special languages exist to trick up an interface without any substance behind it. These interfaces aren't connected to getting any results by computation, and their languages don't seem like "real" languages just because they do no conventional computing operations. But they allow the user to see what kinds of things might appear on the screen.

The UNIX operating system has as an important feature a separation between "kernel" services and "command processes," programs that perform most of the functions of the system. Because it is so easy to write these programs, and to organize their execution into cooperating groups of commands called *shell scripts* (after the primary command process, which is called a shell), "shell-script programming" is a powerful way to do rapid prototyping. It is often possible to begin with a very early pseudocode design, for example, and have it running in minutes with a shell script. An example is given in Chapter 13.

12.2 Support Tools for Programming

Software engineers are heavy computer users themselves. Program development in a high-level language, viewed as a process on a computer, consists of creating and editing files (programs), compiling those files, then linking the compiled (object) files into an executable system. The editor, compiler, and linker are the basic support programs for programming. To distinguish support programs from the program being developed, it is usual to call them "tools," in analogy to the tools that (say) a carpenter uses. Maurice Wilkes has correctly criticized using "tool" to refer to support programs, noting that (say) a hammer is quite unlike a compiler—the hammer is much more general purpose and much easier to use, which Wilkes considers necessary properties of tools—but we will use the word despite its deficiencies.

Software development comprises much more than the mechanics of programming. The software engineer's main stock in trade is knowledge about the software that is being written, and there are many support tools that help to record, analyze, and understand this information. These tools are useful throughout development because they work on information stored in computer files, irrespective of what the files represent. But because program files are the most detailed and complex ones in development, the tools found their first application to programs and continue to be used primarily there.

In order for us to be specific, the tools described in this section will be those available for computers running some variant of the UNIX operating system. (Their UNIX names will be printed here in the "computer" font.) Many of them have versions for other systems, and the UNIX description should be enough to locate what's needed. Most of the tools are in the public domain, and can be found by searching the World Wide Web for downloading free of charge. The descriptions given here are not intended to instruct the reader in making real use of the tools—the manuals, online documentation, and a number of good textbooks are more appropriate for that. Our purpose is to suggest the range of what tools can do, and convince the reader that it is worth looking up the details and using the tools.

12.2.1 Language Analyzers—LCLint

One class of important tools has already been mentioned: language analyzers and preprocessors that compensate for deficiencies in the programming language itself. It may seem a nuisance to use these tools when a "proper" language would not need them, but if the dictated language for development is deficient, it is well worthwhile to systematically employ the compensating tools. When routines are separately compiled, they must be combined for analysis, which is a further nuisance; however, since the interfaces between routines are a notorious source of obscure bugs that are really type errors, again the effort is worthwhile.

The standard checking tool for C is `lint`. In effect, `lint` defines a restricted subset of C and acts as a syntax checker for that subset. Thus many things that are error prone in C, but will compile without complaint on the best of compilers, will be flagged by `lint`. It is a good idea to use `lint` routinely, but there is no excuse for not using it at the first sign of trouble with the execution of any C program.

An extended version of lint called LCLint has been developed at the MIT Laboratory for Computer Science. LCLint can be used as lint is— to check C programs for error-prone constructions. However, by adding "annotations" to a C program (they look to a compiler like comments), the programmer can cause LCLint to perform much stronger checks, which make C appear to be a much safer, more modern language. Sometimes lint is not used because it finds too much: the programmer can't face the plethora of error messages that appear, many not of immediate interest. LCLint has annotations to select which messages will appear.

LCLint checks for unused declarations, violations of strong typing, variables used before being set, unreachable code, function-returned values ignored by caller, likely infinite loops, fall-through in switch statements, and potentially wrong breaks, checks that most versions of lint also make. (If the reader does not see why these checks should be made, chances are that he or she has not been burned by the C deficiency that is being checked. As one example, the break problem was the cause of a huge failure in the AT&T telephone network in 1990.)

With appropriate annotations, LCLint can detect unwanted modification of call state by the called routine, inconsistent use of global variables, memory management errors (leaks and unsafe use of released storage), dangerous aliasing of parameters, dereferencing possibly null pointers, dangerous macros, and unpredictable order of execution. It has the ability to enforce naming conventions for variables. The most ambitious checks that LCLint attempts have to do with the implementation of information hiding in C. LCLint can flag violations of information hiding and encapsulation violations.

It is not too strong a statement to say that with creative use of LCLint, the C programming language is a real competitor for any existing language.

12.2.2 File Utilities

Every operating system has file manipulation commands—for listing the contents of directories—and for copying and moving and removing files. These commands merit some study since they often have somewhat obscure options that help the software engineer. For example, the UNIX "copy" command cp, has an option that preserves time-stamp information about the file copied so that the new copy does not appear to have been created at the time it was copied, but rather at the time the original was created. Using this option makes it easier to remember the origin of files. Another option makes sure that copying does not overwrite any existing file without querying for confirmation, which can prevent expensive mistakes. UNIX has an alias command that allows commands to be redefined, and by redefining cp to have these options always on, the programmer can customize the operating system behavior.

In program development, particularly when many pieces of code are kept in separate files, and these files may each have several versions, the programmer may lose track of what is where. Using a directory hierarchy can be a great help by keeping files in related groups. The time stamps on files in a directory listing are also helpful in sorting out what files contain. Most UNIX command interpreters have a matching facility that can filter file names. For example, if a person wants to look at a file, but remembers only that it is a C program (by convention having a .c extension), and that it has either gen or Gen somewhere in the name, then the directory command:

```
ls *[gG]en*.c
```

will list file names that might be the one wanted. The pattern matching is done using so-called extended regular expressions. These are well worth learning about, and any UNIX system will have online documentation; the manuals for editors also describe them.

12.2.3 Shell Command Scripts

UNIX command interpreters normally accept input from interactive terminals, but have the ability to execute commands from a file. In UNIX jargon, such a file is called a "shell script," and shell scripts are very useful for grouping commonly used commands. The script can use parameters from the command line that invokes it. To give a simple but frequently used example, when a series of commands is repeatedly needed, it makes a useful script. The LaTeX text-processing system requires such a sequence, and the shell script to automate it might look like:

```
#latexIt <file>
# runs LaTeX on <file>.tex, then BibTeX, then creates
# a Postscript file in <file>.ps and tries to view it.
latex $1
bibtex $1
latex $1
latex $1 #LaTeX has to run twice for cross references
dvips -o $1.ps $1.dvi
ghostview $1.ps
```

The intricacies of shell script programming will not be explained here; the UNIX user should avidly read the manual for one of the shells, which run to about 75 pages. (The one used in examples here is the so-called C shell csh.) In the script shown here, # introduces a comment, and $1 is replaced by the first parameter typed on the command line. If this script is properly put into a file `latexIt`, the UNIX user can type:

```
latexIt mybook
```

instead of the sequence:

```
latex mybook
bibtex mybook
latex mybook
latex mybook
dvips -o mybook.ps mybook.dvi
ghostview mybook.ps
```

Simple scripts like this one will go wrong if the LATEX source has an error since the script will blindly continue. It is possible to write a more involved script that handles errors, sends helpful messages to the user, asks the user for direction, and so forth.

12.2.4 grep Searches

When information is misplaced in a file system and file names, dates, and so on, are not enough to recall it, the `grep` family of search routines can be used to examine the contents of files. These search programs locate a given string (which may include regular expression patterns like those in commands) in a group of files. For example, suppose a programmer is trying to find files containing C routines that call a certain function `FooLish`, which has two parameters. The UNIX command

```
grep FooLish *.c
```

might print:

```
fooldef.c: int FooLish (int X, int Y)
calc3.c: seed = FooLish (3,7);
calc3.c: if (FooLish (aBa, AbA) == 0) then
report.c: printf ("%d  %d\n", Index, Foolish (Index,0));
```

which would tell the programmer that the function is declared in `fooldef.c`, used twice in `calc3.c`, and once in `report.c`. If there are spurious matches, for example, against a variable named `FooLish`, the `grep` command could be made to seek a more complicated pattern. But in general, it is safer to use `grep` to search for simple strings and put up with a few false matches—when one attempts to select exactly those strings one wants, mistakes in the regular expression can waste a lot of time and be misleading.

In the time of a television advertisement urging long-distance calls to "Reach out and touch someone," signs appeared on Bell Labs offices of the UNIX development group reading "Reach out and grep someone."

Software engineers are often advised to create and maintain a database of information about each software development project. For all projects but the largest, under the most difficult circumstances, using an actual database program is counterproductive. If the database exists, it is of course easy to query it to find out what one needs to know. But creating the database is extra work, and if mistakes are made, or entries fall behind the other work, a database becomes a liability. The ideal situation would be to create nothing beyond the work itself, reflected in the program and documentation files that are part of the project. In that case, grep can be used to realize most of the features of a database. To find information about any aspect of the project, one searches for strings characteristic of that information, and then looks in the files found by grep to learn whatever is needed. This scheme works much better if some thought is given to placing similar files together in directories, or using a naming convention to make a link between related files. (These tricks will simplify the names that are given to grep to search.) The contents of files can also be exploited. By putting standardized comments or identifier names into files, grep can locate things without using complex patterns. (However, adding nonessential information in this way is like creating a special database: it's extra work, and there is no guarantee that it will be done properly.)

12.2.5 Programmed Searches and Edits

Although grep is a powerful tool, its searches are based on single lines of information, and sometimes what one needs to find or process in files is related to more than one line. For example, one might want to find all the C programs in which a function call extends over several lines of program text. In documentation, one might want to find all the places where the word *where* immediately follows a blank line.

More complicated searches can be done with most interactive text editors (but usually using noninteractive commands that are classed as "expert" usage). UNIX also has a noninteractive editor with the necessary capabilities, called sed. One writes simple "programs" for these editors, telling them to locate something (perhaps using a pattern) and then to continue with other actions.

A second mechanism for processing files is to use a "little language." This name is given to programming languages that are much simpler than C and designed to be easily implemented to accomplish some special purpose. Two well-known little languages whose purpose is text file processing are awk and perl. They have few of the usual language's sophisticated features like data types and block structure, but make up for this with special constructions that make processing lines in files easy. For example, the awk program:

```
/^$/ {getline; print $1 $NF}
```

will print the first word and the last word in any line that immediately follows a blank line in a file.

A person can learn a little language in a very short time; indeed, the manual for awk is only a few pages long and is mostly composed of examples.

Programs like awk and sed make it very easy to do simple file operations that are beyond grep. However, they are in fact general-purpose programming languages, so they can be used to do very complicated things as well. A good rule to follow is to use elaborate programs only when there is a repeating problem. It makes sense to spend hours writing and testing an awk program only if what it does will save hours of more tedious effort; it does not make sense to program up a storm in awk to make a few changes that could be edited by hand.

Too much engineering is not a good thing

12.2.6 Comparing Files

The reason for seeking information in files is often so that it can be changed. After changes have been made, the problem of too many files is multiplied because a prudent person never discards or overwrites the "old" versions, but just adds "new" versions to the file system. "New" and "old" versions also arise because changes to files are imported from outside. For example, software distributed from a central source may arrive in the latest release while the old version is still around. In such cases, it is very valuable to be able to compare two files and have their differences presented in readable form. If one line has been changed in a huge file, the only way to come to grips with what this signifies is to see that line, not the whole file. The UNIX program diff does a pretty good job of comparing text files based on their lines. It prints a minimal set of differences, showing what was in both files. For example, if one.c and two.c differ only in that two.c was obtained by deleting line 95 and fixing a syntax error in line 162, the output from:

```
diff one.c two.c
```

might be:

```
95d94
< for (i = 1; i < 10; i++) { };
162c161
< if x = 3 and x < 9
  .
  .
  .
> if (x == 3 && x < 9)
```

The carats identify the contents of the two files, < for the first file, and > for the second, and the number–letter combinations give the position and action required. When a programmer makes a small change, then can't remember what was done or which file was which, `diff` is the ideal tool to solve the problem.

Files that have the format of a `diff` listing can also be used to "patch" either of the two files into the other one. (Thus it would not be necessary to keep both files to retain all the information; one file and the `diff` between them would have the same content. This is a way that version control systems, described in Section 12.2.8, store multiple files efficiently.)

12.2.7 The `make` Utility

When software is to be constructed from many distinct files, the commands to properly compile and link the complete system can become complicated. Furthermore, when some or all of the files are being updated, perhaps by several different people simultaneously, it is easy to forget to recompile everything that has been changed. When a compilation is forgotten, what usually happens is that the system links and runs properly, but changes in the uncompiled file have not "happened" at all. When just one change was made, this effect merely puzzles the programmer: "Why didn't my fix work?" and is soon corrected. But if many changes were made, the failure to recompile may not be noticed, and the linked system will contain an uncorrected bug that may not be detected for a long time. Worse, when the offending file *is* finally recompiled, a forgotten and untried change will appear in it.

A more subtle problem occurs when sources `#include` one another. When X and Y `#include` Z, and Z is changed, both X and Y have to be recompiled. Current practice in developing systems in C relies on extensive "header" files, usually named with a `.h` extension, that are `#included` in many C sources, supplying declarations and type definitions to them all. Should one of these header files be modified, all the C programs that depend on it must be recompiled, and if some compilations are forgotten, the errors introduced can be subtle and nasty.

The UNIX utility `make` was designed to mechanize the creation of complex systems and to automatically force recompilation as needed. It was designed specifically to solve the problem of properly compiling and linking a set of dependent program files, but it can be creatively used whenever files are interrelated and must be processed in a complicated way when changes are made. For example, `make` could be used to run a series of updating programs prior to generating a report that depends on data being current.

Although `make` is a very important idea in building systems, the tool works by a simple brute-force algorithm. It is driven by a "makefile" that explicitly lists all the files that each other file depends on, and gives the command that must be used to process each file should changes require it. The make user supplies this makefile, and creating it takes time and care. With this information, make can operate in an obvious way, using only the time stamps on files in directories. When make is run, it looks at the dependency information. Suppose that file S depends on file H, and that S is used to create T. If the time stamp on H is later than the time stamp on T, then H has changed, and S must be processed (compiled, if S is a program) before it is used to create a current T. When all the necessary commands have been run to compensate for all the changes indicated by the pattern of current time stamps, the necessary system will have been recreated with all changes in place. In the case of building a system, the last command will be to link all the updated object files. Of course, make can also be used to do other utility work: discard temporary files, move files from one directory to another, etc.

There is nothing magic about make: if there is a mistake in the makefile (for example, a missing or erroneous dependency), make will carefully build the wrong system just as instructed. But once a proper makefile has been created, the programmer need not think about the processing needed for system construction ever again. Like many software engineering tools, make does not come into its own until relatively complicated systems are to be built. For a few source files all kept in a single directory, it is just as good to recompile all the files and relink, every time anything changes.

12.2.8 Version-Control Tools

For a very complex software project, especially when many people are involved, it may be wise to put the project under "configuration management," as described in Section 5.4.2. Tool support can be useful in controlling the versions of files once the management procedures are in place. But once again, heavy machinery may be more hindrance than help in a small or individual project. The basic UNIX tool for version control is rcs, but here we will describe a more recent tool called cvs, which is becoming a standard for the production of "open software," where the source is freely distributed and programmers all over the world contribute their work. (The "Linux" version of UNIX is probably the best known open software system.)

The mechanism of version control is to store one complete file as a "base," and then to store subsequent modifications of that base not as new files with new names, but rather as "versions" of the base file under the same name, as "deltas," in which only the changes are recorded. (The mechanism of diff described in Section 12.2.6 could be used to store the deltas.) The file complex that holds the base file and its deltas is called the "repository." When the base file is large and changes are small, this mechanism saves a lot of disk space. However, the primary virtue of the version control storage mechanism lies in the power it gives its users. They can retrieve from the repository the latest version of the file, but they can also retrieve any earlier

Intellectual control ▶

version without remembering any naming convention. For example, a user can call for a `diff` between the latest version and the previous version to see what change was made.

In the simplest use of version control, files are put into the repository, then edited, and the most recent versions are used to build a system. Occasionally, it is necessary to retreat to earlier versions for some system parts, when changes are in error, for example. The repository serves as backup, and as documentation for changes. Management can track software progress by examining the repository.

Version control comes into its own, however, when more than one person is working on a file. Without version control, multiple file users face the potential problem of conflicting editing, and failure to synchronize file storage may cause work to be garbled or lost. The simplest case is that two people begin editing the same file, both save it at about the same time, and the first person to save loses out because the second save overwrites the first. And if that were not bad enough, no one will even know that the first person's work has been lost. With version control, file conflicts can be controlled. Here is how `cvs` handles things in the simplest case:

> When anyone begins work on a file (by "checking it out" of the repository), the version checked out is noted; for concreteness, suppose version 5 of a file is checked out by two people at work simultaneously. The first person to attempt to put the file back into the repository ("checking it in") will succeed because the version in the repository is the one that was checked out, and the newly stored file will become version 6. Should the second person attempt to check in the changed file based on version 5 (let's call it V), the current version (6) is not what was checked out, so it may not be safe to check V in. To see, `cvs` compares version 6 with V. If the set of changes made by the two people do not textually conflict, they are merged and stored as a new version 7, and a message is logged to that effect. It will appear as if version 7 were created by the second person beginning with version 6 instead of version 5, so nothing is lost. (The person checking in V might be concerned about what is actually in version 6, but can do a `diff` between versions 5 and 6 to find out.) The worst case is that V does conflict textually with the changes in version 6. In that case, `cvs` does not check in V, but provides the second user with a special comparison file Q, which represents a potential version 7. In Q, a `diff`-like syntax is used to display the conflicting changes from version 6 and V. The user can choose which lines should be saved, and when Q has been edited to contain a single change in all conflict areas, it can be checked in as version 7, with a message logged about the resolution.

The algorithms used by `cvs` to resolve conflicts are the least restrictive possible, and of course do not always result in versions that all the people involved would consider best. But no information is lost, and a log records what happened.

It should be evident that configuration management is just as useful for documents associated with requirements, specification, design, and with test plans and tests, as it is for code.

12.3 Adding to the Test Plan While Coding

The basis of a good test plan is the functional test cases that are derived from the requirements, both for normal and "error" conditions described there. These cases are augmented during design to cover additional "functions" that may be invisible to the user, but that the designer has added, notably the "unit tests" for the particular components to be implemented. Fault-based tests also come up in design to check that difficult or error-prone conditions are correctly implemented. Test cases added to the test plan during the coding phase are of much less importance. However, it often happens that a programmer comes up with "worries" while trying to code some routine, concerns that it may not have been done correctly. Each such worry can be the source of a fault-based test case to reassure the programmer.

For example, a table into which several pointers are kept might start out with contents zeroed. The initial zeroes are not supposed to be significant, but a programmer might worry that there is somewhere an implicit reliance on them. A fault-based test to settle this worry might put a few items in the table, remove them, insert one new item, and then try some functions that will yield the wrong result if the zero entries matter.

Not the least important reason for putting "worry" tests into the test plan is to catch maintenance mistakes. The programmer's worry may be unfounded when the code is finished. But if the worry concerned something that really is difficult to get right, it may well happen that another programmer, making a change later, messes it up and will be caught by the fault-based test.

How Does It Fit?

From section 12.1

1. What will be the result if the code fragment with the strong typing errors at the beginning of Section 12.1.1 is run? (If one of its problems obscures the others, imagine that the obscuring problem were removed so that the others would also show up.)

2. Some run-time bounds violations cannot cause destruction of code or data in memory. Give an example, and comment on whether such a violation is worth detecting.

3. If a run-time error is detected during the execution of a production program, and the program is terminated, should a message be printed for the user, or what should be done and why?

4. The Pascal language explored the concept of strong typing for the explicit purpose of preventing the mistakes that no one wants to make, turning them into syntax errors. Pascal made a serious attempt to deal with run-time errors using types. Such an attempt cannot succeed entirely because the computability theory results forbid it, but it was surprisingly effective. If you know Pascal well, explain why it is *impossible* to get an "array out of bounds" message at runtime. Also explain why this language design feature has not been used in other languages (for example, Ada) that are based on Pascal.

5. Explain what is undesirable about a macro definition

   ```
   #define sqr(x) x*x
   ```

   when used as sqr(t + 3).

6. What does a call on vfork() do? Why isn't this routine in the C library online manual section?

7. Consider the two C expressions:

   ```
   X && Y !! Z
   X !! Y && Z
   ```

   Add parentheses to show the way your C compiler interprets them.

From section 12.2

8. Why is an unused declaration an important error to flag?

9. What is "the break problem" for C?

10. Most people who write a routine like:

    ```
    /* append B to A and store in C */
    concatenate(char *A, char *B, char *C)
    ```

    do not think of a call like:

    ```
    concatenate(S, S, S);
    ```

    This is the "dangerous aliasing" that LCLint checks for. What could go wrong here?

11. Consult the C shell manual to discover how to check that a command has terminated in error, and rewrite the LaTeX script to abort with appropriate messages if any step fails. Are there steps that cannot fail?

12. By guessing (or finding out from documentation) how diff works, make up a file and a small change to that file that diff will fail to analyze well.

13. When several people are using cvs for open software development, and one of them is informed of a conflict on check-in, what are the responsibilities of that person? What tools will be useful in carrying out those responsibilities?

From section 12.3

14. In the example of a programmer "worry" about a table being zeroed, suggest an alternative to worrying and fault-based testing.

Review Questions

1. Contrast type errors (detected at compile time) with run-time errors.
2. List the UNIX support tools described in Section 12.2 in a table, and with a few keywords indicate the use of each one in program development.

Further Reading

Anyone interested in programming language design should read C. A. R. Hoare's essay [Hoa73], if only to see that today's most popular languages make far too many of the mistakes that were well understood in 1970. To read (say) the ANSI C standard [AN90] is to weep over the lessons that have remained unlearned after 20 years, and the stupid mistakes in language design that make our best tools so much less useful than they might be.

There are languages specifically designed for software engineering; Eiffel [Mey92] is perhaps the most interesting. C++ is perhaps the most pedestrian of the object-oriented languages [Str97].

ALGOL 68 made many important contributions to the science of programming languages, clarifying ideas like syntax versus semantics, and type definition and usage. It isn't easy to penetrate the defining report [vWMPK69], but aids are available [LvdM71]. Pascal [Wir71] also made important contributions to language design, particularly in its attempt to pull run-time checking into strong type checking.

The impetus for hardware run-time checking came from the first attempts at multiprogramming—running more than one process in the same memory at concurrent times. To hope to succeed with this requires foolproof bounds checking. The first such system was the Ferranti Atlas [KHPS61], which was doing in the 1950s on hardware with a few thousand bytes of memory, what mainstream PC systems are only now beginning to attempt. In the early 1960s, Burroughs developed the B5000 computer system [Cor66], which had only high-level programming languages (its operating system was written in a version of ALGOL), an ALGOL compiler that is a model of step-wise-refinement coding, and complete run-time bounds checking. When a run-time error occurred, the programmer received from the operating system not only the message about which array and subscript, but a dump of the call stack listing routines and their parameter values.

Several people who have done a lot of coding, and thought about it afterward, have written fat books to convey their experience. Perhaps the best of them is McConnell's [McC93]. A good way to learn about books, once you know the title of one on a well-defined subject, is to go to one of the online booksellers like Amazon.com, where they maintain links between similar books. If there is a competitor for McConnell's book, for example, even if it is recent, it will show up under Amazon's "People who bought this book also bought ____."

"GNU" is an
unusual acronym
since it stands
for "GNUs Not
UNIX."

The so-called GNU software distributed (free, of course!) by the Free Software Foundation has a good reputation and is widely used. The licensing agreement that users of GNU software must sign makes interesting reading because it states that although the software is free, it may be used as part of software that is sold, so long as no attempt is made to sell the GNU programs themselves or restrict their distribution.

The World Wide Web is touted for its wonders, but anyone who tries to use it for information gathering soon acquires reservations about its usefulness. But for obtaining software, the Web is an unqualified success. A particular package (like LCLint) can usually be found more easily with a search engine than by trying to remember its URL.

References

[AN90]   (ANSI). American national standard for programming languages – c. 1990.

[Cor66]   Burroughs Corporation. *A narrative description of the Burroughs B5500 disk file master control program*. Burroughs Corp., 1966.

[Hoa73]   C. A. R. Hoare. Hints on programming language design. 1973. Invited address, Symposium on Principles of Programming Languages, Boston.

[KHPS61]   T. Kilburn, D. Howarth, R. Payne, and F. Sumner. The manchester university atlas operating system. *Computer Journal*, pages 222–225, 1961.

[LvdM71]   C. H. Lindsey and S. G. van der Meulen. *Informal Introduction to ALGOL 68*. North-Holland, 1971.

[McC93]   Steve McConnell. *Code Complete: A Practical Handbook of Software Construction*. Microsoft Press, 1993.

[Mey92]   Bertrand Meyer. *Eiffel: The Language*. Prentice-Hall, 1992.

[Str97]   Bjaine Stroustrup. *The C++ Programming Language*. Addison-Wesley, 1997.

[vWMPK69]   A. van Wijngaarten, B. J. Mailloux, J. E. L. Peck, and C. H. A. Koster. Report on the algorithmic language algol 68. *Numerische Mathematik*, 14:79–218, 1969.

[Wir71]   Nicklaus Wirth. The programming language pascal. *Acta Informatica*, pages 35–63, 1971.

Pseudocode

P eople who solve problems using so-called imperative coding—step-by-step instructions on how to solve a problem—often begin by drawing a flowchart, or by jotting down in English a description of the steps to be taken. *Pseudocode* is the name for rough, textual step-by-step descriptions of how to solve a problem. A pseudocode program (pseudoprogram?) looks rather like a C program, except that its "statements" are more like comments than C. Pseudocode is the least formal of formal design methods, but it may be the most useful.

13.1 Designing with Pseudocode

There need not be any precise description of the pseudoprograms that can be written in pseudocode—the designer may just make up whatever notation seems to be useful. On the other hand, it is perfectly possible to define formally a pseudocode "language" as carefully as a programming language is defined. In an extreme case, the pseudocode language would *be* nothing different from a programming language, but presumably a better one for design than the language chosen for coding. In the 1970s, when both the idea of pseudocode and the Pascal language were new, a serious proposal was put forward to use Pascal as a design language. The Pascal programs were to be written down but never compiled, and these program documents were to be used to direct the real programming in FORTRAN. (That there were FORTRAN compilers for most computers, but very few Pascal compilers, made this proposal a little less ridiculous than it seems now.) The idea that pseudocode might be compiled into an executable program is intriguing and deserves further discussion.

Would it be good to have a programming-language–like definition for pseudocode? On the one hand, it appears to be a virtue in any language that

it be precisely defined, and if pseudocode could be executed, it would eliminate one whole phase of the development lifecycle. But from another viewpoint, precision is just what pseudocode *doesn't* need. Pseudocode *ought* to
be fuzzy, as befits its role in design, which is to capture big, high-level ideas.
And without precise definition, there seems no chance of executing pseudocode since execution is the most precise of processes. The fuzzy nature of
good pseudocode can be understood best in terms of "data structures" that
pseudocode uses. To be precise, these should be well defined things like arrays, linked lists, heaps, and B-trees. But if precise structures are used, then
imprecise statements, such as

```
Find the largest account balance
```

are not appropriate. Instead, if the structure containing the account bal-
ances is an array, one ought to write a loop examining all its elements to
find the largest, or keep it sorted, or use some other particular algorithm.
And for the purposes of design, to give such details would be a mistake. The
details do not *have* to be considered immediately, and far better intellectual control results if they are deferred. The need to find the largest balance
comes first, and at that level what comes next is what to do with it after it's
found, *not* the details of finding it.

**Fuzzy into
focus** ▶

There is a compromise position in the conflict between fuzzy pseudocode and precise, programming-language–like pseudocode. The data
structures could be so high level that the algorithms to manipulate them
do not interfere with thinking about the problem to be solved. Mathematical sets are one such data structure because sets have no order, no problems
with duplicate elements, and a direct operation ("member," symbolized
∈) to decide if an element is present. And sets are a perfectly good data
structure for execution—Pascal has them, for example. But the conflict over
executability has not gone away—if precise pseudocode has very high-level
data structures, the conflict has merely moved to a new arena. Set operations can be executed, but not very efficiently, compared to operations on
more usual data structures. So designing with sets is OK, but it is likely that
coding will later be required, using some other data structure. Meanwhile,
if efficiency is not important, as it is not for checking out the functionality
of algorithms, the pseudocode could be directly executed by the designer,
or even demonstrated to a user to check if some requirement were being
correctly handled.

Pseudocode languages that can be compiled into (inefficient) executing code exist, but they are not much used, whether because they are too
inefficient, or too difficult to use easily in design is not clear. The vast majority of pseudocode designers just make it up as they go along, using vague
English words like "store the result" to avoid getting caught up in the inappropriate data structure detail. There is not so much opposition to using
the precise control structures of programming languages, and the usual

NOTE Spelling the closing word of a construction as the reversal of the opening word is an affectation used in ALGOL 68 ETON.

IF ... THEN ... ELSE ... FI and WHILE ... DO ... OD are much used. Most pseudocode uses closing words rather than brackets around a compound construction, as befits a notation that is first scribbled on bits of scrap paper and so not likely to be carefully indented and aligned.

13.1.1 Example of Pseudocode: Zipf's Law

A peculiar relationship has been observed to exist between the words that compose a large corpus of text and their frequency of occurrence in the text, which makes a nice problem to solve using pseudocode. *Zipf's law* can be stated as follows:

> Let the distinct words in the corpus be arbitrarily labeled w_1, w_2, . . . , w_N. There will likely be more than N total words because some will be repeated. Let the number of times that word w occurs in the corpus be $C(w)$. Let $R(w)$ be the rank order of word w, that is, $R(w_k) = 1$ for the most frequently used word w_k, $R(w_j) = N$ for the least frequently used word w_j, and the others are ordered in between. Then the graph
>
> $$\{(C(w_i), 1/R(w_i))|1 \leq i \leq N\}$$
>
> is approximately a straight line.

Figure 13.1 shows the expected shape of the graph.

Zipf's law is intriguing because it does not to seem to depend on the source of the corpus of text. It holds for Shakespeare's plays and for the worst sort of computer manuals, so long as the text is in a natural language. Making a plot of the relationship for a particular corpus of text is a way of checking the law, but it is also a means of understanding the text since the most frequently used words are the important ones that pin down the subject. Hence the calculation of $R(w)$ can be useful in information retrieval.

Based on the careful description of Zipf's law, it is a sensible requirements statement for a piece of software to say:

> Given a corpus of text as input, make a plot of Zipf's law for it and print the words of the text in rank order, each with its count.

What these requirements omit is any detail about the appearance of the graph to be plotted, and more important, the exact definition of a "word." To be useful, a Zipf's law program must deal with punctuation and with the different grammatical forms of the same word. However, using iterative enhancement as a design technique, we could begin with a program in which "words" are just character strings that appear before white space, and later do better with this aspect of the problem.

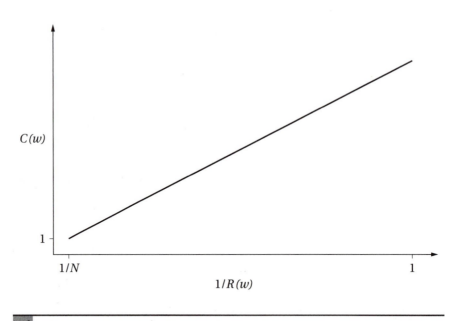

▶ **Figure 13.1**   Zipf's law, word count $C(w)$ vs. inverse word rank $R(w)$.

The pseudocode for the problem is easy to write:

```
WHILE there are unread words in the corpus
  DO
    read the next word W
    IF W is already stored
      THEN
        add 1 to W's count
      ELSE
        store W
        set W's count to 1
      FI
  OD
sort the stored words by their counts,
  largest first, in list V
print V in order
plot the counts against
  the reciprocal of position in V
```

The first part of the pseudocode (the DO ... OD) is explicit in its control structure but very fuzzy about its data structure. The rest of the pseudocode uses well-understood operations (like "sort" and "plot") to avoid explicit control structure, and a more precise data structure (a list) whose properties (its order) are exploited. The decisions about control and data structures are part of the designer's art. The goal is to produce a set of fuzzy instructions that obviously work to solve the problem.

Pseudocode lends itself to a natural decomposition of the problem solution into programming tasks. The interfaces between these program components can be given in programming language syntax to make the pseudocode more precise. In the preceding example, one might imagine four tasks driven by a main program containing the loop. Using C syntax:

```
/* Returns 0 if there are no more words,
   otherwise returns 1
      and the next word in the parameter */
int
GetWord(char *Word)

/* Sorts the words and counts in Vague
   in descending-count order into Lst */
void
Sort(CountsWords Vague[])

/* Prints the words in Lst in order */
void
Print(CountsWords Vague[])

/* Plots the counts in Vague against
   reciprocal position in the list */
void
Plot(CountsWords Vague[])

main()
{
  declare Store V
  WHILE GetWord(W) returns 1
    DO
      /* next word is in W */
      IF W is already stored in V
        THEN
          add 1 to W's count in V
        ELSE
          store W in V
          set W's count in V to 1
        FI
    OD
  Sort(V)
  Print(V)
  Plot(V)
}
```

Thus there are five relatively independent programming assignments here, and the comments (and pseudocode within `main()`) define what the programmers are to do. Programming cannot begin until details are given for the data structures `List` and `Store`, however. If `List` is defined first, then programming of `Print()` and `Plot()` can begin immediately. The main `Store` structure might be a hash table, a linked list, or an array. There is more to do at the design level, but the pseudocode has done its part by describing the main algorithm and its components.

13.1.2 Test Plan for the Zipf's Law Software

Additions to the test plan during design often arise from special cases that were not thought of during requirements analysis, and the tests are often fault based.

For example, in the Zipf's law design, if a hash table is used to store the words, collisions in the hash table are an important special case that should be tested. Another case that might not have been emphasized but is now seen to be a possibility is that two words have exactly the same count—what then is their rank order? The user might have to be consulted, but in any case this is a possible source of difficulties, and should be tested.

13.2 Implementing Pseudocode

The straightforward way of implementing a pseudocode design is to treat the pseudocode as the beginning point for step-wise refinement, and proceed until it is completely converted into code. The refinement steps can be carried out either in pseudocode (and some of them may have already been done in design) or in the programming language that will eventually be executed. Treated in this way, the pseudocode is entirely prescriptive, and the designers can use it to reduce the skill level needed to complete the programming, by making most of the implementation decisions in the design.

However, a pseudocode design can also be used in just the opposite way. It can be viewed by programmers as a description of *what* to do, but one given in a prescriptive way, and therefore flawed. That is, the programmers can see what is to be accomplished by grasping how the design says to do things, and then find their own way to accomplish that same end, perhaps quite differently. If the design is treated in this peculiar fashion, the programmers are essentially doing it over—redesigning—as they go. In a reasonable software development process, it should be agreed at the beginning whether or not programmer redesign is acceptable, and that agreement should be carried out. When an individual is doing both design and code, the agreement is implicitly that there will be no redesign. It seems silly that a person would spend time on design, then ignore the work just done and code it differently. However, having done a design might give the person new ideas, and ignoring rules is what individuals do best.

When design work is done during coding, it may not be recognized as design. The programmer is likely to think, "what does it matter?" and just get on with the job. What will suffer is the documentation. If an existing design document is disregarded, then it must be replaced with what the coder did use. If changes in detail are made, they must be added to the design document. The natural tendency is to put this documentation into code comments, which is entirely inappropriate. Someone (even the single author of both design and code-that-doesn't-follow-the-design) who later has to deal with the software will not be pleased with a design document that tells lies about what really happened. Although it is pseudocode that the coder is most tempted to redesign, these remarks about updating design documentation apply to any changes that come up in coding, whatever design formalism was used.

Pseudocode lends itself nicely to rapid prototyping, and the prototype may very well involve redesign or even respecification to the point of altering the original requirements because of special features of the rapid-prototyping language used. But such drastic changes, of course, do not alter the original documentation. When the real system is coded, the programmer must return to its description in the original requirements, and to the original design, perhaps slightly modified by lessons learned in writing the prototype. Only the latter modifications get recorded in the final project documents. It is sometimes worth separately documenting the prototype. A good place to do that is in its code, with traceable references to the original documents.

13.2.1 C Implementation of Zipf's Law

Working directly with the pseudocode design, we fill in the data structures, turn `main()` into real code, and write several of the routines:

```
#include <stdio.h>
#include <string.h>
#define BIG 1000 /* how many words + 1 */
#define LONG 50 /* longest word + 1 */

typedef struct{int Count; char *Word;} CountsWords;
int NewPlace = 1; /* 1st word must be at subscript 1 */

/* Returns 0 if there are no more words,
   otherwise returns 1
      and the next word in the parameter */
int
GetWord(char *Word)
{
```

```
      int nxtChar; /* getchar() casts char to int */
      int SoFar = 1;
      char *partial = Word; /* save original start */
      /* skip any blanks or newlines */
      while ((nxtChar = getchar()) == (int)' '
             || nxtChar == (int)'\n') ;
      if (nxtChar < 0  /* error, usually EOF */
         || NewPlace >= BIG)  /* stoarge exhausted */
        return(0);
      *Word++ = (char)nxtChar;
      while ((nxtChar = getchar()) != (int)' '
             && nxtChar != (int)'\n')
        {
          if (++SoFar >= LONG)
            {
              *Word = (char)0;
              fprintf(stderr, "Word '%s' truncated\n",
                partial);
              break;
            }
          *Word++ = (char)nxtChar;
        }
      *Word = (char)0;  /* mark end of string */
      return(1);
}


/* Returns the index in All where Word is stored;
   or if not there, the negative of a free location.
   Maintains storage and the free-pointer */
int
LocWord(char *This, CountsWords All[])
{
  int cycle;
  for (cycle = 1; cycle < NewPlace; cycle++)
    if (strcmp(All[cycle].Word, This) == 0) /* found */
      return(cycle);
  /* Not there at all */
  if (++NewPlace >= BIG)  /* GetWord will stop soon */
    fprintf(stderr, "Out of space at %d words\n",
      BIG-1);
  All[NewPlace - 1].Word =
    (char *)malloc((strlen(This) + 1)*sizeof(char));
  return(-(NewPlace - 1));
}
```

```
/* Sorts the words and counts in Vague
   in descending-count order into Lst */
void
Sort(CountsWords Vague[])
{
/* Not yet coded */
}

/* Prints the words in Lst in order */
void
Print(CountsWords Vague[])
{
  int i;
  for (i = 1; i < NewPlace; i++)
    printf("%d %s\n", Vague[i].Count, Vague[i].Word);
}

/* Plots the counts in Vague against
   reciprocal position in the list */
void
Plot(CountsWords Vague[])
{
/* Not yet coded */
}

main()
{
  CountsWords V[BIG];
  char W[LONG];
  int Where;  /* location in the structure */
  while (GetWord(W)) /* exits if too many words */
    { /* next word is in W */
      Where = LocWord(W, V);
      if (Where > 0) /* found */
        V[Where].Count += 1;
      else
        { /* add new word */
        Where = -Where;
        V[Where].Count = 1;
        strcpy(V[Where].Word, W);
        }
    }
  Sort(V);
  Print(V);
  Plot(V);
}
```

In the process of writing `main()`, a utility routine to locate words in storage (and to get and maintain storage) seemed a good idea, so `LocWord()` was added to the design. There are still two routines to code, but a big step has been taken in turning the pseudocode into C.

13.2.2 Implementing Zipf's Law in a Shell Script

The UNIX programmer who begins a C implementation of the pseudocode for Zipf's law can't help recognizing that the code could be written easily using UNIX utilities. For example, there is an excellent `sort` package, and `awk` makes isolating words in the input extremely easy. So a somewhat different implementation comes naturally. Utilities are combined by a "main program" called a *shell script* because the program that executes UNIX commands is called a "shell."

The reader unfamiliar with shell programming will not be able to jump from this example to doing the same on other projects. But by explicitly giving code (even though the details may be incomprehensible), we hope to convince even the novice that such prototypes are easy to write, and that shell programming bears serious investigation for a software engineer's bag of tricks.

The shell script programmer has available all the utility programs that are part of a UNIX distribution, as described in section (1) of the UNIX online programmer's manual. One way to learn what is available is to thumb through a printed copy of the manual, noting interesting programs. Of course, one can write programs in (say) C if they are not available, but usually it is easier to use a more special-purpose language like `awk`. Shell scripts can process files and make good use of streams of information that pass between UNIX programs without actually going into a permanent file, streams that are directed to/from the programs using a construction called a "pipe."

Too much engineering is not a good thing (creeping feature creature) ▶ Because it is so easy to accomplish, the shell script version attempts grammatical processing to count "words" a bit better.

To process a command like

```
zipf <input-file> <output-count-file> <plot-data-file>
```

the following script is placed in the file `zipf`:

```
tr -d [:punct:] < $1 | tr A-Z a-z |
awk '{for(i=1;i<=NF;i++)print $i}' | sort | uniq -c |
sort -nr | tee $2 | awk '{print 1/++i,$1}'>$3
```

(In the file, the script is a single line, broken here only for display purposes.) To describe roughly what happens:

- `tr` is the first program to run, taking as input the first parameter from the command line, in shell scripts written $1. `tr` deletes all punctuation from the file and sends ("pipes," indicated by the vertical bar |) the resulting data to the next program in the script, which is `tr` again, but now translating all uppercase characters into lowercase.

- `awk` runs next, and the `awk` program is given as its quoted argument. This `awk` program decomposes a file of lines into a stream in which each word is a separate line.

- This stream is sent on to the UNIX `sort` program, which orders it alphabetically. This is done only so that duplicate words from the original text will appear together, as input to `uniq`.

- `uniq` counts duplicate lines, and replaces the block of duplicates with a count and a copy of the duplicate text. Thus its output is in the right format for `<output-count-file>`, except that it is not in descending order by count. Another `sort` puts it in this order.

- `tee` (a pun on a plumber's piping) splits the information stream into two copies, one of which goes out to a file (here `<output-count-file>`, the second parameter from the command line).

- Finally, another `awk` program creates the information for plotting (`<plot-data-file>`).

However incomprehensible this prototype is, its entire code comprises just one line. Executing it on the text of Chapter 4 of this book as `<input-file>` produces a `<output-count-file>` that contains:

```
501  the
262  to
209  of
209  a
204  is
167  and
....
 72  are
 63  software
 62  process
 57  as
 55  an
 53  project
 53  not
 48  on
 48  management
 46  but
 44  level
 42  will
```

```
42  can
39  engineers
38  this
37  product
....
```

The most frequent word in almost any English text is "the." But the first technical words indicate the subject of Chapter 4. For Chapter 11, results are

```
674  the
302  of
268  a
....
179  be
178  design
174  in
152  that
119  for
115  it
 89  are
 68  as
 63  system
 59  subsystem
 57  can
 56  requirements
 53  with
 49  will
 46  subsystems
 45  one
....
```

When the Chapter 11 data is plotted (using a UNIX program called gnu-plot), it looks like Figure 13.2 in the region that includes "design." The vertical axis is the number of times a word occurs, and the horizontal axis is the reciprocal of its rank. Zipf's law appears to hold tolerably well, despite the inadequate definition of words of the text.

How Does It Fit?

From section 13.1

1. In the Zipf's law example, it was decided to use iterative enhancement and initially ignore most details of English grammar for "words." In the next

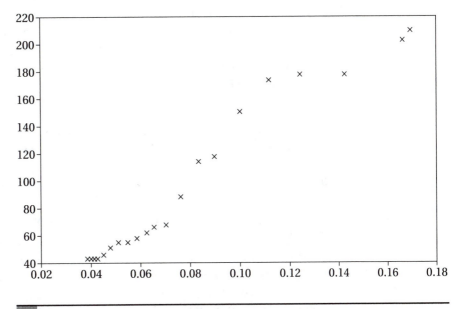

▶ **Figure 13.2** Part of the Zipf plot for Chapter 11.

iteration, keeping the design structure already developed, where should the processing for grammar be placed in the pseudocode?

2. In the graph of Figure 13.1, three points are marked on the axes. (1 on both axes, and $1/N$ on the horizontal axis.)

   (a) What is the meaning of these special values on the graph?

   (b) Why is there no upper value marked on the vertical axis?

   (c) Does the $(1, 1/N)$ point always appear in the graph for a particular corpus of text?

From section 13.2

3. Although the C implementation of Zipf's law isn't all coded, the given code will in fact compile and run. What does it do as is? What general design technique could be in use here?

4. The shell script implementation of Zipf's law includes some grammatical processing that is not in the C implementation. Add the same features to the C code.

5. The C programmer might worry about whether the limits defined by the constants BIG and LONG are being properly handled by the given code. Devise fault-based tests that will set these worries to rest.

6. Refine the shell script for Zipf's law to include grammar processing that:

   (a) Combines singular and plural forms of the same word

   (b) Combines different tenses of the same verb

(c) Eliminates common suffixes like "-tion" and "-ment"

(d) Performs another useful grammatical transformation that you identify by looking at a list of word frequencies produced by the script

(Probably awk is your best ally for this work, using its string-matching and substitution functions.)

7. In the shell script implementation of Zipf's law , suppose that two words have the same count. In what order will they appear in the word list?

8. Use the Zipf's law shell script on a fairly long UNIX command "manual" (man) file (for example, one of the shells), and see if the most frequently used words describe the command.

9. The shell script implementation of Section 13.2.2 doesn't follow the pseudocode of Section 13.1.1.

(a) Write pseudocode that the shell script does follow.

(b) Write a shell script that does follow the pseudocode.

10. Why do the points in Figure 13.2 get closer together at the left?

11. Which point in Figure 13.2 is the one associated with the word *design*?

12. Write a simple shell script that will print a single word as output upon input of a file, where that word is very likely to be the subject of the text in the file.

13. The C implementation includes some error processing for words that are too long, and for too many words, but there is no error processing in the shell script implementation. What limits might exist for the latter, and what will happen if they are exceeded?

Review Questions

1. Are data structures or control structures more likely to be captured by pseudocode?

2. What is a shell script?

Further Reading

awk is so called because those three letters are the initials of the surnames of its authors.

Shellscript programming is an arcane art because it seems to depend heavily on particular details of particular UNIX systems. Nevertheless, everyone works on a particular system whose details can be learned. The lesson in shell scripts is that there are fast, high-powered ways to accomplish difficult tasks, ways that are worth learning. Two of the UNIX gurus have written a good book [KP99].

The UNIX Programmer's Manual [Lab83] includes not only the documentation on commands, but many of the defining descriptions of tools like awk. The shell itself is one of the few programs whose manual is entirely available online as a UNIX man(1) page. There are several different popular shells; the one used here is the so-called C shell (csh on most UNIX systems, tcsh on Linux).

References

[KP99]   Brian Kernighan and Rob Pike. *The Practice of Programming*. Addison-Wesley, 1999.

[Lab83]   Bell Telephone Laboratories. *UNIX Programmer's Manual (2 vols)*. Holt, Rinehart and Winston, 1983.

chapter 14

Finite State Machines

"Internal states" are characteristic of one natural method of computation. At one point in the problem–solution process, some information is saved (in the "state"); later on, the state is examined and the saved information affects the course of the subsequent solution. When only a finite amount of state information is required, such computations can be concisely described by an abstraction called a finite state machine (FSM).

14.1 Designing with FSMs

An FSM design is natural for problems in which there are a finite number of input events (sometimes called stimuli), and for each stimulus, an output event is required. Some variation is allowed: the output can differ depending on patterns in the input, but these patterns are restricted.

FSMs have a long history. They are the "gates" of computer circuit design, and they capture the simplest kind of grammar-based computer languages. Here we need only the easiest beginnings of FSM theory.

14.1.1 Formal Finite State Automata

A finite state machine (FSM) consists of a finite, nonempty collection of *states* (one of which is the special *start state*), and a finite set of *transitions* between pairs of states. Each transition is associated with an *event* of some kind in the problem to be solved—often the arrival of an input. Also associated with each transition is a problem *action* of some kind—often the production of an output. If this description sounds vague, it is because the states, transitions, events, and actions are arbitrary and abstract—they have no intrinsic meaning, but are just made up in each particular FSM.

A conventional diagram is used to give examples of FSMs. Each state is given a circle labeled with the state name. The start state is marked with

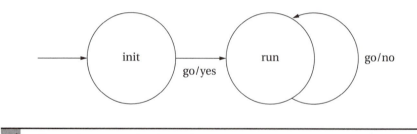

▶ **Figure 14.1**   A simple FSM.

an arrow into it from nowhere. Each transition corresponds to an arrow between two circles. The arrow is labeled E/A, where E is an event and A is an action. E is the event that causes this transition; A is the action that results. Figure 14.1 shows an FSM with two states init (the start state) and run, two transitions (one from init to run and the other from run to itself), one event (go), and two actions (yes and no).

The choice of meaningful-sounding labels for the parts of an FSM (as in the example of Figure 14.1) appears to give it a meaning, but this appearance is false. An FSM always "works" in the same way, as described in the next paragraph, and the names used are immaterial. However, it is a property of good notations that they appear to have a "life of their own," and the experienced designer chooses names to exploit this property.

The FSM moves from state to state in response to events. It begins in the start state. If one of the events that labels a transition arrow leaving the start state occurs, the FSM goes into the state to which that arrow leads. As the state shift is made, the transition's action also occurs. This process is repeated for the new state in which the FSM finds itself, and subsequent events, transitions, and actions. For example, in Figure 14.1, if the sequence of events go-go-go occurs, the FSM goes through the state sequence:

$$\text{init} \longrightarrow \text{run} \longrightarrow \text{run} \longrightarrow \text{run}$$

and the actions yes-no-no occur. When events are inputs and actions are outputs, then the FSM "computes" an input/output transform, which in this example has one pair of values:

$$\text{go-go-go} \mapsto \text{yes-no-no.}$$

14.1.2 Example FSM: The C `scanf()` Conversion

Finite state machines are often profitably used to describe character strings with many intricate complications, and their meaning. Such strings occur as inputs to computer programs, particularly when the inputs are programs themselves. Such a string controls the operation of the `scanf()` input conversion in C programs. In the C statement

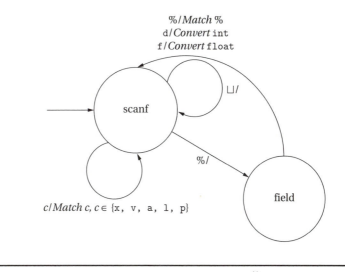

> **Figure 14.2** Design for a part of C `scanf()` control string.

```
scanf ("xval⎵%f⎵pval⎵%d⎵%%", &X,&P);
```

the control string is xval⎵%f⎵pval⎵%d⎵%%: and it specifies that two values are to be extracted from an input similar to:

```
xval⎵3.75 ⎵ ⎵pval⎵22%
```

with the result that the C variable X is set to 3.75, and P is set to 22. (In these strings, the blank character is shown explicitly as ⎵.)

Figure 14.2 shows an FSM design for a portion of `scanf()` conversion sufficient to handle this example. The FSM of Figure 14.2 does not process the input string that the C program reads; it processes the control string in the `scanf()` within the C program itself. (A quite different FSM could be constructed to do the former, which would constitute a means of implementing `scanf()` for C programs.) The actions for the FSM of Figure 14.2 are of two kinds. *Match c* means that the input must contain the character *c*, which is then skipped over. *Convert t* means that the input must contain characters describing an object of type *t*, which must be put into proper form, stored in a variable, and skipped over.

The FSM of Figure 14.2 has no transition arrows for syntax errors in the control string although these could be added. It also answers some obscure questions, but not necessarily correctly. For example, it is not clear from the usual verbal descriptions of `scanf()` whether or not %⎵d can be part of a control string, but in Figure 14.2 it cannot.

The great virtue of the FSM for describing complex situations is that the description is extremely precise; yet, with a little practice, the diagrams are easy to read. Perhaps no other notation does as well in meeting these two conflicting goals.

14.1.3 Designing a Simple GUI as an FSM

GUI (pronounced "gooey") is an acronym for graphical user interface. The idea originated at the Xerox Palo Alto Research Center in the 1970s, and was made the core of the Macintosh system. It is now almost universal in systems designed for use by people without much knowledge of (or interest in) computers for their own sake (that is, almost all computer users!). The "mouse" input device is crucial to these interfaces, which are also called "point-and-click" interfaces.

In a typical GUI, information is collected from the person in front of the screen, information that is then processed to solve a problem. As a very simple example, consider a system to write and send memos in an organization that has a collection of terminals linked by electronic mail. The memo program is to allow a terminal user to compose a memo, and send it to other terminals by e-mail. The system is to have access to a database of personnel addresses for receipt of memos. The details are left to the system designer, who decides to use a GUI and to describe it using an FSM.

To send a memo requires composing it and selecting recipients. Let's suppose that the text of a memo must be placed in a file by an editor not part of the memo system. Further assume that each memo is sent to a single recipient (that is, there are no "address lists"—to send multiple copies of the same memo requires repeated user actions). The designer decides to start with the Memo window shown in Figure 14.3, containing four buttons. Overall control in the system is to be serial—that is, the terminal user

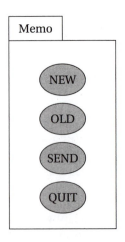

▶ **Figure 14.3**   The main Memo window.

must deal with each window in order and must dismiss one window before another can be used. There is thus at most one "active" window at a time. Rather than continue with an informal description, let us use the FSM to be precise.

The FSM transition diagram is shown in Figure 14.4, and the intuitive meaning of the states is given in Table 14.1. The events are abbreviated on the diagram—a single word in capital letters indicates the event of clicking on a button. For example, in state M, the transition to state B occurs when the user clicks on the QUIT button. Other events are abbreviations of user or system situations as described in Table 14.2, involving parameters of the situation. For example, the event "enter'name'" that triggers transition from state A to state T1, indicates that the user has typed 'name' into the box in the window shown in Figure 14.5. The actions are coded, and described in Table 14.3.

The Name window may overlay the Memo window as shown in Figure 14.5, for example, when the transition from M to N2 occurs because the user clicks on the OLD button in the Memo window. Similarly, the Query window may overlay the Name window as shown in Figure 14.6, for example, on a transition from T3 to Q. When the external editor is invoked, its window (not shown) includes a BACK button.

This complex of information in the window diagrams, the tables of states, events, and actions, but primarily the transition diagram of Figure 14.4, constitutes the FSM design of the memo system.

Some general features of the FSM design are worth pointing out.

"Write-only" work seems so difficult to study that it would be best just to recreate it. Are programs themselves the ultimate write-only documents?

- The transition diagram is not easy to read. A great deal of information is captured in the diagram—it took the designer a long time to make it and get it right. Its virtue is not that the meaning leaps out at the novice reader, but rather that it *is* concise and precise. How many paragraphs of text would be required to say the same things? You should expect to have to study such a diagram for a long time to grasp its meaning.

- Liberties have been taken with the formalism. An action has been indicated on the start-state arrow, which is to mean that this action is taken initially (to display the Memo window). Some actions are missing (for example, on the "enter'name'" transition from states N1 and N2), meaning that no action is taken on such transitions. The example's most serious transgression against FSM formalism is that some of its events and actions are not "finite" enough. For example, in setting the flag "memOK" that means a memo is ready on the T3 $\longrightarrow$ Q transition, the event is a decision about a name stored on the N2 $\longrightarrow$ T3 transition, and the action sets a flag. On the T4 $\longrightarrow$ M transition, the flag is tested. Technically, giving events and actions "storage" of items like user-supplied names makes the FSM nonfinite.

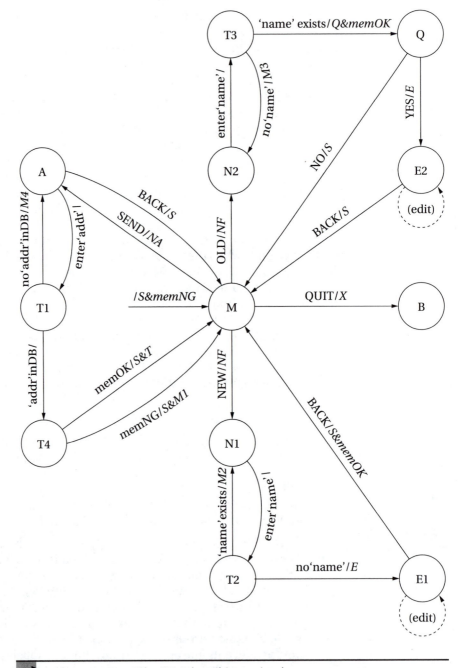

Figure 14.4   The FSM describing a simple memo system.

State Name	Meaning
M	The Memo window is active
B	System terminated
N1	The Name window queries for a new file name
N2	The Name window queries for an existing file name
A	The Name window queries for an address
T1	Check if address is valid
T4	Check if memo is ready
T2	Check if file exists
E1	Edit (create) new file
T3	Check if file exists
Q	Check if the old file is to be edited
E2	Edit old file

▶ **Table 14.1**   Intuitive meanings of the GUI FSM states.

Event	Meaning
enter'addr'	User enters 'addr' in the Address window
'addr'inDB	The given 'addr' exists in the database of addresses
no'addr'inDB	The given 'addr' does not exist in the database of addresses
enter'name'	User enters 'name' in the Name window
'name'exists	The given 'name' file exists
no'name'	The given 'name' file does not exist
memOK	A memo has been previously specified
memNG	No memo has been previously specified

▶ **Table 14.2**   Explanation of the GUI FSM event abbreviations.

- Several of the states appear to be very similar, but are nevertheless duplicated (for example, states N1 and N2 both display the Name menu). FSM states are not subroutines, so to do the same thing under different circumstances requires a new state each time.

- The diagram indicates an informal use of step-wise refinement, in that the states E1 and E2 for editing a memo do not include the edit events and actions. These might be described by another FSM that is not given here.

Given the FSM diagram of Figure 14.4 with supporting tables for its abbreviations and the window layouts shown in Figure 14.3, 14.5, and 14.6,

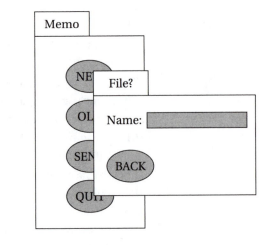

▶ **Figure 14.5**   The overlaid Name window.

Action	Meaning
S	The Memo window appears alone on the screen, replacing any others
X	The screen is cleared and the system terminates
NF	The Name window is overlaid on the Memo window with its label box reading "File?"
NA	The Name window is overlaid on the Memo window with its label box reading "Address?"
M1	Message: NO MEMO SPECIFIED
M2	Message: 'NEW' FILE ALREADY EXISTS
M3	Message: 'OLD' FILE DOESN'T EXIST
M4	Message: ADDRESS NOT IN DATABASE
T	The memo is transmitted to the address
Q	The Query window is overlaid on the Name window
E	The editor is invoked and its window appears
memOK	Flag that a memo exists
memNG	Flag that a memo does not exist

▶ **Table 14.3**   Explanation of the GUI FSM action abbreviations.

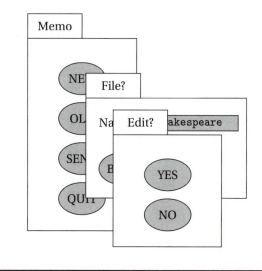

Figure 14.6   The overlaid Query window.

it is possible to trace through any possible behavior of the system described. For example, Figure 14.6 will result from clicking on the OLD button in the Memo window, then entering the name of an existing file in the Name window. Next clicking on the NO button will bring the Memo window back to replace these, and the unchanged file selected will be ready to send. The designer can use the diagram to explore the system long before it is implemented to see if it meets the requirements.

The designer of this GUI has in fact done a slipshod job, as can be seen by considering the state sequence in Figure 14.4:

$$\longrightarrow M \longrightarrow A \longrightarrow T1 \longrightarrow T4 \longrightarrow M.$$

If this sequence takes place as a user's first action, it will probably make him or her angry, but the designer either failed to notice the undesirable behavior or was too lazy to fix it.

14.1.4 Test Plan for the GUI

One large advantage of a design based on an FSM is that it is easy to implement correctly, even automatically, as Section 14.2 will show. FSM implementations can be expected to be perfect, to do exactly what they were designed to do. What is the point of testing them, then?

The trivial case should not be neglected: any implementation, however automatic or by rote, requires transcription from a diagram or a person's mind to a keyboard, and typos are always a possibility. Testing is a good way to eliminate typos. If "coding" for an FSM design is no more than correct use

Length	Possible Sequences
1	M
2	M $\longrightarrow$ B
	M $\longrightarrow$ N2
	M $\longrightarrow$ N1
	M $\longrightarrow$ A
3	M $\longrightarrow$ N2 $\longrightarrow$ T3
	M $\longrightarrow$ N1 $\longrightarrow$ T2
	M $\longrightarrow$ A $\longrightarrow$ T1
	M $\longrightarrow$ A $\longrightarrow$ M
4	M $\longrightarrow$ N2 $\longrightarrow$ T3 $\longrightarrow$ Q
	M $\longrightarrow$ N2 $\longrightarrow$ T3 $\longrightarrow$ N2
	etc.

 **Table 14.4**   Possible FSM test sequences.

of the keyboard, the feedback loop from coding to design for maintenance in the software development lifecycle is trivial. But not so the feedback loop from coding to requirements. It may very well happen that in the extensive effort required to construct an FSM design, the end user's wishes are not correctly captured. Testing the FSM code, which is probably correct for the FSM design, has a chance of exposing the FSM design as being incorrect for the end user. When the user sees the results of a particular test, he or she may see that the design is doing the wrong thing.

An FSM design is a natural map of actions, and sequences of actions, that users of the software (when it is implemented) will perform. The states of the FSM are also natural "modes" for the software to be in between user actions. The user must know the mode to successfully control the software because the same input does not do the same thing in different modes. For example, in the GUI design of Figure 14.4, entering a name in state N2 has quite a different meaning than entering the same name in state N1—the software is in a different mode.

Thus in devising tests from an FSM design, there are two kinds of design structure to exploit:

Sequences of actions.   Tracing the transitions through an FSM design leads to functional test cases that might not have been thought of during requirements analysis. It is even possible to plan a kind of systematic coverage of all possible sequences up to some maximum length. In the GUI example, some of these sequences are shown in Table 14.4.

The inputs to force these sequences and the outputs that should result can be read from the FSM transition arrows of Figure 14.4.

State or transition coverage. To put the software through its paces, it seems necessary to see what happens when it is in any of the possible modes and each possible event occurs. Thus, for example, when the GUI system is in state T2, it is possible for the two events '"name'exists" and "no'name'"' to occur, and both should be tried in this state. To get into state T2, there are many possible sequences, the shortest being of length three, and many others, such as:

$$M \longrightarrow N1 \longrightarrow T2 \longrightarrow N1 \longrightarrow T2 \longrightarrow N1 \longrightarrow T2.$$

A systematic list of the states and events can be constructed and the necessary inputs read from the FSM diagram.

A subtle caution is in order when devising tests to "cover" possibilities in an FSM design. The coverage is valid only if the design is taken as a prescription *and correctly implemented*. In that case, the software *will* have states corresponding to the FSM, and they will be covered by systematically generated tests. However, should a mistake be made in implementation, it can create new "states" of the program, states that have no existence in the FSM, and that can be entered in execution, leading to strange behavior. It is no guarantee of good behavior to test all the FSM states of the *design* if such "hidden" states exist. On the other hand, if an FSM is automatically implemented, as described in Section 14.2, then the only reason to test sequences and state coverages is to see that the requirements are being correctly carried out by the FSM design—one knows without testing that the implementation faithfully follows the design.

14.1.5 Model Checking

Intellectual control ▶

FSM software designs are attractive because their states and transitions are good mental tools for thinking about what the system behavior will be, and thus checking that the design will do what the intuitive requirements say that the software should do. The drawback in any real FSM is that it has far too many states, and although in principle a human being can think about the possible state sequences, in practice the task is too difficult. *Model checking* is an idea and a clever implementation of the idea to aid a person in analyzing FSM designs.

The idea behind model checking is as follows: to see whether or not a particular FSM that has been crafted as a software design is intuitively correct (according to a set of intuitive requirements), it is very helpful to think of "properties" that the intuitive requirements should have, and then to check that the design does have them. This is exactly what a Formal Methodist of the "proof" school, as described in Section 10.5.4, thinks formal methods should do. For example, in the GUI design of Section 14.1.3, the user might think of the property: "No vacuous memos should be sent." Or "Once a memo has been sent, its file should never be changed." To see if these properties are violated (once they are precisely defined in terms of the entities in the FSM design) requires only that the state space of the FSM be exhaustively explored. There are two possible outcomes:

1. There is a sequence of states, inputs, and transitions that violates the given property. (For example, for this sequence, a vacuous memo *is* sent.) In this case, the design is no good because it violates the user's intuition about what should happen. The example sequence that goes wrong is an ideal vehicle for thinking about the situation and correcting the design.

2. There is no sequence that violates the given property—that is, the design is what the user wanted (with regard to one property at least). One might think that this can never be established, but here the nature of an FSM comes into its own: because the FSM is literally finite, its transitions cannot go on and on changing—eventually a state must repeat. And once all the possibilities have come back to some previously occurring state, and the property being explored has not been violated, then it will never be violated. In this regard, FSMs are entirely unlike general computer programs, which need never repeat a state.

A *model checker* is a program that tries all the possible state sequences of a given FSM, and for each state checks a given property. If the property ever fails, the model checker prints the sequence for which it failed; otherwise, it prints that the property always holds. Some very clever computer science research work has made model checkers practical even for quite large FSMs. State-of-the-art model checkers can handle state sizes of about 10,000 in a reasonable amount of computing time, and much larger state counts if the states show strong regularity patterns.

The formalism in which requirements properties are expressed is usually a kind of "temporal logic," so called because it can express statements like, "every time situation X occurs, then situation Y must eventually occur afterwards." The details are not appropriate in a beginning text like this, but it is important to realize that model checking exists and is a major reason why FSM designs may be the best choice for complex systems that must work properly.

14.2 Coding an FSM Design

FSM designs are easy to work with, yet completely formal and hence very precise. Model checking is a powerful analysis tool for FSM designs. In addition to these virtues, an FSM can be coded automatically. When an FSM design is possible, there is every reason to use this technique.

```
Set S to the initial state
REPEAT forever
  Get next event NE
  Find the place for event NE
    and current state S in the table
  IF the pair (NE,S) has no place in the table
    THEN
      print error message and abort.
    FI
  Lookup next state NS and action A
    at (NE,S) in the table
  Do action A
  Set S to NS
TAEPER
```

Figure 14.7   A table-driven FSM specification coded by hand.

14.2.1 Implementation Techniques

When a design uses an FSM, there are several implementation choices, all very satisfactory:

Automatic tools.   FSM diagrams can be given in textual form, by encoding the transitions as tables showing which states, events, and actions are involved. In such a form, it is not difficult to write a program that from the table will construct a program that executes to perform the input/output transformation of the FSM. (This is an example of *table-driven programming* or of a *program generator*: the "programmer" writes the table, and the program is produced automatically.) Perhaps the best known example of automatic FSM tools are the lexical analyzers used in many compilers. The programs that result (the most used generators produce C code) are generated from FSM descriptions, and when they execute, they recognize the reserved words and special symbols of the language to be compiled. The way in which automatic tools work can be understood by thinking about a by-hand implementation, described next.

Hand-coded, table-driven FSM.   An FSM can be implemented by providing the table describing its transitions as a data structure (an array is appropriate), with a program whose pseudocode is given in Figure 14.7. The program part is the same no matter what FSM is being implemented; only the contents of the table change, which is the basis for automatic tools.

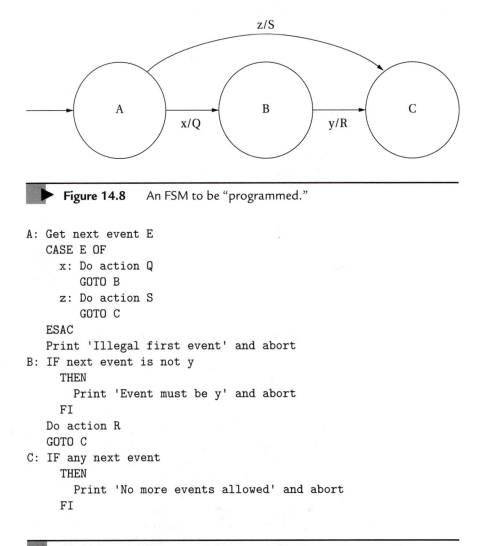

Figure 14.8   An FSM to be "programmed."

```
A: Get next event E
   CASE E OF
     x: Do action Q
        GOTO B
     z: Do action S
        GOTO C
   ESAC
   Print 'Illegal first event' and abort
B: IF next event is not y
     THEN
        Print 'Event must be y' and abort
     FI
   Do action R
   GOTO C
C: IF any next event
     THEN
        Print 'No more events allowed' and abort
     FI
```

Figure 14.9   Explicit pseudocode for the FMS of Figure 14.8.

Coding a specific FSM.   A program can mimic the transitions and actions of an FSM with conditional statements, progressing through all the possible states and transitions. For example, the FSM shown in Figure 14.8 corresponds to a program whose pseudocode is given in Figure 14.9. One reason for writing code like this is the ability to include case-by-case error processing for cases not covered in the FSM.

These implementation techniques each have a place. Automatic implementation reduces the coding phase to a mechanical exercise. The programmer need only transcribe the FSM transition diagram into the table format required by the tool that will then generate the FSM program. Of course, it's possible to make mistakes in the transcription, but the simplest tests usually find them. The only trouble with automatic tools is that they are inflexible—the resulting program will work just as the tool dictates.

Hand coding the table-driven algorithm isn't difficult and returns control of the FSM execution to the programmer. One example case in which hand coding is dictated is for a "sparse" FSM—one with many states and only a few transitions. The FSM table would then best be stored not as the array that most automatic tools use, but as a linked list.

It would seem that an implementation that isn't table driven would never be desirable, but the ability to individually craft error messages is so important that even some compilers forego the automatic implementation.

14.2.2 Implementing Transgressions of FSM Formalism

The FSM formalism is so satisfactory that designers try to use it even when the problem isn't technically finite state. The example in Figure 14.4 illustrated transgressions of events and actions that store and check values in a way that a true FSM cannot do. If an automatic implementation is attempted for such an "almost FSM," the programmer will find that the transition diagram can't be expressed in the tabular form required by the tool.

In a hand-coded FSM like that of Figure 14.9, transgressions will show up as "event _____" or "action _____" and the blanks can be simply filled in with whatever code is needed in the final programming language. So long as this special code is kept isolated and is well documented, for example, by encapsulating it in a procedure, most of the advantages of a true FSM design will be retained.

How Does It Fit?

From section 14.1

1. Use a standard reference such as the Kernighan and Ritchie book referred to at the end of this chapter to find the complete description of the C `scanf()` control string.

   (a) Complete the FSM diagram of Figure 14.2.

   (b) Make a list of issues that came up in doing part (a) that are unclear in the reference you used.

   (c) Explain why it isn't a good idea to experiment with your favorite compiler to answer questions about `scanf()` that aren't clear in the reference.

2. At the end of Section 14.1.2, it is mentioned that %⊔d may or may not be legal in a `scanf()` control string. Explain the way Figure 14.2 makes this string illegal.

3. The discussion in Section 14.1.2 mentions the possibility of describing actual input strings being read by C programs, using an FSM. The scanning of numbers is an important part of such a description.

   (a) Draw an FSM diagram for the %d format.
   (b) Draw an FSM diagram for the %f format.

4. The serious transgressions against the FSM formalism that occur in Figure 14.4 are not all necessary.

   (a) Add states and transitions to the diagram so it is no longer necessary to use the flag "memOK/memNG". Is the resulting complexity worth it?
   (b) Can the "'addr'inDB" flags be similarly eliminated? Explain.
   (c) Can the implicit storage of names and memo contents be similarly eliminated? Explain.

5. In the FSM design of Figure 14.4, is it possible to click on BACK without entering the file name in the name window? Explain.

6. What sequence of user input actions in the FSM design of Figure 14.4 leads to the state sequence

$$M \longrightarrow A \longrightarrow T1 \longrightarrow T4 \longrightarrow M$$

that is said to expose slipshod design in the GUI? Explain why the behavior of the design is undesirable from the user's point of view.

7. Add the corresponding result sequences to Table 14.4.

8. Write a statement of the form:

   Every time _____ happens, then the GUI is required to make _____ happen subsequently, by filling in the blanks to describe some desirable behavior of the FSM design of Figure 14.4. (It is just such statements that can be made in a temporal logic and then given to a model checker to see if they can be violated.)

9. List two interesting state sequences of length six in the GUI design of Figure 14.4, and state in words what they mean to a user. Give the sequences of input events that these tests represent.

From section 14.2

10. The FSM of Figure 14.8 was implemented in pseudocode, but it might have used the hand-coded, table-driven implementation. Contrast the error messages possible in the two kinds of implementation.

11. Improve the error messages in the pseudocode of Figure 14.9.

12. Step through the execution of the sample FSM of Figure 14.8 using the pseudocode of Figure 14.7. Compare the execution to that of the pseudocode of Figure 14.9.

13. If transgressions against the FSM formalism exist in a design as indicated in Section 14.2.2, and the implementation is by hand as in Figure 14.9, then each non-standard event or action can be replaced by explicit code to perform it. What would this code be for the setting and testing of the "memOK/NG" flag in Tables 14.2 and 14.3?

14. If transgressions against the FSM formalism exist in a design as indicated in Section 14.2.2, and the implementation is by a hand-coded table as in Figure 14.7, what difficulties arise, and how can they be overcome?

Further Reading

Finite state machines were once the staple of digital logic design, but silicon chips and the CAD programs that help design them have passed well beyond this "gate" level. Computer science theory makes excellent use of finite state abstractions, but as "finite automata," which lack the "action" ability of FSMs. There are many good textbooks on both [Boo67, HU79]. Model checking is a technique with tremendous potential since it allows exercising a FSM design almost exhaustively, in practical cases [CGP00]. Although FSMs are not as flexible as some other formal design methods, it may be that their use will increase just on the strength of model checking because other methods have no comparable testing technique.

The reference used for C scanf() in Section 14.1.2 is the standard one by the language's inventors, Brian Kernighan and Dennis Ritchie [KR88].

References

[Boo67]   Taylor L. Booth. *Sequential Machines and Automata Theory*. Wiley, 1967.

[CGP00]   E. M. Clarke, Orna Grumberg, and Dovan Peled. *Model Checking*. MIT Press, 2000.

[HU79]   John Hopcroft and Jeffrey Ullman. *Introduction to Automata Theory, Languages, and Computation*. Addison-Wesley, 1979.

[KR88]   Brian Kernighan and Dennis Ritchie. *The C Programming Language, 2nd Ed.* Prentice-Hall, 1988.

chapter 15

Abstract Data Types (ADTs)

D avid Parnas has suggested a way to judge the quality of a design's decomposition into modules. He argues that the "natural" steps of solving a problem tend to follow the execution order of the program being designed. Indeed, this is the nature of pseudocode and the imperative programming language framework: "First, do this, then do that . . . ," etc. These natural steps result in modules that also follow execution order, and Parnas claims (with some support from data on large projects) that the resulting system will be a maintenance nightmare because almost any change will impact all its modules. For maintenance purposes, it would be far better if a change could be confined to one module. Parnas's idea is that by assigning "secrets" to modules, a more maintainable design will result. He calls his design idea *information hiding,* and *abstract data types (ADTs)* are its mechanism.

15.1 Hiding Design Decisions

Information hiding is not a great deal of help in finding the modules into which a design should be decomposed. It is better at judging whether a given decomposition is good. So-called object-oriented design is more help in suggesting modules because it uses natural "objects" that occur in the problem as units, as described in Chapter 16. The corresponding software objects, however, are not very different from the ADTs of this chapter.

Secrets do help to determine a module breakdown, however. Every time a design decision is made, a decision to have the software be or act one way rather than another, it is a potential secret. For example, the decision to use a static array for storage, and to dimension it for a maximum size of (say) 1000 elements, should be secrets confined to one module since it may later develop that the size must be increased or that a dynamic array is necessary or that some more radical change in structure is needed. Once a secret is identified, it can be used to define a module around it. That module at its largest implements all the system functions that need its secret information. But such a maximal module is usually too large and comprises functions that seem intuitively unrelated. A further decomposition requires that other modules be allowed limited access to the internal secrets. The secret-hiding module can be outfitted with *access routines*, which deliver information in such a way that a caller cannot know the internal form, and so the secret is kept. For example, the module whose secret is a 1000-element array for storage might have an access routine whose parameter is a range of values and asks whether any stored element falls within this range. Internally, the array would be searched and the result returned. It would be a poorer design to have an access routine whose parameter was an integer, returning the value stored at that subscript. Such an interface would reveal that the secret structure acts like an array, and would even allow a caller to probe for the maximum allowable subscript.

Parnas originally described the information-hiding idea using an example of text processing. He designed a program to read in information, rearrange it in several steps, and print the result. The "logical" decomposition following execution order is expressed in pseudocode:

```
Read information.
Reformat the information.
Process in new format.
Print processed information.
```

Nothing could be more straightforward. But if each step is to be a separate module, it is implied that there is a data structure to hold the information. The first module will fill that structure, the second and third will modify and use its contents, and the fourth will use it. Central data structures must be passed between modules, either as parameters or by making them global to all modules. What happens if a change in the problem requires a change in central data structures (perhaps because the data volume changes, so memory-resident lists have to be changed to files)? *All* the modules will have to be changed substantially.

Parnas suggests that a data structure be made the secret of a single module, which he calls an information holder. The information holder has access routines that allow other modules to store information (without knowing how it is stored) and to similarly retrieve information. Let module *IH* be the information holder for the input information. Then the "read" module will call *IH* to store the input data and the "reformat" module will call *IH* to retrieve it. The other modules will either call *IH* or another information holder module (depending on how different the reformatted and processed information is from the original data). Now should it be required to substitute files for memory-resident lists, only *IH* need be changed. None of the four routines calling the holders is at all sensitive to the form of the "secret" data structures.

Of course, information hiding works best when the designer can anticipate the kinds of changes that may be required because those aspects can be hidden as module secrets, and changing them will require less work. Unanticipated changes may still cut across all the modules. In the Parnas example, if the change is to add a new field to the input data, a field that alters processing and the form of the printed results, then all modules (including the information holder) will be affected.

Information hiding has an important application to making software easier to develop. Modules that hide part of the design may be implemented in a "quick and dirty" fashion without compromising the whole system forever. Since the poor implementation is the module's secret, none of the rest of the program is influenced in any way. Thus a prototype can be quickly constructed, but a prototype that has a sound design *except in some modules*. If the badly done modules are not important to the system's efficiency, there is no reason to change them. On the other hand, if the prototype performs badly, it may be necessary to improve some modules. The programmer can do so *without changing any other code*.

Divide and conquer ▶

15.2 ADT Signatures and Axioms—Boolean Example

An example is perhaps the best way to introduce the defining elements of ADTs, and the "Boolean" type is as simple as can be. It is a primitive type in most languages, but not in C.

15.2.1 Signature Diagram

ADT syntax can be captured by a *signature diagram* that pictorially shows each collection of values (usually corresponding to a data structure) as a circle labeled with the name of those values, and each access routine as a mapping arrow connecting appropriate circles. For example, in the Boolean type the value collection would be "Boolean," and the access routines might be the logical operations "and" and "not." Constant values in Boolean (that is, {TRUE,FALSE}) take the form of 0-ary functions. Thus the signature for this simple ADT is given by Figure 15.1.

In a signature diagram, all the access routines are pure functions, which means that their results depend only on their inputs—there are no side effects. It may not be possible to implement these in some programming languages, or the possible implementations may be inefficient. The diagram fails to capture the order of arguments to functions. Expressing the signature

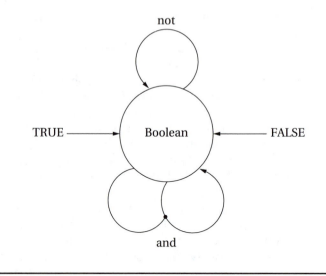

▶ **Figure 15.1**   Signature of the Boolean ADT.

information as subroutine headers in a programming language like C is less graphic but more precise:

```
typedef /* only the name, not the structure! */ Boolean;

#define TRUE /* = only the name, not the value! */
#define FALSE /* = ditto */

Boolean not(Boolean B)

Boolean and(Boolean A, Boolean B)
```

By not giving the details of the Boolean typedef and TRUE and FALSE, the ADT is a nonprescriptive design—the person assigned to code it can choose the details. Its users, on the other hand, have all they need to write code. For example, a user might use a pair of Boolean variables to record two separate conditions and test their conjunction:

```
Boolean P,Q;
P = Q = FALSE;
  .
  .
  .
/* Search for something, and if found: */
P = TRUE;
  .
  .
  .
```

```
/* Search for something else, and if found: */
Q = TRUE;
if (and(P, Q) == TRUE)  /* both searches succeeded */
  .
  .
  .
```

15.2.2 Algebraic Axioms

A second formal device helps to capture the semantics of an ADT. A set of assertions (*axioms*) gives properties of the access routines (from the signature) in terms of each other. For the preceding Boolean signature:

not(TRUE) = FALSE
not(FALSE) = TRUE
and(u,v) = TRUE if u = v = TRUE, otherwise FALSE

Unfortunately, algebraic axioms do not often capture the semantics so well as in this simple, finite case.

15.3 Encapsulation and C

Languages designed for implementing ADTs, like C++, Ada, and Java, have particular syntax mechanisms for expressing ADTs and yet keeping their secrets. C is not so well suited to ADTs. For instance, in the Boolean example, the code cannot be compiled and run until the secret blanks are filled in. One choice might be:

```
typedef /* secret */ int Boolean;

#define TRUE /* secret */ = 1
#define FALSE /* secret */ = 0
```

These declarations must be placed so that their scope includes the module whose secret they are. But their scope must also include all the users of the module. These users may not mean to make use of the secret information, but they *can* use it. A user can write

```
if (!and(P, Q)) ...
```

and violate the secrets yet not be caught by the C compiler. For those particular implementation choices, the user's code is correct.

If ADTs are to be defined in C so that they look like built-in types, providing the ability to declare and allocate storage wherever needed, then there is no way to really keep some secrets. There is a way, however, to completely encapsulate secret data structures in C, by placing them entirely inside a module. An ADT defined in this way can provide only a few "abstract" variables, and it must have additional access routines to set and retrieve their values. As an example, here is a form of the Boolean ADT design that has two built-in values:

```
void setPtoT()
void setPtoF()
void setQtoT()
void setQtoF()
int getP()
int getQ()
int PandQ()
int notP()
int notQ()
```

The names of the access routines suggest what they do; for example, setQ-toT should cause the ADT to assign the (secret) value for *true* to its Q variable. Code using the ADT for the same program fragment as before would then look like:

```
setPtoF();
setQtoF();
   .
   .
   .
/* Search for something, and if found: */
setPtoT();
   .
   .
   .
/* Search for something else, and if found: */
setQtoT();
if (PandQ())   /* both searches succeeded */
      .
      .
      .
```

When the code for these ADT access routines is written, storage for the "variables" that it provides is entirely within the implementing module, and nothing of its form is revealed outside. The internal declarations will have to be static so that they retain their values between calls.

The second kind of ADT in which limited storage is kept inside is inelegant, and it will not be used in what follows. However, it should be noted that this form of ADT design can be used in almost any language, regardless of how poor its type mechanisms may be. (Yes, even COBOL.)

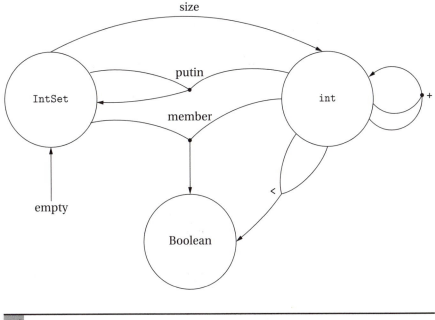

▶ **Figure 15.2**   Signature of the ADT `IntSet`.

15.4 Example: The ADT `IntSet`

As an example of designing a more substantial ADT (and also an example of subroutine design and design-phase test planning), consider the data type "set of integers." The programming language is to be C, which lacks such a built-in data type, but C does have an `int` type which we take to be an adequate form for integers. The ADT `IntSet` is to have access routines to create an empty set, to find the cardinality of a set, to add an integer to an existing set, and to determine membership in a set.

15.4.1 Signature for `IntSet`

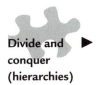

Divide and conquer (hierarchies)

Figure 15.2 shows the signature for the set-of-integers ADT. When a mapping has more than one parameter, the `int` one comes first. Details of the Boolean type are not shown; see Figure 15.1. Only the addition and one relational operation of `int` are shown. It is an important property of ADTs that they can be *composed*—in defining a complex ADT the complexity can be reduced by incorporating other ADTs, which can be defined independently.

15.4.2 English Specification

`IntSet` is an ADT for a set of integers, in the commonly understood mathematical sense. The access routines have the syntax shown in the signature, with the meanings:

Function	Meaning
empty	creates an empty set
size	returns the cardinality of a set
member	returns whether an element belongs to a set
putin	adds an element to a set, returning the new set

Most readers probably know what these set operations are all about; if not, there are many set theory textbooks to consult. But it is also possible to give some of the mathematical meaning using axioms:

size(empty) = 0
size(putin(i,S)) = size(S) if member(i,S)
size(putin(i,S)) = size(S)+1 if not(member(i,S))
member(i,empty) = FALSE
member(i,putin(i,S)) = TRUE
putin(i,putin(i,S)) = putin(i,S)

These axioms do not define the access routines completely, but they do concisely indicate important properties, such as that adding an element to a set has no effect if the element is already in that set (given by the final axiom and the second axiom).

15.4.3 Design of `IntSet`

At the heart of the `IntSet` design is a decision to use dynamic storage for the members of a set, allowing this storage to grow and shrink as the set changes. Thus although the storage representation is first given only as

```
typedef /* internal representation (deferred) */ IntSet;
```

it is expected that the representation will in some way contain a pointer to memory obtained by the C library routine `malloc()`. This decision forces the C headers of the access routines to differ from the signature:

```
void empty(IntSet *New) /*returns New*/
int size(IntSet S)
Boolean member(int i, IntSet S)
void putin(int i, IntSet S, IntSet *NewS) /*returns NewS*/
```

(The Boolean ADT of Section 15.2 is used in `member()`.)

The reason for this violation of the signature is complex—it has to do with deficiencies of the C language and with deficiencies of the ADT formalism, and is worth a digression from designing IntSet. For putin and empty to return an IntSet itself could introduce storage leaks when the ADT is used. Consider calls on the access routines if they were taken from the signature:

```
IntSet X;
    .
    .
    .
X = empty();
X = empty();
X = putin(0,X);
```

The first call would allocate storage, put a pointer to it in the representation of an empty set, and store the representation in X. The second call would do the same thing, and thus the first-allocated set representation would be overwritten. But the representation includes a storage pointer, so that storage would be lost forever. Similarly, the third call would allocate storage for the new set, copy into it the contents of X, and then add 0. But the representation of this new set would then overlay what's currently in X, which includes a storage pointer, causing a second block of storage to be lost.

In languages of a higher level than C (Java, for example), where this kind of storage re-allocation is frequent and expected, there is an automatic mechanism for reclaiming lost storage, called "garbage collection." In C, the programmer has to do all the work, and to do it requires knowledge in the access routines of both the old and new set representations involved. By making the output set a parameter in the headers given earlier, the access functions can use the same storage for a "new" set as is currently in use for an "old" one, when the same variable is used for both; that is, the set can be updated in place.

The access routines whose headers are given earlier with values returned through the parameter list work properly in the example:

```
IntSet X;
    .
    .
    .
empty(&X);
empty(&X);
putin(0,X,&X);
```

The information is present to allow the same storage to be used for X throughout. (That's the end of the digression on storage and updating in place.)

To continue with the design of `Intset`, here are the details of implementing the secret data structure to represent a set, which the designer passes on to the coder:

> Storage is to be obtained for sets in "chunks" of 100 integer values. Initially, `empty` obtains 100 locations, and `putin` gets additional storage (copying and reclaiming the previous storage) if it is needed. The current size of element storage is always the smallest multiple of 100 greater than or equal to the number of elements currently in a set. When a set is updated in place, if it consists of the wrong number of chunks, the old storage is returned and the new set gets the right number.

The `IntSet` example is unusual because it is not necessary to give functional specifications for the access routines. They are required to behave as sets, and set operations are well defined.

15.4.4 Testing `IntSet`

An ADT is never a complete system, but always a part of one. Within the larger system, there will be calls to the ADT, such as the ones that illustrated the potential pitfalls of using `empty()`. These calls will test the parts of the ADT as a part of the complete system, when system tests are conducted. However, during design of an ADT is an ideal time to create a test plan for the ADT itself, as a "subsystem" including a number of interacting subroutines (the ADT access routines). All the difficult design and implementation problems are fresh in the designer's mind, and the design provides exactly enough information to explicitly write test cases. (The subject of subsystem testing will be further discussed in Section 19.3.3.)

Document it! ▶
(record it or
it's lost)

It may seem strange to be writing explicit code for testing an ADT whose coding itself has not even begun. The tests cannot be run until the ADT is coded but the tests *can* be coded, because the ADT routine headers have been designed in detail. So here is a useful driver and test program for the access routines of the `IntSet` ADT:

```
/* driver and test program for the IntSet ADT */
#include <stdio.h>
#define CUPLACHUNKS 400

IntSet mine, yours;

main()
{
    int elem, count = 0;
```

```
/* functional test of empty and size */
empty(&mine);
if (size(mine) != 0)
  printf("Empty size is %d\n",size(mine));

/* fault-based test: does empty set contain 0? */
if (member(0,mine) == TRUE)
  printf("0 falsely in empty set\n");

/* functional test of member */
putin(1, mine, &mine);
if (member(1, mine) == FALSE)
  printf("1 mistakenly absent from {1}\n");

/* functional test of updating in place and putin
     that can be used to try duplicate elements */
empty(&mine);
printf("Enter positive elements ending with EOF:");
while (scanf("%d", &elem) != EOF)
{
if (member(elem, mine) == FALSE) count += 1;
putin(elem, mine, &mine);
}
if (member(elem, mine) == FALSE)
  printf("Failed last-member test\n");
printf("%d =? %d\n", count, size(mine));

/* functional test of putin with distinct sets */
putin(-1, mine, &yours);
if (member(-1, mine) == TRUE ||
  member(-1, yours) == FALSE)
  printf("Failed copy test\n");

/* functional test of multiple-chunk allocation */
for (count=0;count<CUPLACHUNKS;count++)
  putin(count, mine, &mine);
printf("Large set: %d\n", size(mine));

/* functional test of storage return */
putin(-2, yours, &mine);
if (size(mine) != size(yours) + 1)
  printf("Failed overlay of large set\n");
}
```

These functional unit tests have a flavor of fault-based tests because they use "exception reporting" whenever possible. If a test succeeds as the designer hopes it will, nothing is printed.

The driver is deficient in that it uses the Boolean type without any tests whatsoever, and it accepts the results of size and member uncritically. Thus these basic functions should be the subject of other detailed unit tests. Similarly, although the driver has many examples where storage allocation should occur, it does not check this allocation except in very crude ways. To properly check allocation will require unit testing of empty and putin, monitoring the address &S.a for the sets therein. (This driver program could be used with such monitoring in place; see Section 15.5.5.)

When the test driver is being used to test an implementation of this ADT, the tester will have the code of the driver to read, and its comments make the tests and the cryptic printed messages clear. Thus the test plan might say no more than "use this driver to test the ADT." However, more information is better, particularly if the person writing this driver will not be the tester who uses it, or if a long time will elapse between writing and using the driver. For example, the driver's loop for keyboard input could be the basis of several tests, which might be documented in the test plan as follows:

[**test setup 1**].   (give the text of the driver here).

[**test 1.1**].   (functional test of updating a set in place). Run the driver, and at the prompt to enter elements, key in the following:

```
2 3 4 5
^D
```

The result should be 4 =? 4.

[**test 1.2**].   (fault-based test of duplicate elements). Run the driver, and key in the following:

```
2 3 2 2 3 4 5
^D
```

The result should be 4 =? 4.

[**test 1.3**].   (functional test of memory allocation). Instrument the putin routine to print out the addresses and sizes of memory that it allocates and uses (see Section 15.5.5), and the values inserted. Run the driver, and key in the following:

```
2 3 3 5
^D
```

The instrumentation should indicate that the set is first obtained as one chunk (2 inserted). On the next call (3 inserted), no memory should be allocated and the same address used. No change in memory should result from the next call. On the final call (5 inserted), there should be no allocation. The result should be 3 =? 3. Similarly, the tester can watch the memory being allocated and returned in the remainder of the functional tests.

Many other tests are possible using this driver.

15.5 Implementing an ADT

ADTs can be thought of as no more than extensions of a programming language's built-in types. In Pascal, for example, there *is* a type Boolean, with built-in operations of conjunction and negation. The implementation of an ADT should make it look like the language has that type built in, for example, to give C a Boolean type. (Languages like Ada and C++ even support defining the access routines as infix operators.) Variables of the new type may be declared, and used just as any variables are used. C's typedef mechanism provides the way to accomplish the data structure part of ADT implementation.

15.5.1 Implementing a Boolean ADT

The Boolean ADT of Section 15.2 might be implemented as follows:

```
typedef char Boolean;
/* 'T' and 'F' are the truth values */
#define TRUE 'T'
#define FALSE 'F'
Boolean and(Boolean A, Boolean B)
{
  if (A == 'T' && B == 'T')
    return('T');
  else
    return('F');
}
Boolean not(Boolean B)
{
  if (B == 'T')
    return ('F');
  else
    return('T');
}
```

Here the programmer has made the "hidden" choices of typedef and TRUE and FALSE that were left open in the design of Section 15.2.

15.5.2 Encapsulation: Header Files

By adopting a standard mechanism for placing the definitions needed to implement and use an ADT in C, the programmer can mitigate some of the difficulties C has in guarding ADT secrets. It is standard practice in C programs to put type information into special "header" files, and then to preface these files to any code that needs to make use of the types. The #include compiler directive does exactly this, and it is common for programmers not to examine the included files and not to transgress against their intent of hiding information. For example, the header file stdio.h includes the line:

```
#define EOF (-1)
```

Once a programmer has looked at this line, the secret is out: scanf() returns −1 on end of file. But programmers usually pay no attention but dutifully use EOF instead. Thus it makes sense to place into a file (say) Boolean.h the information needed by users of this ADT, namely:

```
typedef char Boolean;
/* 'T' and 'F' are the truth values */
#define TRUE 'T'
#define FALSE 'F'
/* Access routines: */
extern Boolean and(Boolean A, Boolean B);
extern Boolean not(Boolean A);
```

and require that any code wishing to make use of the Boolean type start with the directive:

```
#include "Boolean.h"
```

The assumption is that programmers will make use of Boolean and TRUE, FALSE, but will turn a blind eye on what these are actually declared to be. This header file can be written before ADT implementation by simply omitting the structural parts. It is proper ANSI C to have a typedef with an empty structural part, but not all compilers properly handle it.

Putting the templates for the access routines in the header file allows the compiler to ensure that these are properly used. The implementation of the ADT can #include "Boolean.h" as well, and thus guarantee that the names it implements are the ones being used.

15.5.3 Correctness of ADT Implementations

The whole reason for using and implementing ADTs is to remove the implementation details from further consideration. Once the ADT is defined, its

It is not an acceptable secret for an ADT that it doesn't work.

users in the rest of the code do not care how it is implemented, with one absolutely crucial exception: the implementation must be correct. There are several ways to define what it means for an ADT to be correct, of which the most intuitive is the algebraic commuting diagram.

Imagine that there are two distinct worlds for an ADT. One is the "abstract" or intuitive world, in which a human being has a mental picture of the data type, and intuitive ideas about what its operations mean. In the Boolean example that began in Section 15.2, this intuitive world might be called the "logical" one, in which there are truth values *true* and *false*, and operations usually written as $\wedge$ (and), $\neg$ (not), etc. Human beings who know some logic have a mental picture of "logical" and can think in terms of it. For example, they know that the only time $P \wedge Q$ is *true* is when P and Q are both *true*.

The second ADT world is the "concrete" or implementation world, in which a computer program manipulates bits in its memory to perform computations. It is this world that we talk about when we write code for the ADT. It contains ADT values that "represent" the intuitive ones, and procedures that transform those values into other values, attempting to mimic the intuitive operations. In the Boolean example of the previous section, the values are the characters 'T' and 'F' corresponding to the truth values, and the procedures corresponding to $\wedge$, $\neg$ are and(), not().

An implementation is *correct* for an ADT if it faithfully carries out the intuitive operations. To express carefully what this means requires that an explicit mapping be made between the two ADT worlds. This mapping, called the *abstraction mapping A*, carries the concrete objects onto the intuitive ones. Thus for the Boolean ADT:

$$A('\mathrm{T}') = true \quad \text{and} \quad A('\mathrm{F}') = false.$$

Of course, the mapping A is the first thing the programmer has to think of when implementing the ADT, to write the typedef and choose the constants.

The correctness of an ADT implementation can now be formally described by a *commuting diagram* for each operation. Figure 15.3 shows the commuting diagram for the logical $\wedge$ operation. The diagram shows the two worlds connected by the A abstraction mapping. What is meant by the phrase "and() is a correct implementation of $\wedge$" is precisely that the same result is always obtained going around the diagram in two directions from lower left to upper right. If one starts in the lower left of the diagram (with any concrete values), and follows around the diagram to the right and up to the upper right (to abstract values); then one starts again at the lower left with the same concrete values, but now follows first up and then around to the right; then, the resulting abstract values are the same. It is easier to express this commuting property in a formula than in words. The implementation is correct if and only if for any concrete values c and d:

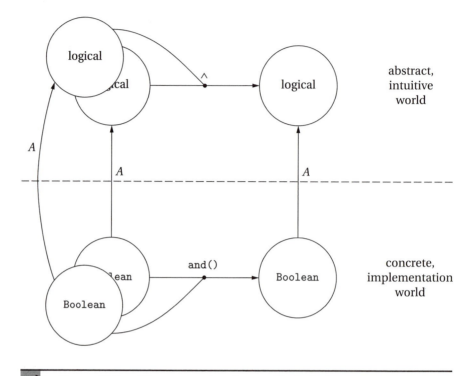

▶ **Figure 15.3**   The commuting diagram for logical ∧.

$$A(c) \land A(d) = A(\text{and}(c, d)).$$

For example,

$$A('\text{T}') \land A('\text{F}') = A(\text{and}('\text{T}','\text{F}'))$$

or

$$true \land false = A('\text{F}') = false,$$

so in this example the diagram does commute.

For this finite Boolean ADT, it is possible to check all the cases of all the operations by hand, and prove that the implementation is correct. For more realistic ADTs, examples are just tests that by no means show correctness by their success.

15.5.4 Implementing the `IntSet` ADT in C

The ADT designed in Section 15.4.3 can be coded in an imperative language, and C has already been chosen (because its subroutine headers were used in the design). Although the memory allocation aspects of the ADT pose some

difficulty, most of the coding is so straightforward that it is faster to write it
than to read it.

The most important choice at the beginning of ADT implementation is
the data structure used to represent the ADT values. The design of Section
15.4.3 left this choice to the implementor, but dictated dynamic storage
allocation in 100-element chunks. The most straightforward structure to
realize this design decision is an array and a counter for the number of
elements already stored therein. Complete details of this data structure are
a primary secret of the ADT, expressed in the typedef for IntSet:

```
typedef /* representation for a set of integers */
struct S {int *a; int c;}
  /* S.a[0], S.a[1], ... , S.a[S.(c-1)]
       contain the set members
     c = 0 for an empty set */
  IntSet;
```

The commentary and the structure are strictly for use by the programmer
who implements the ADT; its users need only to see:

```
typedef /* don't look! */ IntSet;
```

Collecting all the ADT information into an #include file IntSet.h:

```
/* interface for the ADT "IntSet" */
typedef /* representation for a set of integers */
struct S {int *a; int c;}
  /* S.a[0], S.a[1], ... , S.a[S.(c-1)]
       contain the set members
     c = 0 for an empty set */
  IntSet;

/* cardinality of S */
extern int size(IntSet S);

/* truth of i in S */
extern Boolean member(int i, IntSet S);

/* return an empty set through S */
extern void empty(IntSet *S);

/* return a set (S union {i}) through nS */
extern void putin(int i, IntSet S, IntSet *nS);
```

This header should be included with any code using the ADT. In particular,
the test driver given in Section 15.4.4 needs it.

With the ADT header information recorded, the implementation can proceed.

There is an immediate problem, which is common to any data type, built into a language or defined: between the time that a variable X is declared and the execution of a statement setting the value of X, it makes no sense to use the variable; it is "uninitialized." Languages designed for ADT implementation have special constructions that allow ADT variables to be initialized on declaration, but C has nothing of this kind. For IntSet, the operations that set values are empty() and putin(). What happens if an IntSet should be used (say, as a parameter to size()) before either of these has initialized it? The implementor of the ADT must answer this question, which is seldom considered when an ADT is specified or designed.

For this implementation, it is decided to tie initialization to the allocation of the dynamic array in the IntSet structure. Because C initializes all nonlocal variables to zero, a test for zero can be used, as captured in the following:

```
/* An unallocated set X is assumed to have
    a pointer value X.a of 0 */
#define NONEXIST(S) (((S).a) == 0)
```

Too much engineering is not a good thing (creeping feature creature) ▶ This implementation will print error messages if an attempt is made to use an unallocated set. There was nothing in the specification about this.

The two access routines that follow do not have to deal with the difficulties that memory allocation introduces. The second makes use of the Boolean ADT from Section 15.5.1.

```
#include "Boolean.h"
#include "IntSet.h"

/* returns the cardinality of S */
int
size(IntSet S)
{
  if (NONEXIST(S))
    {
    printf("size(unallocated set).\n");
    /* there is no good return value */
    return(-1);
    }
  return(S.c);
}

/* returns truth of i in S */
Boolean
member(int i, IntSet S)
```

```
{
  int x;
  if (NONEXIST(S))
    {
    printf("member(unallocated set).\n");
    return(FALSE);
    }
  for (x=0; x < S.c; x++)
    if (S.a[x] == i)
      return(TRUE);
  return(FALSE);
}
```

A fault-based test suggests itself here: to be sure that the proper part of the array is being searched, one must look for a unique element inserted last. To find such an element using member proves that the search does not stop too soon. There is already such a test in the driver of Section 15.4.4.

The access routines that must allocate memory are next. These probably require some internal design since there exist the possibilities that (1) a set has not yet been assigned storage, (2) it has been assigned storage, but not the amount now needed, and (3) the update should happen in place. For empty, the cases are straightforward:

```
/* returns an empty set through S */
void
empty(IntSet *S)
{
  if (NONEXIST(*S))
    { /* new set */
      S->a = (int *)malloc(sizeof(int[CHUNK]));
      S->c = 0;
      return;
    }
  if (S->c > CHUNK)
    { /* allocated, more than one chunk */
      /* return storage and reallocate */
      free(S->a);
      S->a = 0; /* make it look unallocated */
      empty(S);
      return;
    }
  /* else allocated at one chunk */
  S->c = 0;
  return;
}
```

The implementation requires a value for the allocation unit (another secret):

```
/* allocation granularity in set elements */
#DEFINE CHUNK = 100
```

The implementation of putin will complete the ADT. It has an "old set" and a "new set." The old set must exist or the result is unspecified. The new set may or may not exist. It is to be updated in place just in case the old set and the new set are the same and adding the new element does not bring things to a chunk boundary. There can be no size change if the new element is already present in the old set. These cases are the ones that structure the code:

```
#define DIFFLOC(S,P) ((S).a != (P)->a)
/* S is an IntSet, P is a pointer to IntSet.
   If their array pointers agree, the storage is
   the same.  But if both arrays are unallocated,
   the two objects will appear to be the same. */

/* returns a set (S union {i}) through nS */
void
putin(int i, IntSet S, IntSet *nS)
{
  int x, nsize;
  if (NONEXIST(S))
    {
      printf("putin(unallocated set).\n");
      return;
    }
  nsize = S.c;
  if (member(i,S) == FALSE)
    nsize += 1;
  if (NONEXIST(*nS))
    nS->a = (int *)malloc(((nsize/CHUNK) + 1)
                              *sizeof(int[CHUNK]));
  else
    if (nsize/CHUNK != (nS->c)/CHUNK) /* wrong size */
      {
        free(nS->a);
        nS->a = (int *)malloc(((nsize/CHUNK) + 1)
                                *sizeof(int[CHUNK]));
      }
  /* here nS exists and is the right size */
  nS->c = nsize;
```

```
/* copy existing set contents if necessary */
if (DIFFLOC(S, nS))
  for(x=0; x<S.c; x++)
    nS->a[x] = S.a[x];
if (S.c < nsize)  /* element not present */
  nS->a[nsize - 1] = i;
return;
}
```

If all this code is linked with the driver routine of Section 15.4.4, the tests described there can be executed (and will all succeed). However, on many earlier versions of the code, these tests did *not* succeed, revealing bugs in the code (mostly in memory allocation) and in the design (improper mixing of pointers and values).

15.5.5 Instrumenting the ADT's Memory Allocation

To insert instrumentation in empty and putin as suggested for [test 1.3] in Section 15.4, it would be appropriate to monitor the use of the allocation/deallocation routines malloc and free. A general way to do this is to make calls to instrumented routines, say, MALLOC and FREE, whose substance is:

```
int
MALLOC(int much)
{
  int store;
  store = malloc(much);
  printf("Allocated %d bytes at address %d\n",
          much, store);
  return(store);
}

void
FREE(int where)
{
  printf("Deallocated storage at address %d\n",
          where);
  free(where);
}
```

There are transgressions on strong typing in this code, as there must be if memory pointers are to be printed as if they were integers. To use (say) MAL-LOC, go through the existing code and change all occurrences of malloc(to MALLOC(. With this instrumentation if place, every memory operation will announce itself for testing. Instead of a function, a #define MALLOC... can also be used. If you use a #define, the instrumentation definition can later be changed to a straight call on malloc, and the calls on MALLOC left in place, without influencing efficiency. The instrumentation might need to be put in and taken out several times.

15.5.6 Local Variables of the ADT Type

Document it! ▶
(know what
you've assumed)

Alas, the code has a serious flaw that the test driver did not expose, but that is likely to appear in any system that uses the ADT seriously. A programmer familiar with the problems of memory allocation and initialization in C might spot the trouble in a formal inspection of IntSet, but the most likely outcome is that the code will go into use and fail in an obscure way. It has been implicitly assumed that all IntSet variables will be declared globally. A variable declared within a procedure in C is allocated space when the procedure is called (and the value contained in the space is not guaranteed); then when the procedure returns, the space is returned and the value lost. C compilers are not required to produce code for local variables that work this way, but most do. Thus a local uninitialized IntSet may not have the zero-valued array pointer that the code requires. And every time a procedure is called and returns, the array space allocated to any local IntSets will be lost when the pointer in the local variable is discarded.

If this bug were discovered after IntSet variables had been used in a system, the only sure fix would be to convert all local variables to global ones. If it were discovered while the ADT was being designed, there are somewhat cumbersome ways to alter the specification and design to make local variables work. Certainly the easiest thing to do is to stamp all the user documentation with the legend:

> **DO NOT DECLARE IntSet LOCAL VARIABLES!**

Unfortunately, though the ADT programmers do their best not to make this information secret, nothing in C stops the ADT user from declaring local variables and trying to use them, with the bad results already described.

How Does It Fit?

From section 15.1

1. If you know how the set data type is implemented in some Pascal compiler, discuss its efficiency and limitations.

2. Using an ADT for the data structure SymbolTable would have been very helpful in the iterative enhancement development of a compiler de-

scribed at the end of Section 11.2.1. Give a brief description of such an ADT, and explain why it might allow easier enhancement of a compiler.

3. In the 1960s, it was generally believed that "modularizing" code by splitting it into many small routines is a good idea, but there was no explicit principle like information hiding to guide the division. It was observed in large systems (the IBM 360 operating system had the first documented case) that when the first changes were made, they impacted only a few of the routines; however, as more and more changes were made, each single change touched more routines until after a while the system became "unmaintainable" in the sense that to make any change, almost all the routines were involved. Explain this observation.

4. How good is the information hiding in the pseudocode example for Zipf's law (Section 13.1.1)? Explain its deficiencies, and redo the design to improve the information hiding.

From section 15.2

5. In the C syntax that corresponds to the signature in Figure 15.1, comments appear instead of certain information. Explain why.

From section 15.3

6. Suppose that an ADT has N access routines each taking one parameter of the type. If a static storage implementation is to act as though it has V internal variables, how many actual access routines will it need?

From section 15.4

7. In the driver and test program for IntSet, there is a #define CUPLA-CHUNKS.

   (a) Explain why this should not be 4*CHUNK.

   (b) Explain why only 4*CHUNK will really do.

   (c) What, if anything, can be done about the dilemma of (a) and (b)?

8. In the driver and test program for IntSet, all the references to the Boolean function member() explicitly compare its value to TRUE or FALSE. A programmer looking at this decides to use 1 and 0 to implement these constants, and then changes the driver code to be more "readable" by replacing, for example

   ```
   if (member(elem, mine) == FALSE) ...
   ```

   by

   ```
   if (not(member(elem, mine))) ...
   ```

   Why is this not OK?

9. Add some functional tests to the test driver for IntSet.

From section 15.5

10. In the Boolean ADT of Section 15.5.1, the representations of the logical constants are given by #defines.

   (a) They might have been initialized constants of the ADT type:

```
Boolean TRUE = 'T';
Boolean FALSE = 'F';
```

   Would this be just as good? (Hint: How often is the Boolean.h file invoked?)

   (b) In the implementing code, the literal values are used instead of the names. Explain why this does or does not matter. Is the ADT secret being violated?

11. The concrete value pair ('T', 'T') was checked for commutativity in Figure 15.3. Do the other cases to prove that the diagram commutes.

12. For the "logical" example of Section 15.5.3,

   (a) Draw the commuting diagram for logical ¬

   (b) Write the equations that state that the diagram of (a) commutes

   (c) Verify that the diagram of (a) *does* commute by trying all possible truth values

13. Draw the commuting diagram for the Boolean function TRUE.

14. It has been suggested that the problem of uninitialized variables should be eliminated at its source by requiring that every variable be given an initial value on its declaration.

   (a) Which is worse, a program in which an uninitialized variable is referenced because a previous statement to read in its value was forgotten, or one in which the variable is initialized when declared, but the read statement is still forgotten? Why?

   (b) Could initialized declarations be used for IntSet variables? Explain.

15. Suppose the memory allocation code in the ADT of Section 15.5 fails to work in just such a way that updates never happen in place, but instead new memory is always allocated.

   (a) Will any functional tests fail?

   (b) If the problem is not caught, how might it eventually manifest itself to a user who is just trying to use the ADT in some system?

16. One early attempt to implement the memory allocation code for the ADT in Section 15.5 checked &S == nS to decide if the last two parameters to putin() were the same set. A student noticed that this code could fail if S and nS were the same variable passed as a parameter to a subroutine.

   (a) Would the tests described in Section 15.5 have exposed this fault? Explain.

    (b) If you know something about the way storage is allocated by C compilers, explain the problem that the student noticed.

17. In the instrumentation using MALLOC in Section 15.5.5, it would be more convenient to leave malloc() in the code, and use a #define malloc ... to replace the call with instrumented code.

    (a) The instrumented code might contain a call on (the real) malloc(). Would this set off an infinite recursion?

    (b) Write a macro that allows malloc() to stay in place.

    (c) When the instrumentation in (b) has done its job and needs to be removed, what should be done?

18. Would it solve the problem of local IntSet variables in Section 15.5.6 to declare them static? (Hint: It would solve part of the problem.)

19. Modify the specification, design, and implementation of IntSet so that it permits the declaration of local variables of the ADT, without loss of storage or the difficulties with initialization mentioned in Section 15.5.6.

20. It would vastly simplify the memory allocation in the coding of IntSet to use just one huge virtual array, partitioned off into large sectors, one for each IntSet variable declared. The operating system would then manage storage allocation. Redo the design in this way, and code putin().

Review Questions

1. What is the relationship between information hiding and abstract data types?

2. Why is it possible to write an explicit test driver for an ADT at design time, when no coding has yet been done?

3. What are the encapsulation conventions for an ADT written in C?

4. What does it mean for an ADT to be correct?

Further Reading

Parnas's article that suggested information hiding [Par72] is not always easy to read, but it is more focused than most seminal work in that its author did not mix several mediocre ideas in with his really good one.

    Fred Brooks reports [Bro75] on data from the IBM System 360 development, concerning modules written without information hiding, and maintenance that quickly escapes from their confines.

    The theory of ADTs has been well worked out. To put it briefly, an ADT is a multisorted algebra with an initial semantics. The mathematics is summarized in a dense paper [GTW78] by three mathematicians. Michael O'Donnell's book looks at the theory of algebraic equations both as specifications, and as a programming device [O'D85]. The theory presented in a paper [GHM87] following Harlan Mills's ideas of "functional correctness" is closer to that presented in this chapter. Its underlying ideas come from Hoare's seminal paper [Hoa72]. John Gutag and Dave Musser were among the early proponents of ADT implementation as practical software engineering. Joseph Gougan has implemented a language called OBJ, which defines ADTs by signature and algebraic equations, and allows them to be executed directly, without an implementation in C or any other programming language. OBJ is particularly suited for the study of hierarchies in ADT definition [Goq00].

References

[Bro75]   Fredrick P. Brooks. *The Mythical Man Month*. Addison-Wesley, 1975.

[GHM87]   J. D. Gannon, R. G. Hamlet, and H. D. Mills. Theory of modules. *IEEE Transactions on Software Engineering*, 13, 1987.

[Goq00]   Joseph A. Goquen. *Software Engineering with OBJ–Algebraic Specification in Action*. Kluwer Academic Publishers, 2000.

[GTW78]   J. A. Goguen, J. W. Thatcher, and E. G. Wagner. An initial algebra approach to the specification, correctness, and implementation of abstract data types. In R. T. Yeh, editor, *Current Trends in Programming Methodology*, volume 4, pages 80–149. Prentice Hall, Englewood Cliffs, NJ, 1978.

[Hoa72]   C. A. R. Hoare. Proof of correctness of data representations. *Acta Informatica*, 1:271–281, 1972.

[O'D85]   Michael J. O'Donnell. *Equational Logic as a Programming Language*. MIT Press, 1985.

[Par72]   David L. Parnas. On the criteria to be used in decomposing systems into modules. *Communications of the ACM*, December 1972.

chapter 16

Object-Oriented Design

The world is composed of objects. Clothes, houses, appliances, toys, books, and garden tools are just a few of the objects encountered by people during a typical day. The human race has found uses for almost every object around, even rocks: they can be used as weapons, collected for their beauty, used to construct roads and buildings. The human mind interacts well with objects, and people are continually synthesizing new objects. For instance, a road is composed of many rocks, brought together into a new form for a new purpose. As a result of human affinity for objects, an *object-oriented* approach to software design is very natural.

Real-world objects are involved in actions. A person *manipulates the object, and the object does things.* This idea is fundamental to object-oriented design. For a moment, think of a cup. A cup can be filled and a cup can be emptied. The actions "filled" and "emptied" are two ways that people use a real cup. In object-oriented design and programming, the word *method* is used to describe actions that involve an object. So, if a software cup object were designed, it would have a method for filling and a method for emptying. Object-oriented design creates software units that act in programs the way real-world objects act. Problems are solved by identifying the real-world objects that enter into the problem situation; software counterparts to these are designed, each with its methods; then the problem solution is expressed as sequences of method invocations among the software objects. The result is a program design that mimics the real world well enough to arrive at the needed results. The designer can imagine that the problem solution is being acted out by objects in the real world, a fiction that is very helpful in designing the solution in software.

16.1 Real Objects and Software Objects

The technical details of object-oriented design describe how software components are constructed to behave like everyday objects.

16.1.1 What is a Software Object?

Software objects are conceptual units that engineers invent in order to describe their interactions. A software object is a collection of data and methods for manipulating data that hide much of the detail in the object container itself. Thus objects are very like ADTs. In an ADT signature (Section 15.2), the circles represent the data, and the arrows represent the methods. (The *inheritance* mechanism for objects is missing from ADTs; see Section 16.3.4.)

Methods can be thought of as algorithms that operate on data contained in an object. This data is often hidden and is sometimes created when the object is constructed although it may also be created by a method itself. The methods are functions associated with this specific set of data.

Intellectual control (language betrays us) ▶ As befits a new idea, object-oriented design comes with new terminology:

Object.   A structure containing data, and a set of functions that manipulate that data.

Method.   A function for manipulating the data in an object.

Class.   A description of the methods and data structures that constitute an object. A class is the template for building and communicating with an object.

Instance.   A specific, concrete member of a class. An instance has actual data assigned to the object.

Subclass.   A child class that inherits methods and data from its parents.

Superclass.   A parent class that provides methods and data to child classes derived from it.

An example may help to explain the differences between objects, classes, and instances. Imagine a class *Car* that describes a passenger car, and the actions that a car is involved in. During execution of a program using *Car,* the instances: *1957 Chevy Bel-Aire*, *1956 Ford Crown Victoria*, and *1993 Ford Taurus* might arise. The *1957 Chevy Bel-Aire* is an object that is an instance of class *Car.*

16.1.2 The Object Paradigm

Paradigm: $0.20.

Mental models of the physical world strongly affect how people get along in that world. A model is a set of ideas and expectations (sometimes called a *paradigm*) about how things fit together, how they are organized, what they really mean. "Objects and their actions" is a world view that people find comfortable because of the way we interact with the physical world. We think of a thing, and what it does comes to us immediately. This natural human bent can be turned to use in software design. Design requires a creative leap from the problem description to the germ of a solution. There are ways to derive software objects and their methods from natural language specifications, and these help the designer get started.

16.2 Object-Oriented Requirements

Requirements are the foundation of any software design. The hard part is getting from the requirements to the first design ideas, and thinking about the real-world objects involved in the problem can help.

16.2.1 Modeling the Physical World

Natural language requirements are written from the user's viewpoint, which allows analysis based on knowledge of the user's experience. Many systems are based on physical analogies that help the user guess what operations might be performed. For example, in the "desktop" paradigm, a computer presents the user with a visual desktop on the screen with files and desk accessories like a clock. The user would guess that a file can be opened or closed and the clock can be set since this is what can be done with these physical objects on a real desktop.

The first rule for object-oriented designers is to *model the physical world* in order to provide the end user with a familiar look and feel. Since the object-oriented approach is closely related to our perception and description of the problem world, it should come as no surprise that an object-oriented design resembles the real physical situation. The analyst should look for real-world descriptions of objects in the requirements.

For example, in the design of a library system, the objects found in a library should be modeled, with operations that can be performed on these objects, such as:

- Book: Check-in, check-out, add-to-library, retire-from-library
- Stacks: Add-to-stacks, remove-from-stacks
- Card catalog: Add-book, remove-book

There are other objects in a library, of course, which would be apparent during a visit to a library itself.

16.2.2 The Role of Requirements

Requirements identify the objects themselves. In the case where the designer is operating outside his or her area of specialty, the requirements are the sole source of input for the design. Fortunately, since the requirements reflect the user's understanding of the problem solution, there are systematic ways to identify the objects in the requirements specification. The objects may be hidden, but the designer can systematically uncover them, and also uncover their intuitive methods.

The approaches for discovering these objects, identifying their methods, and orchestrating their interactions to solve the user's problem are the substance of object-oriented design and implementation. As befits a new and promising technique, object-oriented design has been given several "flavors" by different proponents. Three popular ones are Booch, Shlaer-Mellor, and the CRC method. A CRC example will be given in detail in Section 16.3.

16.2.3 Booch Method

The Booch method is named after its developer, Grady Booch. It focuses on four basic aspects of the design:

- Logical model
- Physical model
- Dynamic model
- Static model

Represented in each of these models is information about the classes, methods, and their relationships. The Booch method provides multiple sets of information, providing the implementer with a rich set of details about the implementation of each object.

16.2.4 Shlaer-Mellor Method

The Shlaer-Mellor method, named after its inventors, uses a different viewpoint for analyzing the system. The Shlaer-Mellor method models three basic aspects of the objects themselves:

- *Object information:* What information needs to be dealt with by each object?

- *Object state:* How does the behavior of the object change with use?
- *Processing/actions:* How does the object behave?

16.2.5 Class-Responsibilities-Collaboration (CRC) Method

The object-oriented design method that we describe in detail uses yet another viewpoint of objects: classes (of objects), their responsibilities (the methods they provide), and the objects that collaborate with them. The CRC method provides a good approach to object-oriented design when the designer begins with a set of unstructured natural language requirements. The resulting object-oriented design must direct the coding phase. In order to implement an object-oriented design, the programmer must understand:

- The classes
- The class hierarchies (inheritance)
- The methods or the responsibilities of each class
- The collaborations between the classes

Intellectual control (language betrays us)

CRC seeks to provide this information.

It's unfortunate, but CRC uses terminology that departs from the normal object-oriented terms:

- *Inheritance classes* are parent classes, which are normally called *superclasses*.
- *Responsibilities* are the things the object must do, which are normally called *methods*.
- *Collaborators* are objects that work together to achieve a specific purpose.

The CRC terminology will be used in this chapter, but it will slowly fade out in favor of the normal object-oriented design terms.

The CRC method consists of these fundamental steps:

1. Identification of the classes by examining the requirements document.
2. Identification of the responsibilities (methods) of each of these classes by finding the actions associated with classes in the requirements.
3. Identification of the relationships (collaborations) among these classes.

4. Identification of inheritance classes (superclasses), which will provide data and methods to their subclasses.

5. Identification of the actual mechanisms for collaborations.

There are techniques and rules for each step, and the best way to give them is in an example.

16.3 Example: A Checkbook System

A simple checkbook-balancing program will illustrate the CRC method in a familiar domain. Most people have a checking account and understand how it works. Starting with a simple description of the checkbook requirements, analysis will lead directly to the object-oriented design.

Natural language requirements:

> *A checkbook system is required for maintenance of checking accounts. This checkbook system must be able to process checking account transactions, such as checks and deposits for several checking accounts. The system must provide a complete listing of all transactions, sorted by date, with a running balance. In addition, the system must accept as input all pertinent data on the check, or deposit slip. This system will run as a batch system, accepting as input the name of the file containing the current set of transactions to be processed, the name of the file containing current account information, and the name of the file for the transaction listing.*

16.3.1 Identification of Classes and Patterns

The natural objects for designing a system are indicated in its English requirements by noun phrases. Here some of them are:

- A checkbook system
- Checking account
- Checking account transaction
- Check
- Deposit
- Listing of all transactions
- Running balance
- All pertinent data on the check or deposit slip
- A batch system
- File containing the current set of transactions

- File containing the current account information
- File for the transaction listing

These are candidates for software classes.

In a large design with many candidate classes, it may be hard to bring candidates into a form where similarities and difference can be identified. Some helpful rules are:

- Look for particular physical objects, not categories of objects.
- Standardize terminology: if more than one term is used for an object, pick the most representative term.
- Adjectives and adverbs can point to object variants, or different ways to use the same object (for instance, *Running balance*).
- Watch out for the passive voice in requirements or system descriptions. The passive voice obscures candidate classes.

Next, the designer begins recording candidate classes on *CRC cards,* which hold the accumulating information of the design. A CRC card is divided into sections that will be filled in during the design effort. An empty CRC card looks like this:

Class:	
Superclass:	
Responsibilities	**Collaborators**

(The "Superclass" section will sometimes be a "Subclass" section.)

The design process creates a CRC card for every software class, on which are identified its superclass, methods (responsibilities), and collaborating classes (other CRC cards). Here is a completed card that might be part of a "desktop" design, which shows the form:

Class: Clock	
Superclass: Timepiece	
Responsibilities	**Collaborators**
set clock	Display
read clock	Display, Preferences

By convention, class and object names are capitalized, whereas method names begin with lowercase letters. This allows the reader to distinguish between objects and methods at a glance.

To begin the design, the following rather arbitrary class choices are made from the list of candidates:

- Account
- Transaction
- Check
- Deposit
- Balance
- Current transaction file
- Account information file
- Listing file

Notice that the *File* objects have been chosen as individually distinct: *Current transaction*, *Account information*, and *Listing*. The *File* attribute is a *recurring theme* that exists in the objects themselves. Here are some themes, often called *patterns*, that can emerge:

- *Naming patterns:* Similarities such as *Account information file, Listing file,* and so on.
- *Attribute patterns:* Similarities such as *pertinent data on the check* and *pertinent data on the deposit slip.*
- *Association patterns:* Similarities in where and how candidate classes work together. In this case, *Check, Deposit,* and *Transaction* work very closely with *Listing file.*

Initially, only the names of the candidate classes are placed on the CRC cards. For instance:

Class: Check	
Superclass:	
Responsibilities	**Collaborators**

It is apparent that there are some superclasses:

- *Transaction:* This is a superclass. The subclasses of *Transaction* are *Check* and *Deposit,* which fits in nicely with the notion of modeling the physical world.
- *File:* This is a superclass. The subclasses of file are *Listing, Current Transactions,* and *Account Information.*

A superclass is entered onto a CRC card as follows:

Class: Transaction	
Subclass: Check, Deposit	
Responsibilities	**Collaborators**

The cross-reference is entered on subclass cards like *Check*:

Class: Check	
Superclass: Transaction	
Responsibilities	**Collaborators**

Here is the class structure so far:

- *Account*
- *Transaction*

    - Subclass: *Check*
    - Subclass: *Deposit*

- *Balance*
- *File*

    - Subclass: *Current transaction*
    - Subclass: *Account information*
    - Subclass: *Listing*

16.3.2 Identification of Responsibilities

Objects have two fundamental aspects: data associated with the object, and operations that can be performed on that data (methods). CRC responsibilities of classes divide the methods into four groups:

- Data mutators: Methods for changing data within the object.
- Data accessors: Methods used for accessing data within the object.
- Implementors: Methods for implementing algorithms or invoking relationships that typically cause the object to change state.
- Managers: Methods for establishing (creating) or deleting objects (constructors/destructors).

These responsibilities typically reveal themselves by examination of the system requirements. Look for:

1. Information that must be maintained.
2. Actions that must be performed.

In the checkbook example, these verb phrases identify responsibilities:

- Process account transaction.
- Provide listing.
- Sorted by date.
- Running balance.
- Accept input (file name).

One possible assignment of responsibilities:

- □ *Account*

    - ⊕ *post transaction*
    - ⊕ *get balance*

- □ *Transaction*

    - □ Subclass: *Check*
        - ⊕ *get check amount*
        - ⊕ *get check date*
        - ⊕ *get check name field*
        - ⊕ *get check number*

    - □ Subclass: *Deposit*
        - ⊕ *get deposit amount*
        - ⊕ *get deposit date*
        - ⊕ *get deposit name field*
        - ⊕ *get cash received*

- □ *Balance*

    - ⊕ *get balance*
        (Note that *get balance* is already a responsibility of *Account.*)

- □ *File*

    - □ Subclass: *Current transaction*
        - ⊕ *get next transaction*
    - □ Subclass: *Account information*
        - ⊕ *get account information*
    - □ Subclass: *Listing*
        - ⊕ *put listing*
        - ⊕ *sort by date*

Notice how easy it is to come up with methods for these classes, from a knowledge of the intuitive objects in the requirements. For example, in the *File* subclasses there must be a way to *get next transaction,* and so forth. Likewise, it seems reasonable to *post transaction* to an *Account.*

At this point, a decision must be made about the *Balance* class. It is possible to continue to model *Balance* as a class, with responsibilities such as *set balance, get balance, deduct check amount, add deposit amount.* But it is also possible to model *Balance* as data that must be maintained by *Account.* If the system were a more elaborate accounting system, a separate *Balance* class would be the right choice, and *Balance* might be reused in different parts of the system, with additional methods such as *compute interest* or *compute penalty.* But for this simple example, *Balance* will be modeled as part of *Account,* and the methods mentioned become responsibilities of *Account.* Two of them are already there as *post transaction,* so the card for *Account* looks like this:

Class: Account	
Superclass:	
Responsibilities	**Collaborators**
post transaction	
set balance	
get balance	

Inspection of an actual checkbook deposit slip and an actual check reveals responsibilities not yet in the description:

- □ Subclass: *Check*

    - ⊕ *get check amount*
    - ⊕ *get check date*
    - ⊕ *get check name field*
    - ⊕ *get check number*

- □ Subclass: *Deposit*

    - ⊕ *get deposit amount*
    - ⊕ *get deposit date*
    - ⊕ *get deposit name field*
    - ⊕ *get cash received*

There is an obvious pattern in these responsibilities: the first three methods are common to *Check* and *Deposit*. Methods shared by subclasses can be *promoted* to their common superclass so that the *Transaction* CRC card would look like this:

Class: Transaction	
Subclass: Check, Deposit	
Responsibilities	**Collaborators**
get amount	
get date	
get name field	

The CRC card for *Check* would now appear as:

Class: Check	
Superclass: Transaction	
Responsibilities	**Collaborators**
get check number	

Duties involving the creation and destruction of objects are implicit in the definition of every class. These are not shown on the CRC cards, nor are they usually described in requirements, but the designer must realize that every object in the design may require storage management.

16.3.3 Identification of Collaborators

To complete the CRC design, the designer must make sure that the classes can fulfill the responsibilities expected by other classes. In short, the objects must be able to work with each other. Collaborators can be identified by thinking of relationship patterns and asking if they hold between classes of the design. For two hypothetical objects *A* and *B*, some relationships are:

- *A* is connected to *B*
- *A* is a kind of *B*
- *A* is like *B*
- *A* knows about *B*

Looking at relationships in the checkbook system, here are some of the collaborations:

- *Account* collaborates with:
  - *Check (post transaction)*
  - *Deposit (post transaction)*
  - *Current transaction (post transaction)*
  - *Listing (post transaction, set balance, get balance)*
- *Check* collaborates with:
  - *Current transaction (get check number)*
- *Listing* collaborates with:
  - *Check (put listing)*
  - *Deposit (put listing)*

When complete, each method in each class should have a corresponding set of collaborators. In the event that a responsibility appears to have no associated collaborators, either the responsibility can be removed (it is not needed) or a class may be missing from the design.

Collaborations are entered on the CRC cards on the line containing the associated responsibilities. Here is the *Account* CRC card:

Class: Account	
Superclass:	
Responsibilities	**Collaborators**
post transaction	Check, Deposit,
	Current transaction, Listing
set balance	Listing
get balance	Listing

The *Account* card is not yet complete; notably, its collaboration with *Transaction* is not recorded.

16.3.4 Polymorphism and Inheritance

On the *Account* CRC card, there is a need to handle two different types of *Transactions: Checks* and *Deposits.* When the *Account* posts the *Transaction* to the *Listing*, the *Listing* will need to know if the *Transaction* is a *Check* or a *Deposit.* This is so the *Listing* can list the check number, if it is a *Check,* or the deposit name field, if the *Transaction* is a *Deposit.* It would be convenient if the *Listing* could accept a *Transaction* as a generic parameter (that is, without knowing whether it is a *Check* or *Deposit*), then query the object about what it really is when it retrieves information for printing.

This particular problem is solved on different levels in modern object-oriented languages by *polymorphism.* Polymorphism means *many forms,* and may mean that there are several forms of the object itself, or that there are many forms of the methods within an object. The *Listing* object has to deal with two fundamental forms: *Check* and *Deposit. Check* and *Deposit* have a great deal in common: they have dates, they have amounts, and they have a name field. However, there are two annoying differences in these two transactions: one has a *check number,* whereas the other has a *cash received* field. The *Listing* object could cover both, except for the *get check number* and *get cash received* methods.

Inheritance allows the designer to define a *Transaction* object, and then derive from it *Check* and *Deposit* objects by using the definition of the *Transaction* object at the beginning. The designer can also use inheritance to build a *Check* object by using everything that was written for the *Transaction* object, and adding the *get check number* method to it. Similarly, the *Deposit* object can add the *get cash received* method to those of the *Transaction* object. By using inheritance, the designers make sure that functionality is implemented in one place, and one place only, for each family of objects.

Document it! ▶
(a place for everything, and everything in its place)

Another aspect of polymorphism is *overloading* of methods. Overloading works as follows: the *Listing* object provides two definitions of the method *put listing*. In one definition, a parameter is defined as a *Check* object, whereas in the other definition, the parameter is defined as a *Deposit*. Whenever the *put listing* method is used, the parameter is one or the other, and the correct method is invoked.

16.3.5 Identification and Use of Persistent Data

Some data used by an object needs to be preserved throughout the object's lifetime. Examples of this for the *Check* class would be the check number, check amount, and so on. This persistent data models exactly what would happen in the real world since a check could be left in a desk drawer for years and the amount of the check would still be readable.

There is no foolproof way to identify persistent data, but it can be found by examining the attributes that allow classes to be distinguished from each other. Consider how a *Check* is different from a *Deposit*. They are mostly alike since they're both *Transactions*, but a *Check* has a check number, and a *Deposit* has a cash received field. Therefore, the designer will have to provide a means to store this information within the objects themselves.

Persistent data must be examined or changed. Accessor and mutator methods are some of the most fundamental in an object's design. These methods often have a fundamental symmetry: where an accessor is present, there will often need to be a mutator and vice versa.

16.4 Checking an Object Design for Implementation

The object design provided for coding must include:

1. Name of class.
2. Name of any superclass from which this class inherits.
3. A list of persistent data and data types, along with any necessary mutators and accessors for this data.
4. List of any protected methods to be provided to subclasses from this class.
5. List of public methods and their parameter lists.

The *protected* methods are sometimes called "helper" methods because they help the subclasses that invoke them. Protected methods can be invoked only by the subclasses and parent class themselves. Public methods are those that are available to any user of the object.

For the most part, the CRC techniques will provide a complete set of information to the implementer. The designer can check for completeness with a technique called "object role playing." A role-playing session brings together a group of designers who act out the interactions of a set of objects. Each designer is assigned objects to represent in the session. The design information is provided to the role players so that they know which objects they collaborate with, what information they have stored internally, and what methods they provide to the other objects for interaction.

In the course of the session, as each object is invoked, the player representing that object can:

1. Ask the requesting object for information (as provided in the parameter list for the various methods).

2. Ask other collaborating objects for information to compute the requested values.

3. Supply information to the requesting object from a method that was invoked by the requesting object.

If the role player determines that an object being "played" cannot fulfill a request, then there is a design oversight. Though role playing may seem elementary, the value of walking through object interactions is not to be underestimated.

The designer should attempt to play out the roles of the objects by themselves before enlisting the help of other designers. As the designer gains experience in role-playing evaluation of object architectures, fewer errors will be discovered in the group role-playing evaluation, saving much time and establishing the designer's reputation in the designer community.

16.5 Object-Oriented Languages

Implementing an object-oriented design can be done using almost any programming language. However, object-oriented languages like Smalltalk, C++, and Java provide mechanisms to make the implementation easier, supporting the major object-oriented concepts. These are:

- Classes
- Methods
- Inheritance
- Polymorphism

These language constructs did not appear all at once. Some are the result of evolution in object-oriented language design, and a brief history will trace their origin. Object-oriented languages are *still* changing, so the final chapter in their history is yet to be written.

The roots of object-oriented programming are somewhat fuzzy. This is probably because objects are a natural way of thinking, and many programmers used an object-oriented approach as a way of managing complexity very early in the history of computing. To use a popular term, the paradigm was to think of program information elements as being related to familiar everyday things, such as *Account, Check, Transaction,* and so on. Data structures and databases reflected the logical association of information within the program. Eventually, it became apparent that in addition to data associations, there are also a logical set of methods for creating and manipulating that information. For instance, it is possible to *get balance* of an *Account.*

16.5.1 Smalltalk

"The best way to predict the future is to invent it."
—Alan Kay

At Xerox PARC (Palo Alto Research Center), Alan Kay put these notions to work in a new language that supported the close association of data and methods. This new programming language, *Smalltalk,* allowed programmers to deal with this association by packaging data and methods together in an *object.* Smalltalk not only supports objects, but it also provides an environment for the development of programs. Finally, it provides the programmer with a set of predefined *class libraries* from which to work. The development environment and class libraries allow engineers to focus on solving problems rather than bootstrapping the development platform. Inheritance allows Smalltalk programmers to add data and methods to existing objects. This proved to be a powerful and effective mechanism for leveraging off existing class libraries and gave a big boost to the idea of software reuse.

16.5.2 C++

Although Smalltalk was (and is) a successful object-oriented language, the software industry could accept only a more familiar language. C++ was developed as a means of providing the programmer with facilities for object-oriented programming, while retaining the look and feel of one of the most widely used languages: C. Today's version of C++ didn't spring immediately into existence, but instead went through a gradual metamorphosis from C, adding provisions for class encapsulation, member functions (methods), and operator overloading. Later versions of C++ allowed for multiple inheritance, a technique for using several superclasses to define a new object.

16.5.3 Java

With the rise of the Internet, the need for a platform-independent language became a pressing issue for the software engineering community. Browsers needed to be able to execute code imported from an unknown Internet host with relative safety. James Gosling at Sun Microsystems developed a programming language that was targeted primarily for consumer electronics, named *Oak*. *Oak* was renamed *Java,* and its application to Internet applications was quickly recognized. Next-generation browsers allowed the execution of Java *applets,* small Java programs embedded in the code (HTML) used by the browsers themselves. Java is one of the most popular programming languages today because of its portability and rich class libraries. Although the Java language implements some of the conceptual features (such as inheritance) in ways that are slightly different from C++, it is easy for C++ programmers to migrate to the Java development world.

16.6 A Brief Introduction to Java

Java is a programming language with a rich set of object libraries, and learning them is a substantial part of learning Java. In this brief section, we look mostly at the language itself, and its constructions for defining and using classes.

Looking at a simple Java program is a good place to start learning about the language. Here is a reconstruction of the classic "Hello, World!" program written in Java:

```
import java.io.*;

public class Hello
{
  public static void main (String[] args)
  {
    System.out.println("Hello, World!");
  }
}
```

In this example, the first line instructs Java to import, that is, allow the use of, a set of class libraries. This program is placed in a file called `Hello.java` by convention. During the processing of the program, a Java compiler will expect to find a class definition for class `Hello` in the file, matching the file name. In addition, within the definition of the class `Hello`, Java expects to find a definition of a method named `main()`, which is used as the main entry point for the program. Within the main routine, there is a call to a method in a library object named System.out. This method (println) is responsible for printing the string Hello, World! to the Java console.

16.6.1 Objects and Classes

Remember the difference between an object and a class: a *class* is the specification of the object, whereas an *object* is an actual instance. Here is an elementary class definition:

```
class Telescope
{
  public double focal_length;  // In millimeters
  public double aperture;      // In millimeters
  public double f_number;      // Unitless

  public Telescope(double flength, double ap)
  {
    focal_length = flength;
    aperture = ap;
    f_number = focal_length/aperture;
  }
}
```

In this class definition, the public variable declaration allows free access by code outside the class definition. There are three floating point double variables: focal_length, aperture, and f_number. These variables represent three attributes of optical telescopes: the length required to focus the image (focal length), the width of the light-gathering opening (aperture) and their ratio, the F-number.

To make an object from this class definition, its *constructor* code is used. The constructor has the same name as the class (in the example, public Telescope()), and appears to be a function, except there is no return type defined, and there is no return statement in the code body. A constructor's only job is to create object instances. The parameter list in the constructor specifies the information required to build an instance of the class Telescope. To construct two instances of the telescope class, the code might look something like this:

```
import java.io.*;

public class Simple
{
  public static void main(String[] args)
  {
```

```
        Telescope MyRefractor;
        Telescope MyNewtonian;

        MyRefractor = new Telescope(1000.0, 90.0);
        MyNewtonian = new Telescope(750.0, 150.0);

        System.out.println("F-number for my refractor:"
                        + MyRefractor.f_number);
        System.out.println("F-number for my newtonian:"
                        + MyNewtonian.f_number);
    }
}
```

In the preceding example, there are two object variables declared for class `Telescope`: `myRefractor` and `myNewtonian`. Each of these object variables is assigned an instance of a `Telescope` object. The constructor for the `Telescope` object, invoked by the `new` operator, calculates the F-number during instantiation (object construction), just before assignment to the object variable. In the code example, the resulting f-number component is printed. The + operator concatenates string values together.

The dot notation used in the code (for example, `MyRefractor.f_number`) is familiar to C and C++ programmers because it is used to access structure members. In a similar way, the dot notation allows access to parts of Java objects, and dot notation is also used to access class methods.

It is worth noting the naming conventions used here. Class names and object variables are usually capitalized to denote that they are object related, and not a user-defined type or structure. In addition, since the class declaration is contained in a file of the same name, the file name is capitalized.

16.6.2 Methods and Parameters

Methods may be thought of as functions or subroutines associated with a collection of object data. Here's an example of a data access method in a revised `Telescope` object:

```
class Telescope
{
  private double focal_length;  // In millimeters
  private double aperture;       // In millimeters
  private double f_number;        // Unitless

  public double get_f_number()
  {
    return f_number;
  }
```

```
    public Telescope(double flength, double ap)
    {
      focal_length = flength;
      aperture = ap;
      f_number = focal_length/aperture;
    }
}
```

In this example, the original `public` variables have become `private` variables. This protects `focal_length`, `aperture` and `f_number` from accidental or deliberate manipulation by code outside the object body. Instead, the access method `get_f_number` is used to return the value of this object's `f_number` variable.

Now the code for printing the value of the F-number looks like this:

```
System.out.println("F-number for my refractor:"
                   + MyRefractor.get_f_number() );
System.out.println("F-number for my newtonian:"
                   + MyNewtonian.get_f_number() );
```

Notice that dot notation for the methods suggests that a method is a member of the object itself. And so it is.

16.6.3 Inheritance and Polymorphism

The `Telescope` class has properties of *aperture, focal length,* and an *F-number* that are common to any focusing optical system. These notions make sense for a camera or magnifying glass. It is possible, then, to specify a parent class, say, `Optics`, that looks very much like `Telescope`. From this parent class, child classes can be defined that inherits its methods.

```
    class Optics
    {
      private double focal_length;   // In millimeters
      private double aperture;       // In millimeters
      private double f_number;       // Unitless

      public double get_f_number()
      {
        return f_number;
      }

      public double get_aperture()
      {
        return aperture;
      }
```

```
    public double get_focal_length()
    {
      return focal_length;
    }

    public Optics (double flength, double ap)
    {
      focal_length = flength;
      aperture = ap;
      f_number = focal_length/aperture;
    }
}
```

A Camera class derived from Optics could look like this:

```
class Camera extends Optics
{
    private String makeAndModel;

    public String get_makeAndModel()
    {
      return makeAndModel;
    }

    public Camera(double flength, double ap,
                  String make_model)
    {
      super(flength, ap);
      makeAndModel = make_model;
    }
}
```

There are several notable things about this new class. That it is an extension of the class Optics is indicated in its declaration by the phrase extends Optics. This means that all the methods and data of the Optics class are inherited by class Camera. So, after declaring a Camera object, programmers can call the method get_f_number(), just as they could for class Optics. The Camera class constructor is simply super, which means "invoke the superclass constructor." The reserved word super is used when it is necessary to refer to a superclass method or data. The Camera constructor also has a string parameter named make_model, which is used for a character string description of the camera's manufacturer and model name. After invoking the parent classes constructor, the local private variable makeAnd-Model is set, and the camera construction is complete. In addition to all the

Optics methods and data, Camera declares a new accessor method get_ makeAndModel. It is impossible to access parent data, such as f_number, directly within Camera objects because these data items are declared private in the Optics object. Private means exactly that: *private.* No one outside the class can use these items, not even child classes. In order to access the Optics object data from the Camera class, we would have to invoke the superclasses accessor method explicitly:

```
double my_f_number = super.get_f_number();
```

However, anyone outside the object could access it by simply invoking the Camera method directly:

```
Camera MyCamera;

MyCamera = new Camera(75.0, 263.0, "Zeiss-Ikon Ikonta");
System.out.println(MyCamera.get_makeAndModel() + ": "
                    + MyCamera.get_f_number());
```

Even though the get_f_number method was not explicitly implemented in the definition of the Camera class, it is inherited from the Optics object, so this code segment would yield the output:

```
Zeiss-Ikon Ikonta: 0.28517110266159695
```

Intellectual control ▶

When object classes are derived from a superclass, it allows the subclasses to be manipulated by other classes in a generic way. Generic processing keeps similar ideas together and eliminates multiple classes that differ only slightly to handle slightly different situations. For example, suppose a print object was needed to handle output for our optical calculation system. It is possible to write a single print method for our Optics class and all its child objects. Suppose we have defined additional child object methods for Telescope and MagnifyingGlass that have special methods for a telescope's configuration and a magnifying glass's manufacturer's name:

```
public void print_optics_parameters(Optics Opt)
{
    double aperture = Opt.get_aperture();
    double f_length = Opt.get_focal_length();
    double f_number = Opt.get_f_number();
```

```
        if (Opt instanceof Camera)
        {
          Camera Cam = (Camera) Opt;
          System.out.println("Parameters of camera "
                             + Cam.get_makeAndModel());
        }
        if (Opt instanceof Telescope)
        {
          Telescope Tel = (Telescope) Opt;
          System.out.println("Parameters of "
                        +Tel.get_telescopeConfiguration());
        }
        if (Opt instanceof MagnifyingGlass)
        {
          MagnifyingGlass Mag = (MagnifyingGlass) Opt;
          System.out.println("Parameters of Magnifying Glass"
                + " made by: " + Mag.get_manufName());
        }
        System.out.println("    aperture:      " + aperture);
        System.out.println("    focal length: " + f_length);
        System.out.println("    f-number:      " + f_number);
      }
```

Here we see the benefit of polymorphism: Optics has several child classes; however, we can take advantage of the many forms of Optics by dealing with the minimum special requirements of each child (in this case, the make or model, configuration, and manufacturer's name).

16.7 Implementation of the Checkbook

The best way to see Java in action is to look at an example. In the following sections, a few classes from the checkbook design of Section 16.3 are used to illustrate Java implementation.

16.7.1 Implementation of the *Account* Class

The *Account* class was assigned responsibility for many of the operations ordinarily associated with a real life checking account. For instance, in real-life, a checking account owner could check the account balance and post a transaction against the account. These basic account operations were included in the design of the *Account* class. The part of the CRC card designed for the class is:

Class: Account	
Superclass:	
Responsibilities	**Collaborators**
post transaction	Check, Deposit, Current transaction, Listing
set balance	Listing
get current balance	Listing

How would an implementor write the *Account* object in Java? Perhaps something like this:

```java
public class Account
{
  private float balance;
  private Listing listing;

  //    Accessor
  public float getBalance()
  {
    return balance;
  }

  //    Mutator
  public void setBalance(float ib)
  {
    balance = ib;
  }

  //    Implementor
  public void postTransaction(Transaction t)
  {
    balance = balance + t.getAmount();
    listing.putListing(t, balance);
  }
```

```
//  Managers
public Account(Listing lst)
{
  balance = 0;
  listing = lst;
}
public Account(Listing lst, float initialBalance)
{
      balance = initialBalance;
      listing = lst;
}
}
```

In this code example, the first statement is a declaration of the class itself: Account. Immediately after the declaration of the class are the declarations of two private variables, balance and listing. The variables are declared private to keep other objects from gaining access to them directly. Instead, under the variables there is a routine labeled Accessor, which allows other objects to read the private information. In the Accessor section of the code, the public method getBalance() returns the current balance directly from the private variable balance. There is no accessor method for listing, simply because the system has no need to access the listing object after it is set in the Account object. In order to preserve simplicity of implementation and design, unnecessary methods should not be implemented merely to preserve symmetry.

Too much engineering is not a good thing ▶

Similarly, the mutator method setBalance() sets the private balance.

The implementor method postTransaction() adjusts the balance of the account, and informs the listing object that a transaction has occurred. The listing object's method putListing() is passed two parameters: the current transaction object t, and the current value of balance. The Transaction object is handled without regard to whether it is a Check object or a Deposit object, a distinction that is unimportant to the Account object since it needs to know only how much to post against the balance. Objects should be handled as high up the class hierarchy as possible.

Immediately after the Managers comment are two constructors, code for creating the Account object. One constructor requires a Listing object, and presumes the initial value of balance should be set to zero. The other constructor, however, allows the object to be built with an initial balance, which is passed into the constructor through the parameter initialBalance. These two constructors are an example of polymorphism: depending on the parameter list used by the code invoking the constructor, the correct constructor is used.

16.7.2 Implementation of the *Transaction* and *Check* Classes

In the design of the checkbook program, the *Transaction* class was a super-class with two subclasses: *Check* and *Deposit.* Their code will demonstrate how to implement inheritance using Java.

Begin with the *Transaction* superclass:

```java
import java.util.Date;

public class Transaction
{
  private float amount;
  private String nameField;
  private Date transDate;

  //    Accessors
  public float getAmount()
  {
    return amount;
  }
  public String getName()
  {
    return nameField;
  }
  public Date getDate()
  {
    return transDate;
  }

  //  Mutators
  protected void setAmount(float amt)
  {
    amount = amt;
  }
  protected void setNameField(String nameString)
  {
    nameField = nameString;
  }
  protected void setDate(Date tdate)
  {
  transDate = tdate;
  }
}
```

Transaction imports java.util.Date. This provides a class named Date, which has useful methods for displaying and calculating dates.

The Transaction superclass consists of a few private variables, some accessor methods, and mutator methods that modify the private variables. The declarations and uses of the private variables and the accessor methods are similar to the Account class, but its mutator methods are not: they are labeled protected. This declaration prevents access to these methods by any object that is not a subclass of Transaction. For instance, the Account object cannot invoke any of the protected items declared here, but Check and Deposit will be able to invoke them. This prevents alteration of any of the private variables' values by any classes other than a subclass of Transaction, and then only through these methods.

The Transaction class has no constructors; Java does not require them for every class declaration. Instead, the designer of this class expects that the subclasses will have constructors that invoke the appropriate mutator methods in the superclass to initialize the object. A brief examination of the Check class will reveal how this is done:

```java
import java.util.*;

public class Check extends Transaction
{
  private int checkNumber;

  //    Accessor
  public int getCheckNumber()
  {
    return checkNumber;
  }

  // Manager
  public Check(Date date, int checkNum, String to,
               float Amount)
  {
    super.setAmount(Amount);
    checkNumber =  checkNum;
    super.setDate(date);
    super.setNameField(to);
  }
}
```

In order to inherit the implementation of the Transaction class, the declaration of the Check class extends Transaction.

The Check class contains only one private variable: checkNumber. This is the only data attribute that sets it apart from the Transaction class.

Since the `Transaction` class has other data attributes, the `Check` class has those attributes as well (`amount`, `nameField`, and `transDate`). Also, the `Check` class provides an additional public accessor method: `getCheckNumber()`.

The constructor of the `Check` class (under the `Manager` comment) sets the `private` variables of its superclass, `Transaction`, using the superclass's `protected` methods, which are available only to its subclasses. This is one standard way of creating subclass objects.

The design of the *Transaction* and *Check* classes did not mention the manager or mutation methods of `Check` and `Transaction`. These methods are part of the objects' creation responsibilities, which is usually left out of CRC design.

How Does It Fit?

From section 16.1

1. What is the difference between an *instance* and an *object*?

From section 16.2

2. Some atheists say that they can't believe in any religion because religions all claim to capture the truth but don't agree with one another. A religious person might reply that there must be something to religions since there are so many versions about which people care so strongly. Recast and add to this discussion with "object-oriented design method" replacing "religion."

From section 16.3

3. In our examples of CRC cards, there is room for no more than six methods on a card. When 3 × 5 index cards are being used, the restriction is not so severe, but the number of methods is definitely limited. The limitation to on the order of ten methods is intended.

   (a) What principle dictates that each object should have only a few methods?

   (b) Give an example of a real-world object that has more than a dozen intuitive actions in which it participates, and hence could not be modeled as a software object on a CRC card.

   (c) What can the object-oriented designer do about a system whose requirements indicate objects with too many intuitive methods?

4. Draw the CRC card for *Deposit*.

5. (a) Might a class have *only* accessor methods and no mutator methods? Explain, with an example.

   (b) Repeat (a) for only mutator methods, no accessors.

From section 16.4

6. In an object role-playing session, suppose that two objects each require the other to provide a certain piece of information, but in fact neither does provide it.

   (a) How would this appear on the CRC cards for the two objects?

   (b) What would happen in the role-play session?

From section 16.5

7. Does the C programming language have *any* of the concepts needed to be an object-oriented implementation language?

8. Are inheritance and polymorphism *essential* to defining class libraries for an object-oriented language? Explain.

From section 16.6

9. It is possible for Java to have "unitialized" objects. Illustrate how this can happen using the code for the `Telescope` class. What happens when an attempt is made to use an unitialized Java object?

10. In the `Optics` example, both `MagnifyingGlass` and `Camera` have methods to disclose a manufacturer, but `Camera` also has model information.

    (a) Restructure the class definitions to move the manufacturer to the superclass.

    (b) `Telescope` has no manufacturer information. How should this be handled?

From section 16.7

11. Write the code for the *Deposit* object.

12. The implementation of `Check` uses a constructor that employs `protected` methods of its superclass. Another way to do the constructor is to give `Transaction` its own constructor, and use it in `Check`.

    (a) Write the Java code for this more straightforward kind of constructor.

    (b) Both methods are used in practice. Discuss the circumstances under which each is appropriate.

Review Questions

1. What are the necessary attributes of a software object?

2. How are prospective objects for a design identified?

3. How are the methods to be assigned to a software object identified?

4. What is inheritance? Polymorphism?

Further Reading

Today's very best buzz-word is "object-oriented" (O-O). Software developers are no different from other people in wanting quick, simple solutions to their difficult problems. This natural desire, and the substantial economic forces behind solving software problems, have led to a series of ideas that are touted by their promoters as the panacea. These ideas are often good ones (high-level programming languages and structured coding are two of the previous ones), but they can never live up to the hype surrounding them. Perhaps the best way to understand O-O is to go at it from the programming languages side, and Alan Kay's introduction to Smalltalk philosophy is a good starting point [Kay77]. Tim Budd has written a beginning Java textbook that emphasizes the principles of objects and makes good use of the Java object library [Bud97]. For more details about Java, a standard text [KAH00] can be consulted. The Java class libraries are more extensive than the language itself; one of the richest contains the input/output classes, and it has its own book [Har99].

Part of the appeal of the CRC method is that it is done with pencil and paper on 3×5 index cards. To supplement the brief discussion in this chapter, the reader should consult an introductory treatment [Wil95].

References

[Bud97]   Timothy Budd. *An Introduction to Object-Oriented Programming*. Addison-Wesley, 1997.

[Har99]   Elliotte Rusty Harold. *Java I/O*. O'Reilly and Associates, 1999.

[KAH00]   James Gosling Ken Arnold and David Holmes. *The Java Programming Language*. Addison-Wesley, 2000.

[Kay77]   Alan Kay. Microelectronics and the personal computer. *Scientific American*, pages 230–244, 1977.

[Wil95]   Nancy M. Wilkinson. *Using CRC Cards: An Informal Approach to Object-Oriented Development*. Prentice-Hall, 1995.

Data Flow Diagrams

One of the first design methods developed was *structured design*. Coupled with its analysis method, *structured analysis*, the pair were known as SA/SD. This approach has weathered the test of time quite well and is still popular today. The strength of SA/SD is that it captures a way of thinking about system structure that is not the most obvious: it models the *flow of data* rather than the *flow of control*. This viewpoint can be confusing for a novice, who spends time looking for ways to represent "*this* happens before *that*." The eventual order of execution is not an immediate concern of SA/SD, but it *does* get resolved at a later stage in design.

The data flow diagram (DFD) is a form of SA/SD that comes from an architectural block diagram of the way data moves in a system and the functional transformations data undergoes.

17.1 Elements of Data Flow Diagrams

Data flow diagrams consist of:

- *Data transforms* (sometimes called *processes*)
- *Information flows*
- *Information sources and sinks*
- *Information stores*

Figure 17.1 gives the graphical representation of each of these elements. Figure 17.2 shows a simple example of a complete DFD (which might be the design for a system to register college students) using these elements.

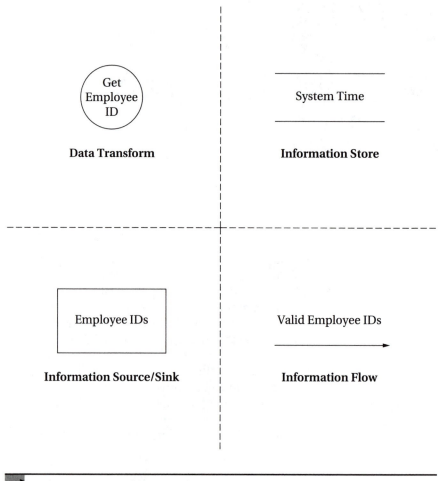

▶ **Figure 17.1**   Elements of data flow diagrams.

17.1.1 Data Transforms

DFDs model the flow of data through the entire system. The steps at which data is converted into another form are called *data transforms*. A data transform is represented by a circle and described by two pieces of information:

- *The name of the transform:* The name describes succinctly what is being done within the transform.
- *Heritage identifier:* The identifier is used to document step-wise refinement of a DFD, as described in Section 17.2.2.

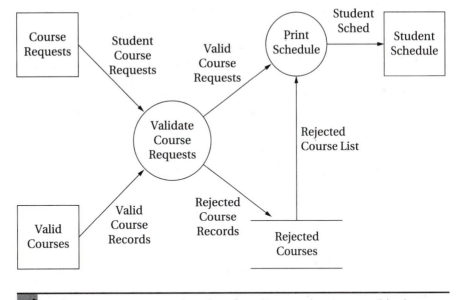

Figure 17.2   A complete data flow diagram showing possible elements.

In Figure 17.2, the data transforms are *Validate Course Requests* and *Print Schedule*, but no heritage numbers are shown.

17.1.2 Information Flows

Information flows describe the information being exchanged between DFD elements. These information flows are represented by labeled arrows in the direction of the flow. The label describes the information being transferred. In Figure 17.2, the information flows are *Student Course Requests*, *Valid Course Records*, *Valid Course Requests*, *Rejected Course Records*, *Rejected Course List*, and *Student Sched*.

17.1.3 Information Sources and Sinks

Information that comes from outside the system is called a *source*. Sources may be hand-generated forms that are keyed into the system by data entry operators, or they may be information generated automatically by another system. An information source is a starting point for a system, and is represented by a box, with a descriptive label describing the information being brought into the system. Similarly, *sinks* represent information leaving the system, to appear on a screen or form a printed report, and so forth. In Figure 17.2, the information sources are *Course Requests* and *Valid Courses*; the sink is *Student Schedule*.

17.1.4 Information Stores

Information stores are locations where information is kept for use by the system at later steps. These stores may be temporary databases, global storage within a program, scratch files, and so on. An information store is transient, meaning that the information is no longer needed after the program has finished its work. Database systems and files that are kept after a program has run are usually represented as system sources or sinks. In Figure 17.2, *Rejected Courses* is a store.

17.2 Example DFDs: A Payroll System

Data flow diagrams are at their best in designing so-called data processing systems, in which collected information is transformed into reports and other summary documents. A simple payroll system is a good example of DFD design.

System inputs are:

1. *Employee Records:* These records contain personnel information such as employee name, address, previous pay history, and identification number.
2. *Employee Timecards:* Timecards are employee work records for a week.

Two sets of outputs are produced:

1. *Paychecks and Stubs:* These are negotiable checks for the employees, and check stubs that show pay and deductions from pay (such as taxes withheld, amd savings bonds purchased).
2. *Accounting Report:* This report contains accounting information for the finance department. It contains information on tax and social security withholdings that need to be sent to the government, among other things.

A *level-0 DFD* shows the payroll system at its highest level, as a single data transform with all the system information sources and sinks (Figure 17.3). At this highest level of abstraction, the inner workings of the payroll system are hidden from view in the main data transform. The level-0 DFD shows what the entire system requires for inputs and outputs.

Input/output ▶ is the essence of software

17.2.1 Refining DFDs

A data transform may be refined to expose more details of its working, creating lower-level DFDs. The decomposition occurs in a systematic manner:

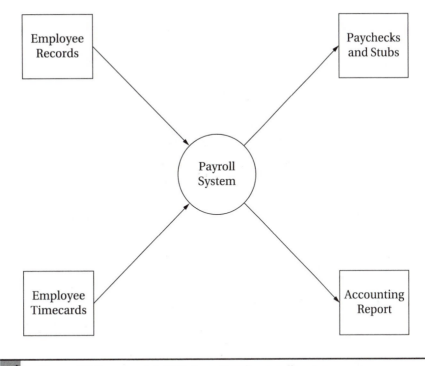

Figure 17.3   Level-0 DFD for a simple payroll system.

- Lower-level DFD inputs and outputs must match those of the upper-level DFD being refined.
- Transforms are broken out on the basis of known information flows, not arbitrary information.

Figure 17.4 shows the first level of refinement (level-1 DFD) for the payroll system. The level-0 data transform of Figure 17.3 has been decomposed into several transforms that reflect the natural progression of data through the system. This decomposition is based on the analysis of requirements as described in Section 11.3. For example, the two output-formatting transforms arise from requirements for the form and content of paychecks and of the accounting report.

Most of the data transforms in Figure 17.4 are *primitive*—they cannot be further decomposed because they have a single input flow or a single output flow. However, data transform 3 (*Calculate Withholding*) is not primitive and can be the source for a second level of refinement, a level-2 DFD as shown in Figure 17.5. This level-2 DFD still contains one nonprimitive transform (*Compute Net*) that could be refined to the next level.

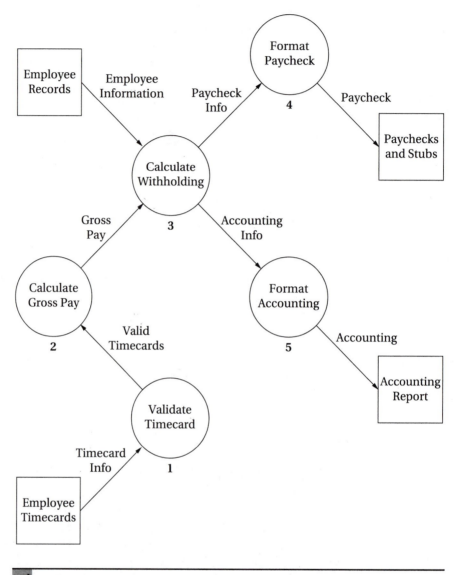

▶ **Figure 17.4**   Level-1 DFD for a simple payroll system.

17.2.2 Heritage Numbers

With complex systems, the number of data flow diagrams can be large. This poses a problem for understanding the position of each DFD within the system. We could end up with hundreds pages of data flow diagrams for some industrial applications. *Heritage numbers* can be used to describe the ancestry of each DFD. Each data transform in the level-1 DFD is numbered,

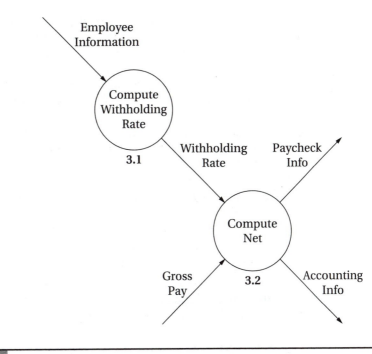

Figure 17.5   Level-2 DFD for a simple payroll system.

as in Figure 17.4. Then in the level-2 DFD for transform number k, the transforms are numbered $k.1$, $k.2$, and so on. Thus the level-2 DFD of Figure 17.5 has transforms 3.1 and 3.2, to show that they came from transform 3 at level 1. Further refinement, say, of transform 3.2 in Figure 17.5 would produce a level-3 DFD with heritage numbers 3.2.1, 3.2.2, and so on.

Heritage numbers allow us to find descendants of a DFD as well as its ancestor.

Document it! ▶
(traceability)

17.2.3 DFD Terminology

Intellectual ▶
control
(language
betrays us)

Data flow diagrams make use of many different notations, and there is a wide variety of terminology for the DFD elements. Many software houses have modified the notation to fit their unique needs.

17.3 The Data Dictionary

As data flow diagrams are refined to include more and more detail, details about the information flows must also be captured. At level 0, it is fine to say that *Employee Records* is an input, but at level 1 or level 2 the transforms need to know what the corresponding information flow *Employee Information* really is. If, for instance, a record consists of employee name, identification number, and rate of pay, that needs to be documented.

In large systems, where several software engineers can be working on DFDs at the same time, it is important to have a repository defining the data elements in each information flow. The *data dictionary* is a common device for recording the information. A data dictionary is exactly what its name suggests: a place to look up definitions of data elements.

To understand how to build a data dictionary, consider how it might be used. When looking at a DFD, an engineer examining a transform with an input information flow labeled *Employee Information* would want to know what sort of information was being used, for the following purposes:

- *Locate the entry:* The data dictionary should be alphabetical.
- *Read a natural language description of the item:* There should be an explanation in concise, clear, and nontechnical terms.
- *Read a formal definition of the elements of the item:* There should be a definition of each element of the item, including initial value and permissible values for each element.

Here are two possible entries for the *Employee Information* part of a data dictionary:

Employee Information	Employee information for payroll only. Excludes items such as address. Taken directly from the employee database.
Employee name	30-character alphanumeric field (ASCII).
Initial values	From employee database.
Valid values	First, middle, last separated by one blank, each name composed of letters A–Z and a–z and hyphen (-).
Identification number	8 digit integer.
Initial values	From employee database.
Valid values	00000000-99999999.

17.4 Checking DFDs—CASE Tools

Since data flow diagrams are a formal method, it should come as no surprise that there are mechanical techniques for checking them. The following checklist can be used to verify the consistency of a collection of DFDs:

1. Is each requirements function represented by a data transform somewhere in the DFDs?

2. Is each system input and output represented in the DFDs?

3. Is each input and output from higher-level DFDs reproduced correctly in any lower-level refinement DFDs?

4. Is each transform in the lowest-level DFDs a primitive one?

5. Do all transforms have unique heritage designators?

6. Do all information flows have labels that correspond to an entry in the data dictionary?

7. Do all the data dictionary entries appear in some DFD?

If an entire DFD design is recorded in a form that can be computer processed, a sophisticated aid for the software designer is possible. Such a tool can do much better than simply checking the designer's work—it can perform many of the design tasks directly and force consistency in parts of the design. The name for such tools in electrical and mechanical engineering is computer-aided design (CAD) tools. By analogy, we have CASE tools, for computer-aided software engineering. A CASE tool based on data flow diagrams has the following parts:

Graphical DFD editor. The graphical editor helps its user to draw DFDs interactively on a workstation, using a *point-and-click* interface. The resulting diagrams are standardized and appear neat and tidy. The real virtue in the graphical editor is not, however, that it makes drawing pretty diagrams easy—it is probably easier to sketch them by hand. The editor brings DFDs into a computer so that they can be further processed automatically. All the DFD elements are recorded by type, with all connections, labels, heritage numbers, and so forth.

Data dictionary editor. Again, a standardized format is enforced on items in the data dictionary, and again the purpose is not really to make entering the items easier, but rather to give the CASE tool control over the information and its format.

Analyzers. The big win in CASE tools is analysis. Many of the mechanical checks listed earlier can now be automatically performed. For example, checking that the data dictionary and the set of DFDs correctly correspond is a simple matter of comparing the files created by the graphical and data dictionary editors.

Synthesizers. Computer-aided design comes into its own when the tool actually takes on some of the engineer's design tasks, and CASE tools can do a little of this. (They are not anywhere near as helpful as are the CAD tools for chip design, however.) For example, consider the creation of a level-2 DFD from a level-1 DFD. The graphical editor can initially present the level-1 DFD on the screen, and the user can click on one of the data transforms to be refined. The editor can then present a blank screen on which to draw the new DFD. But it can also place on that screen all the proper inputs (from the level-1 DFD), and as new transforms are created, can give them correct heritage numbers. Thus two of the checklist items will not need to be checked—they will be created correctly by the CASE tool.

Some software engineers swear by CASE tools and believe that they are essential to design productivity. But others swear *at* CASE as a waste of time. The real argument is not about CASE—everyone agrees that it is a good idea with promise. Those who don't like the tools are really objecting to design using DFDs. If in fact DFDs don't help much with the design, then neither will CASE tools help much. And CASE doesn't come free: the tools themselves are expensive; they run best on expensive workstations; and most important, they take time to learn and use, time that might be better spent in creative design *not* using DFDs.

17.5 Structure Charts

Structure charts are a way to determine the system's high-level architecture from data flow diagrams, bringing designers one step closer to the actual system implementation. The charts provide designers with:

1. Names of the major system modules.
2. A map of the arrangement, or structure, of major system modules (hence the name).
3. Information on what data is passed to the modules.
4. Information on what data is returned from the modules.

Structure charts are derived mechanically from data flow diagrams. Their systematic derivation is one feature that makes data flow diagrams an appealing formalism. (To see what a complete structure chart looks like, look ahead to Figure 17.9.) To construct a structure chart from a DFD is an analysis process that helps the designer to understand the system structure.

17.5.1 The Central Transform

Construction of a structure chart from a DFD begins by identifying the *central transform* of the DFD, which requires separating data transforms into two types:

- *Data synthesis:* This transforms combine data from input streams to create data that did not previously exist.
- *Data refinement:* This transforms either validate, select, or merge inputs; or, they select, merge, or format output.

The central transform is that portion of the DFD in which the main calculations of data synthesis take place, after data refinement. It is identified on a DFD as follows:

- Trace each input stream in toward the center of the DFD.
- Mark the point where the input stream has been refined to its highest point of abstraction (that is, after the stream has been validated or merged but before any actual data synthesis has been done).
- Trace each output stream back toward the center of the DFD.
- Mark the point where the output stream is refined to its highest point of abstraction, (that is, after the stream has been synthesized but has not been merged or formatted).
- Draw a boundary through the marks, enclosing the central transform where data synthesis occurs.

17.5.2 Constructing Structure Charts

The process for deriving the structure charts is straightforward:

1. Start with the level-1 DFD.
2. Identify the central transform.
3. Draw a single box at the top of a blank page, and label it with the same name as the level-0-DFD transform.
4. Draw boxes underneath the top box, one for each input refinement transform, one box for the central transform, and a box for each output refinement transform.
5. Label each box with its transform name, and fabricate a name for the central transform.
6. Connect each of these boxes to the top box with a line.
7. Draw a box underneath the central transform box for each transform that is inside the central transform boundary.
8. Label these boxes and connect them to the central transform box.
9. For each data flow, draw and label arrows along the lines connecting the modules to indicate the data flow. All data between transforms at the highest level will flow through the top module. If there are several data items flowing to a transform, only a single arrow is shown, labeled with them all.
10. For each level-2 DFD, a structure chart is constructed in the same way, with its level-1 transform serving as the departure point for the development of subordinate modules and data flows.

17.5.3 Example Construction

To illustrate the construction of a structure chart from a DFD, look back at the DFD constructed in Figure 17.4. Figure 17.6 shows the identification of its central transform, as follows:

- *Input streams:* There are two input streams to trace toward the center of the DFD; they originate in the sources *Employee Records* and *Employee Timecards*. For *Employee Timecards*, the first transform encountered is *Validate Timecard*. This is only a refinement transform, so continue to the next transform *Calculate Gross Pay. Calculate Gross Pay* is certainly synthesizing new data that will be passed on, so a cut line is drawn between these two transforms. On the input stream for *Employee Records*, the very first transform encountered (*Calculate Withholding*) converts the data; therefore, no cut line can be placed for this input.

- *Output streams:* There are two output streams that end at the sinks *Paychecks and Stubs* and *Accounting Report*. The first transform encountered tracing back from *Paychecks and Stubs* is the refinement transform *Format Paycheck*. However, the flow between *Calculate Withholding* and *Format Paycheck* should be marked, because *Calculate Withholding* is a synthesis transform. Similarly, tracing *Accounting Report* back toward the center results in a cut line on the *Accounting Info* data flow.

The central transform boundary passes through these cut lines and includes the entire *Employee Records* stream that had no cut line.

Figure 17.7 shows the developing structure chart. It is begun with a box at the top of the page containing the system name. Next, a box is added for each input flow, the central transform, and each output flow.

It is clear from examining the central transform that its primary purpose is to calculate gross pay and deductions. Therefore, the designer could label the central transform box *Calculate Net Pay*. The next step is to arrange the modules of the central transform under *Calculate Net Pay*, as shown in Figure 17.8. Notice the addition of a module at the lower left. By convention, *Get* modules are added to a design when it is necessary to represent a source itself, and they are named for the data stream, not the source. Similarly, a sink might give rise to a *Put* module.

The structure chart for the level-1 DFD is completed by labeling the data flows. The final chart is shown in Figure 17.9.

At this point, it is possible to continue refinement of the structure chart. The transform *Calculate Withholding* has a level-2 DFD that could be expanded into a structure chart underneath the *Calculate Withholding* module in Figure 17.9. However, the diagram quickly becomes too large. The

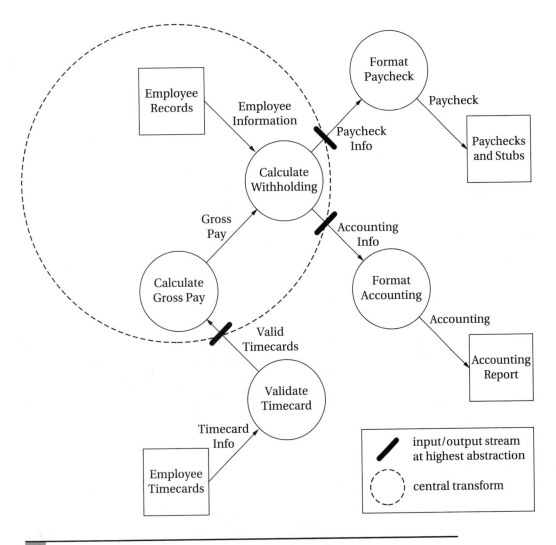

Figure 17.6   Identification of the central transform.

heritage numbers of DFDs can be used to organize structure charts into a hierarchy of charts that appear on separate pages.

It should be obvious how a CASE tool can aid the designer in constructing a structure chart. The tool would display the level-1 DFD, and the designer would point and click to mark the central transform. The tool could then construct everything in the chart except for the name to be given to the central transform module.

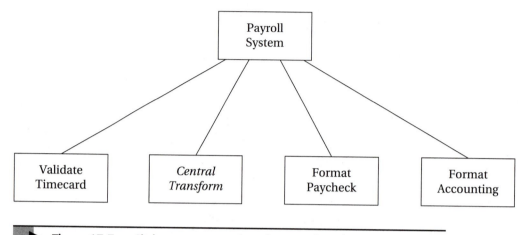

Figure 17.7   Skeleton structure chart for payroll system.

17.6 Implementing a DFD

To implement a DFD design, the structure chart derived from the DFS and associated entries in the data dictionary provide the coding assignments. As an illustration, the structure chart of Figure 17.9 will be coded in C.

First, define the major data structures to be used. In this example, most details of the input format are sketched or omitted.

```
/* Maximum allowable name length */
#define MAX_NAME_SIZE 60

struct time_card
{
  char workers_name[MAX_NAME_SIZE];
  int hours_worked;
  int sick_hours;
  /* other time card information omitted */
} time_card;

struct gross_pay
{
  /* relevant gross pay information omitted */
} gross_pay;

struct employee_info
{
  char id[ID_LENGTH];
```

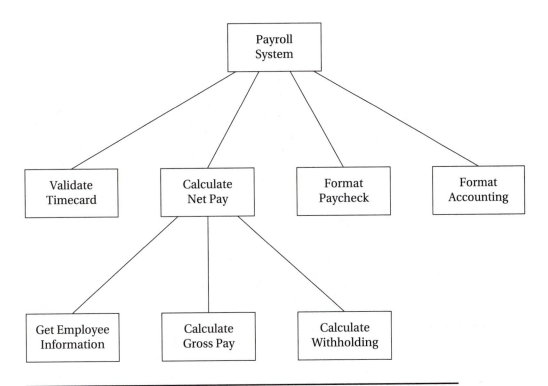

Figure 17.8   Structure chart showing expanded central transform.

```
  char full_name[MAX_NAME_SIZE];
  float pay_rate;
  int exemptions;
  /* other employee information omitted */
} employee_info;

struct paycheck_info
{
  /* Paycheck printed information, omitted */
} paycheck_info

struct accounting_info
{
  /* Accounting report printed information, omitted */
} accounting_info
```

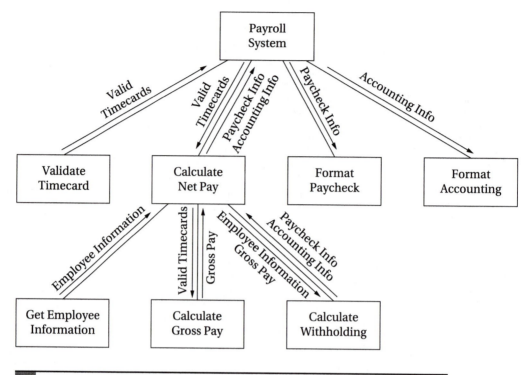

Figure 17.9   Final level-1 structure chart.

Next, the interface parameters can be induced from the level-1 structure chart of Figure 17.9. We give only a few routines in the top tier of the diagram:

```
int
validate_timecard(struct time_card *);

int
calculate_net_pay(struct time_card,
                  struct paycheck_info *,
                  struct accounting_info *);

int
format_paycheck(struct paycheck_info);
```

Input parameters are passed by value, whereas output parameters are passed by reference as pointers.

Having defined the data structures and interfaces, the simplest code for the main module might look like:

```
main()  /* Simplest Payroll System */
{
  int finished = 0;
  FILE * input_file;

  input_file = fopen(INPUT_FILE,"r");
  finished = feof(input_file);

  while (!finished)
  {
    validate_timecard(&time_card);
    calculate_net_pay(time_card, &paycheck_info,
                      &accounting_info);
    format_paycheck(paycheck_info);
    format_accounting(accounting_info);
    finished = feof(input_file);
  }
}
```

This implementation looks adequate at first glance, but it does no error checking. Each of the called routines should have the capacity to signal an error if one is encountered. A better implementation would provide an error code upon return from each routine:

```
main()  /* Better Payroll System */
{
  int finished = 0;
  FILE * input_file;
  int ec;  /* error code */

  input_file = fopen(INPUT_FILE,"r");
  if (input_file == (FILE *) NULL)
  {
    perror("Error encountered while opening file\n");
    exit (1);
  }

  finished = feof(input_file);

  while (!finished)
  {
    ec = validate_timecard(&time_card);
    if (ec != 0) handle_error(ec);

    ec = calculate_net_pay(time_card, &paycheck_info,
                           &accounting_info);
```

```
    if (ec != 0) handle_error(ec);

    ec = format_paycheck(paycheck_info);
    if (ec != 0) handle_error(ec);

    ec = format_accounting(accounting_info);
    if (ec != 0) handle_error(ec);

    finished = feof(input_file);

  }
}
```

In this example, an error code is saved in a local variable and passed to handle_error(), which then has the option of:

- Terminating the program if the error is fatal, or of sufficient severity.
- Printing a diagnostic message and resuming execution. The diagnostic message may include a dump of all the system variables, such as paycheck_info and accounting_info.
- Doing nothing at all, if no action is warranted.

Subsequently, the remaining level-1 functions could be implemented directly from the knowledge of the parameters and the transforms that are to performed on them. The central transform of our structure chart, calculate_net_pay(), could be implemented in a similar way (with more terse parameter names, however):

```
int
calculate_net_pay(struct time_card tc,
                  struct paycheck_info *pi,
                  struct accounting_info *ai)
{
  struct gross_pay gp;
  struct employee_infor ei;
  int ec, lc = 0;

  ec = get_employee_information(&ei);

  if (ec != 0)
  {
    handle_error(ec);
    if (ec > lc) ec = lc;
  }
```

```
    ec = calculate_gross_pay(tc, &gp);
    if (ec != 0)
    {
      handle_error(ec);
      if (ec > lc) ec = lc;
    }

    ec = calculate_withholding(gp, pi, ai);
    if (ec != 0)
    {
      handle_error(ec);
      if (ec > lc) ec = lc;
    }

    return lc;
}
```

The error-handling strategy of this routine is to return the largest error code encountered.

How Does It Fit?

From section 17.1

1. If one DFD element had to be eliminated without doing too much damage to the design method, which would it be?

From section 17.2

2. Write a brief set of requirements for the payroll system in narrative style.

3. The information flows are missing from Figure 17.3. Fill them in.

4. Figure 17.3 does not have any hierarchy numbers. Could they be given? Why are they omitted?

5. Do the information flows in Figure 17.4 agree exactly with the ones in Figure 17.5? Explain.

From section 17.4

6. Define a data structure (or, equivalently, a file format) for the information to be recorded by a graphical DFD editor and data dictionary editor, sufficient for use by DFD analyzers and synthesizers.

From section 17.5

7. The source *Employee Records* that lies inside the central transform is represented in the structure diagram of Figure 17.8 by a *Get* module, but the other source is not represented, nor are the sinks represented by *Put* modules. If these were to be represented, how should they appear? Add them to Figure 17.9 along with the appropriate data flows.

8. Suppose that in identifying the central transform of a DFD, a chain of data synthesis transforms is identified before the point of highest abstration is reached. How should these appear in a structure chart, and where will the associated data flows be shown?

9. One philosophy of program design has it that the first step in design is to identify the heart of the needed processing, and to design this central algorithm, before starting on the less important routines that will go with it. What is the relationship between this philosphy and DFD design?

10. Carry out the central transform construction on the example DFD of Figure 17.2, using the suggestive names on the diagram to figure out what the data transforms should do.

11. Using the structure chart of Figure 17.9, trace the data flow starting with the source *Employee Records* and ending with the sink *Accounting Report*. Make a sketch of Figure 17.9 showing just the boxes and lines, and draw the flow on your sketch as a continuous line.

From section 17.6

12. Give the header with parameter types for the routine `format_accounting()`.

13. If the *Get* and *Put* modules were added to the structure chart as in exercise 7, write the code to incorporate them in the first version of `main()`.

14. Why do `main()` and `calculate_net_pay()` use the routine `handle_error()` differently?

Review Questions

1. Describe DFDs as a hierarchical design mechanism.
2. What aids does a CASE tool provide for the system designer?
3. For what main purpose is a structure chart constructed?

Further Reading

CASE tools are the subject of many books [Gan90], but probably none is interested in presenting a balanced case pro and con. Data flow diagrams have so many variants that one can get into an argument over which book to read [Ste91], much less the actual DFD terms.

References

[Gan90]   C. Gane. *Computer-Aided Software Engineering: The Methodologies, the Products, and the Future*. Prentice-Hall, 1990.

[Ste91]   W. P. Stevens. *Software Design*. Prentice-Hall, 1991.

chapter 18

Wrapping up Design and Coding

Chapters 13–17 have described good design ideas and their implementation in detail. We hope that the novice—faced with learning and using one of these ideas—can start by reading the corresponding chapter, which carries an example through from start to coding. We also hope that software engineers—whether novices or old hands—will use these ideas.

18.1 Additional Design Ideas

Some currently popular design ideas are more sweeping than the techniques that we have explored in detail. Design ideas come and go at a great rate because there is a tremendous need to find a magical solution to the design problem. The experienced software engineer becomes leery of each new panacea, having enthusiastically embraced previous ones only to find them less wonderful than their inventors and promoters said they were.

18.1.1 The Universal Modeling Language (UML)

Software developers would like to emulate the success of computer hardware chip designers in their use of computer-aided design (CAD). The essential underpinnings of CAD tools are formal description languages and diagrams for the objects being designed, and over the years there have been a number of proposals for such aids to software design. Most of these have been based on block diagrams in one form or another, for example, the CASE tools for DFDs described in Section 17.4. Software design tools have not been very successful because the formalisms on which they were based did not capture the semantics of a design. Frequently, the tool was very good at manipulating boxes on a screen but provided no support for describing just what a box represents or what it does. In addition, the learning curve for tools was quite steep, and the combination of weak support and slow acquisition of expertise made them unattractive.

The latest in software design notations is the Universal Modeling Language (UML), whose basis is in object-oriented design. It is a technique for recording and analyzing O-O designs, and as such has a better starting point than any of its predecessors. The language is too new to know how well it will ultimately be accepted or whether it will really help practicing designers. In its present state of development, it has been changing so quickly that it is hard to believe in it as a standard. A two-year-old textbook is little help in understanding today's UML.

A primary UML diagram is called a *class diagram*. It is an overview of the classes in a design, the information each encapsulates, their methods, and the relationships between them. The origin of class diagrams is in the lowly block diagrams sketched on the back of an envelope. But by inventing and standardizing graphical notation, UML seeks to make these high-level descriptions precise and communicable to people other than the author.

Figure 18.1 captures part of the checkbook design of Section 16.3. The boxes in the figure are the classes, whose names head the box. Below the name is a list of the class's encapsulated data, sometimes called its *attributes*. In Figure 18.1, only *Account* has an attribute (*balance*). Below the attributes is a list of the class's methods. Lines connecting the sides of boxes show *associations*, relationships between classes. Lines pass down from a superclass to its subclasses. Finally, a descending line starting at a diamond indicates *composition:* the upper class is composed of several instances of the lower class, and the numbers are written at the ends of the line.

Use case is the UML name for an example of how the designed software will be used. Before UML, these would have been called something like "typical use scenarios." They describe not isolated actions, but coordinated activities in which a user accomplishes some purpose in the applications domain. Thus a use case is precisely a functional test case of an important sequence of operations, but its purpose is to illuminate and sharpen requirements rather than to test the software.

A picture is worth 1000 words, but there are very few collections of 1000 words that any picture describes.

Use cases are often easier to describe in words than with a diagram, but UML includes use case diagrams in which stick-figure people have arrows going from them to ellipses around words for what they do.

Finally, *sequence diagrams* relate use cases to the software design. A sequence diagram shows how the objects of the design carry out the use case, in particular how objects are created and methods invoked among them.

The UML notations and diagrams are normally used to explore requirements and come up with a design, in a way parallel to that presented in Chapter 16 for the CRC method. It is evident that a UML class diagram is a good way to record and check an object-oriented design, and that use cases could direct a role-playing session. Sequence diagrams are a way for an individual to work out the results of the role playing.

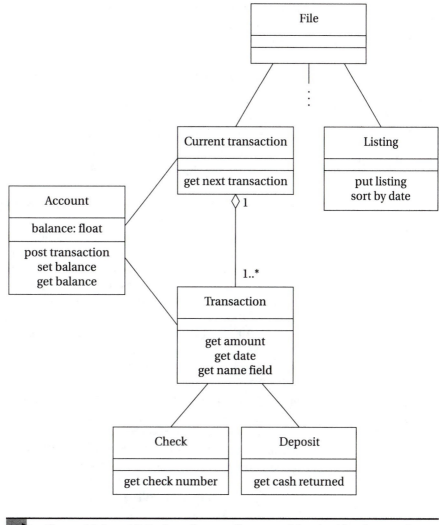

Figure 18.1   UML class diagram for part of the checkbook example.

18.1.2 Client–Server Design

In the days of computer mainframes, there were either no connections between the central machine and other devices or no more than connection to local terminals or to phone lines leading to remote terminals. Early "networking" between computers took the form of a few machines with directly connected memories or processors, in which one machine performed a service for the other. Two examples from the 1960s: IBM had a pair of "direct-coupled" mainframes—a 7040 and a 7090—in which the 7040 did

The 7090 instruc-
tion calling for
7040 service was
HEY STUPID.

A PDP-8, work-
ing flat out, could
handle about a
dozen terminals
at about 0.1 kilo-
bits/sec each.

all the I/O operations for the 7090, including using most of its memory as buffers. Many of the early DEC timesharing systems—PDP-10s—used satellite computers—PDP-8s—to handle remote terminals, the satellite doing all the character echoing and modem control.

A modern computer installation is a network of many, many computers, communicating over very fast lines (10–100 megabits/second), using standard protocols that allow machines to be easily added to the local network. The interconnection networks extend outward to the whole world over hardwired, microwave, and switched telephone lines, forming what is usually called the Internet. In this situation, there is a natural design technique that breaks the design of an application into two pieces:

Server. A server is something like an ADT whose operations are available to any other program over the network. The server program may run on a dedicated computer, but by and large its users are elsewhere, and they send it orders via the network. The server has many secrets, and they are protected by its isolation. Servers range from programs that are almost like standalone device drivers that manage (say) a printer, to database management systems that accept queries into a database they control, to point-of-sale systems that track and record activity. Almost any application can have some or all of its functions collected into a server. Sometimes a server is called an "engine" by analogy to a ship where the engines are isolated in the hold, and orders are sent to them from the bridge.

Client. Callers of the ADT-like operations that a server provides are its "clients." A client program may have almost no functions, doing nothing but formatting, sending, and receiving server requests and perhaps translating them into more readable form for a human user. It is common for a client to have a graphical user interface that allows a person to communicate with it easily. Or a client may have a great deal of functionality, but still use a server (or several servers) for doing some of its work.

The primary advantage of client–server systems over a design in which the system is a single program is that in the client–server form, two isolated programs are running in two different computers, so they can process in parallel, and they cannot interfere with each other. Unfortunately, that is also the primary disadvantage of this design technique since thorny timing problems can arise in parallel execution, problems that a single program never encounters.

Designing a client–server application is different from a conventional design only in that the first step of high-level design is to divide the system functionality between the two programs, and define the interface between them as messages over the connecting network. Then in detailed design and implementation, much attention needs to be paid to timing, sequencing, and cooperation between the programs.

18.2   Choosing Design Techniques

The essential part of design is creative, an art of finding problem solutions in programs, learned through experience, that is difficult to describe. Those who know the art would understand a description but would not need it; those who do not know the art would not understand. Furthermore, the art is different in different application areas—designing (say) business accounting software is unlike designing real-time control software. So most of the techniques we have described are concerned with the *inessential* part of design: recording and formalizing the results of the creative work.

18.2.1   Recognizing a Design

However hard it is to describe the art of designing, it is easy to tell after the fact if one *has* a design. A design consists of:

1. A list of "modules," meaning self-contained, independent programmer assignments in the programming language to be used.
2. A precise description of the interfaces between modules, usually as subroutine headers in the programming language and associated documentation.
3. A functional description (specification) for each of the modules, usually in English, or English supplemented by some formal notation, sufficient for a programmer to carry out the task of writing the code for each module, and sufficient for a tester to unit-test each module.

And—oh yes—these modules, if correctly coded and linked, should solve the problem posed by the system requirements and specification.

In practice, many designs are done "by the seat of the pants," as described in Section 11.3. Such a design may be entirely informal, but nevertheless documented by diagrams, tables, pseudocode, and so on. Abstract data types for information hiding (ADTs, Chapter 15), data flow diagrams (DFDs, Chapter 17), and FSMs (Chapter 14) are general techniques that provide some direction to a design, and record its progress. Object-oriented design can be a real help in identifying important parts of the code-to-be and defining these objects, starting from rather vague requirements, as explained in Chapter 16.

All design techniques can make use of step-wise refinement (Section 11.2.2), for example by:

- Breaking pseudocode into a hierarchy of segments
- Making one FSM appear as a single state in another FSM
- Including ADTs within ADTs (as `Boolean` was a part of `IntSet` in Section 15.4), or one object as part of another

DFDs explicitly use step-wise refinement in their successive levels.

Iterative enhancement (Section 11.2.1) stands outside all the other techniques in being part of the creative process. It actually helps the designer to solve the problem, not just document the solution. The preliminary stages of iterative enhancement, the early systems that solve parts of the problem, are not necessarily saved. Once they have served their purpose of finding and trying basic solutions, they might be discarded. But the wise designer documents and keeps these early systems because they succinctly describe fundamental ideas and their implementation, and the designer may need to start with them on another occasion for a similar problem. Nothing is more valuable than easy-to-understand code that gets to the heart of some difficult aspect of a system.

Reuse past work ▶

18.2.2 Which Formal Technique(s) Should I Use?

The easy answer to this hard question is: "Use whatever helps." But to apply that advice, the designer has to have experience with the possible techniques, to develop a feeling for what *will* help. In the heat of an actual development is no time to be trying something for the first time—it may help, but if it doesn't, irreplaceable time will be wasted. What goes wrong with software design in practice, leading to projects that are abandoned, or badly overrun their budgets, or miss schedule deadlines, or are delivered lacking major required functions, might be described as follows:

> The designers choose methods that won't work, but discover that they aren't working only after substantial time has been devoted to the attempt. Then it is necessary to start over, and this may prove impossible.

The fewer design tricks are in the designer's bag, and the less experience the designer has with each one, the more likely it is that this disaster scenario will occur. In the worst case, the designer has no options but "seat-of-the-pants" trial and error, and if the problem is too hard for that to succeed, the project is doomed.

At the risk of giving obvious advice, here are some guidelines for choosing design techniques:

- If at any time there is doubt about how to accomplish what the system is required to do, immediately use iterative enhancement to reduce the problem and solve it. Never begin systematically working on a problem whose solution has known holes in it. The result will be a system that doesn't work because it has those holes still, and all the other work will be wasted.

- Use formalisms you understand and with which you have successful experience. This advice would seem to tell the beginner that formalism should never be used at all. But its intent is rather that formalisms should be learned and practiced before they are needed.

Document it! ▶

- Use formalism notations only when necessary. If the way to problem solution seems clear, pass to code as directly and quickly as possible. But describe the modules and interfaces, and record their functional specifications. Pseudocode is a good choice when more abstract methods aren't needed.

- Add to the test plan whenever possible during design, whatever techniques are used. Fault-based tests should be directed at hard design problems to later prove that they have been properly solved.

Expect to ▶
deal with change

- Use information hiding when there is any indication that changes in the system will be required. Try to guess what might be changed, and make it the secret of a module. This advice applies to potential changes in the requirements, but also to changes in the design itself. When parts of the design are unclear, or of dubious quality, they are likely to change as development progresses. Hide them in as few modules as possible.

- Object-oriented design is ideal for simulationlike problems, in which the software is required to model interactions taking place among real objects.

- FSMs are most useful for interactive, continually running systems that operate in a cycle of responding to events. Process control systems and other real-time applications often benefit from FSM descriptions.

- DFDs are most useful for batch, information processing systems in which input data is processed and rearranged to form output. File update systems and other business data processing systems are the ones for which DFDs were designed.

18.3 Wrapping up the Code

If the design is very prescriptive, few choices are left in the coding phase. The programming language has been chosen, the breakdown into individual routines has been chosen, and each has been specified. All the coder has to do is systematically work through these routines, completing each one and putting it onto the pile of finished parts. A design may leave more creative work for coding, but that work is always done in the context of a given language and the restricted functionality required of particular routines. The coder who has been given a somewhat vague design does have additional options and responsibilities, however.

18.3.1 Documenting Choices

The first coding responsibility is documentation. Choices left to the programmer will be made as the work proceeds, and if they are not recorded, the whole project goes out of control. The designers almost certainly intended such choices to be limited to details of each routine. The place to record exactly how the routine works is in commentary at the head of the code itself. But designers are human and make mistakes. It can happen that the coder finds herself or himself making more wide-ranging decisions. The specification for a routine being coded may be incomplete or ambiguous. Worse yet, the interface for the routine may have to be changed. These more sweeping programmer choices and changes affect the coding of other routines, and require that the design documents themselves be changed. Furthermore, those other routines may have already been coded, and they and their documentation will also have to be changed. In a large project where many programmers are working in parallel, it takes careful management to avoid creating a mess where incompatible routines fail to work together. This is the primary example of change management, as described in Section 5.4.2.

18.3.2 Defensive Coding

Take responsibility ▶

Walt Kelly: "We have met the enemy, and he is us."

Famous last words: "Mistake? I don't make mistakes!"

When the programmer knows exactly what to do—when the routine could be "coded in my sleep"—then there's no more to be said. But such certainty isn't common. To the extent that the programmer is unsure whether the routine is going to work, it is worthwhile putting in extra effort to avoid trouble later. The techniques described in Section 12.1 can be used to control the most dangerous foe in coding: yourself. Assertions and other kinds of checking code will help to locate something amiss when the code runs. A diagnostic subsystem (Section 11.4.1) is invaluable for collecting information about problems in execution. Even if there is no predefined subsystem for taking snapshot dumps, for example, establishing a small table, and recording a few values in it as a hedge against those values going wrong in unforeseen ways, can be a life saver.

For some reason it is very difficult for most people to put defensive code into a routine. Perhaps the reason is that programming is difficult enough without having to continually worry about how it might go wrong. Perhaps it's economy and optimism: if nothing does go wrong, writing defensive code is a dead waste of time. But later on, when things don't work, a little time spent on getting ready will pay off handsomely. And if there's one thing it seems safe to bet on, it's Murphy's law.

Divide and ▶
conquer (7 ± 2)

When an individual is coding a complete system, the coding task itself can be organized as a sort of iterative enhancement. The main program is coded first, and in a good design the main program will be short. Then the smallest possible subset of its subroutines are chosen to code. The subset is selected so that with these routines in place, the complete program does something that can be tried. In the ideal case, only one subroutine needs to be coded. The other routines are coded as stubs—each no more than a header and an immediate return statement. As each selected routine is being written, the programmer keeps track of any doubtful aspects of its implementation, and when the system including that routine is tried, the programmer checks each issue to see that any doubts are resolved. The tests that resolve doubts are fault-based cases as described in Section 6.2, and of course, they belong in the test plan. When the programmer is satisfied that no issues remain for the partial system constructed so far, and any changes have been made and documented, it is time to proceed to the next iteration, adding a few more routines to the system and making sure that they are OK. This procedure is a mini-version of a particular integration and test strategy, described in more detail in Chapter 19.

Document it! ▶
(record it or it's
lost)

18.4 Managing the Design and Coding Phases

As software development moves toward its more technical aspects, a manager has less to do, and must trust the technical expertise of the engineers actually doing the work. Design is the beginning of this "real engineering." Design's management problem is one of gauging the abilities of available engineers, and distributing the work among them at the coding stage to follow. There is less chance than in requirements or specification that engineers will be tempted to prolong or cut short the necessary processes of design. There is no difficulty about recording the design details because they have an engineering life of their own, and engineers are trained to know what to do.

The design that emerges has two distinct aspects for a manager. First, it is a work breakdown for the coding phase, from which a number of programmers can be assigned to work independently. The number of independent modules or routines to be written of course depends on the workforce that will be available, and to a certain extent the schedule can be speeded up by preparing to use more programmers. The second aspect of design is also dependent on the programming talent to be used: the individual assignments must be defined and specified according to the needs and abilities of those who will have to carry them out. At a minimum, each module assignment has to be an adequate functional description. It must tell the programmer who will work from it exactly *what* the code is to do. To a variable degree, it also tells the programmer just *how* the code is to do the job. When the programmers are well trained, most of the "how" can be left to them; they will

Identify the ▶
customers

find appropriate algorithms, fast enough but no more complex than need be; they will make tradeoffs between space and time used by the code; and so on. Particularly when the designers themselves will be doing the programming, it is efficient to defer all details to coding. However, when the programmer is a novice or lacks background, the designer may need to spell out just how the code is to accomplish its task.

As the only person in the development project who knows the staffing, the manager must tell the engineers what workforce will be doing the coding so that they can adjust to fit the number of routines to be written and the detail with which those routines are described. Inspection, with participation from the design team and from the prospective programmers, will be the manager's way to learn how the design is progressing. The testers should also be represented in inspecting a design because they will have to use the functional specifications of modules for testing them in isolation.

In principle, there should be very little management needed in the programming part of a software development project. The design is a technical description, in terms that programmers understand, of the coding task(s) to be accomplished. Programmers have their assignments, which have been adjusted to take account of each person's training, experience, and skill. The manager should be able to sit back and let them get on with it. What could go wrong? In such an ideal world—nothing. But in real coding, things do go wrong, just because the design and its management aspects are imperfect. For example, a programmer may be given a too difficult assignment (or an impossible one), either because the design of that part of the system was not properly done or because the assignment is beyond his or her capabilities. Just because the work seems so straightforward, it may not be recognized that this programmer has been set up to fail until so far into the coding phase that the whole project is thrown off schedule. In the worst case, parts of the coding will be of poor quality, but it will not be known which parts these are, and finding the system's problems will become an intricate puzzle for the testing phase to piece together.

Thus management of coding is an activity of checking for problems and trying to catch them early enough to keep on track.

Code inspection is one technique that works although it is expensive. Inspection was originally invented to apply to code, and code checklists are the most precise and useful. However, where the inspection of a requirements or specification or a design involves a single large document, code comes in many small chunks, and the overhead of inspecting each routine is substantial. To give an illustrative example, a system of about 100,000 lines of C code (roughly the size of a compiler) might have on the order of 1000 routines. Inspecting one routine's code takes several hours of time from each of about five people. Thus the inspection consumes about the same resources as the coding itself. Even if there is sufficient staff to run two inspections simultaneously, about five inspections per working day would be the limit, and that would mean a total elapsed inspection time of about a year. Most projects cannot afford such an overhead. The manager must therefore choose routines to be inspected with care, and many cannot be inspected.

It is possible to use unit testing (described in Section 19.3.1), conducted by the person who programmed each unit, instead of inspection. Unit testing can be very inexpensive, particularly if the programmer doesn't do a very thorough job, but it is much less effective than inspection, particularly at catching problems that may arise later at the system level, but originate within one code unit.

A scheme that originated in the shrink-wrap software industry, and said to be used routinely at Microsoft, is to code so that the complete system can be compiled and linked daily. The code headers for each module are provided by the design, or if not, are coded immediately, and then as code is filled in, a "daily build" is required. The system that is "built" may not be able to do very much near the start of coding, but linking it provides a check on interface consistency and requires programmers to work in small increments. Microsoft adds a unit-testing twist: each programmer may be assigned to work in a pair with a tester. As the programmer of the pair builds each day's code into the system, the tester of the pair tries it out. This "incremental unit test" should be effective at finding yesterday's mistakes since they are fresh in everyone's mind. It does, of course, exactly double the cost of coding, but does not add to the schedule time.

Fred Brooks: "Adding personnel to a late project makes it later."

When a coding manager finds a problem, the only resources available to solve it are staffing adjustments. If one programmer is having trouble, another can be assigned to help. If one module seems more difficult than the others, people can be brought in to inspect it. Assignments can be adjusted so that better people do more of the work. As a last resort, programmers can be added to the project to reduce the workload on the team, but this step may backfire in that the new people may take more from the project than they add because things need to be explained to them before they can be productive.

How Does It Fit?

From section 18.1

1. A UML design will be built around a number of use cases. After the design is completed, can you suggest something to do with the use cases other than file them away?

2. The Internet is fertile ground for clients and servers. Consider a person using a browser such as Netscape, to access a search service such as Yahoo.com, by connecting a modem to a local ISP (Internet service provider). In client–server terminology, describe what happens when a search is requested. What part of the operation runs on which machine?

From section 18.2

3. Which of the design techniques in Part III makes the best use of a hierarchy?

4. Some design techniques are clearly a bad fit to a particular problem. Consider:

   (a) A DFD design for the memo system in Chapter 14.
   (b) An FSM design for the payroll system in Chapter 17.
   (c) An O-O design for the Zipf's law problem in Chapter 13.

   Which techniques and problems are an acceptable fit, and which are hopeless?

From section 18.3

5. Here is a defensive coding trick for a program that works by reading an item from a file, processing it, and repeating until the file is exhausted:

   Just after the read statement, update a new file by appending to it the item just read. Do this is such a way that the new file is always properly closed just after the item is appended.

   (a) Illustrate how this trick could prove useful in debugging.
   (b) Describe a similar trick for recording the index variable of a loop.

From section 18.4

6. In the Microsoft coder–tester pair method, is the tester member of the team more an insider (as the coder would be) or an outsider (as an independent tester would be)? What are the advantages of both positions?

Review Questions

1. List the design notations given in Chapters 13–17:

   (a) In order of increasing difficulty of use
   (b) In order of increasing precision and formality
   (c) From most prescriptive down to least prescriptive

   Are the orderings about the same?

2. What are the three essential parts of any design?

3. What is "defensive programming"?

Further Reading

New design techniques like UML are initially described by their promoters, who often have a considerable financial and personal stake in making them successful. This does not result in early publication of critical analysis of the techniques. The wary software engineer can only read the promotional material and try to evaluate the substance between the lines of hype. The introductory bible for UML [KSB99] is probably not the best book to start with, but its readers agree that it's the best brief reference when details are needed. A better book for beginners intertwines the subject of object-oriented design with the UML notation [PJC99]. UML design is part of a formal process (what else besides the *Unified Software Development Process*?) that is commercially defined and supported by tools (for example, for drawing class diagrams).

Operating systems have long been designed as client–server systems, with the processes of the system all the servers and the "network" just internal message passing. What is new about the client–server idea is the use of multiple computers that have no mechanism for cooperating except their network communication and the artifice of two particular programs [OHE99]. Testing these systems is a challenge, but there is a good practical book [Bou97].

Any textbook on coding will include some defensive techniques. Two of the best books [McC93, Maq93] are full of practical advice.

References

[Bou97]   Kelly C. Bourne. *Testing Client/Server Systems*. McGraw-Hill, 1997.

[Maq93]   Steve Maquire. *Writing Solid Code: Microsoft's Techniques for Developing Bug-Free C Programs*. Microsoft Press, 1993.

[McC93]   Steve McConnell. *Code Complete: A Practical Handbook of Software Construction*. Microsoft Press, 1993.

[KSB99]   Martin Fowler, Kendall Scott, and Grady Booch. *UML Distilled: A Brief Guide to the Standard Modeling Language, 2nd ed.* Addison-Wesley, 1999.

[OHE99]   Robert Orfali, Den Harkey, and Jeri Edwards. *Client/Server Survival Guide, 3rd ed.* Wiley, 1999.

[PJC99]   Meilir Page-Jones and Larry Constantine. *Fundamentals of Object-Oriented Design in UML*. Addison-Wesley, 1999.

Testing
▼

Software testing is a subject full of contradictions. It has the potential for being the best organized, most engineeringlike part of development; yet, it is often the most disorganized part, performed by staff with the least training and experience. A good deal of testing theory exists because testing is a technical problem that can be treated theoretically; yet, the theory isn't often applied, and some people believe it is useless.

As it is used today, testing is an activity of looking for trouble. Tests are supposed to expose cases in which the software does not work properly, cases that lead to finding and fixing deficiences. The implicit model is that mistakes are "injected" into the code, and testing is to find them so they can be removed. There is a wider role that testing can and must play, of quantitatively measuring the degree to which the user can trust that no trouble lurks in the software. But this certification aspect is largely missing from practical software development today.

chapter 19

Software Testing

Testing a program ought to be more fun than designing and coding it, certainly more fun than negotiating with its users about the requirements. For the first time in development, you get to see it work! There's no denying that watching all that information processing horsepower in action is interesting, even exciting. After so much work, running the program should be a reward.

Maybe the reason testing is not always thought of as fun is that there's a flip side: the program may not work. In the earlier parts of development, things can go wrong, but failures are not as absolute and graphic as they are in testing. A developer can even (unconsciously or on purpose) sweep problems under the rug during requirements, specification, design, and coding—but when those problems show up as failed tests, it's no longer possible to kid yourself.

Or maybe the fun of testing diminishes if it isn't your own code being tried. But testing is still detective work that would be a serious challenge for Sherlock Holmes. The program and its specification and design documentation contain the clues to the crime (the lurking crashes), and the tester must find them as a triumph of deduction. Then again, not everyone likes detective work, and many people have no talent for it. Dr. Watson had none.

19.1 Get out the Test Plan

Document it! ▶
(record it or it's lost)

Testing that begins from scratch when code is ready to be executed is almost guaranteed to be inadequate. Not only will the many potential problems that arose during development have been forgotten or muddled, but the testing task is so formidable that it intimidates anyone facing it without prior preparation in hand. So the first rule of testing is: "Get out the test plan and follow it." It is a sad fact that although few developers advocate omitting the testing phase, most do not seriously prepare a test plan. If you must start from scratch, it is best to try to catch up on what was not done—to build a test plan, using the information from earlier development phases, after the fact. The heart of testing is "functional"—putting software through its paces. The functions are described by requirements and design documents, so if tests were not planned while these were being constructed, those phases must be revisited.

The code itself can also be a source of test cases, but it is not a wise place to start. To see why, we must examine the purpose of testing.

19.2 What Should Testing Accomplish?

Textbooks written before the 1980s often expressed the obvious goal of software testing something like this:

- **(Upbeat!)** Software testing is intended to verify that software meets its requirements.

Leaving aside the difficulty that requirements can impose *unlimited* constraints on software (for example, "for all inputs, the program shall . . . ") while tests can check at most a limited number of actual executions, this early textbook purpose is still misguided. It arises from the analogy to mass manufacturing (always a dubious source of wisdom for software). In the mass manufacturing process, testing is intended to show that all is well. A great deal of effort is expended in "setting up" the manufacturing process so that it correctly produces a product, say, a toaster. The toasters "coming off the line" are tested, and they are expected to work. While the process is being set up, defective toasters may result, but each defect points directly to something in the manufacturing process that should be fixed, and in the end, defects appear only if the production line breaks down.

The manufacturing analogy is a poor one because software is not "stamped out" in thousands of identical copies by a simple fabrication process. That may happen in copying for distribution, but the real software "manufacture" is one-of-a-kind, idiosyncratic development of a program, whose text is later copied. Furthermore, although it is fairly easy to see if a toaster works (all it takes is a piece of bread), the software tester has much more to check. The main difference, however, is that simple products like toasters have a small number of *failure modes*, each directly connected to the manufacturing process. If the toaster element doesn't get hot, there are only a few causes to explain why (for example, defective cord, broken heating element, bad connections or switch). For software, there seem to be an infinity of failure modes, only tenuously connected to the development process. All too often, what goes wrong is very peculiar indeed, and has no explanation other than "someone made a mistake." It isn't sensible to expect

After the extensive 1990 telephone outage caused by a mistakenly placed C break in the multimillion-line program that had crashed, an AT&T official made the public statement that such a thing would never happen again. Perhaps he thought that the engineer who did it had been shot dead.

trial and error to correct a process with unlimited failure modes—as fast as one is corrected, another entirely different one can appear.

In the late 1970s, Glenford Myers recognized the essential difference between software development and mechanical fabrication, and gave a quite different goal for testing:

- **(Downer!)** The purpose of software testing is to find errors.

Myers's pessimistic view has carried the day.

> **A notational aside.** It is useful to distinguish two aspects of software "error." The first is *failure*: the software does something wrong, that is, contrary to its specification. The second is a *fault*, which is something in the program text from which failure arises. Words like "bug" or "defect" usually refer to faults. Although it may be clear (after a lot of hard work called *debugging*) what can be done to fix a program that has failed, the fix does not define a unique fault. Programs are flexible enough that there are a myriad of ways to fix the same failure, and hence pinpointing "the" fault requires subjective judgment.

This terminology of faults and failures is enshrined in an IEEE glossary, and we will try to use the correct terminology in this chapter. But to show how hard it is, what did Myers mean by "error"? Did he mean that the purpose of testing is to find failures, or to find faults? About the best we can do is to paraphrase him as follows:

- **(IEEE-speak.)** The purpose of software testing is to find failures so that once the software has failed under test, faults responsible for the failures can be found and fixed.

Myers's insight was profound because of human psychology. People tend to find what they are looking for. If they are seeking to show that software is all right, they likely will do that; if they are looking for trouble, they will find it. What Myers recognized is that software is usually *not* all right, so unless the tester wants to be fooled, it is better to look for trouble. For an individual who is both developer and tester, the case is even stronger because of another piece of psychology: people are relatively blind to their own mistakes. A designer who misinterprets a requirement, for example, will then code the same mistake into the program, and will not try a test case that can expose the mistake. If the test case does get tried, the designer may not notice that the result is wrong! The best defense against the truths of psychology is to adopt a "mindset," and Myers's suggested mindset is negative: try to find something wrong.

In one experiment, testers overlooked 25% of the failures that plainly appeared on their tests.

The separation of concerns that put the "what" in software requirements and specification, the decomposition and high-level "how" in its design, and the details of "how" in the code can help the tester to achieve the proper mindset. Studies have shown that by far the most common faults in code are those of "omission"—something gets left out although it was needed. This need is directly expressed in the requirements, as a function the software is supposed to have. If test cases are devised from the requirements, functional test cases, then they have a chance of exposing code omissions. Test cases derived from the code itself are not likely to uncover what is not there. Hence if a test plan must be constructed too late, it is essential to return to the requirements document to identify functional tests.

Chapter 6 introduced functional testing; more information is given in Section 20.1.1.

19.3 The Testing Process: Unit Testing Versus System Testing

Functional testing works well at the "system" level, that is, on a complete piece of software. The test inputs to such software are rather like those that its eventual users will give it, and users have described them in the requirements. However, there is also reason to conduct testing at what is usually called the "unit" level, involving only pieces of the whole. No matter how diligently system-level test cases are devised, or how scrupulously the test plan is constructed, a complex system is hard to test, and no test engineer ever feels really comfortable and in control at the system level. This uneasy feeling, along with the way code is produced in development, leads naturally to a two-level testing process:

1. As each module is completed by its programmer, it can be *unit-tested*, by the programmer or another person, in complete isolation. If any problems are uncovered, they are fixed immediately. Iterating the test-and-fix cycle produces software units in which the developers have high confidence.

2. Modules are combined, first into subsystems, and finally into the complete system, to be *system tested*. There will necessarily be a time gap between completion of the first units and linking the whole system, so the programmers (who may still be busy) are not the best people to do system test. Instead, specialized test engineers are involved, perhaps working for an organization that did not do the development. This separation in time and personnel makes a test-and-fix cycle work much less well than in unit testing.

19.3.1 Unit Testing

Divide and conquer ▶

Testing only parts of a software system is an example of solving too large a problem by decomposing it. Unfortunately, the problem decomposition is not ideal. Testing pieces separately does find failures in the pieces, but when all these have been fixed, the whole system still can fail, in ways not attributable to one piece or another, but rather to their interactions.

The most obvious "units" of software are its subroutines. The design method of step-wise refinement makes heavy use of the subroutine encapsulation mechanism, both for intellectual control of the design and for storage efficiency of the resulting code. Unfortunately, the design of subroutines may not be accompanied by careful specification. The routines may be documented only by a brief comment in the code, which is nothing like what is needed to construct functional test cases. The code may be viewed as "self-documenting" because its requirements are simple and were well understood (but not written down) at the time of coding. But if mistakes were made, self-documenting is another way of saying "fault concealing"—when the code is its own definition, it cannot be judged independently.

The necessity of generating functional unit test cases is the strongest argument for providing, as part of software design, functional specifications for its parts that are as detailed as the specification for the whole system. Subroutines have very restricted functionality compared to the complete system, and that functionality is directly accessible through the subroutine parameter lists. Once a subroutine has been integrated with the others, its role is complicated by their presence, and some aspects of its functionality may be difficult to invoke. Inputs come to the complete system, and control passes through its code in complex ways, so that it is problematic whether or not a given subroutine will even be called. Thus testing a subroutine in isolation is much easier than testing it *in situ*. (Of course, an isolated test is also "unrealistic" in that real failures may arise from the very interactions that are missing in unit test.)

19.3.2 Test Harness and Stubs

There is an immediate practical problem in testing only part of a software system. The unit (it is appropriate to think of it as a subroutine) is not directly executable. To execute it requires:

Stubs. The subroutine may call other routines that are not present during unit test. They may not be coded yet, or they may be excluded just to keep the size of the tested unit small. To create an executable program, the calls must be linked to "stubs," dummy routines that simply return without doing much. But the idea of a stub is inherently a weak one. If the stub does literally nothing, the unit under test may not work properly, or its operation may be trivialized. But if the stub is made to act something like the real routine it replaced, then the tested "unit" grows. It is a compromise to make each stub an interactive interface with the human tester. When the stub is called, the human being is prompted to supply values as the missing routine should have supplied them. These values are then returned to the calling routine that is under test.

If a subroutine needs a functional stub (say) int subA(char *X), then it could be interactively instrumented by adding the code:

```
int subA(char *Input)
{
  int Output;
  printf("subA called, param %s; give int value: ",
          Input);
  scanf("%d", &Output);
  return(Output);
}
```

A test harness.   To execute a subroutine, it must be called, and the call supplies its argument values. This problem of unit testing has several nice solutions and opens up the prospect of "automated testing." In the simplest solution, the "test harness" for function ToBeTested() that has (say) one real parameter and returns a real value is a main program with the following structure in C:

```
main()
{
  float t, ToBeTested();
  while (!scanf("%f", &t))
    /*testing ends with an EOF*/
  printf("Result on input %f is %f\n",
          t, ToBeTested(t));
}
```

Linking this harness with ToBeTested() (and any stubs it requires) will yield a program that when executed reads test values and prints them along with corresponding results.

A person impatient with a long list of values to check after using an interactive harness will quickly take the next step. The test inputs and outputs can be put in files, and the test harness can then read a test input, pass it to the routine to be tested, check the result against the correct value in the file, and print a message to the human tester only when there is a failure. The construction of such test harnesses can itself be automated, with a program writing the harness (and basic stubs, as before) on being given the source code of the unit to be tested. Of course, constructing the input and output files is the creative work of finding test cases and what they should do; automation doesn't help with that.

19.3.3 Subsystem Testing

A *subsystem* can be defined as a relatively self-contained program unit. That is, it is small compared to the whole system, but not so small that it needs many stubs (the routines that would have been stubbed are incorporated), nor does it require too elaborate a harness (most complex data structures needed are internal to the subsystem). ADT modules and object-oriented classes are almost ideal subsystems.

Testing Abstract Data Types

The program module that is an encapsulated abstract data type (ADT) would seem to exactly fit the definition of a perfect subsystem for unit testing. All its subroutines (access functions) lie within the ADT, so no stubs are required. Furthermore, all important data structures also lie within the ADT; indeed, these are often part of its "secret" and so cannot be external. Perhaps most important, the functional specifications of ADTs are much better than the usual subroutine documentation because the ADT is meant for use by outsiders who do not read its code. In some cases, that code is considered part of the ADT secret, and is literally hidden from people who will incorporate it in their software.

An ADT *is* a subsystem, however, not a subroutine. Its access functions often call each other, so what is being tested is the whole, not each function in isolation. One routine's failures may be masked or distorted by another routine. Any subsystem displays this testing problem.

The information hiding of an ADT, its very reason for existence, unfortunately also complicates the testing problem. The problem caused by keeping internal data "secret" is that the outcome of tests cannot be seen— the results are hidden in the internal data structures. For example, think of an ADT implementing `IntSet`, with operations `member()`, `putin()`, `empty()`, `size()`, as in Section 15.4. Perhaps the actual `IntSet` values are stored in an array as they were in Section 15.4—that will be a secret of the ADT. How then are we to test (say) an access with `putin()`? No test harness can examine the array; to do so would be to violate the ADT boundaries. In a language like Java or C++ such an attempt constitutes a syntax error. So the tester is reduced to using `member()` to see if `putin()` worked properly. But the two routines share information, and they might also share faults. It could happen, for example, that both of them are off by one in the position of the last element used in the array. If so, `member()` will tell the tester that `putin()` worked properly; but, if (say) `size()` does not share the off-by-one fault, the ADT is buggy. Its routines appear to work in isolation, but sequences like `putin(0,X) ... size(X)` will fail.

What's usually done in practice is to add a special access function to the ADT for testing, and to remove it when the software is released. This function prints out a human-readable version of the hidden internal structures. Sometimes exposing the secrets in this way is called "improving the testability" of the code.

It is interesting to think about "faults" that might be *universally* shared by ADT access routines. If, for example, the ADT design documentation describes the `IntSet`-array last element one way, and all the access routines violate that description consistently, no test will fail. But later when a maintenance change is made, it will follow the documentation, and *everything* in the ADT will stop working.

▼
Is a universal fault really no fault at all, just another secret?

Testing Object-oriented Code

For the purpose of testing, an object-oriented class is little different from an ADT. Its methods are the access routines, and there is the same difficulty with examining hidden data. However, the inheritance mechanism does sometimes simplify testing. If a superclass method that is inherited by subclasses has been unit-tested, there is no need to retest it in each subclass.

There are pitfalls in inheritance, too, many related to retesting after a maintenance change. For example, a subclass might provide its own method `my_own()`, which is also available in its superclass. Removing `my_own()` from the subclass requires retesting because that exposes the superclass method, never tested in the subclass context.

Sequences of Inputs to Subsystems

What distinguishes a subsystem from smaller units is its more self-contained nature, which is achieved by using internal stored data. That is, the subsystem can be independent of the context in which it is used by maintaining its own data structures, which persist between interactions with the larger world of a whole software system. For an ADT or object-oriented class, the internal stored data is often hidden. Testing a subsystem with stored data is much more difficult than testing a unit that has no "memory" because results (and failures) depend on the *sequence* of tests. When a test point fails, the reason may involve an interaction between the input and the internal data state that existed when that input arrived. Indeed the internal state, not the test, may be responsible for the failure: the state may be wrong so that *any* next input would fail.

There is not much theory available for the generation of test sequences, as opposed to single, presumed independent, test points. As usual, functional testing based on the requirements is the best place to start. The requirements may identify "states" that the software must handle (sometimes these are called "modes"). For a command-decoding user-interface subsystem, here is a typical example of a requirements state:

[**2.5.7**].   When a user has supplied more than three consecutive commands that resulted in error messages, the system must go into "dumb-user" mode.

[**2.5.8**].   "Dumb-user" mode is terminated by a sequence of two consecutive commands that do not result in error messages.

$\vdots$

[**2.6.1**].   In "dumb-user" mode, the "help" screens for each user command are displayed before the command is executed, whether or not the system is in the "verbose" mode, and the user must confirm the command execution before it is actually attempted. If the user elects to abort the command, it does not count for the purpose of terminating "dumb-user" mode.

Functional testing of these requirements must put the system into dumb-user mode (and also, testing of combinations involving "verbose" mode are called for, which we ignore). The test sequences to reach dumb-user mode involve commands that result in error and nonerror responses, with the obvious combinations on the number of such responses. Once the system has been forced into what should be this mode, then there are further test sequences that try what should happen there, and terminate the mode.

Test sequences constructed from the requirements in this way are covering "states," but states *of the requirements*, not data states of software that tries to implement the requirements. It may well happen that an actual subsystem stores a value in some data structure that flags the program as *being* in dumb-user mode, yet the program *should not* be there. By doing the function test sequence, the tester stands a chance of exposing such a problem, but only a chance. The functional test might succeed even though the internal state is wrong. All functional testing has this potential problem since it tries only a small sample of the possible inputs for each "function." For this example, imagine a subsystem implementation that leaves the counter of error responses at 1 upon exiting dumb-user mode. Then this implementation will incorrectly go back into dumb-user mode too soon. To expose this problem will require a test sequence in which the mode should be entered, exited, and three commands follow, the first two with error responses. Such a sequence is not necessarily dictated by functionally testing dumb-user mode.

For an ADT or object-oriented subsystem, every internal state corresponds to a sequence of calls on the access functions (methods). Since those functions are an explicit part of the design (given in the signature for an ADT), the tester can construct a list of all single-function invocations, all invocations that are a sequence of two function calls, all three-function-call sequences, and so on. It may be possible to exhaustively try this list up to some maximum sequence length, as a kind of sequence "coverage" of the subsystem. (As usual with coverage ideas, each covering point is only a representative for a possible infinity of similar points, which differ in the parameter values supplied to the function calls in the sequence.) It is natural to think of objects and ADTs as having a finite collection of (requirements) "states," and as passing among these states (rather like an FSM that isn't finite) when the access functions (methods) are called. Then it is natural to think of tests that try each of the state possibilities and each transition. This coverage is subject to the difficulty that the module implementing the object may not in fact have the correct data states, and that the functional tests of the requirements' states might not expose failures in the program's data state.

An FSM has explicit states, and its defining diagram lets the tester explore sequences of inputs that will cover the states. However, these are again states that the designer intends the program to have, not states that the program actually has, and covering them may not have the desired effect of exposing failures.

Modes and mode combinations are useful abstractions for finding functional tests. The tester must try to avoid the trap of thinking that the program necessarily has the required modes. Myers's mindset is the key: in testing, seek to discover that the program modes are *not* exactly as specified.

19.3.4 System Testing

Ultimately, an entire software system is assembled from its units and subsystems, and must be tested. In one sense, no previous tests really matter because the complete system is all that its users ever see—they will never know about successes or failures of the parts, unless these are reflected in the behavior of the whole. This truism has led to the suggestion that most or all testing be done at the system level. For finding failures, however, "system test only" is a bad idea. As the software being tested grows, less can be learned, less understanding is available, and tests may not probe deeply. Thus fewer failures will be found. The advocates of system test only might respond that then users would not experience such failures, so they do not matter. Developers are wary of this argument, and feel unsafe neglecting unit and subsystem tests.

System testing is sometimes called "integration testing" because the software components must be integrated into a whole. The *incremental* method of integration begins with the most self-contained units (usually subroutines), and tests these in isolation. Then the smallest self-contained subsystems are formed and tested. Larger and larger subsystems are formed and tested, using only already tested components, until finally the complete system is built from a handful of large subsystems. In contrast, the *big-bang* method of integration immediately links all the parts, without trying to go through intermediate testing stages. (The name is descriptive of what usually happens: the system fails in some spectacular, explosive way.) However integration is accomplished, at some point the tester is faced with the complete system, just as users will see it upon release.

The big advantage for system testing is that requirements describe what a complete system should do, so functional testing is most natural at the system level. Functional system tests were the first ones in the test plan. In most cases there is an addition to the requirements and specification documents that is invaluable to the tester: a user's manual. User manuals are really no more than readable (well, sometimes they are!) versions of the requirements. They often contain examples that are the very best of functional tests, since they illustrate what the software should be able to do, and users are almost certainly going to try them. At the same time, by passing to the full system, the tester gives up a great deal. At the unit and subsystem level, it is possible to examine the code in detail, and to make a satisfactory catalog of fault-based and broken-box tests that seem to explore all the possibilities. For a large system, this detailed understanding is literally impossible. Section 20.1.2 will discuss "structural" testing based on code, and it will be seen that code-based testing is least satisfactory at the system level. If a good test plan has not been accumulated throughout development, it is system testing that will suffer most.

The problem of test *sequences* described for subsystems arises in spades for system testing. It now has the added difficulty that it may not be clear how to actually put the system into a given mode for test. For example, it is common to have a requirement like:

[**9.9.2**]. If a hardware error is detected, the operation will be retried three times, and if not recovered, the offending command will be terminated with an entry to the system log.

When the retry subsystem is being tested, it may not be too difficult to supply it with parameters that correspond to hardware failure, nor will it be difficult to try the possible combinations that can occur for retry and recovery. But when only the entire system is available for test, this function can be tried only if the actual hardware error can be made to occur on demand, and there may be no way for the tester to know if the retries are being correctly done the correct number of times. In general terms, it may be difficult or impossible to force the system into a required state, and it may be equally difficult to know the internal data state that actually exists in the program being tested.

19.4 Inspection Versus Testing

Code inspection at the module level and unit or subsystem testing at this level have a common purpose: to find faults in code units. The processes are very different, however, and it is natural to want to compare them. The experiments needed are difficult to conduct since they involve contrasting complete cycles of development, in which many confusing factors enter:

Cost. The overhead on inspections is high, but so is the payoff—problems found in the text of code are immediately localized, and can be fixed before testing begins. It would be expected that the cost of finding and fixing a problem would be lower for inspection, and experiments have shown this to be so. However, although unit testing can be done very cheaply, as haphazard tests during coding, and still uncover some defects, inspection requires training, organization, and discipline to do any good at all. Thus in the short term, testing is cheaper. The published comparisons involve organizations that have invested in making inspection work, and compared the cost after it was in place.

Effectiveness. As befits people who prefer technical work, most programmers do not want to believe that the "soft" methods of inspection work better than the "hard" methods of testing. But a number of studies have shown just that. The clearest results were obtained in organizations where a comprehensive inspection process was in place throughout development, not just for code units but for requirements and designs. It was found that following all these inspections, unit testing seldom uncovered *any* failures, and the results support eliminating unit test from development altogether. The experiments may seem unfair because the inspections had first crack at the code; however, that's the best way to do it since it realizes the earliest detection and would save not only the test cost but the cost of developing stubs and harnesses. In unconnected research, it has been suggested that structural coverage testing, the kind most often used at the unit level, seems to work best at finding shallow faults, program "typos" (like the use of the wrong variable name in an expression), so perhaps there is not much required of inspection to replace unit testing.

Programmers are not at all happy to think about abandoning unit testing, but their motivation is suspect: most people would rather test their own code in private than face their co-workers in a formal inspection. Intuitively, the strength of unit testing lies in fault-based tests and in checking for "worries" that arise during coding. Anyone who has been through code inspections realizes that many of the faults that inspectors look for could be found mechanically, so perhaps the future will bring a synthesis of unit testing and inspection. One could imagine that prior to inspection, mechanical unit-test analyzers would have to be run on the code; and, during the inspection, the code would be available online in a test harness to answer questions that might arise.

19.5 Managing the Testing Phase

Probably the most difficult part about managing testing is to see to it that it happens at all. As the final phase in software development, testing can be squeezed out of the process by schedule slips, until an almost untested product must be released. The best defense against losing testing time is to do as much of the work as possible along with the earlier phases of development, and the test plan is the mechanism to use. All the time spent on the test plan is time that must be spent in the test phase if no plan is available.

Testing is an activity that lends itself perfectly to being carried out by several people working concurrently. Each person can have a copy of the software to be tested, a separate computer system to use, and a part of the test plan to do. No communication or coordination is needed between them. But the test plan is essential; lacking it, a group of testers cannot work without telling each other which cases they are doing.

A manager who sees the schedule slipping and testing time disappearing can prepare for the worst by finding additional staff, dividing up the planned tests, and getting ready to do a big job in a short time. Unfortunately, there is no way to similarly compress the time needed to fix the problems that will be uncovered. Unless there is time for debugging, the testing phase will do no more than show everyone that the software is failing, without allowing it to be fixed. The unfortunate fact that debugging is not an activity whose time can be estimated in advance shows the importance of quality work throughout development: unless the software has attained a reasonable standard when it enters testing, a long debugging period whose end is not predictable will have to follow. Projects that wildly overrun their budgets and schedules apparently do so precisely because they *are* tested, they fail badly, and then they enter a cycle of debug and retest that drags on and on.

If there is enough time for testing and debugging, and a solid test plan, the manager doesn't need to do more than keep an eye on progress through the plan, adjusting staff to cover any problems that arise. If the testing includes different methods such as those listed in Section 21.5, it may be necessary to see that the priority order is observed. Engineers may enjoy unit testing more than functional testing, but it is less important. The manager has an obvious measure of progress in the number of test cases planned versus the number executed (and any failures seen repaired, with retest).

How Does It Fit?

From section 19.1

1. Suppose that a development project arrives at the testing phase not only without a test plan, but with no requirements document. What should the testers do?

From section 19.2

2. After a fault has been fixed, it is possible to characterize it, say, as "incorrect parenthesis order in expression." However, it has been observed that different debuggers, trying to fix the same failure, often produce entirely different fixes.

   (a) Give a simple example of a failure that could be fixed in two very different ways.

   (b) In cases like (a), "the failure" is well defined. But is "the fault"?

3. Find a copy of the IEEE glossary defining testing terms, and look up "error." What is the definition?

4. Give arguments pro and con for why the person who codes a subroutine should also unit-test it.

From section 19.3

5. In the stub example of Section 19.3.2, why are the format characters in the `printf` and `scanf` statements `%s` and `%d`?

6. When testing an ADT, explain why sequence tests obtained from the signature are sufficient to cover all "modes."

7. For the `IntSet` ADT of Section 15.4, write a special testing-only access function that prints out the contents of the internal array. Things to think about:

   (a) Is it better to translate the array into setlike terms when printing, or just to dump the raw values? In particular, should the printing stop at the array element that is supposed to represent the last set member?

   (b) Where does the information needed to understand the internal structure come from? (Hint: see Section 15.5.3.)

   (c) Suppose an ADT has an access function to print its central data structure. If the ADT's secrets change, will this routine have to be changed?

8. Give an example of how a system's internal state can be wrong during testing, yet no failure has occurred.

9. What is the difference between testing an FSM to cover its sequences of transitions and similarly testing an ADT?

10. The examples given in a system's user manual should be tested since users will almost certainly try them. Whose job should it be to test these

examples—the manual writer or the system tester, and why? How can the development process be set up to be sure that they are tested?

From section 19.4

11. If you are familiar with a "code inspection checklist," the things that inspectors are supposed to look for in inspections, count how many of its items could be eliminated by using mechanical analysis and unit testing to be sure that the code being inspected does not have those faults.

12. In a code inspection, do you think it would be a good idea to allow (require?) the author to express "worries" about the code and ask the inspectors to check them? Explain.

Review Questions

1. Why is it better to have a test plan ready when coding is finished rather than beginning then to construct one?

2. What are unit testing, subsystem testing, and system testing?

3. Describe test stubs and drivers. When are they needed, and why?

Further Reading

Testing is generally thought to be the most time-consuming part of software development. (Unless, of course, the time runs out, and then testing takes no time at all.) It is strange that so important a subject has received so little attention in textbooks. Perhaps the reason is hinted at by a title: Glenford Myers called his book [Mye79] *The Art of Software Testing*. It's hard to write about an art. For those who seek textbooks, Myers small book would be perfect except that it is more than 20 years old. A modern overview [Bei90] and a practical how-to text [KFN93] are available. Brian Marick has a very detailed book [Mar95] on subsystem testing for C.

References

[Bei90]   Boris Beizer. *Software Testing Techniques, 2nd ed.* Van Nostrand Reinhold, 1990.

[KFN93]   Cem Kaner, Jack Falk, and Hung Quoc Nguyen. *Testing Computer Software, 2nd Ed.* Van Nostrand Reinhold, 1993.

[Mar95]   Brian Marick. *The Craft of Software Testing*. Prentice-Hall, 1995.

[Mye79]   Glenford J. Myers. *The Art of Software Testing*. Wiley, 1979.

chapter 20

Coverage— "Systematic" Testing

W hen searching for anything—a forgotten quotation from Shakespeare or a ship at sea—there is just one "systematic" method. The possible locations must be marked off and examined one after the other. The necessity of checking off parts of a search space arises when there are too many possible places to look. Finding a Shakespearian quotation once took an army of readers, each assigned to perhaps one scene of one play. (Nowadays, a CD-ROM can be searched exhaustively.) The ocean must still be divided into sectors to find a lost ship. And some information structures will always remain too large to search by brute force—for example, the possible moves in a chess game, or, to come back to our subject, the possible test inputs for a program.

The complication in large searches is that they can fail. The subdivisions are made, each is examined, but the result is not sure. The missing ship may never be found because the search craft cannot perfectly cover their assignments. Similarly, a person skimming a Shakespearian scene might miss the quotation sought, and so a program tester may miss a failure even though it is there. All one can do is to make the best subdivision possible for searching and cover its pieces as well as possible.

20.1 Dividing the Input Space for Failure Search

For program testing, the search space for failures is the collection of all possible inputs to the program, which in most cases is unimaginably large. For example, a mathematical subroutine with one integer parameter, which is to use double-word arithmetic on a 32-bit computer, has $2^{64} - 1$ possibilities. To try them all at one per second would take more than 500 billion years— too long! Similar calculations for the number of possible input strings for a compiler, the number of possible transaction records for an accounting program, and so forth, come up with equally hopeless input counts. The search space for faults is not so large—it is merely the program text that might contain those faults. But there is no use in considering the program text because testing cannot search it except indirectly. To try a program, an input has to be supplied.

So testing (trying to find failures) is a search problem requiring division of the search space (possible program inputs), in which the coverage is at best imperfect. The "systematic" testing methods are all really methods of subdividing the input space into a small number of subdomains, and imperfectly covering the subdomains with tests. One "method"—*exhaustive testing*—takes each possible input as its own singleton subdomain. When there are only a few possible inputs, the method works perfectly, finding any failures that are there to find. But most of the time exhaustive testing isn't feasible. Other methods are careful to keep the number of subdomains small so that it is possible to cover them all, but they then suffer from an inability to properly explore any one of these (big) subdomains.

The intuition behind subdomain decomposition is that all the elements in a subdomain are somehow "the same," and therefore there is no reason to try them all—one element or a few elements should be representative. The crucial "sameness" for testing is relative to failure. What a tester does *not* want in a subdomain is the following:

> The elements of the subdomain appear the same. For example, the coder believes that they all use the same case in the program's algorithm, so the program should either work for them all or fail for them all. Alas, it is not so: the program works for most of them, but fails on a few, perhaps because the common algorithm is inappropriate for those few. Now the tester tries some subdomain points, almost certainly gets ones that succeed, and the failures go unnoticed.

Unfortunately, these unsatisfactory subdomains are the rule. After all, no one knows where in the input space the failures lie, so "failure" can't be used to define a subdomain.

20.1.1 Functional (Specification-Based, Black Box) Testing

As described in Chapter 6, during the development phases that produce an executable program, there are many opportunities to record functional test cases, at the complete system level and for units (subroutines) that make up the system. The functions define subdomains of the input space—all inputs that correspond to a function. The test cases are probes into these subdomains. For example, in a command-driven program with 12 commands, the inputs may be thought of as divided into 12 subdomains, one for each command. Functional coverage (based on the commands) is obtained by selecting at least one input from each subdomain (that is, trying each command). All the commands can be "covered," by 12 tests, but of course these 12 do not really cover all inputs because there are typically a vast number of "versions" of each command, selected by parameter values, by the history of commands issued prior to the one being tested, and so on. Thus the 12 functional subdomains can be *refined* by breaking them down into sub-subdomains, such as one defined by a certain command with a certain representative parameter value. (Again, there will usually be too many parameter values to test them all, so the sub-subdomains will be "covered" by at most a few samples.)

Broken-box testing is another way to refine the subdomains of a functional test. Usually, it is just a better way to choose special cases of a function, cases that correspond to information found by peeking inside the program black box. Instead of selecting parameter values at random to subdivide a functional subdomain, it may be possible to group parameter values that cause the program to use distinct algorithms, perform some common actions, or otherwise "do the same thing." These groups define the broken-box sub-subdomains, from which "typical" values can be selected to get test coverage.

Devising a good collection of tests that cover the functions that software should perform is not easy, particularly if nothing is done until the code is ready to execute. There is a cheap way to accomplish something like functional testing, however, with almost no difficulty. For software with a large consumer base (from previous releases), developers can use something called beta testing. (This follows what is presumably alpha testing, which for those trying to get off cheaply, often amounts to a small volume of haphazard tests.) In beta testing, the software is "prereleased" to a selected set of customers, who are using the previous version, and who have volunteered to try the new one. In exchange for the privilege of doing the developer's testing for free, these people are expected to carefully report any problems they encounter. They use the new software to repeat things they have done in the past, and they try out its new features. Beta testing does find failures, and they can represent just what customers would experience (because the testers *are* customers).

Fault-based tests (whose name derives from the IEEE terminology) are a kind of negative functional testing. Fault-based subdomains consist of all those inputs on which the program would fail, *if* some fault were present. But the test was devised before the program or any particular faults in it even existed, so "fault" refers to *any* fault that would lead to a certain failure. The tester picks one input from a fault-based subdomain, and if the program does not fail on that input, the tester concludes that there is no such fault. Here is an example of the search space being imperfectly defined because the subdomains are seldom composed *only* of inputs that *must* fail if a certain fault is present. More commonly, other inputs are mixed in, inputs on which the fault may be present, but the failure is not certain. Thus the tester

Identify the customers ▶

can be fooled into thinking there is no fault. Fault-based subdomains can also be refined with broken-box techniques, and adding program information often sharpens the sub-subdomains so that faults are found.

One variant of functional testing deserves special mention because it is something like fault-based testing without the hard work of isolating the fault. It has long been observed that extreme and exceptional cases are easy to neglect in design and coding, and such cases arise in software at the "boundaries" of specification or broken-box subdomains. Boundary value testing, or *special-values testing*, consists of choosing test inputs that probe where requirements meet or overlap, or at their extremes. Often, these inputs are failure prone. The extremes are the easiest to isolate. Whenever a requirement gives a range or restriction, like "the value must be an integer between 1 and 1000 inclusive," or "valid characters are lowercase letters," it defines special values to test, *viz.* 1, 1000, a, z. It is wise to enlarge the special-values set to include values adjacent to the extremes, here 0, 2, 999, 1001, Z, b, y, A. Boundaries can also be identified by cases in the requirements like: "In dumb-user mode the system shall . . . ." The test cases here involve inputs for which the system has just gone into and out of dumb-user mode. Broken-box conditionals like:

```
if (x <= 0.001)  /* use polynomial for accuracy */
   .
   .
   .
else /* library routine is good enough */
   .
   .
   .
```

suggest special values for x of $0.001-\epsilon$, 0.001, $0.001+\epsilon$, where ϵ is the smallest available floating point change.

20.1.2 Structural (Code-Based) Testing

Caution about the source of test cases—especially when a test plan has to be created too late—is needed because there is a seductive shortcut that the tester must avoid. This shortcut goes under the name of "structural testing," or sometimes "program(code)-based testing," or even the misnomer of "systematic testing." The idea is that tests can be generated without much knowledge of what the software is supposed to do, and without knowledge of its design.

Here's how after-the-fact, code-based testing (the "statement-testing" version) works in practice:

Haphazard testing.   There is no test plan, but executable code has been produced, perhaps for an implicit (unwritten) specification, by trial-and-error design and coding. The programmer, now acting as tester, assembles a few haphazard test cases, the first ones that come to mind. These are run, and the results examined cursorily. If the program crashes or gives obviously wrong answers, it is changed and the same tests repeated. When the haphazard tests have been made to succeed, the code is examined to see if all of it got "covered"—all of its statements got executed—by these tests. The examination is facilitated by the use of a tool like an execution profiler, which flags statements that were never executed. The tester then studies the code and adds test cases specifically designed to force execution of any previously unexecuted statements. If any new failures come to light, the code is changed and all tests repeated. When finally all the statements have been executed for some test case, and no failures have been noticed, the software is declared to be "adequately tested."

In the extreme, the tester begins with an empty set of test cases and, by trial and error, generates a collection that covers all statements.

20.1.3 Generating Code-Based Tests

The subdomains of code-based testing are collections of inputs that all execute the same part of the code. In this section, we describe statement coverage testing, in which all elements in a subdomain execute the same statement of the program being tested. Other kinds of code-based testing use more elaborate "parts" to be covered. These will be discussed in Section 20.3.

To find a test input that will execute an arbitrary statement Q within a program source, the tester must work backward from Q through the program's flow of control to an input statement. Each conditional branch is analyzed to force it toward Q. The desired test input is one that takes the branches in succession and winds up at Q. For simple programs, the calculations are straightforward. They amount to solving a set of simultaneous inequalities in the input variables to the program, each inequality describing the proper path through one conditional. Since conditionals may be expressed in local variable values derived from the inputs, these must figure in the inequalities as well. As an example, consider the code fragment:

```
int z;
scanf("%d%d", &x, &y);
if (x > 3)
  {
    z = x + y;
    y += x;
    if (2*z == y)
      {
        /* statement to be executed */
      .
      .
      .
```

The inequalities are:

$$x > 3$$
$$2(x + y) = x + 1$$

with the solution $x > 3$, $y > -1$. Then the (x, y) value $(4, 0)$ (among an infinity of others) will force the statement to be executed. Such calculations can be carried out mechanically; the process is called *symbolic execution*.

Unfortunately, the presence of loops or recursion in the program code makes it impossible to write and solve the inequalities in general. The difficulty is that each pass through a loop may alter the values of variables that figure in a following conditional, and the number of passes cannot be determined by static calculation. However, a person can often guess values that will result from a loop.

Code-based testing does find software failures, and a great deal of research effort has gone into trying to discover the "best" kind of coverage to use. But at the same time, all testing that does not derive from the functions of the specification is fundamentally misguided. People do not use software in order to execute its statements; rather, they invoke its functionality. Although there is a rough correspondence between each function and a block of statements implementing that function, it is all too easy to execute all the statements yet miss some functions. (An example is given in Section 20.1.4.) Should this happen, the tester will be misled into thinking that everything a user might do has been tried, when in fact the first user to invoke some function will be in unexplored territory.

20.1.4 Misleading the Tester

As an example of the way in which structural coverage is inferior to functional coverage, and can mislead the tester, consider a program that is supposed to insert information into an internal data structure, then be able to retrieve it. Suppose that the information is correctly inserted, but when searching the structure for retrieval, the program fails to examine the last item inserted. (This could happen, say, because a counter is off by 1.) Thus information can be found, but only after new information has come in after it. Finally, suppose that a "change A to B" function is implemented by inserting B as a copy of A's information, then removing A. Testing using *only* the "change" function will execute all the code for insertion (because B is inserted), all the code for searching (for A, to remove it, but only after B has come in after it), and all the code for removal (of A); however, the test will actually not have tried an "insert," "search," or "remove" function. Each of these functions can still fail, as shown by the following plausible examples, despite executing all the code:

Case 1.   The user tries "insert X," then discovers the information was wrong, and so does "remove X."

Case 2.   The user tries "insert Y," takes a coffee break, and then can't remember if Y has been inserted, so does "search Y."

Case 3.   After inserting U and several other items, the user tries "change U to V," then in order to be sure that it worked, does "search U" and then "search V."

The example shows that achieving code coverage does not do a very good job of achieving functional coverage, and code coverage may not expose failures that functional coverage would expose.

It would be stupid not to insist that tests achieve code coverage. After all, if some particular statement has never been executed during testing, it could contain the most dreadful blunder, and no one would know about it. If some untested statement is so badly flawed, then as soon as it *does* get executed, there will be a failure. But it does not follow that if we avoid one kind of stupidity, nothing can go wrong. As the preceding example shows, executing all statements is no guarantee that software cannot fail. The intuitive structural reason is simple: coverage guarantees that each statement has been executed *once*, using one particular set of internal data. But each statement has the potential for being executed with many different internal data values. Just because one set of internal values works properly does not mean the others (untried) must also work. As a simple example, the expression X+X, if executed when the internal value of X is 2, will produce result 4. If the expression *should* have been X∗X, 4 is nonetheless correct, for *one internal value* of X. But for most other values, X+X and X∗X will differ, so the execution using 2 misleads a tester. This particular fault is addressed by *mutation coverage*, described in Section 20.5.2, but there is no general solution to the problem of a coincidentally correct result from faulty code.

20.1.5 Test Oracles

A test plan *must* include information about the test cases to be tried. If the actual input values are not given, at least an indication must be there about how the inputs will be determined. Outputs, on the other hand, are more problematic. The test plan could just say: "See the specification." There are good reasons not to be so lazy, the best being that the tester may not bother to work out the expected result, and may accept results that are not correct. Another reason to supply output in the test plan is that during testing, time is likely to be in short supply, whereas the test plan is being developed up front, where time is less critical.

However, there is an ideal situation in which test case outputs do not need to be part of the test plan—there may be an effective *test oracle*. An oracle is the name given to any procedure for checking that a test output conforms to the specification. So if the tester is expected to check the output, then the oracle is a human being. If the test plan does have output values, then the plan itself is the oracle. An oracle is *effective* if it is some mechanical means of checking the result. It is not common to have an effective oracle, but it does happen. One important example is in code/decode problems, or communication protocols. To see if a result of coding value X is correct, all that is needed is to decode the result and check if it's X back again. Of course, if both coding and decoding software are being tested, the decoding may not be trustworthy, but in some cases, one direction is so simple that it really serves to check the other.

Some functions have inverses that are trivial to calculate compared to the problem itself. For example, it may be very difficult to factor a huge input integer, but to check that the factors are correct requires only multiplication. An easily calculated inverse is an effective oracle. Sometimes, there is an independent way to obtain the result of a specified computation, and that method constitutes an effective oracle if the output of the program being tested is compared to the other source. This happens when a problem is being reprogrammed (perhaps to improve the execution speed), but the old program can be trusted. It happens when there is some physical measurement that can be made to determine if the program being tested is right. For example, results of a wind tunnel experiment could be used to check a flight simulation.

The greatest promise of formal specification methods may be that they serve as effective oracles, as indicated in Section 10.5.7.

20.2 Structural Test Adequacy and Marick's Recommendation

There is general agreement that functional testing, not structural testing, is at the heart of a good test plan designed to uncover failures as Myers advises. Structural coverage may look attractive when the test plan was let slip, but it is *not even available* at the time when the test plan should be under construction. Functional test cases can be derived from requirements and design, but structural cases must wait for the code to be completed. Nevertheless, it would be stupid not to make sure that tests achieve code coverage. Elaine Weyuker proposed that structural testing be used as a way of *evaluating* functional test quality. Brian Marick has given a particularly cogent presentation of this idea. Figure 20.1 shows Marick's proposal for generating test data, which has the following essential features:

1. Functional tests are generated from the requirements or specification and design, with the intent to try every function, and particularly to explore potential functional difficulties.

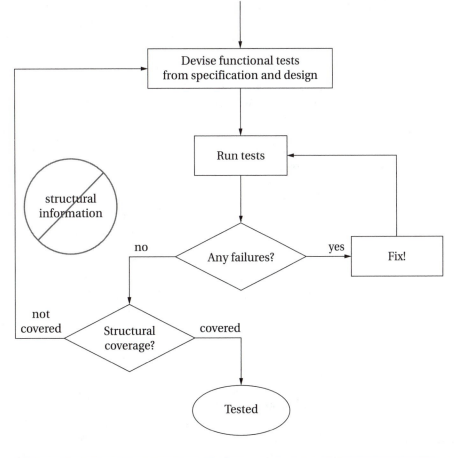

Figure 20.1   Flowchart of Brian Marick's testing method recommendation.

2. Structural coverage is examined only *after* the tester is satisfied that the functional test collection is adequate.

3. When structural coverage is imperfect, the tester does *not* use program details to improve it. Instead, more functional cases are generated.

Thus structural coverage is used as an *adequacy measure* for functional tests. When there is less than 100% structural coverage, then clearly there is a functional coverage problem: the uncovered code must have some purpose, and that purpose has not been invoked, so some function is untested.

There is no good argument to justify the reverse implication. Why should functional testing be adequate just because structural coverage has been attained? As we saw in Section 20.1.4, functions can remain untried despite 100% statement coverage. The only argument (and it is a weak one) that can be given to support structural coverage implying functional coverage is an appeal to the "diversity" of the methods. If the functional tester is studiously *not* thinking about structural coverage, yet attains it, then it seems to mean something.

Marick's recommendation doesn't appear very different from the structurally based "haphazard" method described in Section 20.1.2. Both generate test data, check structural coverage, and add to the data to improve the coverage. But the "mindset" is profoundly different. Marick is consciously looking for failures, and using the functional approach to systematically seek them. The haphazard method of Section 20.1.2 ignores functions in the first part of its test generation, and additional tests are conceived not by function, but by code study. Certainly faults of omission will more likely be found by Marick's method.

Marick recommends "mining" the requirements and the design for functional "clues." Each requirement, and each design decision, suggests a situation to try. This clue can then be turned into a specific test case for that situation. If a test plan is constructed as the specification and design are created, these clues are exactly the right thing to record; the actual test cases can be constructed later if that is more convenient. If a test plan has not been part of the ongoing development until too late, then looking for these clues is a good way to build one; better late than never.

The hardest part of using Marick's recommendation is to avoid the use of structural information when seeking additional coverage. Of course, structural information does enter. Statements not executed are the clue to finding new functions to test. An example will illustrate the difference between generating additional tests from the code, or from the specification, by function. Consider the following fragment of C code:

```
  :
  :
/* Purge items dated before yesterday */
while (X = OutofDate(L, TodaysDate - 1))
  Remove(L, X);
/* See if the list is getting too small */
if (ListLess(L, 3))
  printf("Data pool is dangerously low!\n");
/* Continue to process commands */
  :
  :
```

Suppose that statement coverage indicates that the `printf()` statement was never executed. A "code analysis" would probably proceed as follows:

> The procedure call `ListLess(L,3)` must be always returning *false*. Studying its code shows that this happens when the list L has less than three entries. So we need to use a small list as test data. Let's try one with a single entry.

And indeed, beginning with a list with one entry, which naturally enough will have today's date (so `Remove()` does nothing), the `printf()` statement is executed, and all is well. But is it? Marick would instead proceed like this:

> What function is not being tried? The unprinted message gives a clue, and consulting the specification, we see that there is a requirement:
>
> > Outdated items shall be removed from storage, and after an item is removed, a warning message should be issued if less than three items remain.
>
> This suggests two functional tests: (1) Try a case of a list with initially less than three items but nothing removed; there should be no warning message. (2) Try a case in which a list is purged below three items, and the warning message should appear.
>
> (Furthermore, how about the case (3) in which a list of initially two items is purged to one item? This should have come up during requirements analysis!)

Notice that test (1) is the same as suggested by the code-based analysis, but that *the correct outcome is different*. Evidently the programmer has misunderstood the requirement, and always printed the warning, instead of printing it only when removals shorten the list. Thus the code-based analysis leads the tester astray, whereas Marick's use of the same test exposes a failure.

Test (2) in Marick's analysis seeks to try the actual function that the code should be implementing. Suppose that there is a fault in `Remove()` such that a counter used by `ListLess()` is not being properly decreased, so that the conditional guarding the warning message cannot succeed. Then test (2) will expose this failure (as the code-based test did not because it was not even trying the specified function).

The reason why solely structural determination of additional cases often finds nothing is that the new cases are trivial ones that aren't related to what a user might actually try. It is obviously more difficult to follow Marick's recommendation than to analyze the details of the code; it is also more likely to expose failures.

20.3 Variations on Coverage Testing

Statement coverage is the simplest and most intuitively appealing of structural coverage criteria. But over the years, testers have invented many other kinds of "coverage." Perhaps the process of invention goes something like this:

> When coverage is used to judge the adequacy of testing, the tested software can still fail. When it does fail, a test engineer naturally asks the question, "Why didn't I catch that?" Sometimes the blame can be put on the details of coverage, which did not require the failure-finding test case. Then the engineer may invent a new kind of coverage that *would* have forced that case to be used and the failure detected.

All such "improvements" in the notion of structural coverage are at cross-purposes with Marick's recommendation, where the study of functional clues in the requirements and design are central. Nevertheless, more elaborate structural coverage criteria can be used to judge the adequacy of functional tests, and complex criteria may be harder to satisfy, so they may make the functional tester work harder and find more failures. However, there is also a reason *not* to use more complex coverages because an elaborate method may not connect well with the specification and may encourage superficial code-based analysis. For example, the "mutation coverage" idea described in Section 20.5.2 has proved very hard to use as Marick suggests; on the other hand, methods like dataflow testing (Section 20.5.1) may actually help the tester identify missed functional clues.

20.3.1 Control-flow Graphs and Their Coverage

In the heyday of assembly language programming, flowcharts were the programmer's "blueprints." The flowchart was a good abstraction of low-level coding. But flowcharts have fallen into disrepute, largely because a properly formatted program in a modern high-level language looks rather like a flowchart (that's what the "structured programming" revolution was all about). Most programmers now think that it's a waste of time to draw a flowchart, when the same logic can be accurately transcribed as program syntax and documented with a pretty printed listing.

In testing, however, flowcharts live on, under the name of *control flow graphs* or simply *flowgraphs*. A flowgraph doesn't use the special symbols that flowcharts used but is technically just a restricted kind of labeled directed graph. Formally, a flowgraph (like any mathematical graph) is a collection of *nodes* and *edges*. The nodes are a finite, nonempty set N, which intuitively corresponds to the collection of statements in a program. Each node is labeled with the program statement to which it corresponds. The edges E are ordered pairs of elements from N. An edge (b, e) directed from node b to node e, intuitively corresponds to the possibility that control might pass from statement b to statement e. (More on the meaning of control that "might pass" later.) One special node (the *exit node*) has no edges leaving it; another special node (the *entry node*) has no edges coming into it. For languages that do not have `case` constructions, at most two edges leave any node: two for a conditional, one for an unconditional statement.

Although the rules for constructing a flowgraph from (say) a C program have not been given exactly, and there are some sticky cases to consider about procedure calls and nodes where control rejoins, we will not need to consider such complications. Those who construct testing tools (see Section 20.4) do need to build correct flowgraphs from programs, and there are straightforward algorithms to do so.

The flow of control captured by a flowgraph is only possibilities because flowcharts don't take into account more than the program syntax. For example, consider the C program fragment F:

```
if (x > x)
    x = 1;
else
    x = 2;
printf("%d", x);
```

Its flowgraph fragment has nodes:

$$N = \{n_1, n_2, n_3, n_4\},$$

where n_1 is the `if`, n_2 and n_3 are the assignments in order, and n_4 is the `printf`.

$$E = \{(n_1, n_2), (n_1, n_3), (n_2, n_4), (n_3, n_4)\}$$

is the set of edges; that is, control might pass from n_1 to n_2, and so on. This information is conventionally represented by a diagram like Figure 20.2.

The fragment F will always print 2; that is, control cannot actually pass from n_1 to n_2 nor then from n_2 to n_4, but those edges are included in the flowgraph anyway. Thus this flowchart contains "dead code" (the assignment statement n_2), which is located on an "infeasible path" (paths are formally defined in Section 20.3.2). Dead code is not always so easy to spot and can be a problem for the tester trying to cover all statements. Dead code can never be covered by any test, but after many tests have *not* covered some statement, it can still happen that the statement *can* be covered, and the tester may spend a good deal of time in analysis (particularly if using Marick's recommendation) to distinguish the truly dead code from code that is just executed in very unusual cases.

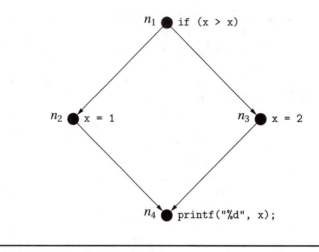

Figure 20.2   Flowgraph of the program fragment *F*.

In flowgraph terminology, the testing method that requires each statement to be executed by some test is *node coverage*.

20.3.2 Path Coverage

A flowgraph is a concise representation of the control flow possibilities in a program. Control might pass along any edge of the graph in the direction of the arrow. At each conditional statement node, there is a choice about which way to go. Following the arrows and making choices defines a *path* through the flowgraph, a sequence of nodes (and edges, but it's sufficient to give the node sequence to define a path) that intuitively corresponds to a sequence of statements that might be executed. Some people believe that each path represents something important a program might do, something distinct from every other path, and hence something that should be tested. The name for this testing is *path coverage*.

Path coverage seems like an awful lot, and it is. The number of paths in a program can be very large, in principle without limit. When there is a loop, one path skips it entirely, another path goes through the body of the loop once, another goes through the body of the loop twice, and so on without end—there is an infinity of potential paths, each for a different execution possibility. Hence no one can be expected to cover them all, and in practice, repeated loop paths are ignored except perhaps for iteration counts of 0, 1, and some arbitrary larger count.

Path testing (even with reasonable restrictions to handle the loop problem) is the most elaborate method described in this chapter, but it's worth remembering two points:

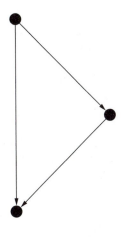

Figure 20.3   Flowgraph for which branch- and statement testing differ.

- More elaborate isn't necessarily better. The purpose of testing is to find failures, and if a test method is too complex, it may detract from that purpose. There are certainly cases in which one is better off with statement testing than with path testing.

- Just because path testing (without restrictions for loops) can't be done, doesn't mean that it would be perfect if it could be done. If it were possible to test every path, which it sometimes is, a fault might still escape detection. (See Section 20.5.2.)

20.3.3 Branch Coverage

"Branches" in programs occur at conditional statements, where the flow of control can go more than one way in execution. Branch coverage of a program requires that test data be provided that, taken together, causes all control possibilities to be realized. For the constructions if ... then ... else and case with else for missing cases, branch coverage is not different from statement coverage; attaining either one forces the other. For the conditional tests in looping constructions, if the loop is not endless, then entering it will result in branch coverage (because it must be exited), so again there is no difference from statement coverage. (And the case of missing the loop body altogether, the conditional initially being *false*, is not forced by either statement or branch coverage. See Section 20.3.2.) The place where statement and branch coverage differ is in an if statement with no else. The case that the conditional is *false* and the protected statement not executed is required for branch coverage, but not for statement coverage. The flowgraph for this case is shown in Figure 20.3.

Marick advocates using branch testing as the primary coverage measure for assessing functional coverage. The special case in which it differs from statement testing is a good source of clues for additional functional tests. The expression that was never *false* can be traced to the requirements, and the case to which this corresponds can be found. It is a common programming error to use an `if` without an `else` and erroneously "fall through" into following code where it is assumed that something from the `then` branch has been done; if this fault is present, exercising the corresponding function has a good chance of exposing it.

A number of variations on branch coverage are thought by some to do a better job at the cost of being more complex. For example, in *multicondition/decision* coverage, the tester is required to force each branch to follow the *true* and *false* edges in the flowgraph as in branch testing, but in addition, if the conditional expression is built from subexpressions using AND or OR operators, test cases must force every possible combination of *true* and *false* for these subexpressions. There is no evidence to establish that multicondition/decision coverage is better at finding failures than branch coverage. All we know is that it seems harder to achieve. The argument supporting its use is that all combinations within the expression should be tried, but whether that is worth the difficulty of doing so is an open question.

20.4 Testing "Tools"

In Marick's method, people generate test cases because the translation of requirements concerns and design problems into specific cases to try out the software in those areas is difficult. Human creativity is essential, and the negative mindset of looking for difficulties fits some people better than others. That is, there are good, bad, and indifferent testers, and the skills or training needed by a good tester is not obvious. But mechanical aids, by an abuse of language called "testing tools," are available to help with the testing process.

20.4.1 Tools to Manage the Testing Process

A tester needs, most of all, bookkeeping help. It is provided by what is called a "test scripting" tool, which comes with a "test-description" language. The language is very simple, providing a standardized way to write down test details: what input values, results, and so forth constitute each test. The tool takes a list of such descriptions, and executes the program to be tested, giving it the inputs and checking the results. Once the test script has been prepared, actual running (and rerunning) of the tests is automatic. (See Section 21.3.)

20.4.2 Structural-coverage Measuring Tools

To apply structural coverage measures to a collection of tests, as Marick suggests one do in order to find deficiencies in the functional testing coverage, requires tool support. Although a person can figure out what parts of a program have been exercised if the program and the coverage criterion are simple enough, this is a task far better done by a program since the book-keeping operations required are just what programs do well and people do badly.

The essential idea behind measuring coverage during test executions is *instrumenting* the code, that is, inserting into the running program probes to record what happens. The most elegant way to accomplish instrumentation is with a hardware co-processor. The co-processor monitors the memory bus of the computer in which testing is taking place, and by recording the pattern of memory usage, permits calculation of which statements, branches, and so on are being taken. The virtue in using a co-processor is that there is minimal intrusion into the running program—the distortion of its activity amounts to stealing fractional bus cycles. Without a co-processor, larger distortions must be introduced. For example, to measure statement coverage in a language like C, the instrumentation amounts to inserting counters at each statement. Given C code like:

```
1   main()
2   {
3       float x, y;
4       scanf("%d", &x);
5       y = x + 3;
.
.
.
86      printf("Bye now.\n");
87  }
```

(the lines are numbered for reference only), imagine the following modified code in which change lines are not numbered:

```
1   main()
2   {
        int markit, mark[88];
3       float x, y;
        for (markit=1; markit<=87; markit++)
          mark[markit] = 0;
4       scanf("%d", &x);
        mark[4] = 1;
5       y = x + 3;
        mark[5] = 1;
```

```
        ·
        ·
        ·
86      printf("Bye now.\n");
        mark[86] = 1;
        printf("Statements never executed: ");
        for (markit=1; markit<87; markit++)
          if (mark[markit] == 0)
            printf("%d ",markit);
        printf("\n");
87   }
```

It is assumed that identifiers mark and markit were not used in the original program. When the modified code runs, it does just what the original did, but in addition, at the end of execution it prints a list of the statement numbers of statements never executed. That is, instrumenting in this way is the basis for a rudimentary statement coverage tool. The processing of source code needed to create the modified program is easy to automate, and even easier to add as a compiler option since the compiler is already parsing the source to find statements.

Statement and branch coverage analyzers are commercially available for most popular languages. Commercial tools have clever interfaces, for example, displaying and highlighting the parts of the source that are not covered. In the public domain, tools are less flashy. The GNU C compiler has options to measure branch and statement coverage in conjunction with a tool called gcov.

Most statement coverage tools work by instrumenting the source program just as the preceding sample indicates. As the code size increases, so does the magnitude of the bookkeeping task they carry out. So long as the resources needed are roughly linear in the size of program units, there is no difficulty using these tools on large programs. For example, the table needed to store information about which statements have been executed gets larger only in direct proportion to the statement count, and the overhead of recording statement executions is a constant per statement.

20.5 More Complex Structural Coverage Criteria

Statement coverage, and its modest extension to branch coverage, are old ideas with obvious intuitive appeal. Path coverage is also appealing, but appears impractical because programs have too many potential paths. The search for a better technique that will magically uncover all program faults has led researchers to try more elaborate kinds of coverage.

20.5.1 Dataflow Coverage

The rationale for path coverage (Section 20.3.2) is that each path corresponds to a unique program action that should be tested. A stronger case can be made for trying some particular paths, as follows:

> On some paths, a program variable is first given a value, then the variable (that is, that value) is used farther along the path. Such a path should be tested because it is the programmer's intent to follow it for some special purpose.

"For historical reasons" is code for "It's dumb, but we're stuck with it."

For historical reasons, setting a variable's value is called a *def*, and the combination of setting and using the same variable is called a *def-use* or *DU pair* for that variable. A DU pair for variable V consists of two program locations, one where V is set to some value, and another where that very value of V is used.

To "cover" a DU pair for variable V in testing thus requires a program execution that follows some path between setting and using V, with the value of V undisturbed between these points. A collection of test data that covers every DU pair for every variable in a program achieves *all-uses dataflow coverage*. For more of those historical reasons, it is not called "DU coverage" because it would be confused with a slightly different kind of coverage that insists on covering *all* the paths linking each DU pair, not just some path. When someone speaks of "dataflow testing," usually all-uses is meant.

Intellectual control (language betrays us) ▶

All-uses dataflow coverage seems a particularly good way to assess the adequacy of functional testing, as Marick recommends. When a DU pair is not covered, it should be easy to identify the requirement the program is trying to satisfy by setting and later using a variable, and hence to find a new functional test to cover that DU pair.

Testing tools to measure dataflow coverage are much less common than tools for statement and branch coverage, and not readily available commercially. Part of the reason is that the potential DU pairs of a program are not as obvious as its statements and branches. A tool must calculate the pairs in order to check whether they have been covered. In the worst case, this calculation is not linear in the size of the source program. Dataflow testing is seldom used in practice, partly because tools are not readily available. But perhaps a deeper reason for the neglect of dataflow is that the ideas involved are more difficult for people to grasp. A cycle is set up in which there is low demand for tools, preventing their development, which in turn reinforces the lack of demand.

20.5.2 Mutation Coverage

Software testing attempts to address a hopelessly difficult problem. A small number of tests are supposed to stand in for the infinity of possible things that a program might do. All the structural coverage schemes are an attempt to define "representative" tests by isolating some finite aspect of the program (its statements, branches, DU pairs, some of its paths, and so forth) and trying these representatives. Then one hopes that the infinity of other inputs that have not been tried will be "the same" relative to failure so that the test representatives will find failures if there are any. Of course, this hope is in general a foolish one. Imagine some particular statement S in a program, where a statement coverage test has executed S, say, with input t_S. Why should t_S, among a possible infinity of other inputs that execute S, necessarily excite a failure?

Control flow testing goes wrong when the covering tests succeed, but some other inputs could fail. How could that happen? The answer lies in a program's "data state." At each program control point, the program variables could take on a vast collection of values. One test passing through probes *one* element of a huge data-state space. If only some of the data states at that point lead to failure, then the coverage can be meaningless—the test got there, but not with a troublesome data-state value. To improve control flow testing, some way is needed to "cover" the data-state values that might arise at each control point.

In *mutation testing*, program locations (statements) are considered one at a time. A small change is imagined in the syntax of the statement, creating a *mutant* program. Test data *kills* the mutant if the data state differs between the original program and the mutant. When a mutant is not killed by a test, it means that the data state going into the change is poorly covered by the test because even a changed statement has no effect. Another way to look at a "live" mutant is that if in fact the original program is faulty, and should have been the mutant program, the test data would not detect the fault. Test data achieves *weak mutation coverage* if it kills the whole collection of mutants (each arising from a different change), at every program location. The collection of mutants represents a myriad of small program changes, applied throughout the program one at a time. Mutation coverage requires that the whole collection be killed. (There is also a *strong* mutation coverage, which requires that to be killed, the mutant must produce an *output* different from the original program. Weak mutation is the more practical version.)

If every possible program change were allowed as a mutant, mutation coverage would be a perfect test method that could not miss any potential failure. If the program being tested were faulty, one (actually, many) of the mutants would be a correct program, and the test data is required to kill this mutant; that is, the test data must expose the failure in the original program. But this ideal scheme isn't practical. There are an infinity of possible mutants, even if the changes are inserted one at a time (and of course real bugs are not so simple). And even the simplest mutations require significant testing time. The original program and *all* mutants must be executed for (perhaps) all test points—far greater overhead than for any of the control flow coverage schemes.

The mutants allowed in implemented systems are very restricted. For example, it is common to change each operator and each operand in expressions to all the other possibilities. The mutants of a C program containing the statement

```
x = y + x;
```

at a control point *L* where the only other accessible variable is v, would contain at *L* each of the following (among many others):

```
x = y - x;
x = y * x;
x = y / x;
x = x + x;
x = v + x;
y = y + x;
v = y + x;
```

Killing these mutants requires rich enough test data to reach *L*, to distinguish them all from the original statement.

Mutation was an idea that occurred to a number of people at about the same time. Kenneth Foster came to it by analogy to fault detection in hardware gates. He suggested that software test data should distinguish all the relational operators from one another so that in C,

```
x < y
```

say, would be seen to have a different outcome than any of:

```
x <= y
x == y
x >= y
x > y
x != y
```

Marick says that he "cannot recommend" using this feature of his own tool because it is too difficult to understand the error messages it produces.

This is fault-based testing at its best—if all the mutants are killed, the tester knows that there cannot have been a mistaken use of the wrong operator. One public domain coverage tool (Brian Marick's GCT) implements weak mutation of relational operators as a special case; other tools are only research prototypes.

Mutation tools are heavy users of computing resources, and their non-trivial bookkeeping algorithms make them difficult to write. As is the case for dataflow testing, a difficult concept linked to a shortage of tools keeps mutation testing from being used. Nevertheless, the idea sheds some light on the mechanism by which simple program faults turn into execution failures.

20.6 Which Coverage Is Best?

If the purpose of testing is to find failures, then obviously the coverage most likely to do so is best. A good deal has been written in an attempt to prove that one kind of coverage is better than another. These "proofs" are often fallacious, based on circular reasoning. The inventor of a clever coverage scheme confuses real failure finding with mere satisfaction of that scheme. In one study, quality of testing was defined by the percent of program branches executed, and it was "proved" that branch testing was best since it got the highest quality!

20.6.1 The "Subsumes" Relationship

It may happen that attaining one kind of coverage *forces* another kind to be attained. For example, it is impossible to attain branch coverage in a test without at the same time attaining statement coverage with that same test. However, it doesn't work the other way around, as the example in Section 20.3.3 shows. When this happens, we say that one method (like branch testing in the example) *strictly subsumes* the other method (like statement testing). It is natural to think that "subsumes" means "better," but it is not necessarily so. For any two methods B and D, where B strictly subsumes D, it can happen that failures are exposed by a D coverage test that isn't a B coverage test. A plausible "quality" relationship like subsumes has to be examined with great care to see if it is actually related to the goal of testing to find failures.

For some programs, the subsumed method is more likely to find failures. In the following subroutine, the comments indicate the position of statements with certain failure properties:

```
void
Q(float X)
{
  if (X < 0)
    {
      /* initialization statement (never fails) */
    }
  /* statement that fails 1/10 of the time if
    and only if initialization not performed */
}
```

Consider the potential statement coverage of this program by small testsets. The coverage depends on only the signs of the test points. For testsets of size two, there are four equally likely combinations of input signs, as shown in the table:

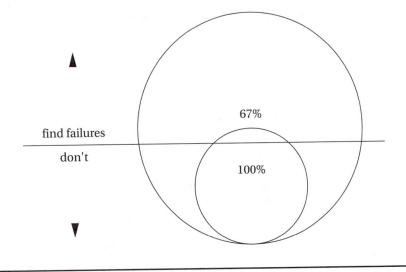

find failures

don't

67%

100%

▶ **Figure 20.4**   Coverage is not failure detection.

Input Signs	Statement Coverage	Failure Probability	Detection Probability	Size Three Detection
+ +	67%	.2	.1	.15
+ −	100%	.1		
− +	100%	.1	.07	.11
− −	100%	0		

A testset with two positive points covers only two of the three statements, whereas any testset with a negative point covers them all. 100% coverage strictly subsumes 67% coverage, and seems obviously "better." Yet as
the table shows, the chance of actually seeing a failure when a 67%-coverage
test is run is .1 (four possibilities at .2, .1, .1, 0), whereas for a 100%-coverage
test it is .07 (three possibilities at .1, .1, 0). (For testsets of size three, four, . . .
the disparity is less and less.)

The subsumes anomaly comes from the variety of different tests that
satisfy each method, as Figure 20.4 indicates. What is important is not how
much is covered, but rather how likely testsets with that coverage are to
accomplish the goal of finding failure. There is an additional psychological
disadvantage to seeking coverage: people tend to pick misleading tests when
they are not concentrating on failures. They choose unrepresentative test
points that simplify the coverage criteria.

Using coverage as Marick recommends (Section 20.2), the subsumes
relationship is of more use. When B strictly subsumes D, for Marick it's not
that B is better at finding things than D because neither B nor D is being
used to find failures. B is harder to satisfy, so the functional tests required

to cover it should be more demanding, and the functional tests should find failures.

20.6.2 Choosing a Testing Method in Practice

In practice, the choice of testing method is determined more by mundane factors than by theoretical superiority. The following are important:

Software developers are notable, incurable optimists so they are often behind the schedule they set.

Testing process. Testing is the final step in a software development process, a step linked to the other development steps by a test plan. The process itself is the most important factor in determining what test methods can be used. If the development process is poorly defined and carried out haphazardly, there will be no test plan, and no ready collection of functional testing cases to apply when implementation is done. If development is behind schedule, there may be little time for testing, and certainly no time for an elaborate method. The structural testing that Marick counsels against (Section 20.1.2) may be the only possibility, and the simplest coverage criterion is dictated. (There may be no testing tools available to help.) On the other hand, a well-defined development process may provide a functional test plan and testing tools. Structural coverage as a check on the quality of the functional tests (Marick's recommendation) is a relatively small investment, an investment that is almost independent of the method used (although perhaps mutation is significantly more difficult to use than the control flow methods).

When testing time arrives, it is far too late to convert a poor process into a good one, so the choice of testing method may be limited long before testing is begun.

Resources available. The generation of good test cases is a labor-intensive process. Running the tests can be routine, but requires constant attention to detail because the bookkeeping task is immense. Some of the process can be automated by testing tools, but it remains true that the single most important factor in good testing is the availability of people time. The simpler testing methods are easier for people to use, and tools supporting them are easily available.

Feasibility issues. There is no algorithm for predicting how an arbitrary program will behave in execution, so the problem of deciding if a given test is structurally adequate necessarily lacks a solution. If a given test collection has not attained coverage, it may be that additional cleverness is needed to augment the tests and achieve coverage; or it may be that it is impossible to cover the program. It is an undecidable problem to decide which is the case in general. For structural methods based on control flow, the technical difficulty takes the form of "infeasible paths." (Mutation has a similar—but more difficult—problem in identifying "equivalent mutants" that cannot be killed.) Suppose Marick's method is being used, and some path U (or statement or branch or DU pair) is not covered by the initial set of functional tests. Effort directed to examining neglected requirements, or to studying the program in violation of Marick's recommendation, *may* come up with data to force execution of U, but not always. It can happen that U is *infeasible*—it cannot be executed by any input. (Another way to say this is that the infeasible path contains "dead code.") The tester trying to achieve structural coverage must devote analysis time to identifying infeasible paths, or risk spending forever searching for tests to execute them. More complex methods like dataflow and mutation testing require more analysis.

These practical issues point to the simplest, most intuitive kind of structural coverage (that is, statement or branch coverage) as the most useful. It is undeniable that more complex methods are harder (and more expensive) to use. Until it is shown that there is a clear payoff, they will not be popular, even among people willing to work hard to do better.

The larger issue is a comparison between functional and structural testing, and here functional testing has an overriding advantage: in functional testing, the software developer tries the very things that software's users are expected to try. Any failures detected are difficulties that will almost certainly be experienced by those users. Users do not like failures, and the simpler the failure situation, the less they like them. Functional testing usually finds at least the simplest failures. Once the decision to use functional testing has been made, Marick's argument is that a structural check on the quality of the functional test is easy to apply, and it would be stupid to omit it.

Identify the customers ▶

How Does It Fit?

From section 20.1

1. Fill in the blanks:

   (a) _____ searches the input space for _____ .

   (b) _____ searches the program text for _____ .

2. A person who volunteers for beta testing is taking a risk because if the new software is used for real work it may cause serious damage, for example, destroying valuable files. Explore the implications for the quality of testing that results.

3. In the three failure cases for insertion and searching given in Section 20.1.4, explain for each what should happen, and what does in fact happen because of the assumed fault in the program.

4. In special values testing, what is the rationale for including test points "next to" the special values? Would any different values do as well?

5. Give an example (different from the one using X + X and X∗X at the end of this section) in which a program has faults, but all its statements can be executed under test without a failure occurring.

From section 20.2

6. At the end of this section, a comparison is drawn between Marick's recommendation and examining code to find additional test cases. Make that discussion more precise by writing a careful specification for what the given program fragment should do, and then altering the code to do that.

7. In view of the way test cases are structurally generated to force execution of a given statement, explain why those tests are often trivial and unlike any real user executions of the program.

From section 20.3

8. Technical questions about branch testing:

   (a) Is it possible for a branch condition to be *neither* true nor false for some test execution? Explain.

   (b) Is it possible for a single test point to cause a conditional statement to take *both* true and false branches? Explain.

9. Give an example of a program that can fail, but for which complete path coverage will not necessarily excite the failure. (Hint: let the program have just one path.)

10. Give an example of a program in which an if has no else, but should have one in order to meet its specification.

11. (a) Prove that branch testing strictly subsumes statement testing, using a particular control flow graph to establish the result.

    (b) With reference to Marick's recommendation for using structural clues to find new functional tests, why does your example in (a) make branch coverage give better clues than statement testing?

> When asked to give an example of failure behavior, what is expected is (i) a specification, and (ii) a program that does not meet it. Resist the temptation to give only a program and point to a fault in it.

From section 20.4

12. In the example of statement coverage instrumentation using an array mark [], the instrumented program will not do quite what it should. What will go wrong, and how could it be corrected?

13. How would instrumentation for branch coverage work?

From section 20.5

14. A dataflow coverage analyzer can detect patterns other than DU pairs. For each of the following possibilities, explain whether the pattern is sensible

or whether it should be flagged as necessarily indicating some kind of error.

   (a) DUU (that is, a def followed by a use followed by another use without a second def)
   (b) U (with no def)
   (c) DD
   (d) D (no use)

15. As in all control flow analysis based on flowgraphs, some of the DU associations identified are not real in the sense that there is actually no input to the program that can cause the association to be executed. Give an example.

16. The first weak mutation system worked by actually trying the mutants, and observing the internal state just after the mutated statement to see if it had changed (and thus if the mutant had been killed). Foster recognized that this trial and error wasn't necessary for relational operator mutations. Instead, he came up with a rule for picking test data that is *guaranteed* to kill all relational operator mutants, so nothing need be tried. What is this rule?

From section 20.6

17. Show that (a) path testing strictly subsumes branch testing, but (b) there are programs and tests from branch coverage that find a failure, but these are not path coverage tests.

   Hint: Figure 20.5 is a very useful flowgraph for demonstrating relationships between path coverage criteria.

18. Show that the subsumes relationship is transitive: if C strictly subsumes D and D strictly subsumes E, then C strictly subsumes E.

19. Suppose that an FSM implementation as described in Section 14.2 is tested, and statement coverage is attained. Discuss whether this coverage means anything (and, if so, what) for the cases:

   (a) An automatic implementation
   (b) A hand-coded, table-driven implementation
   (c) A specifically coded FSM, as in Figure 14.8

20. Suppose that a subsystem such as the `IntSet` ADT is being tested with a driver as in Section 15.4.4. For each of (a)–(c), explain why the named routine(s) should or should not be instrumented for structural coverage:

   (a) The driver routine itself
   (b) The routines of the `Boolean` ADT
   (c) The routines of the `IntSet` ADT
   (d) Suppose the coverage in (c) is inadequate. What does this mean, and what should be done?
   (e) Do you think that branch coverage of (c) *will* be inadequate?

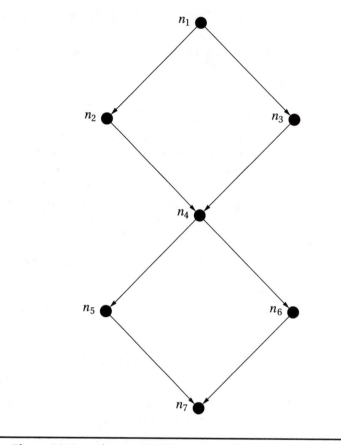

Figure 20.5 Flowgraph with two branches and four paths

Review Questions

1. What does it mean to say that one kind of test coverage is "better" than another?

2. Which is better, functional or structural test coverage, and why?

3. What are the most popular kinds of structural coverage?

4. What is a structural-coverage testing tool?

Further Reading

Brian Marick's book on subsystem testing [Mar95] exemplifies his advice on the use of structural coverage adequacy, and gives detailed examples of using the clues it provides.

It isn't easy to read the technical papers on details of the structural coverage methods. Weyuker is the authority on dataflow [FW88]. Weak mutation has two sources, in Foster's analogy to hardware testing [Fos80] and in an early testing tool [Ham77]. Simeon Ntafos has generalized the idea of structural coverage to arbitrary "elements" of a program [Nta88], and in particular, to a kind of dataflow coverage in which DU associations transfer to one another through a program, making patterns that might be represented as $D(x)U(x)-D(y)U(y)-D(z)U(z)$ in which a def of variable x is passed through y to z and the required DU association is $D(x)U(z)$.

Careful experiments are beginning to appear in which structural methods are compared [FW93]. However, the significance of the experiments is called into question by the toy programs that have so far been used.

References

[Fos80]   K. A. Foster. Error-sensitive test cases analysis. *IEEE Transactions on Software Engineering*, pages 258–264, May 1980.

[FW88]   P. G. Frankl and E. J. Weyuker. An applicable family of data flow testing criteria. *IEEE Transactions on Software Engineering*, 14:1483–1498, 1988.

[FW93]   Phyllis G. Frankl and Stewart N. Weiss. An experimental comparison of the effectiveness of branch testing and data flow testing. *IEEE Transactions on Software Engineering*, 19(8):774–787, August 1993.

[Ham77]   R. G. Hamlet. Testing programs with the aid of a compiler. *IEEE Transactions on Software Engineering*, pages 279–289, 1977.

[Mar95]   Brian Marick. *The Craft of Software Testing*. Prentice-Hall, 1995.

[Nta88]   S. Ntafos. A comparison of some structural testing strategies. *IEEE Transactions on Software Engineering*, 14:250–256, 1988.

chapter 21

The Future
of Testing

M yers's advice to test with the intent of finding failures is the basis for most practical testing in the world today. It is certainly the best advice for engineers looking for individual testing skills. But there is an additional dimension to software testing—there is more to it than Myers suggests. Imagine being successful at testing according to the best practice. That practice might be software development in which sufficient time and talent were devoted to the requirements, specification, and design documents, which were carefully inspected, and a careful test plan constructed at the same time. Then a method such as Marick's might be used for functional testing with structural adequacy. Not so many mistakes as usual would be made in such a development, and more of them than usual would be found by inspection and testing. But the question can still be raised:

Would you trust the resulting software? Can it still fail?

The question is not academic. Software is crucial to the operation of much of the modern world, and the time is not far off when a substantial number of people will be betting their lives on software working. A small number of people are already in this position, and not all of them won the wager. To give only the most obvious example, the next generation of commercial airliners will not stay in the air without the correct operation of their flight-control computer programs.

It is easy to see why testing to find failures does not necessarily make software trustworthy. Unless it is known in advance that no failure can escape our testing methods, we can apply them as diligently as possible, yet still miss something. Here the theoretical impossibility of doing perfect testing comes back to haunt us. Just as there are ways in which bugs can elude the structural methods, so can functional testing (or any other kind) go wrong. Any piece of software has a vast number of potential behaviors, a practical infinity of possibilities for how it will respond to inputs. Any practical collection of software tests is not only finite, but minuscule in size compared to the input possibilities. To expect that the tiny number of tests we conduct, however cleverly, will somehow uncover every possible failure among the infinity of possibilities seems foolish.

21.1 Random Testing

Focusing the testing effort on finding failures almost guarantees that testing will not have much significance when no failures are found. The better a testing method is at bug exposure, the less representative of normal operation its tests are likely to be. Special values testing is an extreme example. By selecting unusual, error-prone inputs, it is very good at detecting problems. But testing *success* on unusual inputs means little—they are seldom used. Every testing method (even fault-based testing) has this same problem of low significance on success—*except* functional testing. Functional testing does try what a program's users will try.

For "success significance"—proving something when failures are *not* found—what's needed is a kind of weighted functional testing, seeking to be a true sample of what users will eventually ask of the software. The crucial word here is "sample," and this kind of testing is called *random* testing.

Two elements are essential to random testing, a *user profile* and a *random input* generator. Roughly speaking, random input values are generated according to a weighting that reflects expected usage, and executed. As with any testing method, an oracle is required to examine the results for success or failure. For random testing, the oracle is more difficult to obtain because the inputs are not "nice" ones for which the result is easy to determine, and there are many more tests than usual.

21.1.1 User Profile

A test will be a valid sample of eventual use of software only if it conforms to the pattern of that use, which might differ between users. It is evident that if user W concentrates on one function of the software, while user V uses mostly another, then a test predicting what W will see must be different from one to predict for V. The *user profile* is a description of what a user will try, as a probability distribution over the software's input space. That is, a user profile gives the probability $d(x)$ that x will be the user's input. Figure 21.1 shows a made-up profile for a numerical (real) input space in which negative values are not used, nor are values greater than 7, and the usage concentrates around input 2 and input 5.

In practice, no detailed probability distribution could possibly be obtained for a real user—it contains far more information than even the most introspective person could supply. However, an approximation to $d(x)$ might be obtained by breaking down the input space by function. If a software system has (say) three distinct commands, it might be possible to ask

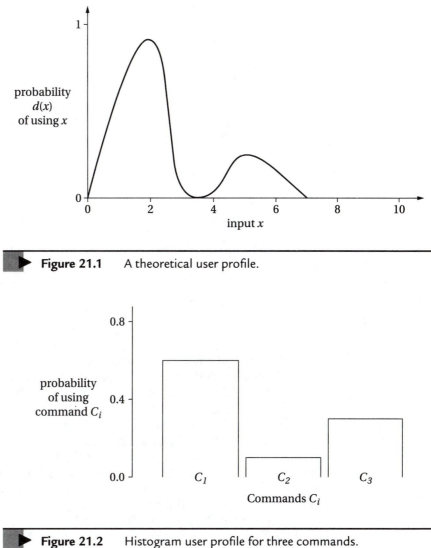

Figure 21.1 A theoretical user profile.

Figure 21.2 Histogram user profile for three commands.

users for estimates of how frequently each command will be used. The resulting histogram, which might look like Figure 21.2, can be turned into a user profile by assuming that different examples of the same command are equally likely over all the inputs for that command.

The best user profile a developer can obtain is a crude approximation to what any user actually does in practice with actual software. Unfortunately, testing with the wrong profile invalidates the test results. If tests concentrate on one function, but the user winds up using another most of the time, the test might as well not have been done—its predictive power is nil. Or if the rough histogram profile is correct, but within one of its bars the user concentrates on a few particular values, then testing is wrong that was spread across all possible values for that bar.

21.1.2 Random Input Values

"Random" is an adjective redefined in computing to have a meaning different from the one in the dictionary. In computing, "random" is often used to mean "haphazard, without sense." The technical meaning is quite different: random selection is choice without bias, independent, uncorrelated. The best example to follow is the theory of measurement errors: *random* error is the opposite of *systematic* error. In making a series of measurements, if the errors are random, then they can be expected to cancel out in an average; if they are systematic, on the other hand, they will reinforce each other.

The testing methods previously described are all "systematic" in this sense—the test points selected serve some purpose and are not independent. Indeed, these systematic testing methods explicitly guide the tester in making "informed" choices, based on the details of requirements or program structure, with the intent of uncovering failures. But just as it is better for measurements to have random errors than to have systematic ones, it may be better to choose tests explicitly devoid of purpose. The users of a program are not searching for failures, so why should failure-seeking tests tell anything about what users will experience?

The essence of random sampling is that there must be no correlation between the sample points. For testing this means that test inputs must be explicitly unrelated. A "pseudorandom number generator" attempts to create uncorrelated values. The essential idea behind pseudorandom generation is to select nonsignificant bits from a computation of some kind. For example, starting with a large odd number k, and repeatedly multiplying to get k^2, k^3, ..., then extracting from these the three bits starting at the 13th-last bit position in the binary representation, will yield a sequence of integers in the range 0–7. The successive integers selected in this way seem to be unrelated to each other, but they are related since they were obtained algorithmically. It isn't easy to obtain good statistical properties for the sequence, but it can be done.

Most programming languages come with a library function to generate pseudorandom numbers, and the documentation tries to describe its "randomness," which may not be very good. Better random numbers can be obtained from chaotic physical processes, such as the noise in electronic circuits. If a program input value is numerical, then a pseudorandom-number generator can be used to generate test data for that input. Things are more difficult when inputs are non-numeric: what is a "random English sentence," or a "random C program," for example? But we ignore these hard questions, and assume that there is a means for generating "random" test data.

21.1.3 An Ideal Example of Random Testing

Random testing is best explained using an ideal example. Consider unit testing a subroutine for computing the cube root of a floating point number, over the range [−10,000, 10,000] with a required accuracy of 1 part in 10^5. This subroutine will be used in such a way that 80% of the time, the inputs will come from the interval [−1.1, 1.1]; 10% of the time, the inputs will come from (1.1, 100]; 5% of the time, the input will be greater than 100, and 5% of the time, the input will be less than −1.1. The example is ideal for three reasons: (1) the input is numeric and falls in a limited range, (2) the user profile is very simple, and (3) there is an effective oracle. The oracle is available because the cube root function has a simple inverse. To see if a result R that should be the cube root of X is correct, it is only necessary to see if the cubes of numbers in a 10^{-5} interval around R bracket X, which requires only four multiplications and two comparisons. (The floating point accuracy of most machines will be adequate for this oracle because of the restricted interval over which the computation is required.)

Then random testing with 1000 test points is done as follows:

Choose 800 random numbers uniformly distributed in [−1.1, 1.1], call the subroutine with each, and check the result using the oracle. Repeat with 100 random numbers in (1.1, 100], and 50 random numbers in each of (100, 10,000] and [−10,000, −1.1). The software passes the test only if all 1000 results satisfy the oracle.

21.2 Predicting Software Quality

If random testing were used as all the other testing methods we have described are used, then there would be no more to say—random testing would be just another failure detection technique. In fact, random testing for failure detection has its advocates. They argue that the user profile directs effort toward what users will most need, and random input choices avoid any possibility that the tester will be tricked by the specification or code structure into missing something important. Advocates of random testing also point out that for them the problem of generating test input data, which is a major people-intensive aspect of other kinds of testing, can be left to a mechanical pseudorandom-number generator. But random testing is not often used to find failures in practice. The reason probably has to do with the oracle. Somehow, having spent a great deal of trouble to come up with a few clever test points, people do not mind struggling to discover what the result should be. Faced with the same task for points generated at random, they balk.

21.2.1 Reliability

Random testing has its primary purpose beyond finding failures. It can be used to make a prediction about future behavior of the tested software, something that no other testing method can do. The standard engineering parameter that describes a prediction of future behavior is the *failure probability*. A failure probability is the number of times that the software can be expected to fail, expressed as a fraction of the number of times it is tried. For example, a failure probability of 10^{-3} failures/demand means that the failure fraction is $\frac{1}{1000}$, so out of (say) 6000 executions, a program with this failure probability can be expected to fail about six times. Another similar statistical parameter is the *mean time to failure* (MTTF), which is (under certain assumptions) the reciprocal of the failure probability. A MTTF of 1000 means that on average 1000 executions can be expected before the program will fail. These statistical parameters can be estimated from trials (that is, testing runs) of the software. When an estimate is made, it can be trusted more if the sample involved is large. One way to express this trust factor is with an *upper confidence bound* for the test run (often shortened to "confidence"). A confidence of (say) 90% in some particular result means that if the measurements that led to that result were repeated a large number of times, the result is expected to be the same nine times out of ten.

If a random test should fail, the program is repaired, and the test repeated (with different random choices for the inputs). Eventually, the random test does *not* fail. Suppose that N test points have been chosen at random from the user profile, no failures occur when executing these N tests, and that the tester wants to predict that the failure/demand will be less than f, with a confidence C. The formula connecting these quantities is:

$$C = 1 - (1 - f)^N.$$

Figure 21.3 shows the behavior of the confidence on the number of tests and on the desired bound on the failure probability. The shape of the curves is in line with intuition: to get higher confidence in a certain failure probability such as h in Figure 21.3 takes more tests, and for any given number of tests, one has more confidence in a less demanding failure probability such as h'. No matter how many tests are run, the confidence in perfection (that is, in $f = 0$, no failures ever) is always 0, whereas one always has 100% confidence that the software is no worse than worthless (that is, $f = 1$, it fails every time).

As a rule of thumb, the formula predicts that to get around 90% confidence in a MTTF of M executions requires more than M tests. That is, there is no magic in random testing: if you want to be sure that software will work for years, you have to test it for years. Thus, although random testing is in principle a means for assessing the true quality of software, if high quality is needed, it will be impractical to make the assessment. For extreme safety-

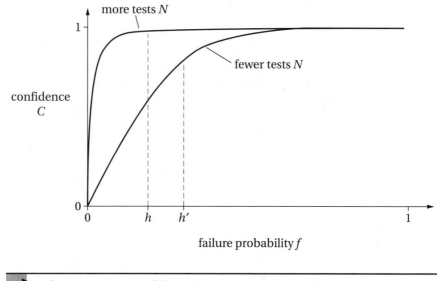

Figure 21.3   Confidence based on test size and failure probability.

critical applications like flight-control software, a MTTF of 10^9 is often taken as the standard. To conduct 10^9 tests at one per second would take about 100 working years.

Software engineers speak loosely about the "reliability" of software, referring to the failure probability, as in "we need reliability of 10^{-5}." But technically, the engineering term has a more complex definition. *Reliability* of something man-made is the probability that it will fail in normal operation in a given time period. The software analog of "normal operation" is "when used according to the user profile," and the analog of a time period is a number of executions. The reliability R for K executions of software with failure probability f failures/demand is:

$$R = (1 - f)^K.$$

The interesting thing about this formula is that for enough executions, the reliability always goes to 0. That is, unless the failure probability is 0, the reliability is a steadily decreasing function of how much usage the software gets. No matter how good software is (short of perfect), use it enough in different ways, and it will fail.

21.2.2 Dependability

Reliability is the standard measure of engineering excellence, but as usual, software is just a little different from other products. Unreliable machines, when they fail, mostly do so completely, or so we consider what we choose to call their failures. An unreliable car drops parts on the road and strands you on the way to work; an unreliable dishwasher leaves the dishes dirty and water all over the floor; and so on. Software failure seems more problematic —when the spreadsheet fails, there is probably some way to get around it, maybe just trying it again. So we classify software failures by severity, on a scale of "cosmetic only" to "catastrophic," and define software as *dependable* if it can be trusted never to fail at the catastrophic end of the scale.

Unfortunately, testing, even random testing, is not much use in predicting failure classifications. The past history of failures found isn't a good predictor of the future—after all, past failures have all been fixed. A responsible development organization does not release software with known catastrophic failures, and the prediction of failure probability and confidence bound gives no idea what these unseen events will be like.

Thus testing comes back to reliability. Developers can try to make software perfect, even at the cosmetic level, and can use random testing to predict possible deviations from perfection. If they measure high confidence in a very low failure rate, then even the worst case, that the first failure some user experiences is a catastrophic one, likely won't happen. By paying attention to potential problems throughout development, with particular care about the severe ones, the developer can believe that it will be better than that.

Take responsibility ▶

21.3 Automated Testing

The label *automatic* gets applied to almost anything in which there is mechanical aid to human action. "Automatic door locks" on an automobile are not terribly different from pushing down the buttons by hand (although some people think them wonderful); an automatic dishwasher really does do the dishes, except for people who need to wash them before putting them in; an "automatic screw machine" is an amazing device that takes a roll of wire and turns it into bolts or screws or nails at a rate that has to be seen to be believed, while its "operator" is free to stand about and tell bad jokes about the machine's name. At one time, using a high-level programming language was called "automatic programming." "Automated testing" also spans a range from the trivial to something that may one day be very important.

The dream of true automatic testing is that a testing system would take as input a program alone, apply some magical algorithm to it, and thereby generate a set of test data, which when run would uncover any and all failures to which the program might be subject. The people who imagine such a system are willing to let it use a vast quantity of computer time, to "let it run all night." Their dream is missing one crucial ingredient, though, because the program's specification *must* enter in. Without the specification, there is no way to know if what the program does is correct. But there *are* automatic test systems. The ingredients are no more than an accurate user profile, a random input generator, and an effective test oracle. Inputs are generated according to the profile, the program is executed on them, and the oracle judges the results. After the automatic system has "run all night," formulas like those of Section 21.2.1 can be used to predict a MTTF. Not many systems today have an accurate user profile or an effective oracle, but there is nothing in principle to say that these could not be developed. A number of current research projects are working hard on the many practical problems that must be solved.

Today's practice, however, is nothing like true automatic testing. The mechanical test generation schemes that exist generate test data for structural coverage, and most of them exist only as "research prototypes," analyzers that fail to handle the peculiarities and scale of real programs. That no one sees fit to develop more capable commercial versions indicates that the ideas are either not understood or not seen to be of value. The formal methods for which effective oracles exist are little used. Instead, automated testing in practice means bookkeeping assistance for running tests.

One version is the *capture/playback* tool that aids testing (or retesting, see Section 21.4) of GUI interfaces. It records sequences of mouse positions and clicks and keyboard input so that these can be "played back" as if they were happening again. Capture/playback tools also record program responses, and can compare them on different playback runs. These tools save a vast amount of time and bring GUI testing under control because the tester does not need to repeat elaborate sequences of input actions. However, it is not testing that is automated, but the repeating of tests. Useful as that is, the quality of the work lies in the intellectual effort of finding good test sequences in the first place.

A second version is the *test-scripting* tool, which does its "recording" using a textual language. Its user creates scripts describing test cases (essentially the inputs to be used and the outputs to be expected, along with how the program is to be run), and the scripts are processed by the tool into executable test cases. Once the scripts are prepared, the rest *is* automatic: the tool runs the tests and produces a report on the outcomes. Again, the real work of testing lies in creation of the scripts, however much help the tool is in converting these to actual executions.

21.4 Regression Testing

As practiced today, regression testing refers to a complete retesting of a software system following some substantial maintenance activity. It is assumed that information is available about testing that was previously conducted—in the best case, the original tests are stored and can be repeated mechanically. This kind of large-scale retesting raises two issues:

1. How can the retest time be shorted by omitting previous tests whose outcome cannot be different for the changed code?
2. What new tests and test editing are needed for the changes?

The same issues come up when testing smaller-scale changes. Code changes during development; for example, to fix a failure caught in system testing, or to add a new layer of functionality in iterative enhancement. If regression testing were better understood, we would know what to do in these circumstances. As it is, retesting is even more an art than testing a system for the first time, and many of the most spectacular software failures—the Ariane-5 rocket, the 1990 AT&T outage—can be blamed on a failure to test changes. The most frequent disaster scenario is one in which the developers decide *not* to retest because the task is so daunting, and the change so small that it "doesn't have to be tested."

Research in regression testing has not gone much beyond the obvious. All the techniques of original testing can be applied to the new code: coverage of new functions using specification-based tests, structural coverage of new code, random testing with a profile weighted to emphasize the changed functions. If there is time, the full original test plan can be applied after it is altered to fit any changes in specification. Some old inputs may have become illegal, or different outputs are required. There is no need to run any test sequence that never passes through changed code—it cannot possibly come out differently than it did originally. Making this determination requires tool support—only a program can keep track of the paths and changes. But although tools help with the bookkeeping, regression testing isn't a very satisfactory technical activity. A careful tester can do a good job of probing what is known to have been added or changed. Where regression testing goes wrong is on what is not known: mistakes made in maintenance result in unexpected failures in cases where there should have been no change. These failure points are related to peculiar interactions between changed code and original code, and are unlikely to be explored by the original tests or by added tests. The result is that the regression test succeeds, then the changed software fails in use in some way that apparently has nothing to do with the change.

21.5 State of the Software Testing Art

It is reported that software testing is the most time-consuming part of the software lifecycle, responsible for about 40% of development time. The statistic hides a big assumption: testing takes a lot of time *if it is seriously attempted*. It is certainly possible, particularly in individual development efforts, to spend almost no time testing, but to release software that has been tried on only a handful of undemanding system tests. Without a serious testing plan, under a tight time schedule, the likely scenario is: no testing. We have recommended that construction of the test plan be carried on in parallel with the whole of development, arguing that opportunities will be missed and information lost if thinking about tests is deferred to the testing phase itself. For small projects, advance test planning isn't really required, however. An individual or a small development team may find it distracting to divert effort from design and coding to devising tests, and may have no difficulty recalling potential problems for testing by looking at the requirements and design documentation. For larger projects with large development teams subject to staff turnover, the test plan developed in parallel *is* essential.

We believe that the best software will fail, and that without testing a poorer product will be released. But the different kinds of testing take different amounts of effort and have different payoffs. When resources are limited, testing activities should be performed in a priority order:

(1) **Elementary system functional testing.** The highest-level functional system tests most directly duplicate what users will actually do with the software. Concentrate on "normal," not exceptional or error cases, and self-contained, independent test points, not sequences. If some information about a user profile is available, begin with the most likely cases. If there is a user's manual or requirements document that includes specific examples, be sure to use them as tests.

(2) **Extended system testing.** Continue with less likely system tests, with a lower payoff in directly duplicating what users will try first. Look at error situations and sequences of test inputs to exercise system "modes." If the complete system is small enough, use the simplest coverage tools (that is, statement or branch coverage) to assess the quality of the complete functional test, and try to fill gaps in the coverage as Marick recommends.

(3) **Unit and subsystem testing.** There are two ways to order the testing of system components: by ease and by failure payoff. Some routines and subsystems are easier to test because they have better specifications, are more self-contained, or require simpler test harnesses. In a limited time, more testing of these components can be accomplished. However, more failures will be uncovered if the components are ranked by likelihood of failure. When a difficult algorithm is being coded, or when the designer or coder was unsure of intellectual control (or just plain tired), those routines are more likely to fail. If they are tested first, more problems will be found in less time. These two orderings are not necessarily in opposition: it can happen that the error-prone components are easy to test—then the optimal strategy is clear.

(4) Random testing for reliability.   Reliability testing should be undertaken only when functional and structural testing no longer find failures. It is not indicated at all unless the software operation is critical to life or property. There must be some kind of user profile available, and an oracle to judge results. Then random testing can be used to estimate the failure probability. If there is no call for such an estimate, then the considerable difficulty of random testing should be avoided.

No matter what testing you plan, leave time for debugging. The tests *will* find failures, and if there is no time to fix them, the testing effort has no point. However, be judicious in fixing just as in testing if time is limited. A problem you can quickly document and work around, that requires large design changes to repair, should be low on the list of bugs to fix. Quick, sure fixes should be done first. And, of course, every fix should be retested, which makes it imperative that you organize and record your tests so that repeating them is much easier than doing them initially.

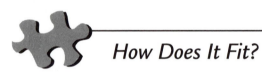

How Does It Fit?

From section 21.1

1. Here is a sequence of pseudorandom numbers obtained by repeatedly multiplying 6,921,185 by itself and extracting two bits at positions 11 and 10 (the units place is position 0):

   2 3 1 0 0 1 3 2 2 3 1 0 0 1 3 2 2 3 1 0 0 1 3 2 2 3 1 0 0 1

   The number of times each digit occurs is roughly the same.

   (a) Do you think the sequence is random? Why?

   (b) Suppose that instead the starting number had been 6,921,184. What will happen?

   (c) Suppose that instead the last two bits (positions 1 and 0) had been extracted starting with the original number. What will happen?

2. Here are two ways of getting "random C programs": First, a pool of programs is obtained either by (i) collecting them systematically from users or by (ii) generating them using a C grammar. The programs collected are numbered arbitrarily, say, from 1 to N. Second, pseudorandom numbers are generated between 1 and N, and used to select programs from the pool.

   (a) Compare methods (i) and (ii) for creating the pool. Can you think of an "automatic" way to do (i)?

   (b) Comment on how "random" the resulting programs will be.

From section 21.2

3. When a functional coverage test of N points has been conducted, all the faults that caused failures have been fixed, and the same test repeated successfully, why can't we predict that the MTTF is about N runs?

4. Derive the formula used to plot Figure 21.3.

5. Why don't we talk about the reliability or dependability of "natural" (or "God-made") objects instead of confining ourselves to things made by engineers? For example, is a flower dependable?

6. Although companies do not release the information, they may record the severity of failures discovered throughout software development by inspection and by testing. If you had access to this information for two different competing products, which would you buy, the one for which many severe failures had been fixed, or the one with few severe failures recorded? Why? Would other information be helpful in making the choice?

From section 21.3

7. Suppose that the problems with loops in generating test data to execute every statement of a program (Section 20.1.3) had been solved so that a tool existed to take as input a program and produce as output a testset that executed every statement. Would this tool constitute a true automatic testing system? Explain.

8. A mutation testing tool takes a program and a testset as input, generates the mutants, executes them on the testset, and produces error messages for each mutant not killed.

   (a) Is this true automatic testing? Explain.

   (b) Suppose, in addition, there were a program to generate test data from a program, test data that in practice kills most of the program's mutants. (There is in fact a research prototype of such a generator.) Could a true automatic testing system be constructed using the test generator and a mutation tool together?

From section 21.4

9. Suppose that changes have been made to a program that had previously been tested for all-uses dataflow adequacy. (That is, its original testset achieved dataflow coverage.) Which DU associations should be retested following maintenance, and which would be of no use to retest? Could a tool automatically select the right tests from the original set?

10. "Perfective maintenance" can be defined as program changes that do not alter the functionality or performance of a program, but only improve some subjective property of the code. For example, a subroutine might be rewritten because it was difficult to understand how it worked, or a data structure might be changed because the new structure was easier to expand (for a subsequent anticipated change, say).

    (a) What changes in an existing test plan would be *required* to run it on a program that had undergone perfective maintenance?

(b) Suggest clever ways to regression-test perfective maintenance changes. What problems might arise, and how would you detect them?

From section 21.5

11. Give an argument for interchanging the top two items in the list of testing activities, and then give a rebuttal to your own argument, for keeping the list as it is.

12. Give an argument for promoting unit testing to top priority in the list of testing activities. Why do you think it has been placed third on the given list?

Review Questions

1. What is the most important difference between random testing and the testing methods described in previous chapters?

2. How is a user profile used in random testing?

3. Can reliability information like the MTTF be obtained from structural test results?

Further Reading

Although random testing and the reliability it measures are not yet widely accepted in practice, they are theoretically important. An encyclopedia article on random testing [Ham94] is a good place to start. Michael Lyu has collected much of the content of "software reliability engineering" (SRE) in a handbook [Lyu96]. John Musa was for years a tireless advocate for SRE within the AT&T organization, where the methods achieved considerable success. Musa devoted a great deal of attention to obtaining user profiles in practice [MIO90, MFIK96].

The limitations of random testing for reliability have been laid out by Butler and Finelli [BF93]. They consider many ways to attempt to circumvent the simple result that to learn anything about a time T of software usage, it will take roughly test time T. They conclude that there is no way out, and thus that "ultrareliable" software that almost never fails cannot be tested to learn if it is satisfactory.

David Parnas has been a supporter of software dependability over reliability as the relevant parameter in engineering safe software systems. He does not believe that testing is the essential ingredient in achieving dependability; rather, he advocates development using particular formal methods, and his research group at McMaster University is engaged in laying the foundations for these and in developing tools to support them. It is well worth looking up his research group on the Internet.

References

[BF93]   R. W. Butler and G. B. Finelli. The infeasibility of quantifying the reliability of life-critical real-time software. *IEEE Transactions on Software Engineering*, pages 3–12, 1993.

[Ham94]   D. Hamlet. Random testing. In J. Marciniak, editor, *Encyclopedia of Software Engineering*, pages 970–978. Wiley, New York, 1994.

[Lyu96]   Michael Lyu, editor. *Handbook of Software Reliability Engineering*. McGraw-Hill, New York, 1996.

[MFIK96]   John Musa, Gene Fuoco, Nancy Irving, and Diane Kropfl. *The Operational Profile*, pages 167–216. In Lyu [Lyu96], 1996.

[MIO90]   John Musa, Anthony Iannino, and Kazuhira Okumoto. *Software Reliability*. McGraw-Hill, New York, 1990.

The subjects of these questions are not necessarily important parts of the chapter, but the questions explore details only hinted at in the text, or difficult points that might have been misunderstood. Sometimes it is said that such questions "make you think."

If you can easily answer most of the questions without looking back at the chapter (or by looking back quickly without struggling with the material they refer to), then you probably understand the point the question is making. (But the answer should not seem *too* easy since the questions are intended to be "tricky.") Teachers who value cleverness often use this kind of question on examinations, especially on open-book examinations.

Solutions and hints are provided capriciously for some questions (and without indicating which ones). The value of these exercises is lost if you look only at the ones with solutions, or if you peek at the solution before you have made a serious attempt to answer the question. But solutions are a guide for just how tricky the authors think they have been.

Chapter 1

5. (a) When coding a particular subroutine with a parameter X, the programmer discovers that some values of X require special treatment, and that these need to be flagged for subsequent special attention, but that there is no place in the designed X data structure to put such a flag. The problem is traced to the requirements where the special case was mentioned, but it was not clearly stated what should be done. Had this been discovered during discussion with the user, the matter might have taken an hour to settle. But now, with design completed and coding in progress, the time required is that hour, plus time to contact the user and arrange a meeting, plus time for everyone to remember the context of the earlier requirements meetings, plus similar study and correction of the design, plus recoding of all modules that involve the data of parameter X, some of which may very well have been completed without noticing the problem. This extra work could well take the eight or so hours shown on the graph.

(b) A logarithmic cost axis means that the growth is exponential—when the lifecycle time is roughly doubled (say, specification to test versus specification to design), the cost is squared. Exponential growth results from a process in which things not only have to be done over, but each thing done over causes several other things to have to be done over, too. Then the effect cascades, like a branching tree, in which the number of leaves grows exponentially in the depth of the tree. This explanation is not terribly precise, but it is far better than one that merely argues that the cost "increases" as development time moves on. Such an "increase" might be linear instead of exponential, which would produce a very different curve.

8. In a data structures class, the assignments often take the form of implementing a nontrivial storage/retrieval structure (for example, a heap). If the assignment is done as a general-purpose subroutine (or converted to that form afterward), it can be used in a subsequent assignment where this structure is needed. The personal program that one author has reused most was an assignment in a UNIX operating systems course, to write a simple interactive interface to UNIX system calls. The interface allowed an arbitrary system call to be invoked from the terminal and was subsequently used whenever an obscure system call problem arose (for example, the proper use of UNIX sockets).

9. (a) As a subsequent question suggests, two possible places are between requirements/specification and design, and between design and coding. (And part of the answer to that subsequent question is in part (b).) A third possibility is between coding and test—by then the test plan must be done. In (bad) practice, the third place is chosen by putting the work off as long as possible. However, by that time the work isn't planning but really testing without any plan at all. So it would be best to start as early as possible, after requirements. Getting the work done while requirements are still fresh in the developers' minds would perhaps compensate for not including tests that arise in design.

(b) Any separate test plan phase incorporated into the waterfall model is a mistake, for two reasons of timing: (1) Waiting until an earlier phase is complete (which is the essence of the waterfall's separation of concerns) loses the information that should be captured in tests as the earlier phase proceeds. (2) Holding back the subsequent phase is unnecessary since nothing in the test plan impacts that subsequent phase—it can start as soon as the original previous phase (not the test plan) spills over. This second problem is the more severe.

14. Consider two word processor programs, W_1 and W_2. W_1 has a problem in managing its screen image—if the lines become too long for the window, part goes off the screen, and the remainder of the page may be shifted in strange ways. However, W_1 has never been known to accidentally destroy a file on disk. W_2 has no known systematic problems, but every few weeks it trashes a file being edited. If these word processors are used 10 times a day, then the reliability of W_1 may be only about 50% over a day if a long line comes up in half the edits. W_2's reliability is about 99% over a day, since it fails only once in about 100 uses. But W_1 is clearly more dependable.

Chapter 2

4. Suppose the problem to be solved is sorting a list of names. It seems to make sense to decompose the problem by splitting the list into sublists and sorting each one. (Indeed, some elegant recursive sorting algorithms begin this way.) However, if no thought is given to how to merge the resulting smaller sorted lists, the subsorts have accomplished nothing. And in the limit, as the size of the sublists goes to a single name, the work shifts entirely to the merge.

9. Perhaps the reason that writers are cautioned to ignore their public is that the creative part of writing is the most important, and too much attention to the "market" will produce only what the market knows and wants, which is not at all creative. If the writer's concern is art, that must be separated from the market's concern of sales. (This is also the essence of the answer to a previous question about thinking that is too "customer oriented.") Software engineers are creative, too, but their creativity finds its way into the *performance* of the software, not its documentation or code listing. The documents are not for the user, but for the developers—other engineers will read them. Hence the writer loses little by thoughtfully providing for the audience. Some of the same forces operate in any kind of exposition. When a writer is trying to explain something, to have the reader understand, then it is all-important to write as the audience requires, and not as the writer wishes. People read novels mostly because they want to; they read instructions and other exposition mostly because they are required to. So the writer of exposition starts out with a restive audience and must help them as much as possible. Should software engineers ever write for themselves alone? Some possibilities suggest themselves: (1) In coding under extreme constraints, for example, in trying to fit a bootstrap loader into a minimum number of instructions, the results will not be "read" except by machine, and the CPU does not care about style. (2) Some people program for the fun of it, and then they will certainly please themselves. (And they may very well suffer for it later if they ever pick up and try to read their own code.) (3) Some of the best documentation ever produced, so-called narrative documentation, at a high conceptual level, requires talent to conceive, and perhaps it can be done only by novelists.

Chapter 3

1. I bought this toaster at the hardware store and took it home. It seemed to work fine until I tried to put a sliced bagel in it that was a little too fat. It burned the bagel, but then it got stuck, and after I pried it out with a wooden spoon, the toaster lever wouldn't stay down and the element didn't get hot. So I took it back to the store. They told me they couldn't do anything. The company knew about the problem, and they were redesigning the toaster to fix it. (The new one was also going to have a fancy new thing on the side that showed the color of the toast. It was, unfortunately, going to be twice as big as the old one.) But it wouldn't be ready until next year, and until then I'd just have to make my toast in the oven. So I asked for a certificate or something to get a refund or a new toaster when it did come out, but they told me I would have to buy an "upgrade" that would cost more than the old one did. I asked if they had any other toasters, but they didn't.

2. Like computer science, mathematics lacks the connection with the physical world. There are no "laws" of mathematics that rest upon observation and could ever be falsified by data. We believe that $2 + 2 = 4$ not because we did experiments with a bunch of rocks or sticks, but because we accept axiomatic definitions from which that equality is deduced using rules (that we also accept). Those who crowned mathematics Queen (Compte was one) probably did so by looking at the deductive part of science, which is similar to what happens in mathematics.

3. There is no question about which way to bet: the problem of deciding if software will abort rests only on definitions, and there is no possibility of "solving" it. The definitions might be changed, but that would make a different problem. Perpetual motion, on the other hand, is impossible only if energy must be conserved, a fact that rests only on observations of the world. If some obscure part of the world comes to light for the first time, the "law" might be violated there.

Chapter 4

3. In today's world of software development, it is far easier to demonstrate an acceptable level of process. The difficulty is that real measures of product quality are not known. However, the demonstration must go well beyond pointing to "company policy" that pays lip service to doing things well. In court, it would be necessary to demonstrate that the company policy is actually followed, and that some effort is made to audit operations and record what has been done. This emphasis on demonstrating compliance with a process standard can lead to some strange activities. For example, engineers may be required to follow, document, and report on process activities that everyone agrees are useless and a waste of time, just because nothing better is available, and the company lawyers must have something to point to.

Chapter 5

5. (a) Does the document use any jargon that would make it hard to understand by either the end user or the software developer?

(b) Are both normal and exception cases covered?

(c) Are input values checked so that subscripts cannot go out of range?

9. Although scheme (a) will fix the bug (unlike the others that won't do so in general), it certainly isn't a good idea. The program has failed for some reason—it contains at least one mistake. It is likely that its mistakes will result in failures on inputs other than x, and the code must be studied (starting in the case of input x, of course) to find the mistake in question, which must then be fixed.

Chapter 6

2. The first time the program is given input X, it produces a certain result that depends on the internal variable Hold, which was initialized to 0. In the process of the calculation, Hold gets set to 13, and is not reinitialized. The second input X, using the same calculation, may not get the same answer.

This problem of repeatability is a bad one in testing—in this case, the program may contain a bug (say, if Hold *should* have been reinitialized), or it may be correct to give the differing results. But how many times must the tester repeat an input to be sure? What is usually done is to restart the program, which will consistently give the first answer. This is certainly not a good idea if the tester is trying to find bugs.

3. (b) Suppose the program has a bug that causes it to miss the LF terminator, and to examine further characters up to the first alphabetic character that next occurs, but that it correctly processes the input if there are fewer than 16 characters before the LF. If the program has a buffer of (say) 100 characters, then it will get a bounds violation (which may be a fatal error on some systems) on an input of 13 Xs followed by LF followed by 88 7s, but will be all right on many other such inputs. Hence it will be necessary to try arbitrarily long inputs to be certain that some such bug does not exist in the program.

7. The only obvious thing to do is make a systematic division of the input range, including the boundary cases. Because the range is so large, it would be good to learn how the routine will be used and concentrate on high usage regions. For example, some applications might mostly be computing exponentials in [0,1,000], so points might be concentrated there, and scattered widely over the rest of the input space. Examining the code for broken-box testing might show that the subroutine uses several distinct algorithms in different ranges, such as a power series approximation near zero, a fitted polynomial approximation for several distinct small ranges, and an asymptotic approximation for large negative inputs. These regions and their boundaries can then be used in functional tests.

Chapter 7

1. (b) Hint: the stacking is not the simplest thing you might expect.

4. In Chapter 8, the problems will be called (a) inconsistency, and (b) incompleteness.

7. (b) The most likely thing is that some employee will get in trouble. The ones most at risk are the clerk that talked to you, or a supervisor or manager who brought your letter to some superior's attention. The least likely to suffer will be the person who did the software requirements, if only because that person cannot be identified!

8. (b) Using the smallest allowed box size, ten boxes won't fit on the same line in the required page size. Six boxes is enough to show that staggering them would allow more to fit (and it is easier to draw).

(c) Allowing staggered boxes will certainly make the programming harder as indicated by the problems with crossing lines, and so on. But it also raises the issue that there is then no standard form for the tree—there are many ways in which the stagger can be done (and more yet if box size is considered along with stagger), and perhaps the user has strong opinions about some of them being better than others, opinions that may be hard to articulate until a tree is shown and disliked.

9. The boxes should be bigger.

11. Here's one: give the input for Figure 7.3, check the output for correct labels, structure, and layout. (That is a functional test, needed to see if the software handles a simple case.) Also examine the output for box size and typeface, which is more a fault-based test looking for the very mistake that was made in the figure. The assumption is that if the box size and typeface are right for any figure, they are probably right for all.

13. (a) Hint: what input should produce this tree?

(b) It should work to simply allow an empty list of subnodes under a head node. Then all the nodes needed for placeholders in an arbitrary structure can appear. (Could the developer or user claim that this is actually allowed already? Who has the most at stake in not changing this part of the specification?)

(c) "Empty" situations are always dangerous and need to be carefully tested.

15. (a) The usual implementation does it this way (is there any other?): when the editor is started normally, it copies the file being edited to a backup under a special name. As editing proceeds, the backup file is rewritten to reflect changes. When the editor successfully saves the file being edited, the backup is deleted. If the editor starts working on a file, and finds the specially named backup in existence, it knows that the previous edit was aborted, and to recover it substitutes the backup for the file.

16. Tigger is the user, and the rest are the development team. Each has only one program to offer, until Christopher Robin sees that Kanga is better prepared. Finally, Tigger's problem is solved by accident.

17. Suppose that the output format depends on the input values, for example, in that the number of output columns is an input parameter, and that for some special value (like 1) the user decides that the output isn't useful, and so 1 should be made an error input.

Chapter 8

3. Here are some lines of output:

```
... 2 ... 4 ...
... 7 ... 3 ...
```

The first is OK, the second is not OK. This could mean that even numbers (or powers of 2) are OK, but odd numbers (or primes) are not. Or it could mean that the smaller numbers have to come first. How many examples would it take to resolve all such questions?

4. Completeness, because if the user doesn't quite know what is wanted, things will be left out; however, the developer knows very little about the user's domain and so is unlikely to think that there is any difficulty.

10. (a) Inconsistency requires that two different results *both* are required to come from the same input; multiple correct results means that any *one* of them will meet the requirement.

Chapter 9

3. When shouting a warning, (B) it's important to be forceful and quick, and so if accuracy suffers, that's OK. Hence warnings are certainly (A) incomplete: the speaker wasn't careful to say which guy, which wheel, or what to do about it. Anyone who has ever said "I love you," or heard it said, knows very well that (A) incompleteness (and too often, incorrectness) are the essence of those words, and that (B) both parties to the conversation would probably much prefer it that way.

5. The jargon needed to cover internal system errors would probably not be understandable to the end user. Such a requirements document would also probably be prescriptive since to know that the error is possible, and what to do about the error, implies a knowledge of the circumstances under which it occurred, which is definitely part of the "how" of design.

Chapter 10

1. Perhaps the largest communication gap arising from background occurs when the people involved are of different sexes. Alan Turing, in his famous "Turing test" to see if a computer displays intelligence, exploits the sexes' poor knowledge of each other to give the machine a leg up (so to speak!).

6. Hint: after you have replaced *perm*() with an appropriate uses of *countdup*(), don't forget to put back the two assertions involving all the members of X being members of Y and vice versa. If you forgot to do this, what would be a test case on which the predicate would give an intuitively incorrect result?

7. The WFF is very precise, and it is in principle possible to study any logical consequence of it. But the user, who is the judge of "correct," does not have a precise idea, and may be unable to understand some of the WFF's consequences. Thus the WFF could be wrong and the user will not know it.

10. (a) This argument is more plausible than certain—it is very difficult to really prove that something is impossible. But here goes: the outermost quantifier of a Horn clause is always $\exists$. The given formula could be converted into an equivalent one that begins with $\exists$, but that would introduce a negation inside, something else that Horn clauses lack.

(b) Hint: it might help to put the database in the list format.

14. Hint: try it! If it works there is nothing to explain; if it doesn't, maybe the example you try will show you why.

15. The order does influence the backtracking and the speed of execution. The first form gets a permutation and then checks the order; the second gets a correct order and checks if it's a permutation. There are many more possibilities in the latter, so it may be much slower. (Try it.)

19. (a) Since Prolog can't express negation, the situation in (b) isn't possible. There are numerical predicates that allow this:

```
ans(X,Y)  :- X<Y,Y<X.
```

Any query using X as an input and seeking Y should then give no answer. What happens on your Prolog? (If it uses resolution theorem proving as most implementations do, there will be an obscure error message. But a "constraint" Prolog will just answer "no.") So perhaps the right answer is that contradictions are hard to arrange in Prolog, and when contrived, just lead to specifying that there is no output for some inputs.

(b) The WFF: $Y = 1 \land \neg(Y = 1)$ is sufficient to derive the logical consequence: $\neg(1 = 1)$ (or, in fact, any other WFF, false or true). That means that a contradictory specification says nothing—any results follow from it.

21. (c) The Formal Methodist would first give the questioner a look that conveyed he had completely missed the point, and then say something like: "Of course the 'sorting' you have in your head is unique, but the formal *sorting* that has been defined may not be because it may fail to capture what you had in mind. By proving that the formal definition does have properties that are needed, we can gain a little confidence that the formal idea is the right one."

22. There need be no difficulty. Given the result to check, try the Prolog answers one by one, and if any of them agrees with the result, it is OK. (This specification has multiple correct results.) On the other hand, if the user did not want some of these results—that is, they are not correct—then blindly using the oracle will hide the fact that the specification must be wrong.

Chapter 11

2. (c) All of them can be made to apply without so much change that the essence is lost. Perhaps the most difficult to alter is "nonprescriptive." Designs are *supposed* to be prescriptive. However, it is to everyone's advantage if the design tries not to make unnecessary decisions, but leaves as much to later work (more detailed design, coding) as possible.

6. Indeed the "date variables" might be hard to identify; however, the problem is harder than that because the code that sets and examines those variables may work only for two-digit values. The whole Y2K problem is much worse than this question indicates because dates are also stored external to programs, for example, in historical files and databases. These must also be changed, and vast systems of programs, files, and the procedures to use them must be simultaneously switched from the old versions to the new versions.

9. (b) If the diagnostic subsystem has been coded (and tested!) the programmer with the problem can use it for snapshot dumps, and so forth. But if it isn't ready, the programmer will have to fall back on less useful aids, or will have to write special dump routines that are like those of the diagnostic subsystem. In either case, time is wasted just because things were done in the wrong order.

17. Hint: what is the chain rule for derivatives? Leibniz's notation makes the variable of differentiation explicit; Newton was doing physics and only needed t (for $t$ime).

Chapter 12

4. Hint: Pascal controls the types of subscripts, permitting them to be only finite types (not `integer`, for example), and has no dynamic array bounds. Thus only one run-time check is required: to see that a variable of a finite type does not assume values outside its limits. This check occurs on assignment to such variables. To make this type of checking work across procedure boundaries, it is necessary to make the subscript type of an array passed as a parameter be part of the parameter type, and this has unpleasant consequences for writing "generic" routines that can process arrays of different sizes.

7. (Comment) If you ran a test using particular values for X, Y, Z, then you have devised a fault-based test to see that code using these Boolean operators is in fact correct.

13. `diff` and `grep` will be invaluable in finding out what all the check-in conflicts signify so that the person can fulfill the responsibility of keeping all the correct work of all the people whose changes figure in the conflict. But it may be that the only really helpful tool will be study of paper listings of the areas of conflict. Paper spreads out on a table much more nicely than text on a screen, and allows people to do things no program can do.

Chapter 13

7. Hint: the only two possibilities seem to be "alphabetical" and "in the order found in the input." Devise a test that distinguishes between these. Suppose that there is in fact a third possibility. What would your test prove in that case?

Chapter 14

13. A variable will be declared in the C program (say MemOK), and assigned 1 or 0 for the OK or NG actions. Pseudocode statements like IF event memOK occurs ... will be replaced by C code if (MemOK) ....

14. The difficulty is in making a table that can handle nonstandard events and actions. One way to do so is to make the table a two-dimensional array whose subscript position [Event, State] contains a function pointer as the action (along with a new State index). When a table entry is selected, an arbitrary function is called through the pointer. Each event is assigned a unique value, which is a row index into the table. When the event is a standard one, this value is directly assigned. When the event is a nonstandard one, a function is called that determines if that event has occurred, and if so, sets the index value. Care must be taken to see that at most one of these functions can make an affirmative return at any given time.

Chapter 15

1. Hint: in compilers whose object code is to run on a 32-bit machine, the implementation often limits Pascal sets to 32 members. That is enough information to figure out how the implementation is intended to be done. Incidentally, if the Pascal specification included the 32-member limitation, what principle of good specifications would be violated?

14. (a) When the uninitialized variable is referenced, the program will abort (if the compiler has been clever enough to arrange it). The potential problem would be detected by LCLint. On the other hand, with mandatory initialization there is no run-time error, but the program uses the initialized value, which is very likely to be wrong and cause it to get the wrong result.

(b) There is certainly no way in C to write an initialized variable declaration that allocates storage to the declared structure. The zero value for the array part of the ADT implementation could, of course, be arranged with a declaration like

```
IntSet S = {0, 0};
```

but this would require that the programmer make use of a knowledge of the hidden structure, violating the ADT's secret.

15. (a) Except for a (long-delayed) problem described in (b), functional tests will not fail because whether or not the updates happen in place is immaterial to the value of results. Of course, it strongly affects the efficiency of the implementation.

(b) A user who is repeatedly storing into a single set, instead of using roughly the amount of memory needed to just hold the data, will require much more. (Exactly how much more? Give a rough formula.) This user is then likely to get some peculiar message about storage being exhausted, and will be unable to understand why this should happen so soon.

19. The pedestrian solution is to require the programmer to call an initialization routine right after a local declaration, and to free the array storage in each local variable before the procedure returns. These two operations could be added as access routines of the ADT. They could be made available more easily to the programmer by #defines that declare (and initialize) storage, and (free storage) and return. Then the programmer would not be so likely to forget to do the necessary operations. Can you think of a way to use the same form to declare all ADT variables, global and local?

Chapter 16

5. (a) It makes no sense to use hidden data without mutator methods since it could never be initialized. If the data is not hidden, then it can be altered without mutators, but this would be in violation of the object paradigm. There are tricks of initialization that might give the data a value and the designer might then want it to remain unchanged. (However, such a "constant object" seems something of an overkill.) There are also complications introduced by inheritance, where a class appears to have no mutators, but uses its superclass to initialize or modify data, exemplified in the implementation of the *Check* object in Section 16.7.2.

(b) Unless the data object is not hidden, mutators without accessors makes no sense. To stretch a point, a class might have a logging function that makes changes in hidden data without access to it, and then sends the final log to some kind of external storage. But the latter operation is really just a peculiar kind of accessor.

8. Class libraries may very well make use of these features; however, it is perfectly reasonable to write class libraries without ever using inheritance or polymorphism. (The latter would be the greater loss since generic classes make good library classes.) But in a language lacking inheritance, the class library is not nearly as useful as if that feature were available. Without inheritance, the programmer cannot extend or adapt library classes, and this is the most important property of a class library.

Chapter 17

9. This "inside out" philosophy is directly opposed to DFD design. In the latter, the central transform, which is like the heart algorithm, is identified not at the beginning, but at the end of design, and far from being a major intellectual activity, finding it is a mechanical process. It is not surprising that critics of DFD design say that it produces poor designs for precisely this reason: the important things are not thought about first. The defenders of the method would reply that for the routine problems on which DFD design is used, there *are* no important things, and it is a waste of time to try to think about them when the DFD technique will produce a satisfactory result by rote. The latter argument is very much in the spirit of engineering practice.

Chapter 18

5. (b) Create an internal array, and at the beginning of the loop body, store the index into the next position of the array. When the storage runs out, start again at the beginning, in a circular fashion. If the program crashes, a symbolic debugger can be used to look at the array and discover the loop index that probably caused the crash. (Why is it better to use an array and a debugger rather than writing the index to a file?)

Chapter 19

2. (a) Suppose that for a unique input the answer is wrong. One way to fix this is to put a conditional statement just before the result is returned, testing for the special case and giving the correct result. Another way to is check for the special input just after it is read in, and return the correct result immediately. Still another is to call a new procedure that does the checking and takes special action.

(b) It is evident that "*the* fault" is not a well-defined idea. What is well defined is "the fix" as made by some person. Unfortunately, even counting "faults" is not sensible since when there are many failures, a clever person may find a way to fix many of them with a single code change, whereas a more pedestrian debugger would have a separate fix for each failure. The latter would then have "found more faults" (and get a promotion?), contrary to common sense.

8. Suppose the system employs a linked list data structure and contains a bug that, when the list grows and then is pruned back to an empty list, the pointer to its head is destroyed. After a test sequence has placed items in the list and then removed them all, no failures will have been seen. But at this point the internal state has a bad pointer, and the next use of the list is likely to fail with a memory violation.

9. Hint: where does the "finite" of the FSM enter the picture?

Chapter 20

1. (a) Testing . . . failures
(b) Inspection . . . faults

8. (a) The conditional statement might not be executed by the test(s).
(b) Hint: the conditional statement might be within the body of a loop.

12. The example fails to account for lines that are not on any statement, such as the ones indicating bare braces. It will claim that lines 1, 2, 3, ..., 87 were never executed. This could be fixed by setting the mark [] element for these as if they were statements, when control reaches the line. Care is required to put the instrumentation on the right "side" of the brace, and keep it outside comments.

16. One of the needed test points makes the two compared expressions equal. Two others are needed, in which the first is less than the second, and in which the second is less than the first. These three cases cause every one of the relational operators to take somewhere a different truth value. Thus if the result of the comparison is correct for these three tests, the wrong relational operator cannot have been used. That is, those tests are guaranteed to weakly kill all the relational operator mutants.

19. (b) The coverage will be of the code that looks things up in the FSM table. That code will likely be completely covered because it will have looked things up in all the ways they can be looked up. This means nothing at all about the particular FSM being "run" through its table.

Chapter 21

1. (b) After one multiplication, there will be at least two zeroes at the end of the result because the starting number is even. (Are there in fact more than two?) Then the next multiplication will make it three. After 10 multiplications, bit positions 10 and 11 will both be zero, and will remain so.

4. Suppose that the failure rate is f, and that N independent tests succeed, drawn from the operational profile. The probability that one test succeeds is $(1 - f)$, that two both succeed is the product $(1 - f)(1 - f)$, and that all N succeed is $(1 - f)^N$. So the probability that the test set sees at least one failure is $1 - (1 - f)^N$. This is in fact the chance that the measurement goes wrong—that the test does *not* succeed, so it is precisely the upper confidence bound C.

Index

logic programming, 181–183,
    186, 207
logical connective, 176–177
logical consequence, 201
logical model, 328
logical relationship, 182, 186
look-and-feel, 327, 343
loop, 111, 418, 426–427
lore of design, 222
lost wanderers, 178
low-level design, 11, 16
lower-level DFD, 362, 367
ls, 254
Lyu, Michael, 457

M

machine language, 171
machine shop, 67
machinist, 231
Macintosh, 284
macro, 246
    argument, 246
    capability, 245
    dangerous, 253
mainframe, 18
mainframe computer, 383
mainframe software, 22
maintainability, 21
maintenance, 13, 15–16, 27, 43,
    53, 95–97, 299, 404
    adaptive, 16
    cheap, 13
    corrective, 16
    feedback, 91
    hidden role, 13
    history, 13
    mistakes, 261
    phase, 13, 36, 99
    problem, 40
make, 258–259
makefile, 259
malloc(), 161, 306, 319
management, 388
    complexity, 80, 343
    control, 68
    engineering, 5, 74, 82

hierarchy, 73
incentive, 79
infrastructure, 72
practice, 65, 68, 259
process, 73
requirements, 70
scientific, 66, 81
skill, 68
task, 24
team, 65
    large, 80
    vs. technical, 4
manager, 335, 389
    competence, 23
    development, 22, 136
    engineering, 4, 137
    invented software
        engineering, 98
    project, 23, 68
    subordinates, 79
    training, 22
managerial matrix, 72
manager's hat, 4
manager's responsibility, 137
manager's toughest job, 20
manual
    test case, 407, 411
manufacturing process, 398
mapping requirements to
    subsystems, 89
Marick, Brian, 108, 411, 433
    testing method, 420–422,
        424, 428, 435–436
market for automobile, 21
marketer, 20
marketing representative, 10
mass transit, 195
mathematical
    abstraction, 127
    idea, 172, 200
    induction, 188
    language, 172
    library, 223
    precision, 200–201
    proof, 199, 202
    training, 171, 174

mathematical error, 199
mathematical specification.
    See specification
mathematics, 172, 174, 193,
    198, 201–202, 207, 220
    antithesis, 198
    direct application, 174
    hard-to-use, 174
    intellectual exercise, 194
McMaster University, 456
mean time to failure. *See* MTTF
measurement error, 446
measurement of changed
    process, 80
mechanical drawing, 163
mechanical engineer, 19, 52,
    90, 163, 174, 231
mechanical support, 226
megawidget, 78
member function, 344
memmem(), 247
memo FSM, 284
    diagram, 285
memo window, 284, 287–288
memory
    dynamic, 109, 223, 237
    out-of-bounds, 241
memory allocation, 161, 250,
    311, 317
mental model, 327
message
    diagnostic, 376
    error, 130, 139, 153, 160, 162,
        164, 223, 253, 295
        syntax, 153
    log, 245, 260
    system, 160–161
    time-stamped, 146
message content, 160
metamathematics, 202
method, 326, 343–344
    abstract, 387
    accessor, 349
    as function, 326
    as subroutine, 346
    Booch, 328